2 0 1 1
STATE OF THE WORLD
Innovations that
Nourish the Planet

Worldwatch publications available from Earthscan

State of the World series from 1994 to 2011
(an annual report on progress towards a sustainable society)

Vital Signs series from 1992 to 2006
(a report on the trends that are shaping our future)

2 0 1 1
STATE OF THE WORLD
Innovations that Nourish the Planet

A Worldwatch Institute Report on
Progress Toward a Sustainable Society

Danielle Nierenberg and Brian Halweil, *Project Directors*

Royce Gloria Androa	Mario Herrero	Qureish Noordin
Charles Benbrook	Marcia Ishii-Eiteman	Sandra L. Postel
Marie-Ange Binagwaho	Nancy Karanja	Chris Reij
Louise E. Buck	Anna Lappé	Andrew Rice
Roland Bunch	Brigid Letty	Sara J. Scherr
Marshall Burke	David Lobell	Alexandra Spieldoch
Christopher Flavin	Saidou Magagi	Tristram Stuart
Dianne Forte	Serena Milano	Abdou Tenkouano
Samuel Fromartz	Anuradha Mittal	Ann Waters-Bayer
Hans R. Herren	Mary Njenga	

Linda Starke, *Editor*

publishing for a sustainable future

LONDON

First published by Earthscan in the UK in 2011

Copyright © Worldwatch Institute, 2011

A catalogue record for this book is available from the British Library

ISBN: 978-1-84971-352-8

Book and cover design by Lyle Rosbotham
The text of this book is composed in Galliard, with the display set in Scala Sans.

For a full list of publications please contact:

Earthscan
Dunstan House, 14a St Cross Street
London, EC1N 8XA
Tel: +44 (0)20 7841 1930
Fax: +44 (0)20 7242 1474
Email: earthinfo@earthscan.co.uk
Web: **www.earthscan.co.uk**

Earthscan publishes in association with the International Institute for Environment and Development

This book was printed in the UK by MPG Books,
an ISO 14001 accredited company.
The paper used is FSC certified.

Mixed Sources
Product group from well-managed
forests and other controlled sources
www.fsc.org Cert no. SA-COC-1565
© 1996 Forest Stewardship Council
FSC

Acknowledgments

The Worldwatch Institute could not assemble a book as ambitious as *State of the World 2011: Innovations that Nourish the Planet* without an amazing global network of advisors and contributors. For the past two years, we have attempted to understand not only the connections between hunger, poverty, and environmental degradation but also sustainable solutions to these problems. We've been reporting on what we've learned at www.NourishingthePlanet.org, sharing the stories of farmers, farmers' groups, journalists, scientists, and donors with our growing network of readers all over the world.

We owe tremendous thanks to the Nourishing the Planet (NtP) Advisory Group. They have been trusted advisors for the past two years, pointing us to projects on the ground and giving feedback on different components of the project, including the NtP blog. The Advisory Group includes the following distinguished individuals: Bina Agarwal, Lorena Aguilar, Dave Andrews, Shayna Bailey, Charles Benbrook, Jake Blehm, Louise Buck, Ben Burkett, Olivier De Schutter, Jim DeVries, Amadou Diop, Alan Duncan, Sue Edwards, Tewolde Berhan Gebre Egziabher, Charles Erhart, Cary Fowler, Dennis Garrity, Hans Herren, Jackie Hughes, Dyno Keatinge, Gawain Kripke, Loren A. Labovitch, David Lobell, Luc Mougeot, Mark Muller, Sam Myers, Sudha Nair, Arivudai Nambi, Eliud Ngunjiri, Diamantino Nhampossa, Jan Nijhoff, Tim Ogborn, Thomas Pesek, Jules Pretty, Chris Reij, Raj Rengalakshmi, Mike Robinson, Sara Scherr, Christina Schiavoni, Alexandra Spieldoch, David Spielman, Steve Staal, Abdou Tenkouano, Norman Uphoff, Edith van Walsum, Swarna S. Vepa, and Jacob Wanyama.

In addition, we want to thank the Worldwatch Institute Board of Directors for their leadership: Chairman of the Board Tom Crain, Vice-Chairman Robert Charles Friese, Treasurer Geeta B. Aiyer, Secretary Nancy Hitz, Worldwatch's President Christopher Flavin, Ray Anderson, L. Russell Bennett, Marcel Brenninkmeijer, James Cameron, Cathy Crain, James Dehlsen, Ed Groark, Satu Hassi, Jerre Hitz, Jeffrey Lipton, Akio Morishima, Sam Myers, Ajit Nazre, Richard Swanson, Izaak van Melle, and Wren Wirth. Our Emeritus Board members are Øystein Dahle and Abderrahman Khene. Sadly, Andrew E. Rice, our longtime board member and former Chairman, passed away in 2010 after a courageous battle against cancer. Andy's lifelong passion for economic and social development would have made him particularly pleased with the focus of this year's *State of the World*.

State of the World would not exist were it not for the generous financial contributions of our many supporters. More than 3,500 Friends of Worldwatch fund nearly one third of the Institute's operating budget.

Worldwatch's research program is backed by a roster of organizations and foundations. We are indebted to the Bill & Melinda Gates Foundation for their assistance in allowing us to report from the field and for helping us focus *State of the World* entirely on innovations that help alleviate hunger and poverty. Our special thanks go to Haven Ley and Brantley Browning, our program officers at the Foundation. They provided both advice and encouragement throughout the project, and we are deeply grateful for their help.

We are also grateful to a number of other foundations, governments, and institutions whose support over the past year has made the Institute's many other projects possible: the American Clean Skies Foundation; the Apollo Alliance Project, with funding provided by the Rockefeller and Surdna Foundations; the Heinrich Boell Foundation; the Casten Family Foundation; the Compton Foundation, Inc.; the Del Mar Global Trust; the Energy and Environment Partnership with Central America; the Ministry of Foreign Affairs of the Government of Finland; Sam Gary and Associates, Inc.; the German Federal Ministry for the Environment, Nature Protection and Nuclear Safety; the Richard and Rhoda Goldman Fund and the Goldman Environmental Prize; the Hitz Foundation; the Steven C. Leuthold Family Foundation; the MAP Royalty, Inc. Sustainable Energy Education Fellowship Program; the Marianists of the USA Sharing Fund; the Renewable Energy & Energy Efficiency Partnership; the Shared Earth Foundation; the Shenandoah Foundation; the Flora L. Thornton Foundation; the United Nations Foundation; the United Nations Population Fund; the Wallace Genetic Foundation, Inc.; the Wallace Global Fund; the Johanette Wallerstein Institute; and the Winslow Foundation.

We are indebted too to our international network of publishing partners, who bring *State of the World* to a global audience. They provide advice, translation, outreach, and distribution assistance. We give special thanks to Universidade Livre da Mata Atlântica in Brazil; China Environment Science Press in China; Oy Yliopistokustannus University Press in Finland; Good Planet and Editions de La Martiniere in France; Germanwatch, Heinrich Böll Foundation, and OEKOM Verlag GmbH in Germany; Evonymos Ecological Library in Greece; Earth Day Foundation in Hungary; Centre for Environment Education in India; World Wide Fund for Nature and Edizioni Ambiente in Italy; Worldwatch Japan; Africam Safari, Televis Verde, SEMARNAT, and the Universidad de las Americas Puebla in Mexico and Latin America; Editura Tehnica in Romania; Worldwatch Norden; Center of Theoretical Analysis of Environmental Problems and International Independent University of Environmental and Political Sciences in Russia; DOYOSEA-Korea Green Foundation in South Korea; Centre UNESCO de Catalunya for the Catalan version and Fundacion Hogar del Empleado and Editorial Icaria for the Castilian version in Spain; Taiwan Watch Institute; Turkiye Erozyonla Mucadele, Agaclandima ve Dogal Varliklari Koruma Vakfi in Turkey; and Earthscan in the United Kingdom.

Worldwatch's longest publishing relationship is with W. W. Norton & Company in New York. Thanks to their team—especially Amy Cherry, Laura Romain, Devon Zahn, and Louise Mattarelliano—*State of the World*, *Vital Signs*, and other Worldwatch books make it into bookstores and classrooms across the United States.

Our readers are ably served by the customer service team at Direct Answer, Inc. We are grateful to Katie Rogers, Marta Augustyn, Colleen Curtis, Lolita Guzman, Cheryl Marshall, Katie Gilroy, Ronnie Hergett, and Valerie Proctor for providing first-rate customer service and fulfilling customers' orders in a timely fashion.

Authors of this year's *State of the World* benefited from intensive review by other authors, members of the Advisory Group, and other experts, as well as several anonymous reviewers. Thomas Prugh, former editor of *World Watch Magazine*, provided feedback on nearly every chapter, helping us give substantive recommendations to authors early in the editing process. Sophia Murphy and Worldwatch staff editor Lisa Mastny also provided intensive review and editing on many of the pieces, helping prepare them for final editing.

Food and agriculture experts Mark Bittman, Chad Dobson, Joan Gusow, Anna Lappé, Francis Moore Lappé, Raj Patel, Michael Pollan, and Roger Thurow also generously lent their expertise to the project in its early phases, pointing us to particular people and projects.

For this edition of *State of the World*, we enlisted a record number of leading thinkers, advocates, journalists, farmers, activists, and scientists as authors and contributors. In addition to the insightful and accomplished chapter authors, a wonderful group of academics and journalists contributed the short articles that appear between chapters. These FROM THE FIELD articles describe particular agricultural innovations and organizations working in agricultural development. And several other writers and researchers provided Boxes for various chapters.

Throughout 2009 and 2010, the Nourishing the Planet project was supported by an amazing and brilliant group of interns. Abby Massey worked diligently on Chapters 1 and 13, helping track down information and co-authoring a text box. Abby also has been an important part of the NtP team, writing blogs, helping plan our meetings and visits, and working on the agricultural innovations database. Kristina Van Dexter helped early on during the project, and Stephanie Pappas helped find information on agricultural funding flows. Ronit Ridberg used her research skills to track down information for Chapter 12, while Alexandra Tung spent her summer finding interesting statistics and innovations for Chapters 4 and 8, as well as helping with Chapter 1. Her contributions to Chapter 4 were particularly helpful to author Sandra Postel. Daniel Kandy helped with Chapters 9, 10, and 15; Matt Styslinger provided assistance for Chapter 7; Vanessa Acara was a huge help in researching and drafting a Box for Chapter 7; Janeen Madan worked on Chapters 3 and 14; and Abisola Adekoyo, Elena Davert, and Daniel Kane all fact-checked chapters to make sure that the statistics and data were consistent throughout the book.

Many of our authors also benefited from the help of their colleagues or staff: Chris Reij would like to give special thanks to the partners of the African Re-greening Initiatives in Mali and Burkina Faso, and in particular to Mary Allen and Mathieu Ouedraogo; Pay Drechsel wishes to thank Philip Amoah, Ben Keraita, Robert Abaidoo, Kwame Nkrumah, and Terry Clayton for their help for his FROM THE FIELD piece on wastewater irrigation.

In addition, this book could not have been written if not for the dozens upon dozens of experts, academics, journalists, businesswomen and men, cab drivers, bus drivers, hotel owners, farmers, and everyday citizens who provided advice and assistance as we traveled throughout sub-Saharan Africa over the last year. Special thanks goes to the following people: Jules Adjima, Pierluigi Agnelli, Leila Akahloun, Dr. King David Amoah, Stephen Amoah, Dr. Kwasi Ampofo, Festus Annor-Frempong, Emmanuel Antai-Taylor, Raymond Auerbach, Eric Biantuadi, Diallo Bineta, Mark Bittman, Donna Bryson, Madou Camara, Argent Chuula, Maimouna Coulibaly, Madyo Couto, Dr. Rosa da Costa, Matty Demont, Joseph DeVries, Raoul DuToit, Felix Edwards, Bishr El-Touni, Moussa Faye, Gregory Flatt, Mariam Ouattara Gnire, Bill Guyton, Richard Haigh, Rick Hall, Getrude Hambira, Jan Helsen, Dee Hertzberg, Eric Holt-Gimenez, Momodou Mbye Jabang, Chris Johnson, Calestous Juma, Susan Kaaria, Daniel Kamanga, Elizabeth Katushabe, Dr. Charles

Kayumba, Sabera Khan, Yacouba Kone, Diana Lee-Smith, Suzanne Lenzer, Mark Lesiit, Dale Lewis, Mia MacDonald, Seck Madieng, Mohamedou Ould Mohamed Mahmoud, Esther Mjoki Maima, Annalisa Mansutti, Sainey Marenah, Santiago Medina, Katlella Abdou Mai Moussa, Rob Munro, Roni Neff, Kristoff and Stacia Nordin, Charles Onyoni Onyando, Osabarima, Nancy Ayesua Out, Fatouma Sophie Outtara, Dov Pasternack, Raj Patel, Steve Power, Charles A. Ray, Jill Richardson, Albert Rouamba, Pap Saine, Aïssatou Seck, Kamuturaki Seremos, Lindiwe Majele Sibanda, Ruth N. Simwanza, Paul Yempapou Sinandja, Salibo Some, Noel Kokou Tadegnon, Joe Welsh, Mark Wood, and Denise Young. We'd also like to thank Joyce Nierenberg, Stuart Pollack, and Barbara Sabbath for accepting late-night collect phone calls from Africa and for their general support of our endeavors.

Buoyed by these marvelous funders, contacts, friends, advisers, volunteers, and colleagues, the Worldwatch staff bring their own dedication to *State of the World*. The Institute would not be able to function without Director of Finance and Administration Barbara Fallin, who has kept the office running smoothly for 22 years. We would also like to thank Darcey Rakestraw, Worldwatch's communications manager, who left the Institute in 2010 to share her expertise at Food and Water Watch. Darcey left her tasks in the very capable hands of Julia Tier, who just before the book was finished left Worldwatch to begin an adventure teaching English in Thailand. Ben Block, Worldwatch's staff writer and Web manager, also left the Institute in the fall of 2010 for a Fulbright in Peru. In addition, Alice Jasperson, *Vital Signs Online* Manager, decided to leave her data-intensive desk job to work in El Salvador. And Juliane Diamond left her position as Development Assistant and Assistant to the President in order to pursue her interests at the Wildlife Alliance.

Molly Theobald, our Food and Agricul-ture Research Fellow, joined the Nourishing the Planet team in 2009. Molly became a Jill of all trades, editing video, writing blogs, and contributing two FROM THE FIELD articles to the book. She was joined by NtP Communications Assistant Amanda Stone during the summer of 2010. Amanda has done a tremendous job reaching out to reporters around the world, as well as improving NtP's social media profile via Twitter, Facebook, Tumblr, and other emerging media. Bernard Pollack, Danielle's partner and traveling companion, contributed to the project as an NtP communications consultant.

Early discussions of this book were enriched by the participation of many Worldwatch staff members, including Vice President Robert Engelman, who has inspired NtP and the Institute with his leadership. Patricia Shyne, Director of Publications and Marketing, was helpful in putting NtP in touch with Worldwatch's international partners. Senior Fellows Gary Gardner and Michael Renner also gave feedback, advice, and suggestions throughout the research and writing for both the blog and the book.

Our development team, which maintains Worldwatch's ties to its supporters, also actively supported this book. We welcomed the creativity of Mary Redfern, Manager of Foundation Relations, and Trudy Loo, Friends of Worldwatch Program Manager. We were also boosted by the new Development Assistant and Assistant to Worldwatch President, Alex Kostura.

Lisa Mastny took time away from editing Worldwatch reports to trim the timeline in this book that was compiled by Kelsey Russell, while Alexander Ochs, Erik Assadourian, John Mulrow, Saya Kitasei, Sam Shrank, Amanda Chui, and Worldwatch's new China Program Manager, Haibing Ma, all provided helpful advice on chapters and other aspects of the project. Corey Perkins and his team of IT consultants also helped keep the NtP Web site and blog on the cutting edge.

As always, we are indebted to independent editor Linda Starke, who helped authors turn their final drafts into polished chapters. This is Linda's twenty-eighth year editing *State of the World*, and we are tremendously grateful for her expertise and dedication. In addition, graphic designer Lyle Rosbotham rapidly turned 15 scattered chapters and numerous short articles into a book with eye-catching photos.

The Worldwatch family continues to grow. Last year, Worldwatch Senior Fellow and Co-Project Director Brian Halweil and his wife, Sarah, welcomed the newest addition to their family, Cyrus Halweil. And Lisa Mastny and her partner, Steve Conklin, welcomed Elsa to their family. Both Cyrus and Elsa remind us of our hopes for a more just, environmentally sustainable world free of poverty and hunger.

Danielle Nierenberg and Brian Halweil
Project Directors

Worldwatch Institute
1776 Massachusetts Ave., NW
Washington, DC 20036
www.worldwatch.org
www.NourishingthePlanet.org

Contents

Acknowledgments vii

Foreword xvii
    Olivier De Schutter, United Nations Special Rapporteur on the Right to Food

Preface xx
    Christopher Flavin, President, Worldwatch Institute

State of the World: A Year in Review xxiii
    Kelsey Russell and Lisa Mastny

1   Charting a New Path to Eliminating Hunger 3
     Brian Halweil and Danielle Nierenberg

FROM THE FIELD: Measuring Success in Agricultural Development 13

2   Moving Ecoagriculture into the Mainstream 15
     Louise E. Buck and Sara J. Scherr

FROM THE FIELD: Innovations in Rice Breeding in Madagascar 25

3   The Nutritional and Economic Potential of Vegetables 27
     Abdou Tenkouano

FROM THE FIELD: Developing Innovations in School Cultivation 36

FROM THE FIELD: The One Acre Fund Puts Farmers First 38

4   Getting More Crop per Drop 39
     Sandra L. Postel

FROM THE FIELD: Rainwater Harvesting 49

5   Farmers Take the Lead in Research and Development 51
     Brigid Letty, Qureish Noordin, Saidou Magagi, and Ann Waters-Bayer

FROM THE FIELD: Grain Trading in Zambia 58

6   Africa's Soil Fertility Crisis and the Coming Famine 59
     Roland Bunch

FROM THE FIELD: New Cassava Varieties in Zanzibar 69

7   Safeguarding Local Food Biodiversity 71
    Serena Milano

FROM THE FIELD: Threats to Animal Genetic Resources in Kenya 81

FROM THE FIELD: The Benefits of Solar Cookers in Senegal 82

8   Coping with Climate Change and Building Resilience 83
    An Agnostic Approach to Climate Adaptation, *David Lobell and Marshall Burke*
    Investing in Trees to Mitigate Climate Change, *Chris Reij*
    The Climate Crisis on Our Plates, *Anna Lappé*

FROM THE FIELD: An Evergreen Revolution for Africa 97

9   Post-Harvest Losses: A Neglected Field 99
    Tristram Stuart

FROM THE FIELD: Turning the Catch of the Day into Better Livelihoods 108

10 Feeding the Cities 109
    Nancy Karanja and Mary Njenga

FROM THE FIELD: Promoting Safer Wastewater Irrigation in West Africa 118

FROM THE FIELD: An Agricultural Answer to Nature's Call 120

11 Harnessing the Knowledge and Skills of Women Farmers 121
    Dianne Forte, Royce Gloria Androa, and Marie-Ange Binagwaho

FROM THE FIELD: Using Theater to Help Women Farmers 130

FROM THE FIELD: What Is an Appropriate Technology? 132

12 Investing in Africa's Land: Crisis and Opportunity 133
    Andrew Rice

FROM THE FIELD: Better Food Storage 141

13 The Missing Links: Going Beyond Production 143
    Samuel Fromartz

FROM THE FIELD: Churches Moving Beyond Hunger Relief 153

14 Improving Food Production from Livestock 155
    *Mario Herrero, with Susan MacMillan, Nancy Johnson, Polly Ericksen,
    Alan Duncan, Delia Grace, and Philip K. Thornton*

FROM THE FIELD: Small-Scale Livestock Production in Rwanda 164

15 A Road Map for Nourishing the Planet 165
    Innovations in Understanding Complex Systems, *Hans R. Herren*
    Innovations in Evaluating Agricultural Development Projects, *Charles Benbrook*
    Innovations in Institutions to Support People and the Planet, *Marcia Ishii-Eiteman*
    Innovations in Governance, *Anuradha Mittal*
    Innovations in Policy Reform, *Alexandra Spieldoch*

Notes 183
Index 221

BOXES

1–1   Global Hunger and Agricultural Trends 4
2–1   Examples of Agroecological Farming 17
3–1   Plant Breeding Innovations: Necessity and Promise 30
3–2   Indigenous Food and Climate Change 34
4–1   Solar Market Gardens: Increasing Access to Energy, Water, and Food 45
5–1   Sharing Innovations in Ethiopia 56
7–1   Diversity in the Food System 75
9–1   Food Waste in Asia 102
10–1 Pushing the Limits of Urban Agriculture 114
11–1 Social Capital Investments: An Innovation to End Poverty 123
11–2 Engaging Cocoa-Growing Communities to Support Women's
      Empowerment 125
13–1 A Better Deal 145
13–2 Phone Banking 151
14–1 Controlling Newcastle Disease in Poultry in Mozambique 161
15–1 Agricultural R&D: New Public-Private Sector Dynamics 170

TABLES

1–1   Putting Sub-Saharan Africa in Perspective 11
4–1   Selected Low-cost Innovations that Improve Water Access and Efficiency
      in Agriculture 42
7–1   Selected Endangered Foods in Africa and Efforts to Save Them 77
10–1 Innovations That Nourish Cities 111
12–1 Selected Proposed and Completed Foreign Investments in Land
      in Africa 137
14–1 Livestock, Livelihoods, and the Environment 157

FIGURES

1–1   Food Prices, 1990–2010 6

2–1   Elements of a Biologically Based, Integrated Soil-Plant-Animal
        Cropping System 16

2–2   Increasing Farm Production and Protecting Forests and Wildlife in
        a Densely Populated Agricultural Landscape 18

2–3   Managing Blue Water and Green Water in Agricultural Landscapes 19

4–1   Percentage of Cultivated Land That is Irrigated, Selected Regions and
        World, circa 2005 41

4–2   Annual Economic Growth and Variations from Mean Monthly Rainfall
        for Niger, 1961 2000 41

9–1   Estimated Losses, Conversions, and Wastage in the Global Food Chain 107

10–1 Urban Households Participating in Agricultural Activities,
        Selected Countries 112

13–1 Maize Production and Area Planted in Zambia, 2002–10 147

13–2 Area of Maize Planted That is Harvested and Total Yield in Zambia,
        2002–10 147

Units of measure throughout this book are metric unless common usage dictates otherwise.

Foreword

Olivier De Schutter
United Nations Special Rapporteur on the Right to Food

We live in a world in which we produce more food than ever before and in which the hungry have never been as many. There is a reason for this: for too many years we have focused on increasing food availability while neglecting both the distributional impacts of food production and their long-term environmental impacts. We have succeeded, remarkably, in increasing yields. But we must now realize that we can produce more and yet fail to tackle hunger at the same time, that increases in yields—while a necessary condition for alleviating hunger and malnutrition—are not a sufficient condition, and that as we spectacularly boosted overall levels of production during the second half of the twentieth century we created the conditions for a major ecological disaster in the twenty-first century.

This thinking is part of the reason that the global fight against hunger and malnutrition has been increasingly grounded since the 1996 World Food Summit on the right to adequate food. In 2000, the United Nations established the mandate of the appointment of the Special Rapporteur on the right to food, whose role is to update it on progress—or lack thereof—toward eliminating hunger. And in 2004, governments agreed to support the progressive realization of the right to adequate food in the context of national food security. These developments are evidence of the international community's conviction that we need to address the problem of global hunger not as one of production only but also as one of marginalization, deepening inequalities, and social injustice.

The right to food seeks to improve accountability and to ensure that governments do not mistake the challenge of combating hunger and malnutrition for the challenge of increasing yields. But accountability is also a tool to ensure that public policies will be guided by the needs of those at the bottom of the social ladder and that policies will be permanently tested and, where necessary, revised. In an increasingly complex and fast-changing world, learning becomes vital to sound public policies—learning that revises our values and presuppositions, the very paradigms under which we work and our ways of framing the problems we address.

In agricultural and food policies, three important developments make such learning not just urgent but indispensable. First, we realize how fragile our current food systems are. As a result of both demographic growth and a lack of investment in agriculture in a number of developing countries, particularly in sub-Saharan Africa, many countries' dependence on international markets has increased significantly. That represents a heavy burden, particularly when prices spike as a result of speculative bubbles forming on the markets for agricultural commodities—and especially since higher food bills are typically combined with higher prices for oil.

Second, there is mounting evidence that climate change will significantly affect agricultural production. Indeed, climate change is already threatening the ability of entire regions, particularly those with rainfed agriculture, to maintain former levels of agricultural production. According to the U.N. Development Programme, by 2080 the number of additional people at risk of hunger could reach 600 million as a direct result of climate change.

In sub-Saharan Africa, arid and semiarid areas are projected to increase by 60–90 million hectares, and the Intergovernmental Panel on Climate Change has estimated that in Southern Africa yields from rainfed agriculture could be cut perhaps in half between 2000 and 2020. Losses in agricultural production in a number of developing countries could be partially compensated by gains in other regions, but the overall result would be a decrease of at least 3 percent in productive capacity by the 2080s and of up to 16 percent if the predicted carbon fertilization effects (an increase of yields due to higher carbon dioxide concentration in the atmosphere) fail to materialize.

Third, as noted earlier, we now understand that increasing the production of food and eradicating hunger and malnutrition are two very different objectives—complementary perhaps, but not necessarily linked. It took a generation to understand that the "Green Revolution" package of irrigation, mechanization, high-yielding seed varieties, and chemical fertilizers may have to be fundamentally revised in order to be more sustainable, both socially and environmentally. In 80 percent of the studies of the Green Revolution over 30 years, the researchers who considered the equity dimension concluded that inequality increased as a result of the technological shift.

The Green Revolution did not reach the poorest farmers working on the most marginal soils. It largely bypassed women, because women had less access to credit than men, received less support from extension services, and could not afford the inputs on which the technological revolution was based. It sometimes locked cash-strapped farmers into a dependence on high-value external inputs. It switched from labor-intensive forms of production to a capital-intensive agricultural model, accelerating rural flight in the absence of alternative jobs.

Some clear conclusions are emerging from all this evidence. We need to improve the resilience of countries—particularly poor, net-food-importing countries—vis-à-vis increasingly high and volatile prices on the international markets. We need to encourage modes of agricultural production that will be more resistant to climate change, which means that they will have to be more diversified and use more trees. We need a kind of agriculture that mitigates climate change. And we need to develop agriculture in ways that contribute to rural development by creating jobs both on farms and off them in the rural areas and by supporting decent revenues for farmers. That much is generally recognized across ideological and geographical boundaries. The challenge, however, is to draw the lessons from these three developments together rather than to treat them separately. Fortunately, *State of the World 2011* shows that alternatives exist that can offer a response.

The ability of developing countries to feed themselves can be improved by supporting agricultural production that respects the environment and benefits the poor in rural areas. Agroecological approaches move away from the twentieth-century tendency to reduce nature to its separate elements. Instead, they recognize the complexity of food production. They see the plant in relation to ecosystems. They reward the inventiveness of farmers, who move from being passive recipients of knowledge developed in laboratories to being co-inventors of the knowledge they need.

Agroecology is generally characterized by a low use of external inputs, limiting dependence on high-priced fertilizers and pesticides. Inputs such as manure or compost are mostly locally produced, and when leguminous plants or trees are used to fertilize the soils, diversity on the plot helps make these systems self-sustaining. Often, agroecological techniques require a close link between the farmer and the land, and they can be labor-intensive. But this is an asset, not a liability: the creation of employment in rural areas can benefit rural development, particularly if combined with encouragement of local agro-food processing capacities and the increase of off-farm jobs.

But systems that rely primarily on locally produced inputs, on the expertise of farmers, and on sustainable modes of production will not flourish without strong public policies that encourage such a shift. Agroecological modes of production can be highly productive per hectare, and they are very efficient in their use of natural resources. Because they are generally labor-intensive, however, they cannot easily compete with larger-scale highly mechanized and capitalized forms of production. Without strong support from the state, they lose.

Governments can support these systems by giving priority to sustainable agriculture in public procurement programs or by fiscal incentives that tax the externalities produced by large-scale heavily mechanized plantations and that reward production that contributes to poverty reduction and environmental sustainability. And governments have a role, too, in providing the public goods that agroecology needs in order to flourish: extension services that work in combination with farmer-to-farmer transmission of knowledge; storage facilities and infrastructure linking farmers to consumers and allowing farmers to bypass intermediaries; the organization of farmers into cooperatives that help them increase their bargaining power, achieve certain economies of scale in processing and marketing, and improve the speed at which each farmer can learn from others. Where governments are ill equipped to perform these tasks or neglect to fulfill their duties, the private sector should be made aware of its own responsibilities not to further increase our debt to the future.

The full realization of the right to food, which includes a dimension of sustainability, cannot be left simply to the mechanisms of the market. It requires the presence of the state. And it requires that we invest in accountability mechanisms and monitoring for results that improve public governance. This is why I encourage governments to implement national strategies on the realization of the right to food, building on the U.N. Food and Agriculture Organization's Voluntary Guidelines on the right to food. The human right to adequate food, after all, has not only a symbolic value. It refers both to a legal duty and to an operational framework. The right to food must reach food security laws, policies, and programs. It will complement the agricultural development model that is sketched here and in this book. It will ensure that we are on the right track to fight hunger.

Preface

Christopher Flavin
President, Worldwatch Institute

The heat wave that swept western Russia in the summer of 2010 seemed at first like a local crisis. Temperatures soared to 40 degrees Celsius or more for several weeks, making Moscow feel more like Dubai. A population that largely lacks air conditioning suffered in the sweltering temperatures. Conditions deteriorated further when the heat wave caused extensive forest fires that destroyed suburban neighborhoods and left Muscovites choking on heavy smoke for over a week. Before the calamity was over, Prime Minister Vladimir Putin had taken the controls of a firefighting plane in a theatrical effort to show that the government had not lost control of the situation.

For other parts of the world, the unusual Russian weather seemed at first to be a television spectacle—until it became clear that the heat wave and accompanying drought had devastated the country's wheat crop. Within days, Russian officials announced the suspension of wheat exports, which immediately sent world prices soaring by more than a third, with follow-on effects on corn, soybeans, and the rest of the world food market.

This second spike in world food prices in just two years was a harsh reminder of the vulnerability of a world food system striving to feed nearly 6.9 billion people amidst a host of environmental limits and an increasingly unstable world climate. The frontlines of this agricultural crisis are occupied by the world's 925 million undernourished people—many of them children living in Africa and South Asia—who face the prospect that their lives will become even more precarious in the months ahead.

Ironically, world agriculture has in some respects been an impressive success story in recent decades. Efforts to raise crop yields by investing in new agricultural technologies and infrastructure have met many of their immediate goals. Productivity has risen steadily in major grain producers such as Australia and the United States, while large areas of Asia, including China, have succeeded in raising yields and thereby reducing rural poverty and hunger.

But that is only part of the story. Agriculture has advanced little in much of South Asia and sub-Saharan Africa, where national governments and the international community have underinvested in agriculture over the past few decades. The failure to advance agriculture in some of the world's poorest regions has made it impossible for rural economies to develop, leaving hundreds of millions of people stuck in a cycle of poverty. Agriculture provides jobs for 1.3 billion small farmers and landless workers and is the main source of livelihood for an estimated 86 percent of the 3 billion rural people in developing countries. A better future for them will depend heavily on what happens on farms in the most destitute parts of the world.

Until recently, most policymakers believed that the only route to advancing agriculture in Africa was to double down on the Green Revolution—provide more productive seeds and fertilizer and thereby raisie yields. This is a seductively simple formula, but in many cases it has not worked. The seeds and fertilizer are often too expensive for the vast majority of poor farmers, or they are simply unavailable. And the benefits of many such projects go to a small number of large farmers who may produce abundant food but do little to promote rural development.

Fortunately, the notion that world hunger can be eliminated with money and technology alone is being discredited not just by its own shortcomings but by exciting evidence that new approaches to building a sustainable, nourishing agricultural system can effectively supplement or replace the innovations found in the standard agricultural toolbox. This is particularly true in sub-Saharan Africa, where thousands of small farmers are drawing on ancient cultural wisdom, along with clever new technologies, to produce abundant food while devastating neither local soils nor the global ecosystem.

That is the story of this book and of Worldwatch's Nourishing the Planet project. During 2009 and 2010, co-project director Danielle Nierenberg traveled across 25 African countries, visiting with farmers and learning about their successes with everything from drip irrigation to rooftop gardening, agroforestry, and new techniques for protecting the soil. Back in Washington, our team of researchers has been using the Internet to locate and analyze an ever wider array of innovative agricultural projects and passing that information on to a rapidly growing audience of Nourishing the Planet blog readers, YouTube viewers, and followers of Twitter.

The picture they paint is an exciting one.

Although we tend to think of innovation in terms of the latest search engine or video game, poor African farmers are demonstrating that innovation is occurring in some of the world's poorest communities—and that it may have a greater impact on people and the planet than most high-tech innovation does. By empowering small farmers—particularly women, who dominate farming in Africa—with simple but transformative innovations, rapid and productive change is possible. If even a fraction of the resources now being spent on factory farms in the United States and soybean plantations in Brazil were invested in innovative small farmers, the world would not be making such meager progress in meeting the U.N. goal of halving world hunger by 2015.

The stakes involved in addressing the world's agricultural problems go far beyond the immediate problem of hunger. At a time when the world is beginning to run up against limits of arable land and water in many areas, rising agricultural productivity will be even more essential to meeting food needs than it has been in the past. And cheap oil will no longer be the easy replacement for degraded renewable resources that it was in the twentieth century. That is why innovations such as using green cover crops as natural fertilizer or locally produced biofuels as a substitute for diesel fuel are so exciting.

Agriculture also has an enormous impact on the natural world. Many of the innovations described in this book can reverse the damage that food production often does to water and soils—and to the ecosystem services that we all depend on.

The world food economy is at the center of global environmental problems as well. Today's agriculture, with its heavy dependence on fossil fuels, not only contributes to global warming—some of the carbon now in the atmosphere was once embedded in the deep prairie soils of North America and Central Europe—it is at grave risk from a changing climate. The summer of 2010 was the hottest ever recorded, and scientists say that the extraordinary weather events that accompanied it—including floods 2,000 kilometers south of Moscow in Pakistan that inundated 1.4 million acres of rich cropland—would have been improbable without the 30-percent increase in the atmospheric concentration of carbon dioxide that occurred since the Industrial Revolution.

One bit of encouraging news that comes across clearly from the agricultural innovations documented in this book is that new approaches to agriculture can contribute to a range of urgent development priorities, from protecting threatened supplies of fresh water to restoring fisheries and slowing climate change. Agricultural innovation also contributes to improved human health, not only by feeding the world's poor but by reducing the epidemic of obsesity that is spreading from the rich world to the poor world.

We have been extremely pleased to partner with the Bill & Melinda Gates Foundation on this literally groundbreaking Nourishing the Planet project. By combining the foundation's commitment to raising agricultural productivity with our focus on finding environmentally sustainable approaches to agriculture, we are building a new bridge that may open a better future for hundreds of millions of poor farmers in Africa and beyond.

Nourishing people and nourishing the planet are now as inextricably linked as they are essential to our future. We hope that *State of the World 2011* will contribute to thinking more systemically—and more radically—about the future of the food system. We must dispense with simple truths like "bigger is better" and avoid the search for silver bullet solutions to complex problems. If we do that, agriculture may once again become a center of human innovation—and the goals of ending hunger and creating a sustainable world will be a little closer than they are today.

Christopher Flavin

State of the World: A Year in Review

Compiled by Kelsey Russell and Lisa Mastny

This timeline covers some significant announcements and reports from October 2009 through
September 2010. It is a mix of progress, setbacks,
and missed steps around the world that are affecting environmental quality and social welfare.

Timeline events were selected to increase awareness of the connections between people and the
environmental systems on which they depend.

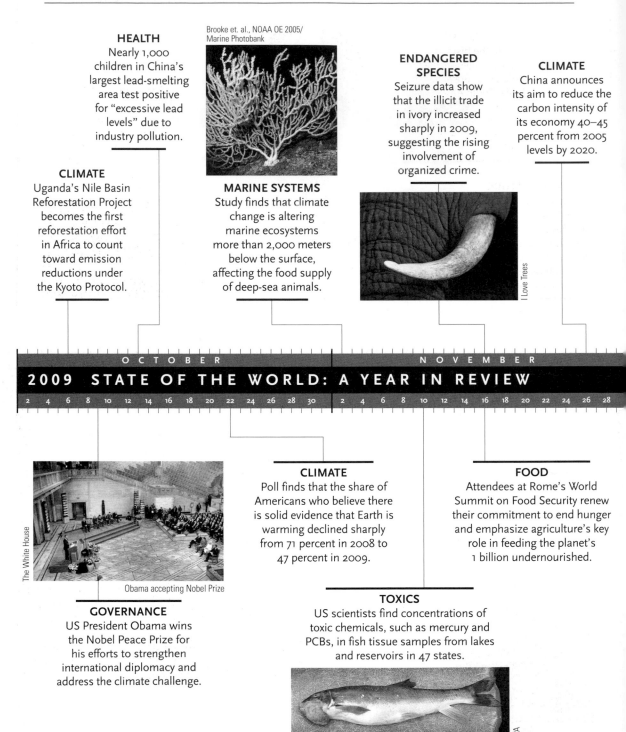

HEALTH
Nearly 1,000 children in China's largest lead-smelting area test positive for "excessive lead levels" due to industry pollution.

Brooke et. al., NOAA OE 2005/ Marine Photobank

ENDANGERED SPECIES
Seizure data show that the illicit trade in ivory increased sharply in 2009, suggesting the rising involvement of organized crime.

CLIMATE
China announces its aim to reduce the carbon intensity of its economy 40–45 percent from 2005 levels by 2020.

CLIMATE
Uganda's Nile Basin Reforestation Project becomes the first reforestation effort in Africa to count toward emission reductions under the Kyoto Protocol.

MARINE SYSTEMS
Study finds that climate change is altering marine ecosystems more than 2,000 meters below the surface, affecting the food supply of deep-sea animals.

I Love Trees

OCTOBER   NOVEMBER

2009   STATE OF THE WORLD: A YEAR IN REVIEW

2 4 6 8 10 12 14 16 18 20 22 24 26 28 30   2 4 6 8 10 12 14 16 18 20 22 24 26 28

The White House

Obama accepting Nobel Prize

CLIMATE
Poll finds that the share of Americans who believe there is solid evidence that Earth is warming declined sharply from 71 percent in 2008 to 47 percent in 2009.

FOOD
Attendees at Rome's World Summit on Food Security renew their commitment to end hunger and emphasize agriculture's key role in feeding the planet's 1 billion undernourished.

GOVERNANCE
US President Obama wins the Nobel Peace Prize for his efforts to strengthen international diplomacy and address the climate challenge.

TOXICS
US scientists find concentrations of toxic chemicals, such as mercury and PCBs, in fish tissue samples from lakes and reservoirs in 47 states.

EPA

growth on long-nose sucker

CLIMATE
At the historic Copenhagen climate conference, Brazil, China, India, South Africa, and the United States agree to a non-binding accord to reduce carbon dioxide emissions.

AGRICULTURE
In conjunction with the twentieth anniversary of Slow Food, 1,000 communities in 120 countries take part in events to encourage agricultural diversity and sustainable food production.

MARINE ECOSYSTEMS
Massachusetts becomes the first US state to develop a comprehensive plan to protect its marine resources.

TRANSPORTATION
Industry group says the Toyota Prius was Japan's best-selling car in 2009, marking the first time a hybrid vehicle has topped annual auto sales.

Toyota

DECEMBER   JANUARY

2010

2 4 6 8 10 12 14 16 18 20 22 24 26 28 30   2 4 6 8 10 12 14 16 18 20 22 24 26 28 30

NATURAL DISASTERS
UN reports that 36 million people were displaced by natural disasters in 2009, with more than 20 million forced to move due to climate change-related factors.

L'Aquila earthquake, Italy

CONSUMPTION
Washington, DC, implements a "bag tax," requiring businesses that sell food or alcohol to charge 5¢ for every disposable paper or plastic carryout bag.

TRANSPORTATION
Report says Americans scrapped more automobiles than they bought in 2009 as the recession reduced demand and some major cities expanded mass transit service.

NATURAL DISASTERS
Haiti experiences its worst earthquake in more than 200 years, a 7.0 magnitude tremor that leaves some 250,000 people dead and 1 million homeless.

lemur-poaching, Madagascar

lemming

BIODIVERSITY

More than 100 countries sign a new UN agreement to protect seven migratory shark species from threats, including illegal fishing, pollution, and climate change.

ENDANGERED SPECIES

Scientists report that nearly half of the world's 634 primate species risk extinction due to deforestation, illegal trading, and commercial bushmeat hunting.

ENERGY

Study reports that the Middle East and North Africa region has the potential to generate more than three times the world's current power demand by developing its renewable energy sector.

BIODIVERSITY

Scientists report a 26 percent decline in lemmings, caribou, and other High Arctic vertebrate species between 1970 and 2004, due in part to warmer average temperatures.

FEBRUARY   **MARCH**

2010 STATE OF THE WORLD: A YEAR IN REVIEW

2   4   6   8   10   12   14   16   18   20   22   24   26   28   2   4   6   8   10   12   14   16   18   20   22   24   26   28   30

FOOD

UN Secretary-General highlights the vital role of small-holders and rural producers in global food production and calls for new and varied partnerships to overcome hunger and poverty.

WATER

Flow levels in Asia's Mekong River reach record lows, posing threats to water supply, navigation, and irrigation for millions of people in Thailand, Laos, and China.

ENERGY

Canadian company successfully captures carbon dioxide emissions from a cement plant and uses them to produce nutrient-rich algae, in a milestone for advanced biofuels.

TRANSPORTATION

Study reports that global production of cars and light trucks dropped 13 percent in 2009, the second consecutive year of such declines.

NATURAL DISASTERS

South China suffers its worst drought in decades, leading to water shortages and crop losses that affect some 51 million people.

Bernard Pollack

African banana harvest

Charles Dawley

cement plant

CLIMATE

Scientists report that thawing permafrost in the northern hemisphere can release as much nitrous oxide as tropical forests, a leading source of the potent greenhouse gas.

POLLUTION

BP oil rig explodes in the Gulf of Mexico, killing 11 workers and triggering the release of some 5 million barrels of oil over three months—the largest accidental oil spill in history.

Patrick Keller, US Navy

ENERGY

India pledges to replace 400 million incandescent bulbs with energy-efficient CFLs, avoiding 40 million tons of carbon dioxide emissions in the largest carbon credit project.

CLIMATE

Some 60 countries commit to spending more than $4 billion over three years in a new partnership for Reducing Emissions from Deforestation and Forest Degradation.

TJ Watt

Vancouver Island clearcut

APRIL

MAY

2 4 6 8 10 12 14 16 18 20 22 24 26 28 30   2 4 6 8 10 12 14 16 18 20 22 24 26 28 30

anjči

NATURAL DISASTERS

Ash from an Icelandic volcano affects air travel in Europe and causes the loss of millions of dollars of African food and flower exports due to grounded cargo planes.

ENERGY

US government approves the $1 billion Cape Wind project off the coast of Massachusetts, the nation's first offshore wind farm.

CLIMATE

US government regulates greenhouse gas emissions from large stationary sources, including oil refineries and coal-fired power plants responsible for 70 percent of US emissions.

Walter Siegmund

FORESTS

Diverse stakeholders form the Forest Legality Alliance to reduce global demand for illegally harvested forest products and support production of legal wood and paper.

MARINE ECOSYSTEMS

Study reports that closing fishing areas and regulating the use of fishing gear can result in more profitable catches that boost fishers' incomes.

©IFAD/Franco Mattioli

pumping water in Ethiopia

ENERGY

UNEP reports that in 2009, China surpassed the US as the country with the greatest investment in clean energy development and technology.

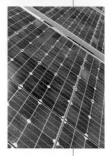

CLIMATE

European agency reports that EU-27 countries experienced their fifth consecutive year of emissions declines in 2008, with greenhouse gases down 11 percent from 1990 levels.

WATER

Water security index of 165 countries finds that 10 nations, including five in Africa, are at "extreme risk" due to shortages of clean, fresh water.

BIODIVERSITY

Russia announces plans to establish nine new nature reserves and 13 national parks by 2020, expanding the nation's protected areas to 3 percent of its territory.

WATER

UN General Assembly declares access to clean water and sanitation a human right, voicing deep concern that nearly 900 million people worldwide lack access to safe drinking water.

JUNE   **JULY**

2010 STATE OF THE WORLD: A YEAR IN REVIEW

2 4 6 8 10 12 14 16 18 20 22 24 26 28 30   2 4 6 8 10 12 14 16 18 20 22 24 26 28 30

FORESTS

Scientists report that deforestation in Brazil's Amazon is creating better habitat for mosquitoes, leading to a 48 percent increase in malaria cases in one surveyed county.

CLIMATE

US agency reports that June 2010 was the 304th consecutive month with above-average temperatures as well as the warmest June since record keeping began in 1880.

GOVERNANCE

UNESCO removes Galapagos Islands from its endangered world heritage list, citing strong action by Ecuador to mitigate threats from tourism, immigration, and invasive species.

ENERGY

Report says that Italy surpassed the United States in solar photovoltaic installations in 2009, making it the world's second largest PV market after Germany.

NATURAL DISASTERS

Russia's worst heatwave in 130 years destroys nearly 10 million hectares of crops and prompts the declaration of a state of emergency in 17 regions.

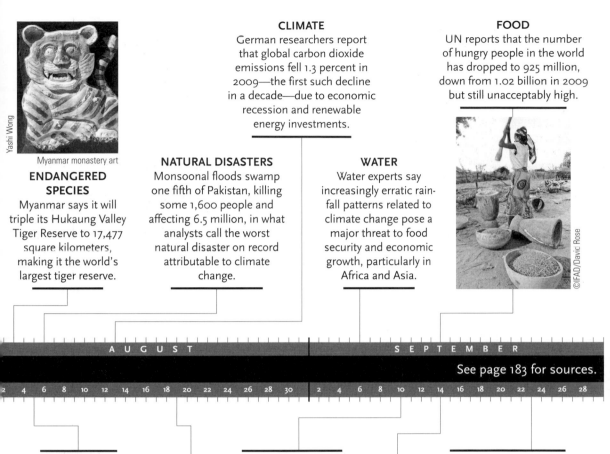

Myanmar monastery art

Yashi Wong

CLIMATE
German researchers report that global carbon dioxide emissions fell 1.3 percent in 2009—the first such decline in a decade—due to economic recession and renewable energy investments.

FOOD
UN reports that the number of hungry people in the world has dropped to 925 million, down from 1.02 billion in 2009 but still unacceptably high.

ENDANGERED SPECIES
Myanmar says it will triple its Hukaung Valley Tiger Reserve to 17,477 square kilometers, making it the world's largest tiger reserve.

NATURAL DISASTERS
Monsoonal floods swamp one fifth of Pakistan, killing some 1,600 people and affecting 6.5 million, in what analysts call the worst natural disaster on record attributable to climate change.

WATER
Water experts say increasingly erratic rainfall patterns related to climate change pose a major threat to food security and economic growth, particularly in Africa and Asia.

©IFAD/Davic Rose

AUGUST   **SEPTEMBER**

See page 183 for sources.

2 4 6 8 10 12 14 16 18 20 22 24 26 28 30   2 4 6 8 10 12 14 16 18 20 22 24 26 28

CLIMATE
An ice island four times the size of Manhattan breaks off of Greenland, which scientists say is the Arctic's biggest ice loss since 1962.

Greenland glacier

ENDANGERED SPECIES
Scientists report that more than 40 percent of the planet's freshwater turtle species are threatened with extinction due to habitat loss, hunting, and a lucrative pet trade.

ENERGY
World's largest offshore wind farm opens off southeast UK coast with 100 turbines and 300 megawatts of generating capacity, enough to power more than 200,000 UK households.

FOOD
Researchers say that distributing new varieties of drought-tolerant maize to African farmers could save more than $1.5 billion and boost yields up to a quarter by 2016.

MARINE ECOSYSTEMS
Researchers say overfishing has deprived the food industry of at least $36 billion annually and prevented nearly 20 million poor people a year from receiving adequate nourishment.

Phil Hollman

2 0 1 1
STATE OF THE WORLD
Innovations that Nourish the Planet

Member of a women's group waters their cabbage, Zimbabwe.

CHAPTER 1

Charting a New Path to Eliminating Hunger

Brian Halweil and Danielle Nierenberg

Along the shoreline of the Gambia River, a group of women has achieved rare success in reducing hunger in their communities. It revolves around a certain briny mollusk. To boost their incomes and safeguard a source of nourishment, the 15 communities in the Women's Oyster Harvesting Association—a total of nearly 6,000 people—agreed to close one tributary in their oyster territories for an entire year and to lengthen the "closed" season in other areas.[1]

These steps were difficult in the short term. But by the following season the oysters were bigger, and so was the price they commanded. Customers, primarily other local merchants or women who want to make fried oysters for their families as a protein-filled treat, have so far been willing to pay a little bit more. Meanwhile, the harvesters—many of them immigrants from surrounding nations and the poorest of the poor in The Gambia—are also putting on plays about mangrove restoration and building hatcheries to further boost the wild stocks, as well as eyeing upscale markets in hotels and restaurants that cater to tourists.[2]

Oysters are not necessarily what come to mind when confronting the task of eliminating hunger and poverty around the globe. After all, according to the latest U.N. Food and Agriculture Organization (FAO) report, 925 million people are undernourished. (See Box 1–1.) That is 98 million fewer than in 2009.

Box 1–1. Global Hunger and Agricultural Trends

In September 2010, FAO released its latest report on hunger, finding that 925 million people are undernourished—98 million fewer than in 2009. (See Figure.) While the lower number is encouraging, it is still unacceptably high—and nowhere near the Millennium Development Goal of halving hunger by 2015. Ghana is the only sub-Saharan African country on course to cut its prevalence of hunger by then.

Globally, the 2010 hunger figure marked a decline of 7.5 percent from the 2009 level. The reduction was mostly concentrated in Asia. FAO estimates that 80 million fewer people were hungry there in 2010. Gains were much smaller in sub-Saharan Africa, where one third of the population was hungry. Furthermore, the overall number of hungry people in sub-Saharan Africa has increased over the last decade. In Burundi, Comoros, the Democratic Republic of the Congo, and Eritrea, chronic hunger affects at least half the population.

Overall, women and children account for the highest proportion of the chronically hungry. High food prices and lower incomes put poor households at an additional risk of not providing expectant mothers, infants, and children with adequate nutrition. Indeed,

more than one third of child deaths worldwide are related to inadequate nutrition.

Most of the men and women, usually farmers, who live on less than $1.25 a day are found in rural areas, lacking land tenure, infrastructure, and access to health services or electricity. Increasingly, however, cities are not immune to hunger. In the 1980s and 1990s the urban population of Africa increased by 4 percent each year, while poverty levels continued to increase as well. The population of slum dwellers is also growing worldwide—at almost 1 percent each year. Rising food prices during the 2007/08 world food price crisis were especially hard on the urban poor. In Kenya, for example, FAO estimated that 4.1 million urban poor in 2009 were "highly food-insecure" and as many as 7.6 million were unable to meet their daily food needs.

While world food prices have fallen since 2008, they remain well above pre-2007 levels, and the trend continued steadily upward in 2009 and 2010. Many food aid programs have not been able to purchase as much food, and the recession has meant less money for food aid. The U.S. Agency for International Development reported that it was only able to donate

But a child still dies every six seconds from undernourishment. Oysters alone cannot address this tragedy.[3]

What can? Typically the solutions cited are higher-yielding seed varieties, dams to irrigate vast areas, and mountains of fertilizer to rejuvenate depleted soils. Yet seafood provides about 15 percent of the calories and a third of the protein that people worldwide consume—and more than that in poorer nations, including much of West Africa. So fisheries will in many regions be lasting sources of food and income for poor communities. But seafood is just one neglected part of the food chain that might provide

answers where fertilizer or irrigation or a focus on boosting grain production alone has not.[4]

It was on a journey to find such neglected solutions that we came upon this group of oyster harvesters. The context, and the basis of Worldwatch's Nourishing the Planet project, was this: Agriculture has come to a crossroads. Nearly a half-century after the Green Revolution, a major share of the human family is still chronically hungry. In addition, much of that revolution's gains have been achieved through highly intensive agriculture that depends heavily on fossil fuels for inputs and energy—and the question of whether the

Box 1–1 continued

$2.2 billion in 2009, a decrease of 15 percent from 2008.

Funding for agricultural development is down as well. The new multibillion-dollar U.S. food security and agriculture initiative (Feed the Future) proposes to invest $20 billion in African agriculture in the next decade. This is a timely recognition of the urgent need to invest more in this sector—but much of the money still needs to be raised. Agriculture's share of global development aid has dropped from over 16 percent to a meager 4 percent since 1980. Moreover, only nine African nations allocate even 10 percent of their national budgets to agriculture. Most of the continent's poor and hungry people depend on agriculture for all of their livelihoods. Yet public spending on agriculture is often lowest in countries with economies based on agriculture—in other words, farmers are, ironically, the hungriest people of all.

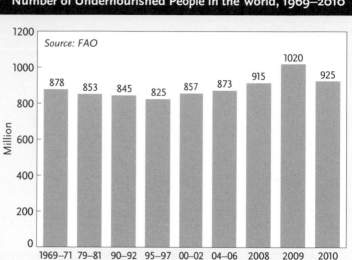

Number of Undernourished People in the World, 1969–2010

Source: FAO

Year	Million
1969–71	878
79–81	853
90–92	845
95–97	825
00–02	857
04–06	873
2008	915
2009	1020
2010	925

Increasingly, over the past two decades, the least developed countries have depended more on food imports. In 11 sub-Saharan African countries, half of the grain they used was imported in 2005–06. In seven other countries, imports accounted for 30–50 percent of their grain.

Source: See endnote 3.

world's croplands can yield more food is being trumped by the question of whether they can do so without compromise to the soils, fresh water, and crop diversity the world depends on. Food prices worldwide are under strong upward pressure (see Figure 1–1), driven by rapidly rising demand for meat in Asia, for wheat in Africa, for biofuels in Europe and North America, and other factors. Climate change is not likely to ease that pressure or make things easier for farmers.[5]

Perhaps most troubling is that investments in agricultural development by governments, international lenders, and foundations are near historic lows. However, the same record food

prices that handicap food-aid organizations and threaten hundreds of millions with hunger are also pushing governments, foundations, and other groups to consider dramatically shifting investments in agriculture. A recent World Bank analysis, for instance, suggested that the Bank has mistakenly neglected this sector and needs to shift resources back to rural areas—which is hands down the most cost-effective investment for reducing poverty and hunger around the world.[6]

Over the last two years we have traveled to 25 sub-Saharan African nations—the places where hunger is greatest and rural communities have struggled most—to hear people's

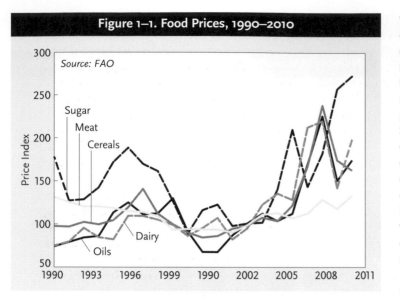

Figure 1–1. Food Prices, 1990–2010

Source: FAO

Sugar
Meat
Cereals
Dairy
Oils

stories of hope and success in agriculture. Africa has among the most persistent problems with malnutrition—it is home to the most nations where more than a third of the people are hungry. In spite of this, the continent is becoming a rich and diverse breeding ground for innovations in agriculture that support farmer income and nourishment for people at the same time.[7]

This journey has paid off in a treasure trove of innovation. On dozens of farms in Malawi we saw yield-boosting techniques used by more than 120,000 farmers, such as planting nitrogen-fixing trees that enrich the soil for the subsequent corn crop and that boost yields fourfold with no other added fertilizer. Across West Africa, we met farmers and shopkeepers using simple storage systems to prevent cowpeas, a major crop in the region, from rotting. If half of the area's cowpea harvest were stored this way, it would be worth $255 million annually to some of the poorest people in the world.[8]

Our aim was to shine a light on communities, countries, and companies that are models on the path to a sustainable future. And beyond the goal of reducing poverty and hunger, we

were guided by some more-traditional Worldwatch criteria. In order to keep feeding humanity for generations to come, and to feed people better, farming must reinforce conservation goals by adding diversity to the food chain and by healing ecosystems. What also becomes clear in visiting farms throughout Africa is that the food production base is in many places being degraded by soil mining, water scarcity, and a loss of the crop diversity that ultimately feeds future farming.

We were also interested in useful models for larger-scale efforts and for applications beyond Africa—even in wealthy nations that struggle with food waste, overeating, and other forms of agricultural dysfunction. A rooftop gardening cooperative that is feeding people in Dakar, Senegal, offers guidance for neighborhoods struggling with food shortages in inner-city New York. Individually, the hundreds of millions of small-scale farmers and their families who are the majority of the world's poor seem to have little power in the face of global issues like hunger, climate change, and water availability. But if each of their individual innovations were scaled up to bring food to the tables of not one farmer but 100 million or more, as well as to the consumers who depend on them, it could change the entire global food system.

But the global connections go beyond Africa. Everyone is in this together, in more ways than one. First, agriculture encompasses such a large chunk of the planet that healthy rural economies are also fundamental to global sustainability. To prevent disastrous climate change, it will help if farmers all over the world are rewarded for building up the carbon content of their soils. Second, even determined "locavores" who try to support local farmers depend on distant regions for coffee, cocoa, fruits, and other daily essentials or out-of-season specialties. The same Americans who are flocking to farmers' markets and pushing agribusiness away from feedlots may emerge as new lobbying allies in matters of international hunger policy. Third, even if people do not get their corn, rice, and beans from African farmers, they are sustained by the crop diversity in those fields. Poorer nations still house most of the world's dwindling food biodiversity, not to mention cultural wisdom that may be a source of enjoyment or better health. Finally, for most people there is also the moral dimension. It is hard to fully enjoy a hearty meal when nearly a billion people elsewhere in the world—perhaps including those nearby—cannot do the same.[9]

There is no single solution. In fact, it is the one-size-fits-all approach that has been so crippling. Past attempts have failed because they squeezed out diversity or depended too much on chemicals and other inputs that farmers could not afford. They also stumbled because they ignored women farmers or neglected to consider food culture as a way to change how they farm. Although a slightly smaller share of humanity is hungry, what the world has been doing about hunger has not really worked. And because attention has been focused relatively narrowly—on a few types of crops, on a few technologies—entire regions and ecosystems, not to mention myriad varieties of crops and rural ways of life, have been ignored.

So, here are three major shifts that we invite farmers, scientists, donors, agribusiness executives, and the global community to consider.

Go Beyond Seeds

The first shift needed is to look beyond the handful of crops that have absorbed most of agriculture's attention and also beyond developing new seeds as the default solution for hunger and poverty. The long-standing focus on seeds is no surprise: they are elegant vessels for delivering new technology to a farm. Whether it is an American corn farmer looking for more drought tolerance or a bean farmer in the Kenyan highlands, buying a new type of seed is a relatively inexpensive and immediate way to try to boost a farm's harvest and income. But this search for just the right seed has tended to erode crop diversity in both rich and poor nations. At the same time, building soils, growing crops other than grains, making better use of rainfed farms, and investing in other elements of the farm landscape have been profoundly neglected. Yet these hold vast promise for raising incomes and reducing poverty.

The Consultative Group on International Agricultural Research (CGIAR) spends 27 percent of its funding on genetic improvement of seeds, and most CGIAR centers are still organized around growing a particular crop—rice, wheat, corn, or potatoes, for instance. But in recent years this global research network has evolved by adding centers focused on agroforestry, integrated pest management, and irrigation; these centers now get nearly 25 percent of the CGIAR's budget.[10]

Because of their relative neglect until recently, the returns on investments in such technologies and strategies can be impressive. That does not necessarily mean they get invested in, however. Developing new seed varieties, for instance, can be a lucrative proposition for seed companies. But few companies have figured out ways to profit from encouraging the rebuilding of soils or aquifers. And the new reality of agricultural investment is that it comes less from public institutions like governments and universities than from private entities. In 1986, for example, of the $3.3 billion that the United States invested in agricultural research, 54 percent came from the public sector and 46 percent from the private sector. Today, in contrast, agribusiness firms—primarily seed and agrochemical companies—have emerged as the majority investors, responsible for 72 percent of the total.[11]

If seeds represent the short-term payoff option, the truly long-term investment with big returns is investing in the soil and water that nourish crops. In Mali and other parts of the African Sahel, soils are severely damaged from overgrazing and drought, but the use of green manure and cover crops can dramatically improve soil fertility without the use of expensive fertilizers. In Chapter 6, Roland Bunch cites recent interviews with farmers from more than 75 villages in six African countries that, like much of sub-Saharan Africa, suffer from well-documented soil exhaustion. "People no longer had any way of maintaining soil fertility," he notes. "Harvests were crashing, dropping 15–25 percent a year." Bunch notes that subsidizing chemical fertilizers, which some African nations are doing heavily (by up to 75 percent in Malawi, for example), has generally not been a good long-term strategy and actually reduces farmers' incentive to invest in more agroecological approaches to nourishing soils. When the fertilizer subsidies end, productivity will drop to virtually nothing. Instead, Bunch maintains that green manure/cover crops are the only sustainable solution to Africa's soil fertility crisis.[12]

Or consider that across much of Africa, only 15–30 percent of the rain that falls on fields gets used productively by crops, and if the land is severely degraded this share can drop to 5 percent. In these places, crop failures may be caused more by "poor on-farm rainwater management than by a shortage of rainfall," notes Sandra Postel in Chapter 4. Only a very small share of African farms currently have access to irrigation—albeit a share that is surging with low-cost, human-powered pumps like the MoneyMaker, the Mosi-O-Tunya ("the pump that thunders"), or the more ubiquitous treadle pump that is used by more than 2.3 mil-

lion poor farmers in Asia and Africa.[13]

But even without irrigation, farmers are finding they can insulate themselves from the worst effects of drought and boost yields dramatically in a rainy year by mulching, reducing tillage, and planting cover crops. As Postel notes, "working with farmers on six experimental farms in Kenya, Ethiopia, Zambia, and Tanzania, researchers found yield gains of 20–120 percent for maize and 35–100 percent for tef (a staple grain of the Ethiopian diet) on farms using such soil- and water-conserving practices versus those using traditional methods." This broad strategy, used in parallel with investing in place-appropriate irrigation, is relevant across the continent's 18 or more distinct growing regions, all of which are predicted to be shocked by more severe rainfall patterns in coming years.[14]

Go Beyond Farms

As Olivier De Schutter notes in the Foreword to this book, eliminating hunger does not just depend on the world's ability to produce enough food. For many communities, the solutions lie in making better use of the food already produced. A new study from the U.K.-based Soil Association suggests that the best way to ensure that everyone gets enough to eat is to change what kind of food is produced and improve its distribution: less meat production, use of more environmentally sustainable agricultural methods that do not rely on petrochemicals, and more local and regional production of food. In fact, many of the farms and organizations we visited seemed to be having the most success reducing hunger and poverty with work that had little to do with producing more crops.[15]

As Tristram Stuart notes in Chapter 9, some 25–50 percent of the harvest in poorer nations spoils or is contaminated by pests or mold before it reaches the dinner table. This amount of loss—sometimes the harvest gets returned to enrich soils, but increasingly it ends up in landfills and trash dumps—is shocking, considering that many experts estimate the world will need to double food production in the next half-century as people eat more meat and generally eat better. So it would make good sense to invest at least as aggressively in making better use of what is already produced as in boosting global production. Simple, low-cost fixes can go a long way in this respect, including inexpensive plastic bags that keep cowpeas dry and pests out, better-built silos for preserving grain, and preserving fruit (and vitamins) through solar drying techniques.[16]

Often food goes to waste because the link from farmer to market is slow, inefficient, or broken. In Zambia, Samuel Fromartz found that corn production was actually in oversupply in 2010 due to good rains and fertilizer subsidies. In theory, this could be profitable, since the excess could be sent to countries in short supply. But Zambia lacks infrastructure and marketing networks to do this, and farmers were simply dumping corn on the market at low prices—thereby entrenching poverty and sending a market signal to all the farmers to grow less. But Fromartz found some exceptions to this, such as Justine Chiyesu, as described in Chapter 13. With the help of the Production, Finance, and Technology (PROFIT) program of the U.S. Agency for International Development, Chiyesu was able to mechanize his farm and increase yields. PROFIT helped him find ways to bypass inefficient marketing networks, allowing him to sell directly to millers and get a better price for himself and the village of growers he represented.[17]

"Add value" has long been the mantra for struggling rural communities from the American Midwest to the North China Plain. That is, process, preserve, or otherwise transform raw commodities into a more valuable product—peanuts into peanut butter, for instance. But Africa has lagged in this realm, partly because of neglect in the off-farm businesses

©IFAD/G. Maurette

A young boy retrieves the day's ration of peanuts from inside a silo, Cameroon

that help farmers add value. In the last half-century, the amount of value-added to agriculture per person has nearly doubled across the developing world; over the same period, it has declined slightly in Africa, where investment in agricultural infrastructure like food processing facilities has lagged. This is partly why the poorest countries in Africa are twice as dependent on food imports today as 20 years ago—a precarious shift because global food prices have also become more erratic.[18]

And while most of the world's poor and hungry remain in rural areas, hunger is often migrating as the world becomes more urban. Where people in cities have jobs and can afford their next meal, the food may come from far away. But for slum dwellers in Kenya and

Ghana, the most reliable source of nourishment is often what they can grow themselves in patio gardens, on vacant lots, or on parcels of land near slums. At least 800 million people worldwide depend on urban agriculture for most of their food needs. Right now the majority of these urban farmers are in Asia, but with 14 million Africans migrating from country to city each year, the residents of Lagos, Dakar, and Nairobi will likely become as dependent on food raised in cities as people who live in Hanoi, Shanghai, and Phnom Penh. Urban agriculture is already an important source of income for millions of Africans. In Chapter 10, Nancy Karanja and Mary Njenga note that the poor in cities are not only supplying food to their own communities but also establishing seed multiplication projects, making their "farms" an important source of local seed for urban and rural farmers alike.[19]

Over the long term, the most important "off-farm" investment may well be making sure that the farmers of tomorrow have the opportunity and the desire to actually become farmers. In Uganda, Project DISC (for Developing Innovations in School Cultivation) has found that teaching students how to grow, cook, and eat spiderwiki, amaranth, and other native vegetables can help give young people a reason to stay in rural areas and become farmers.[20]

Working in schools can also help reduce hunger. In the United States, where 16.7 million children are deemed "food-insecure," the most effective government intervention has been the meals that children get in school. The school feeding programs of the World Food Programme (WFP) now reach at least 10 million girls worldwide, helping to combat gender inequities in education and nutrition. Take-home rations provide an incentive for parents to send girls to secondary school, and improved nutrition helps children develop properly and stay focused during classes.[21]

One thing they can focus on is getting the most out of local foods. Serena Milano from Slow Food International reports in Chapter 7 that teachers and chefs all over Africa are helping families do more with their limited food budgets by documenting, reviving, and teaching traditional recipes and food preservation techniques. In places where indigenous or wild plants are the only crops thriving, Milano suggests investing in preserving wild resources, like coffee and honey, as well as encouraging farmers to "grow" biodiversity in their fields by planting indigenous crops.[22]

Go Beyond Africa

No matter where food comes from—a farmers' market, a discount superstore, a household garden, or even online vendors—people everywhere are tied into a global food system. (See Table 1–1.) In this sense, international solidarity in the realm of food—embodied by everything from fair trade cashews to farmers' groups like Via Campesina and cross-continental collaborations like the Global Crop Diversity Trust—is one of the most hopeful innovations for reducing poverty and hunger.[23]

Food aid in Africa and elsewhere has traditionally come from the United States and other rich nations. But food aid could be much more cost-effective if the United States, the world's major donor, purchased the food in or near recipient countries. The United States currently donates only U.S.-grown crops. These shipments provide much-needed calories to hungry people, but they also disrupt the food supply system by lowering prices for locally grown food and by crowding producers in neighboring areas out of nearby markets. "We are changing how we view the ultimate goal of development," said President Barack Obama on issues of global food security. "Our focus on assistance has saved lives in the short term, but it hasn't always improved those societies over the long term." Europe, the other major food donor, has already modified its aid policy. Today the highways in southern Africa are

Table 1–1. Putting Sub-Saharan Africa in Perspective

Indicator	World	Sub-Saharan Africa
Population	6.8 billion	863 million
Total arable land	1,380,515,270 hectares	179,197,800 hectares
Share of food production that is smallholder	70 percent	90 percent
Urban population	3.49 billion	324 million
Share of population that is urban	51 percent	33 percent
Hungry	925 million (14 percent)	239 million (27 percent)
Children underweight	148 million (24 percent)	39 million (28 percent)
Average age	29.1 years	18.6 years
Per capita added value output of agriculture between 1961 and 2006	Increased 35 percent	Decreased 12 percent

Source: See endnote 23.

filled with trucks carrying food aid across the continent, more and more of it from African farmers selling directly to the World Food Programme. In Liberia, Sierra Leone, Zambia, and several other nations in sub-Saharan Africa (as well as in Asia and Latin America), WFP is not only buying locally, it is helping small farmers gain the skills necessary to be part of the global market. And there is good evidence that the need for food aid will soar in coming years, not only because of higher crop prices but also because of climate-related and geopolitical chaos.[24]

The global impact of farming also extends to agriculture's impact on climate change. African farmers could remove 50 billion tons of carbon dioxide from the atmosphere over the next 50 years, primarily by planting trees among crops and stewarding nearby forests. That is like eliminating an entire year of all the world's greenhouse gas emissions—and it would be a generous contribution from a region that emits a tiny share of these gases. Already roughly 75 projects in 22 countries across Africa are in the works in the hopes of compensating farmers and rural communities

for providing this climate-healing service, including a proposal to create an African Agricultural Carbon Facility that could incubate projects and help connect them with buyers.[25]

Farmers and communities throughout the developing world can thus play an important role in solving certain global problems—a role that could lead simultaneously to income, jobs, and self-reliance. Not all of these experiments will work. But David Lobell argues in Chapter 8 that "we need to be adaptation agnostics, willing to be honest about what we do not know and ready to expend the effort to figure out what actually works....The key will be whether public and private investors can quickly recognize what works and scale it up."[26]

Farmers' groups are already making changes throughout Africa—sometimes through Prolinnova-supported projects where farmers share information via workshops, meetings, photographs, and the Internet, as described in Chapter 5. At the same time, farmer advocacy and activists groups, including GRAIN and The Land Coalition, are mobilizing to prevent corporate and foreign acquisitions of agricultural land in Ethiopia, Madagascar, and other countries. In Chapter 12, Andrew Rice reports that millions and perhaps tens of millions of hectares have been acquired by international buyers, like Saudi Arabia and China, in just the last decade. Currently this land is mostly used to grow crops for people back home or elsewhere in the world.

Even as countries and communities start to invest in local agriculture, people remain tied to a global food system. And even where fewer people are hungry, governments and communities struggle with problems that ultimately relate to what people eat. Consider that the American diet, anchored in a major way to food products made from corn and soybeans, has been implicated in the massive dead zone in the Gulf of Mexico, which is caused partly by fertilizer and manure from midwestern farmland, as well as in rampant public health problems related to meals bulked up by corn syrup, soy oil, and grain-fed meat. The New York–based Feed Foundation's 30 Project is bringing international activists involved in hunger issues together with domestic advocates who are addressing obesity, looking for long-term solutions that will make the food system better for everyone. "Kids in the South Bronx need nutritious foods and so do kids in Botswana," explains founder Ellen Gustafson. Among the organization's goals for the next 30 years are easy access to fresh fruits and vegetables for every person on the planet, global sustainability standards for meat production, and processed food priced to account for all the negative impacts from its production and distribution.[27]

Steps on the New Path

The innovations we uncovered on our African journey represent the kind of radical new thinking that more and more people are calling for. Most recently, the International Assessment of Agricultural Knowledge, Science and Technology for Development suggested that farmers and researchers need to abandon the conventional reductionist approach that separates agriculture from the environment and the environment from meeting human needs. The report noted that there is no uniform approach to solving hunger and poverty, that re-integrating livestock and crop production could dramatically improve rural economies in the most degraded environments, and that "orphan crops" and traditional seeds have more potential than previously assumed. These are the types of innovations that will help nourish people and the planet alike.[28]

Needless to say, we have great expectations for the world's food producers in Africa and beyond. Agriculture is emerging as a solution to mitigating climate change, reducing public health problems and costs, making cities more livable, and creating jobs in a stagnant global economy. In the most hopeful future—one that is entirely achievable—countries that are currently food-short could begin to feed themselves and generate surpluses to help other countries.

Our hope is that this book will serve as a partial road map for foundations and international donors interested in supporting the most effective and environmentally sustainable agricultural development interventions—and that it will offer some inspiration and support for the rural communities that are the source of these innovations.

Given the limited ability of scientists to find solutions, the finite generosity of donors to support agricultural research, and the overstretched patience of struggling farmers and hungry families, shifting funds and attention in new directions is long overdue.

FROM THE FIELD

Measuring Success in Agricultural Development

After more than 50 years of accumulated experience, the global development community still struggles to measure "success" in agricultural development. Policymakers, scholars, activists, and farmers each have their own sets of indicators and bodies of evidence. Despite these differences, there have been several important innovations in recent history that have substantially reduced hunger and increased productivity. Learning from these successes can help inform policymaking and leverage investments in ways that contribute to both overcoming hunger and conserving natural resources.

The most dramatic successes over the last 50 years have occurred in Asia. Beginning in the mid-1960s, governments in South Asia introduced policies and accelerated investments in science, infrastructure, inputs, and food price stabilization, in what became known as the Green Revolution. The result was a doubling of cereal output and yields between 1965 and 1990 as well as improvements in food security for some 1 billion people between 1970 and 1990.[1]

Beginning in the late 1970s, policy and technological innovations in China similarly accelerated growth and development. Between 1978 and 1984, China reintroduced household farming after more than 30 years of collective agriculture, providing farmers with the incentive to market their surplus. By returning more than 95 percent of China's farmland to some 160 million households, the reforms helped increase rural incomes by 137 percent, reduce rural poverty by 22 percent, and increase grain production by 34 percent.[2]

But agricultural development is not just about boosting yields and output; it's about innovation on how we produce, distribute, and consume food. Modern dependence on chemical inputs, combined with overuse of soil and

water resources, has encouraged innovation in more sustainable farming techniques. In some of the same villages where the Green Revolution first took hold, farmers are now cultivating wheat using zero-tillage techniques that help return nutrients and moisture to the soil. An estimated 620,000 small-scale wheat farmers have adopted some form of zero tillage since the mid-1980s, accounting for about 1.8 million hectares of land in South Asia and generating average income gains of $180–340 per household, particularly in the Indian states of Haryana and Punjab.[3]

Agricultural development is also about collective action. At the local level, this means vesting communities with a stake in the ownership of a development process, tapping local knowledge, and involving communities in project consultations, policy deliberations, and scientific research. In Burkina Faso, innovations in resource management have helped resource-poor households expand the cultivation of food staples such as sorghum and millet. In the wake of repeated droughts, some farmers began innovating based on traditional practices: managing indigenous trees and crops, collecting manure and rainwater in planting pits, and constructing stone contour bunds to control runoff and erosion. Support from community leaders and nongovernmental organizations contributed to the rehabilitation of 200,000–300,000 hectares in the Central Plateau, which translates into roughly 80,000 tons of additional food per year—enough to sustain a half-million people. In southern Niger, similar efforts are estimated to have transformed approximately 5 million hectares of land, improving food security for at least 2.5 million people.[4]

At the global level, collective action means

pursuing agricultural development through cooperation and partnerships. In Asia and Africa, concerted efforts to control the spread of rinderpest—a livestock disease capable of killing 95 percent or more of the animals it infects—through cattle vaccination, quarantine measures, and disease surveillance have played an important role in securing the livelihoods of small-scale farmers and pastoralists, preventing substantial financial losses in terms of milk, meat, animal traction, and livelihood assets.[5]

What sets these—and many other—developments apart is that they are all relatively large-scale, long-term successes backed by rigorous and well-documented evidence of positive impact and sustainability. More important, these proven successes have demonstrated that agriculture can be a key driver of growth and development. Still, the changing realities of the global food and agriculture system and the persistence of hunger indicate that more successes are needed. Agriculture is increasingly driven by market demand, consumer preferences, and regulatory scrutiny. Emerging information, communications, and biotechnologies are providing new opportunities for farmers and consumers, while climate change is imposing new constraints. New demographic concerns are emerging with the continuing HIV/AIDS pandemic, changing age structures, and growing urbanization and migration.

Given these changing realities, a few lessons are worth keeping in mind. First, success is not a substitute for strategy. Sustained success-building is feasible only if countries pursue good strategies, create supporting policies, and encourage appropriate levels of investment and experimentation. Decisionmakers should design and implement strategies that take a comprehensive approach to raising agricultural productivity, increasing incomes, and reducing poverty. This can encourage many intertwined successes to add up to a larger national or regional success story.

Second, success is a process. Agricultural development must address ever-changing priorities and challenges: containing the transboundary movement of diseases and pests, strengthening ecosystem resilience in the face of climate change, improving global trade governance, encouraging investment in developing-country agriculture, and articulating grassroots voices more effectively. As such, successes are generated and sustained through experiential processes. This means discovering by doing, learning from mistakes, and adapting to change.

Third, success is recognizable. For successes in agricultural development to be recognized, they need to be sufficiently supported by strong evidence, ranging from first-hand accounts to large-scale impact studies. Regardless of the type and level of evidence, the key point is that successes in agricultural development—and failures too—need to be systematically documented, examined, and shared so that others can learn lessons, adapt them to different contexts, and avoid similar pitfalls.

Finally, success can be ambiguous. Many successes are characterized by a mix of pros and cons. Increases in food production may depend on the use of harmful chemicals, and productivity gains may generate price collapses that hurt farmers but benefit consumers. But ambiguity should not be an excuse for reducing investment in agricultural development. Rather, it suggests the need for careful consideration of difficult trade-offs. The benefits of interventions that increase the availability, access, and quality of food must be weighed against costs in terms of economic and financial gains, environmental impacts, and sociopolitical importance.

—David J. Spielman and Rajul Pandya-Lorch
International Food Policy Research Institute

A boy in rice fields outside Antananarivo, Madagascar

CHAPTER 2

Moving Ecoagriculture into the Mainstream

Louise E. Buck and Sara J. Scherr

David Kuria points out with pride the new features of the Lari landscape in Kenya. A decade ago, he and the Kijabe Environmental Volunteers, a local group, began mobilizing farmers to protect and restore the threatened, high-biodiversity forests and watersheds in this densely populated area. Now the forest and wildlife are thriving, and the farmers are benefiting too—from healthier soils, higher crop yields, well-fed livestock, and new markets.[1]

A growing enthusiasm for such ecosystem-friendly, locally adapted agricultural systems is sparking widespread innovation—and in some cases large-scale expansion—throughout Africa and around the world. Part of the motivation is the need to restore dynamic rural livelihoods and communities where agriculture's roles beyond production are also valued. There is also growing concern about extensive soil and water degradation due to current agricultural practices. And wild plant and animal species are under threat both from the expansion of cropland into natural forests, savannas, and wetlands and from the push to increase yields in ways that damage ecosystems. In a warming world, agricultural systems and communities will need to adapt to abrupt and sometimes extreme

---

Louise E. Buck is director of the Landscapes Program at EcoAgriculture Partners and a faculty member at Cornell University. **Sara J. Scherr** is president and CEO of EcoAgriculture Partners.

changes in temperature and precipitation and to the higher cost of fertilizers from fossil fuels. And farmers will be called on to help mitigate the effects of climate change by sequestering more carbon in plants and soils.[2]

David Kuria envisions an "ecoagriculture" landscape in Lari—one where agricultural production, rural development, and ecosystem management are mutually supportive. This vision draws on two broad strategies: ecologically suitable production practices on farms and a multistakeholder approach to managing agriculture and natural resources in the landscape as a whole.[3]

Agroecological Farming

Managed well, agriculture "can do more than just focus on production. It can help supply clean water, it can help to protect biodiversity,

it should be managed in a way that manages our soils sustainably," according to Robert Watson, director of the International Assessment of Agricultural Knowledge, Science and Technology for Development. To achieve these goals, agroecological farming relies on biologically based, integrated soil-plant-animal cropping systems. (See Figure 2–1.)[4]

Often referred to as regenerative agriculture, this approach is rooted in knowledge of how to manage the complex dynamics among plants, animals, water, soil, insects, and other micro-fauna in order to produce crops and livestock on a sustainable basis. Practices such as applying crop residues as surface mulch, using compost and green manures, intercropping of legumes, and biocontrol of insect pests and diseases are used to enhance yields and sustain soil fertility and health with minimal dependence on outside chemicals and energy.

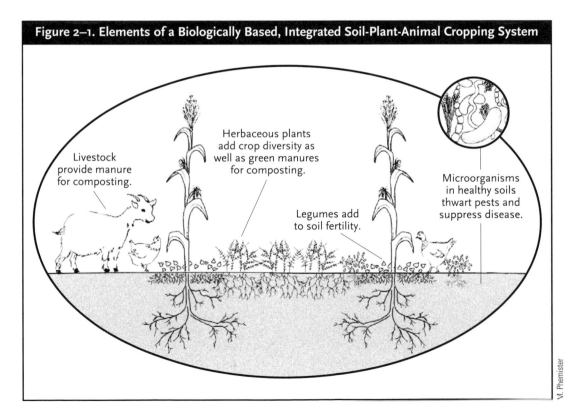

Figure 2–1. Elements of a Biologically Based, Integrated Soil-Plant-Animal Cropping System

Livestock provide manure for composting.

Herbaceous plants add crop diversity as well as green manures for composting.

Microorganisms in healthy soils thwart pests and suppress disease.

Legumes add to soil fertility.

M. Phemister

Agroecological farming aims to increase economic returns not only to land, labor, and capital but also to other factors of production like water and energy and to meet a range of local household and community needs as well as supplying markets.[5]

Diversity in farming systems—in crop mixes and varieties as well as livestock—is a key feature of the approach. (See Box 2–1.) Farmers in Lari, Kenya, for example, keep rabbits, chickens, goats, and cattle in confined spaces, gathering manure to compost with crop residues to improve soil fertility. They are diversifying their production systems to include vegetables, beekeeping, and fish farming. They are growing farm trees that provide important nutrients for crop growth as well as fruit, fodder, and fuelwood to use or sell. And they are protecting the seed of local landraces and species to preserve genetic diversity in their cropping systems.[6]

Ecoagriculture Landscapes

But bringing about food security, watershed restoration, biodiversity conservation, and agricultural market development requires more than the adoption of certain practices by individual farmers. Farmers' organizations and agricultural communities need to work collaboratively with other groups responsible for managing forests, water, wetlands, wildlife,

---

Box 2–1. Examples of Agroecological Farming

Organic agriculture seeks to maintain long-term soil health. Farmers use techniques such as crop rotation, green manure, composting, and biological pest control. International certification for organic farming excludes or strictly limits synthetic fertilizers and pesticides, plant growth regulators, livestock antibiotics, food additives, and genetically modified organisms. There are some 530,000 organic producers in Africa, almost half of the world's total, with some 900,000 hectares of certified organic agricultural land (3 percent of the global figure).

Agroforestry mixes trees and shrubs in cropland or pastures in ways that mimic natural forest or woodland in terms of nutrient cycling, pollination, water cycling, microclimate moderation, and wildlife habitat. Some farmers protect naturally regenerating trees; others plant tree species selected and improved for agroforestry. In 2006, more than 417,000 farmers in Malawi, Mozambique, Tanzania, Zambia, and Zimbabwe used agroforestry practices that included nitrogen-fixing "fertilizer" trees for land regeneration, soil health, and food security; fruit trees for nutrition; fodder trees for smallholder livestock production; timber and fuelwood trees for shelter and energy; trees that produce various products; and medicinal trees that combat diseases.

Conservation agriculture uses practices such as zero or minimum tillage, topsoil management, and crop rotations based on principles of minimal soil disturbance, permanent soil cover, and biological disease control for preferred crops. Adaptation of these technologies to smallholder farms in Zambia has helped some 350,000 families increase food production by 30–100 percent, enhance their nutrition, increase their profit margins, and reduce labor requirements.

Evergreen agriculture combines the relatively short-term livelihood gains commonly realized in conservation agriculture with longer-term but sustained crop productivity and environmental resilience derived from leguminous and fruit trees. In Malawi, continuous maize cultivation with *Gliricidia sepium* fertilizer trees and no mineral fertilizers had average yields of 3.7 tons per hectare compared with 0.5–1 ton per hectare in conventional plots.

Source: See endnote 6.

---

and infrastructure in order to expand the positive effects of their eco-friendly agricultural practices to a landscape scale.

Ecoagriculture builds on the science of landscape ecology, which assesses patterns and flows of nutrients, water, people, and wildlife throughout the mosaic of land uses. In Lari, for example, the pattern of forests, farm trees, and compatible farm practices provides essential habitat for birds and other wildlife. (See Figure 2–2.)[7]

Managing the flow and quality of water resources in farming landscapes also requires coordinated land and water management in different parts of the watershed. Water stored in soils and used by plants ("green water") is just as important as groundwater, rivers, and streams ("blue water"). (See Figure 2–3.) Managing green water well in farms and natural habitats can make a big difference in agri-

cultural productivity, community well-being, and economic development.[8]

To achieve such win-win-win outcomes thus requires negotiation and cooperation among the diverse stakeholders in the landscape. Adaptive management—modifying plans in response to changing situations and new knowledge—is a cornerstone of ecoagriculture landscapes.

Although there are costs associated with collaborative action, in many landscapes stakeholders are finding that the benefits are far greater. In a formerly forested area in the lower Tapajós region of the state of Pará in Brazil, for example, indigenous farmers established tree-crop agroforestry around forest protected areas on the periphery of intensive production areas. Their efforts reduce the conversion of natural habitat, improve the habitat value of cultivated areas, and create a

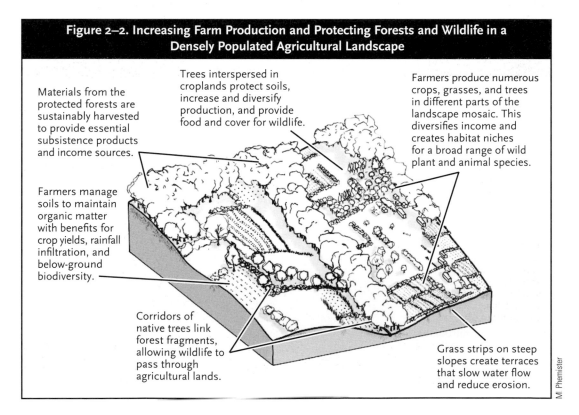

Figure 2–2. Increasing Farm Production and Protecting Forests and Wildlife in a Densely Populated Agricultural Landscape

Materials from the protected forests are sustainably harvested to provide essential subsistence products and income sources.

Trees interspersed in croplands protect soils, increase and diversify production, and provide food and cover for wildlife.

Farmers produce numerous crops, grasses, and trees in different parts of the landscape mosaic. This diversifies income and creates habitat niches for a broad range of wild plant and animal species.

Farmers manage soils to maintain organic matter with benefits for crop yields, rainfall infiltration, and below-ground biodiversity.

Corridors of native trees link forest fragments, allowing wildlife to pass through agricultural lands.

Grass strips on steep slopes create terraces that slow water flow and reduce erosion.

M. Phemister

benign matrix for habitat fragments. The practice of growing rubber in traditional agroforests was revived and adapted to integrate elements of modern production technology that are compatible with the low-input, low-risk logic of the agroforests. A collaboratively designed strategy to improve the system was implemented and scaled up by the inhabitants, with little or no external assistance and at little cost. Their efforts improved the productivity of the resource and the profitability for the indigenous people who manage it, while also enabling them to secure long-term property rights to the land.[9]

Communal grassland restoration in the savanna of Zimbabwe provides another example of strategic planning with a landscape perspective. A 20,000-acre communally owned grazing area in Dimbangombe provides important wildlife habitat within the Hwange and Zambezi National Parks. Mismanaged grazing had degraded forage quality, water

supply, and the biodiversity that sustains agriculture, forestry, livestock, wildlife, and tourism in the region. People's livelihoods were in jeopardy. Innovative land managers introduced a carefully coordinated rotational grazing system for their livestock. They mimicked the natural disturbance of grazing wildlife by increasing stocking densities. This stimulated more hoof action and produced dung and urine that rejuvenated the soil by improving aeration, water penetration, germination of dormant seed, and fertilization. In just two years the landscape had vastly more forage and ground cover. Water retention had improved, and the major river in the area was flowing again. The grazing changes increased livestock production, with previously starving animals becoming well-fed stock. Livestock losses to lions were reduced through traditional fencing systems, even while the land's value as wildlife habitat improved.[10]

Meanwhile, initiatives in Kericho, Kenya, are

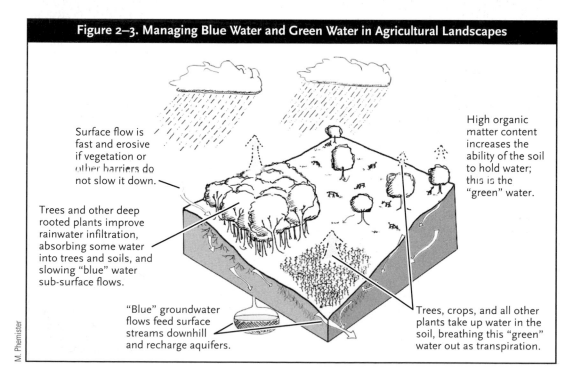

Figure 2–3. Managing Blue Water and Green Water in Agricultural Landscapes

Surface flow is fast and erosive if vegetation or other barriers do not slow it down.

Trees and other deep rooted plants improve rainwater infiltration, absorbing some water into trees and soils, and slowing "blue" water sub-surface flows.

"Blue" groundwater flows feed surface streams downhill and recharge aquifers.

High organic matter content increases the ability of the soil to hold water; this is the "green" water.

Trees, crops, and all other plants take up water in the soil, breathing this "green" water out as transpiration.

M. Phemister

enabling the members of smallholder tea cooperatives to manage 8,000 hectares of tea plantations based on Sustainable Agriculture Initiative Platform principles. The farmers are using mulch and intercrops, which help increase the levels of organic matter in the soil, while bunds (embankments), microcatchments, and drainage systems enhance soil and water conservation. No insecticides or fungicides are used in the tea fields. Dispersed throughout the fields are patches of forests, small wetland areas, windbreaks, and riparian forest buffers that provide fuelwood for tea drying as well as habitat and soil conservation benefits. Unilever Tea Company, which manages the program, is cooperating with the Rainforest Alliance to develop certification schemes that result in a 10–15 percent increase in tea revenues to farmers. Farmers are replicating the management and certification model all over Kericho, with anticipated benefits to the watershed as a whole.[11]

The Potential

What is the potential for agroecological farming systems, in ecoagriculture landscapes, to meet the rapidly growing demand for food? Can they compete economically—and for policymakers' attention—with monoculture fields of high-yielding seeds and agrochemical inputs?

Because ecoagriculture landscapes and their component practices aim to satisfy multiple social, ecological, and economic objectives, they should ideally be evaluated on the basis of these diverse criteria of performance. However, there are still relatively few comprehensive comparative studies, and until more are done it will remain difficult to fully assess the relative advantages of these approaches.

Nonetheless, a growing number of studies have documented significant production, livelihood, and environmental benefits of agroecological practices. In 1999 sustainability researcher Jules Pretty looked at evidence of yield increases from diverse agroecological farming practices in 286 projects in 57 developing countries, representing a total surface area of 37 million hectares. He found that the average crop yield gain was 79 percent over previous production practices. A 2007 review of scientific literature on the biodiversity impacts of agroecological cropping practices found agroforestry, organic agriculture, field hedgerows, and farm woodlots all had positive impacts on at least three wildlife classifications, while studies of agroforestry practices in the humid tropics have shown major biodiversity benefits.[12]

Sustainable rice intensification (SRI) is an agroecological system based on six practices for managing plants, soil, water, and nutrients: plant seedlings at a young age, space plants far apart, use organic matter to fertilize (perhaps with some synthetics), transplant only one or two seedlings per hill, apply small amounts of water and alternate wetting and drying during the growth period, and use manual weeders and integrated pest management. Studies of SRI plots in eight developing countries found that, on average, farmers increased yields by 47 percent using mostly organic fertilizers, while realizing water savings of 40 percent, a reduction of input costs of 23 percent, and an increase in income of 68 percent. The practices increased resource productivity while reducing requirements for water, seed, synthetic fertilizers, pesticides, herbicides, and often labor— especially tasks performed by women. Indian farmer Siddimallaiah noted another advantage: "During the drought of 2009, my SRI crop produced well, when my fields using normal practices and irrigation system struggled in the parched soil and dried up."[13]

Two recent major international reviews of agricultural science and technology for development concluded that many agroecological practices are already performing well and have great promise. Crop yields and production costs compare favorably with traditional and conventional production systems where existing yields are low to moderate. They can be competitive with industrial input-intensive systems in many years and produce higher yields during poor rainfall years. On the other hand, there can be greater local learning and adaptation costs for some practices, and others are more labor-intensive, which is a concern in labor-scarce communities.[14]

Evidence of production, ecosystem, and livelihood impacts of ecoagriculture landscape approaches is even more difficult to measure in an integrated way. There are a few well-documented cases. The Loess Plateau Watershed Rehabilitation Project in China helped farmers reforest steep slopes, control grazing, level crop fields, and diversify production. Per capita grain output increased from 365 to 591 kilograms a year; the annual income of project participant households increased from $70 to $200 per person; and perennial vegetation cover increased from 17 to 34 percent, drastically reducing sediment flow into the Yellow River by more than 100 million tons per year. A silvopastoral program in Matiguas, Nicaragua, that introduced tree cover in degraded pastures and paid farmers for ecological benefits reduced the area of degraded land by two thirds, increased participant incomes, increased effective forest cover to 31 percent across the landscape, and connected 67 percent of forest fragments by at least one route.[15]

Simplified landscape measurement approaches are needed. EcoAgriculture Partners' international *Landscape Measures Initiative* has brought together experts from multiple sectors to develop a landscape measurement framework with indicators that are meaningful in specific landscapes and measurable by stakeholders. Kevin Kamp of CARE International notes that "we need to track how changes in farming practices affect wildlife, watersheds, and climate so that we can adapt our strategies over time."[16]

Realizing the Potential

There are no published estimates of the actual proportion of total land area and production accounted for by agroecological practices and ecoagriculture landscape initiatives. We do know they are found today in many diverse contexts. They are promoted particularly where there is high food insecurity and high pressure for agricultural intensification but industrial inputs are unaffordable, unavailable, or economically risky for farmers. They are also seen where soil degradation is a barrier to agricultural intensification and where ecosystem degradation is threatening agricultural production and sustainability by reducing irrigation water flows or quality, flooding, or the loss of grazing resources. Elsewhere, commercial demand is creating attractive market opportunities for eco-certified cropping systems.

Stimulated by necessity as well as a working knowledge of time-tested practices, farmer and community organizations have been early innovators and leaders in the development and spread of agroecological practices. Farmers have organized and advocated for the grassroots agroecology movement. They were also pioneers in the organic farming movement, which led eventually to certification schemes driven by nongovernmental organizations.[17]

Other grassroots movements have arisen to champion coordinated action on agriculture and ecosystem management. Landcare originated in rural communities in Australia to address diverse types of land degradation threatening agriculture production and local ecosystems; it mobilized a network of over 4,500 voluntary Landcare groups. This model has been adapted through International Landcare in New Zealand, the Philippines, and South Africa, as well as countries in East Africa and elsewhere. Another group, the Community Knowledge Service (CKS), promotes social learning and knowledge-sharing among local and indigenous agricultural, pastoral, forest, and fishing communities who are working to strengthen rural livelihoods and health while conserving culturally and economically important biodiversity. CKS helps local community initiatives in East Africa, South Asia, the Philippines, and tropical America advocate for community voices in policies and programs on biodiversity conservation, agriculture, and rural development.[18]

Integrated landscape initiatives that specifically engage crop and livestock producers are proliferating. A new generation of landscape projects is being promoted by conservation organizations and public agencies for biodiversity conservation with farmers in and around protected areas, such as the African Wildlife Foundation's Heartlands program, and in high-biodiversity-value farming regions, such as the Cape of South Africa. The Ibero-American Model Forest Network is supporting multistakeholder groups in 24 landscapes with mixed farming-forest mosaics to undertake rural development in ways that improve farmer livelihoods, increase food production, and conserve forest resources.[19]

In some places, such land and resource management initiatives have become linked to broader rural development strategies. Territorial development strategies in Latin America have sought to adapt sectoral development planning and investment to local priorities. Indigenous populations who have gained local political control are developing territorial strategies that reflect their values, traditions, and institutions. The food sovereignty movement has brought together small farmers, agricultural workers, fisherfolk, pastoralists, and artisans, particularly in developing countries, to direct control of food production and consumption back to localized food systems. The "local food" movement in the United States, Europe, and elsewhere is revisiting the potential of local "foodsheds" and linking local producers and consumers through improved local value chains.[20]

Agribusinesses and the food industry are also beginning to consider the benefits of agroecological practices. They are concerned about the long-term sustainability of their sources of supply, as well as about responding to consumers' and governments' demand for social and environmental corporate responsibility. The rapid growth of market demand for organic and eco-certified products has attracted the attention of business investors. Public-private partnerships are arising to link sustainable food supply chain initiatives with watershed and biodiversity management. Mars Corporation, for example, is promoting agroecological and agroforestry practices for sustainable cocoa production, as well as genetic improvement and biological corridors to sustain tropical forest biodiversity in cocoa-growing areas. Companies like Nestle are helping smallholder producers in Africa, India, and other developing countries manage local water resources and reduce greenhouse gas emissions.[21]

National governments are setting up programs to support integrated agriculture and ecosystem management. TerrAfrica is a multinational effort to align investments in sustainable land and water management practices across Africa, including a $1-billion multisector investment portfolio. TerrAfrica is putting in place knowledge and information resources to scale up agroecological practices through the coordinated actions of diverse public agencies and civic groups. And in Central America, eight presidents have agreed to promote a Regional Strategy for Territorial Development, with a focus on transboundary territories considered critical for agricultural production, biodiversity and watershed conservation, and poverty reduction. These and numerous other initiatives around the world are accelerating the learning, scaling up the experience, and developing the practice-based evidence that is needed to propel ecoagriculture into the mainstream.[22]

Mainstreaming

The debate on whether agroecological production practices in ecoagriculture landscapes will be able to meet the entire global food demand is misplaced. Evidence available now indicates that these approaches can feed a large portion of the world—while at the same time addressing a host of present and looming problems of environmental degradation, livelihood insecurity, and poverty.

Globally, only a minority of agricultural lands are in large contiguous areas of intensive, high-yield monocultures on the industrial model, though these account for a large share of total production and international trade. A majority of farms are in mosaic landscapes with considerable opportunity to use uncultivated areas for conservation purposes and to help farming communities sustain or restore ecosystem values while increasing agricultural yields and achieving broader rural development goals.[23]

Moreover, only 10 percent of the world's food production enters international trade. Even if this figure grows, domestic production for domestic consumption will still grow in absolute terms and remain dominant in terms of land area and total output, especially in low-income countries with large rural populations. Thus most countries will need to learn how to grow more food while doing better at protecting ecosystem services and sustaining rural communities.[24]

An oft-mentioned rationale for ignoring the local environmental costs of agriculture is that high productivity increases are essential to stop the last remaining tropical forests from being chopped down to make way for cropland. Rising commodity demand and prices, relatively lower production costs, and growing profitability of agriculture are indeed spurring a

rush of land clearing in humid tropical forests, but these require more-targeted policies. Meanwhile, some of the greatest threats to biodiversity are within agricultural landscapes—in the temperate and tropical grasslands and woodlands that are the most attractive for agricultural expansion—and in freshwater and coastal ecosystems that are threatened by the off-site impacts of farming.[25]

Shoveling dried cocoa beans in São Tomé

The alternative to agroecological practices and ecoagriculture landscapes is not the status quo. In some regions that are currently major food surplus producers, such as the Punjab, the Mekong Delta, and northern Mexico, further intensification through high-external-input intensive monoculture methods is clearly unsustainable. Irrigation systems are becoming salinized and groundwater depleted; pests and diseases are overwhelming chemical controls; there is political resistance to further water pollution. And the underlying economics of agricultural production is shifting as energy and fertilizer costs rise, water costs increase, and climate and environmental regulations evolve.[26]

Concerns about climate change will motivate investments in food security resilience, and these will be broader than just improved seed and farm inputs. At some point the value of terrestrial carbon sequestration in slowing climate change will be recognized, and farmers will be rewarded for storing carbon in the soil and vegetation. And it seems likely that climate-induced increases in variability of growing conditions will prompt efforts to increase crop species and varietal and associated wild diversity. So there will almost certainly be major changes in farming systems and landscapes.[27]

At the policy level, expectations about the social, economic, and environmental roles of agriculture are changing. In the July 2010 Dialogue Towards a Shared Action Framework for Agriculture, Food Security and Climate Change in Africa, a group of African leaders argued that while growth in agricultural production and productivity is paramount for the continent, agricultural strategy must contribute to a broader rural transformation. At the national, subnational, and local levels, policy goals will be to sustain viable rural communities, slow or even reverse rural outmigration, and sustain ecosystem services.[28]

If the potentials of agroecological practices and ecoagriculture landscapes are to be realized, strategic investments and enabling policies will need to be implemented on a much larger scale. International action on climate needs to make terrestrial carbon sequestration or emissions reduction in agriculture a priority. Governments and others need to set up financial mechanisms to support farmer innovation, testing, and scaling up. The infrastructure needs to be put in place to systematically develop, disseminate, and adapt agroecological practices, with or without parallel systems for distributing industrial inputs, particularly for smallholders. Market supply chains and infrastructure must adapt to more diversified production systems. Seed selection and breeding for crop improvement and resilience, through both farmer-managed systems and advanced scientific methods, will continue to play a critical role in agricultural development, but with explicit attention to the incorporation of better seeds in diverse agroecological production systems.

As political interest in reinvesting in agriculture globally gains momentum, it is important to invest in a variety of approaches. We know that no single method is suitable for all areas under all conditions. We need to be more sensitive to differences in social and ecological potential and to invest in methods that are most appropriate to different conditions. Indeed, agroecological practices in ecoagriculture landscapes are by definition location-specific. And they are nurtured through multiple sources of innovation, making a singular vision neither likely nor desirable.

Innovations in Rice Breeding in Madagascar

As in many parts of Africa, people in Madagascar depend on rice every day. For the Malagasy people, this staple food symbolizes family, tradition, and rural economy. Rice is grown in nearly every region of the country and accounts for 80 percent of agriculture on the island.[1]

According to recent collecting missions done in some collaborative projects, more than a thousand varieties of rice, including traditional and improved ones, are grown in Madagascar. In every ecosystem, a range of different varieties are available to farmers. In the past, mainly local varieties were planted, which could ensure a stable yield; these included Tsipala in the western region, Makalioka in the Lake Alaotra region, and Rojo in the highlands.[2]

Many of these traditional varieties are tall, with a height of more than 1.2 meters. The high stalks provide straw for both animal feed and bedding, making them a multipurpose crop. In addition, most traditional varieties of rice have a good ability to clump closely together, which enables them to escape the noxious effects of diseases like sheath rot that deteriorate grain quality and can devastate the crops. Fertilizer does not increase yields of these varieties that much; instead, they respond better to the use of manure as a source of nutrients. Although farmers in the highlands prefer red rice varieties because they are more filling, most consumers prefer white rice.[3]

As a result, it is important to work with farmers, helping them develop different rice varieties for different regions and different conditions. The Centre National de la Recherche Appliquée au Développement Rural—the National Center for Rural Development—not only introduces new varieties of rice, it also listens to farmers. The Center works with them to adapt different technologies and innovations to fit their own needs through extension services and on-farm testing.[4]

Good adaptability in diverse environments was the first criterion for a rice breeding strategy. Tolerance to water constraints, disease resistance (mostly to the disease blast in humid regions), high nitrogen fertilization, rusticity, and grain quality preferences were also considered.[5]

But it is not enough to develop an innovation; farmers must be able to practice it. For example, a System of Rice Intensification increases yields but is more labor-intensive and relies on a strict water management; similarly, F1 rice hybrids require a lot of expensive fertilizers. These innovations have a number of benefits but also drawbacks that may make them impractical for local rice farmers.

And while conservation farming practices, such as minimal tillage and the use of compost, can help prevent erosion and improve soils, Madagascar—even with funding from the French government and other donors—cannot be Brazil when it comes to conservation farming. In southern Brazil, cover crops, intercropping, and other conservation agriculture practices are used extensively for maize. But lowland rice is very different than other crops, and while rice can be intercropped with wheat or trees in integrated rice and agroforestry projects, not every farmer will be able to adopt such practices. Enough innovations are available, but they are not applied because of local constraints, including farmers' access to credit or land or markets. Removing the constraints and strengthening farmers' rights must be considered in order to alleviate hunger and poverty.

With the population increase in Madagascar during the last few decades, rice production cannot keep up with demand for food. New technologies are needed to overcome the constraints that limit rice yield, and yields must increase at least 0.5–1.0 ton per hectare in order to respond to rice demand. A better understanding of the rice production system and the rice varietal behavior under diverse ecosystems is essential for increasing rice production.[6]

In many places, late transplanting is observed because of late water irrigation, which often comes from a remote source. Seedlings in the nursery bed become old and are slow to recover after transplanting. For different reasons, a great deal of water is needed during rice growth in the paddy field, especially during the flowering period, with about 10–15 centimeters of depth. However, droughts causing cracked soil and the submergence of rice seedlings due to poor drainage are very common and destructive to rice crops. A change in the habitual water management is needed to improve yield and reduce damage to crops.[7]

Among the great number of varieties, including the semidwarf lines that contributed to the success of the Green Revolution, an improved variety called Mailaka was adopted by farmers in Madagascar. This variety is renowned for its cooking quality, because it swells more than many other varieties and can feed many more people using the same amount of rice grains. On-farm demonstration plots as well as farmer participatory trials during many years and through different seasons convinced farmers of its potential. It actually covers many rice areas, and some farmer organizations are starting to produce certified seeds of this improved variety, strengthening the seed system that is very much needed for rice production increase.[8]

While this variety was introduced, some other lines issued from local crosses were also being adopted and contributing to higher yields. Particularly during the last few decades, the spread of upland rice varieties has facilitated the expansion of upland rice cultivation under improved techniques such as direct seeding on organic or live cover.

—*Xavier Rakotonjanahary*
National Center for Rural Development

At a market outside Niamey, Niger: peppers and onions

CHAPTER 3

The Nutritional and Economic Potential of Vegetables

Abdou Tenkouano

Six decades ago, the world's food supply increased dramatically thanks to the development of more productive varieties of wheat and rice by Dr Norman Borlaug and others. These were better adapted to cultivation, responded better to fertilizers, and allocated more of the soil resources to the edible fraction of the crops. Plant breeders and geneticists changed the genetic makeup of the crops to make them less vulnerable to diseases and other problems. These achievements occurred primarily in Asia and Latin America, two of the most pop-ulated regions of the world, but the effects have been felt throughout the world and have inspired hundreds of agricultural scientists working on other staple crops.[1]

Replicating this Green Revolution in sub Saharan Africa, where the world's poorest and fastest-growing populations live, has proved challenging, however. One reason is that the region often lacks the necessary supporting infrastructure. Another is insufficient under-standing of the local nature of agricultural development. People's attitudes toward new opportunities are driven first by their food

---

Abdou Tenkouano is director of AVRDC–The World Vegetable Center's Regional Center for Africa in Arusha, Tanzania.

choices and second by affordable access to yield-boosting technologies, including improved crop varieties.[2]

Nevertheless, new approaches are now improving the prospects for sub-Saharan Africa's food supply. But while staples such as rice, maize, wheat, and cassava have been the focus of much research and investment, an abundance of these crops will only amount to a "Grain Revolution" if the vegetables required to balance the diet are not equally abundant. The staples are traditionally consumed with vegetables in the region, and a "Revolution of Greens" is consequently necessary as well.

For the sad fact is that while Africa may be adequately fed by staple crops, it will not be nourished until diets improve. Otherwise, millions of people, particularly in sub-Saharan Africa, will remain vulnerable to ailments that compromise their mental and physical fitness. Worldwide, diseases related to imbalanced diets, especially insufficient vegetable and fruit consumption, cause 2.7 million deaths annually and are among the top mortality risk factors.[3]

Micronutrient deficiencies, including lack of Vitamin A, iron, and iodine, affect some 1 billion people and are extremely common among rural and urban populations in sub-Saharan Africa. They lead to poor mental and physical development, especially among children, and cause poor performance in work and in school, further crippling communities already facing other health problems and poverty. Vitamin A deficiency, for example, has been detected in more than 17 million people in West and Central Africa, including nearly 500,000 pre-school children there. This deficiency can lead to permanent blindness in children and suppress the immune system, thereby predisposing children to respiratory tract infections, measles, and diarrhea.[4]

Inadequate intake of iron and zinc is also widespread. In southeastern Nigeria, for instance, as much as 50 percent of children and 61 percent of women suffer from chronic ane-

mia due to iron deficiency. This condition is also linked to learning disabilities, mental retardation, poor physical development, and a reduced ability to fight infectious diseases, ultimately leading to premature death.[5]

Alarmingly, the International Food Policy Research Institute predicts an 18-percent rise in the number of malnourished children in sub-Saharan Africa from 2001 to 2020, yet research on vegetables remains severely underfunded. In 2002, the research centers that belong to the Consultative Group on International Agricultural Research invested $118 million on research on cereals, but just $15.7 million on fruit and vegetable research—about 13 percent as much as on cereal crops.[6]

So research on vegetables is underfunded just when it is most critical. Staple crops, with their long cropping cycles, tend to be more vulnerable to environmental threats and the risk of crop failure. In contrast, vegetable crop species have shorter cycles, are faster growing, require little space, and thus are very dependable. Furthermore, they constitute the necessary ingredients without which staples would be unpalatable. Vegetables are the sustainable solution for a diversified and balanced diet.

Fortunately, a Revolution of Greens is clearly within reach. "Millions of smallholder farmers are poised to deliver long-term solutions to chronic hunger and poverty across the region," said Namanga Ngongi, president of the Alliance for a Green Revolution in Africa. "They have the land, the energy, the experience, and the will to grow the food that Africa needs to end the undernourishment that affects more than one in three Africans."[7]

Listening to Farmers

To be effective, research on vegetables will need to take a particular form. In Africa, like everywhere else in the world, there are cultural preferences for particular ingredients, dishes, and ways of preparing food. Researchers can

use their understanding of the biological characteristics of the ingredients to tease out the
underlying genetic origins and then use that
information to develop new cultivars that
enhance and complement the particular food
preparation. This end-usage breeding can be
scaled up to industrial products aimed not just
at traditional farmers producing for their own
consumption or local village markets but also
at specialty crop growers feeding industrial
processors.[8]

Making this process work effectively requires
farmer input and participation in the research
process. On-farm evaluation requires the development of efficient mechanisms for monitoring progress—and making sure that researchers
and farmers understand each other. The most
effective participatory research programs ensure
the continual flow of information from farmers to researchers and back to farmers—including participatory appraisal, followed by testing
of best bets, identification of best in class, and
multiplication and dissemination of best in
class. (See also Box 3–1.)[9]

The choice of best-in-class varieties has to
be location-specific because different varieties
respond differently in various environments.
And, as just mentioned, there are also cultural
differences in varietal preferences. Cooks in
one region or country, for example, might
prefer sweeter red onions, while farmers elsewhere might prefer growing white onions that
can be stored for a long time. As a result, the
choice of the best-in-class varieties needs to be
done by farmers themselves in order to identify the varieties most likely to be accepted by
growers and consumers in their communities.

This is why AVRDC–The World Vegetable
Center (previously known as the Asian Vegetable Research and Development Center
(AVRDC) in Taiwan) consults with farmers
such as Babel Isack, a tomato farmer in Tanzania, who advises AVRDC about which
tomato varieties best suit his particular needs,
including varieties that do not need chemical

sprays or have a longer shelf life to help prevent food waste. It is also important for farmers to know what consumers want from
different vegetable varieties. Periodic workshops, conferences, or field days, such as the
ones held at AVRDC or by the International
Development Research Centre, can bring farmers, consumers, businesses, and the community
together to find out what varieties of onion,
tomato, eggplant, and okra people actually
like best.[10]

The open field days also train participants
how to produce the seeds they will need. But
to ensure that increased demand for seeds due
to farmers' awareness of new varieties is met,
it is important that research agencies work
with established private-sector seed companies. These companies can evaluate and start
growing the varieties—chosen by farmers—
at their company-run farms. In this way, the
farmers' decisions about the best types of varieties are communicated directly to seed producers and they, in turn, can respond to the
demand. The companies can also start doing
the research necessary to make sure that the
new varieties meet the regulatory requirements for seed production and certification.[11]

In addition, bringing farmers and
researchers together throughout the year—
and making sure that they continue to learn
from one another—helps ensure that both
groups are contributing to the collective dis-
covery of what worked where and why.

Getting Seeds to Farmers

Farmers' voices need to be supported and
amplified so that the seeds of their chosen
varieties are made available throughout sub-
Saharan Africa. In most countries in the region,
the official release system for vegetables either
does not work—and seeds are not distributed
to the farmers who need them—or it is copied
from the systems used to distribute staple field
crops or commercial (industrial) crops. A

Box 3–1. Plant Breeding Innovations: Necessity and Promise

Although plant breeding dates back 12,000 years, the need for it has never been more urgent. Growing enough food to feed an ever-increasing human population—which doubled between 1960 and 2000, reaching 6 billion, and is likely heading for 9 billion or so by 2050—will require extraordinary innovations in plant breeding. For the last 50 years, global food security has been anchored by a 2–4 percent annual increase in crop productivity in the five major crops that feed humankind.

The urgency is perhaps greatest in sub-Saharan Africa, where population pressures are severe but modern varieties of food crops have barely penetrated. In 2003, for instance, growth in annual crop yields from modern varieties accounted for 86 percent of all increases in food production in Asia and Latin America—but for less than 10 percent in sub-Saharan Africa. Modern varieties account for more than 80 percent of crop varieties in Asia but for less than 20 percent in sub-Saharan Africa (with the exception of South Africa). Today plant breeding accounts for as much as 50 percent of yield growth and 40 percent of production growth in Asia and Latin America.

Gains of this order are critical for Africa's future. Fortunately, the history of plant breeding and new knowledge of ways to maximize the spread of beneficial modern varieties offer both tools and inspiration for addressing the challenge of feeding Africa's growing population.

The poster child example of the startling increases in yields that plant breeding has enabled is the U.S. hybrid corn industry. According to the Corn Farmers' Coalition, maize hybrids developed by public-sector corn breeders in the 1930s have produced a sixfold gain in yield per acre since 1931. A more relevant example for the developing world is the plant breeding innovation story of the Green Revolution in Asia and Latin America. This started in Mexico in 1944, when the Rockefeller Foundation partnered with the government to establish a wheat improvement program headed by Norman Borlaug.

The high-yielding and fertilizer-responsive dwarf varieties developed by the program doubled yields in Mexico. It became a worldwide movement when the dwarf varieties were successfully introduced in the early 1960s in India and Pakistan—followed by a tripling of wheat yields there. The success of dwarf wheat varieties was quickly repeated with rice; the semi-dwarf rice variety IR8 developed by the International Rice Research Institute in Manila raised the yield of rice in India from 2 to 6 tons per hectare between 1961 and 1970 and made India one of the world's largest producers of rice.

Of course, hybrids with radically new potential do not tell the whole story of rising yields. Farmers must welcome new varieties for them to spread, and they will not do that unless the new varieties meet their particular local needs. That means getting farmers and researchers to talk to each other, in a process called participatory plant breeding or participatory research.

A good example of this approach is the case of breeding cassava, a tropical root crop, for the semiarid region of northeastern Brazil. The region is characterized by low soil fertility and droughts that last for months. Intense attacks by pests and diseases can sometimes drive loss rates to 100 percent. Although cassava is the principal subsistence crop, yields are much lower than in the rest of the country, and farmers chose not to adopt varieties generated by conventional field-based breeding because they were bred under alien soil, climate, and socioeconomic conditions and gave less-than-satisfactory results.

In the early 1990s, the Brazilian Agricultural Corporation and local extension agents

Box 3–1 continued

began a participatory breeding program in nine communities using nine improved cassava clones and one local control. The following year, the work was extended to another 17 communities using the same nine improved clones. Four clones were selected as a result of this work and distributed in the region. A second stage involved 305 trials in 70 communities and 1,500 farming families. Eight varieties were officially released and multiplied, and a dozen more with high probability of acceptance by farmers were identified. Participatory plant breeding was effective in increasing adoption and, more important, yields within the project period of 10 years.

Participatory research works just as well in Africa. Smallholders there grow more than 4 million hectares of beans annually, providing food for at least 100 million Africans and earning hundreds of millions of dollars. But the early 1990s were a bleak time for bean farmers and consumers in eastern Africa, as root rot disease decimated harvests. In response, scientists from the Pan-Africa Bean Research Alliance (PABRA) identified resistant bush and climbing bean varieties that, when combined with integrated pest and disease management using local farmers' knowledge, proved effective in countering both bean root rot and other diseases and pests. By 2004, a total of 245 new bean varieties had been disseminated in the 18 PABRA countries. Recent impact studies indicated that some 35 million farmers were sowing the new varieties.

Countries in sub-Saharan Africa are mostly agrarian societies where agriculture is predominantly smallholder resource-limited crop production burdened with physically fragile, infertile soils. Such difficult conditions are tailor-made for innovative plant breeding. But as noted earlier, getting farmers to adopt new varieties can be a challenge. Early adopters are critical; if they succeed, they become opinion leaders in a social system of informal communication.

A noticeable trend in sub-Saharan Africa has been the entry into farming of a new class of farmers: mostly middle-aged professionals, some retired, who have taken up farming. These individuals could be the early adopter farmers who introduce innovations in plant breeding that increase productivity. But they need better access to modern varieties adapted to their locales, along with improved production packages. Developing an estimated 1,600 varieties for 16 major crops spread across an entire continent's agroecologies is a daunting task. Given limited spending by the public sector, public-private partnerships have become attractive. Water Efficient Maize for Africa—a partnership between Monsanto, the International Maize and Wheat Center in Mexico, National Agricultural Research Centers in five African countries, and the African Agricultural Technology Foundation—is one such example. Farmers in sub-Saharan Africa need access to the most effective improved crop technology. Facilitating this process will go a long way toward increasing crop productivity in Africa.

Martin Fregene
Danforth Plant Science Center
Source: See endnote 9.

review of national seed regulatory systems is a tedious but necessary way to facilitate the release of new varieties. Better seed laws could also help local seed producers and companies gain access to the very lucrative seed market, which is typically dominated by imports of varieties usually not adapted to local conditions.

Quality is an essential input for the production of healthy and nutritious vegetable crops. Better seeds mean more vitamins in the food, better-tasting food, and ultimately less hunger and malnutrition. And breeding quality seed requires mastery of both the technical knowledge of seed biology (including the skills to overcome any biological restrictions) and the managerial skills to run a seed business. Training seed company personnel in these often-overlooked skills, as well as developing better systems for seed drying and packaging, can make a huge difference in both the quality and quantity of local seed that is sold. Seed dealers in Tanzania, for example, have worked with AVRDC to learn better methods for preserving seeds and then labeling them appropriately so that farmers will know how and when to plant them.[12]

In addition to technical and managerial support, there are policy-related constraints to the supply of quality seeds. The biggest problem may be the private sector's lack of access to the foundation seeds—the earliest seeds available for seed production—from the public sector. Developing innovative strategies that bring farmers, researchers, and seed dealers together will go a long way in helping strengthen vegetable seed systems in Africa and also ensure easy access by farmers to locally adapted, affordable seed.[13]

Although not perceived as profitable by large multinationals, open-pollinated seed varieties (OPVs) continue to be widely planted by sub-Saharan farmers, and for good reasons. Unlike hybrid seeds, they do not need to be purchased every planting season, and they are far less expensive. In most cases vegetable hybrids are too expensive for smallholder farmers. They are also typically designed for higher-input agricultural areas and so often fail to thrive on low-input farms. Thus it is essential that the smaller domestic seed companies continue to recognize the market for OPVs and to stimulate and efficiently meet farmers' demand for them.[14]

A few years ago, for instance, scientists at AVRDC developed two new tomato varieties (Tanya and Tengeru 97) that not only yield more than previously grown varieties but have thicker skins and are a lot less vulnerable to pests and transport damage. They are notably resistant to tomato mosaic virus, fusarium wilt, and root-knot nematodes, and they have a longer shelf life—lasting up to three weeks at room temperature—which helps prevent food waste. Major companies have commercialized the two varieties, and they are also being used as parental lines to produce hybrids with good horticultural traits.[15]

Six years after these new varieties were introduced, more than two thirds of the households sampled in Tanzania were growing them. In 2003/04, the new tomato varieties were found on more than 80 percent of the acreage used to grow tomatoes. Yields jumped up by more than a third, largely thanks to the new varieties' higher resistance to tomato mosaic virus and roundworms. Since the average variable cost of production was 17 percent lower, overall net income rose. In fact, it was 40 percent higher than with the tomato varieties the farmers used to cultivate.[16]

Taking Advantage of Indigenous Vegetables

African indigenous vegetables have long been ignored by mainstream agriculture. In many countries they have received little attention in terms of research and development, resulting in a lot of information gaps. They have unfamiliar names—amaranth, baobab, cowpea, dika, enset, moringa, spider plant—and many are typically thought of as weeds.[17]

Yet these indigenous vegetables and many others provide an important source of nutrients to millions of people. Some have been used for thousands of years and have deep cultural roots, while also helping to increase food security and incomes. But these "weeds," which are a rich source of protein, calcium, and important micronutrients—and which taste good—are typically neglected on the international agricultural resource agenda despite their important potential to help alleviate hunger in sub-Saharan Africa.

As food prices continue to rise on the continent—in some countries the prices are 50–80 percent higher than in 2007—indigenous vegetables are becoming an integral part of home gardens. And as the impacts of climate change become more evident, the hardiness and drought tolerance of traditional vegetables is increasingly important. Many use less water than hybrid varieties, and some are resistant to pests and disease, which are likely to increase as climate change worsens. (See Box 3–2.)[18]

Production has continued to be small-scale, with farmers being the major custodians of the genetic materials and production technologies as they produce mainly for subsistence. But interest in traditional vegetables is surging because of increased awareness and education on their nutritional and overall health benefits, as well as improvements on traditional recipes. This has raised demand for high-quality seed and improved lines and cultivars.

Three improved lines of amaranth, for example, with softer, sweeter leaves than those of local varieties, have created a new industry for small-scale farmers near large cities in East Africa. The new varieties can be harvested in just 21–28 days (other varieties take longer) and can be cooked much more quickly (meaning less work for women and less fuel). National seed companies are commercializing some of these improved lines in Tanzania and Uganda. In some areas, the companies are struggling to meet an ever-increasing demand.[19]

Researchers and farmers are also working together to develop the African eggplant lines Tengeru White and the premium-priced and sweet-tasting DB3, AB2, and RW14. The lines have been popularized in different countries through on-farm evaluations, demonstration

plots, field days in Tanzania and Kenya, and agricultural trade fairs and shows. Breeders' seeds for these advanced lines have also been distributed to partner research institutes, nongovernmental organizations (NGOs), and seed companies for on-station testing followed by multilocational trials.[20]

Shelled cowpeas in Nigeria

The International Institute of Tropical Agriculture

As these varieties have become more widely adopted and commercialized, they are changing the perception that eggplants are "food for the poor." Today African eggplant regularly appears on market and supermarket shelves, especially in Tanzania. Local seed companies have started scaling up seed production, and research groups (including AVRDC) are working with research partners to fast-track the official variety-release and registration process for some of the promising lines.[21]

A recent study suggests the new lines are already making a difference. An assessment of households' participation in growing African eggplant in four villages in Tanzania's Arumeru district found significantly higher incomes and women's ownership levels than in villages not growing eggplant. The DB3 eggplant can be harvested every week for seven months and

Box 3–2. Indigenous Food and Climate Change

In Kenya, a devastating cycle of drought and flood reflects the worst that climate change has to offer and threatens the health and survival of the nation's poorest and most at-risk inhabitants. Although the government is trying to improve the nation's ability to produce food by providing funds for agricultural and rural development projects and for environmental programs, money and agricultural techniques based on western agriculture may not be the answer.

For Mary O. Abukutsa-Onyango, a horticultural scientist, teacher, and researcher at Nairobi's Jomo Kenyatta University of Agriculture and Technology, the problem with using western agricultural methods in Kenya is the loss of the superb diversity that once made indigenous plants a reliable and nutritious native food source. "Of the approximately 200 indigenous species of plants that were used by Kenyans as vegetables in the past," she notes, "most were either collected in the wild, semi-cultivated or cultivated. Now many are either unknown or extinct."

What Abukutsa-Onyango wants is a long-term solution that uses the tools at hand, including the marginal, arid soil of Kenyan lowlands, to bring about a lasting revolution in regional agriculture. She calls this an "indigenous food" revolution. And she is dedicated to seeing Kenyan agriculture survive not as some protected unmanageable offshoot of western monocultural crop techniques but as the traditional approach to food production that operated before Europeans intervened.

To that end, Abukutsa-Onyango has reintroduced such items as African nightshade and vegetable amaranth to regional farmers and has set up a system to put them back into the marketplace. "To date, we have about 100 [contacted] farmers and/or farmer groups...who are trained in all aspects of growing indigenous crops, from seed produc-

tion to processing, using organic methods. The farmers that do well are also taught simple food perseveration techniques like drying, which increase shelf life but retain as much of the nutrients as possible, and are linked to supermarkets to sell their vegetables. Because of their extensive training, they are able to pass on their knowledge of indigenous food growing to others in their communities."

These native foods, after years of being spurned as suitable only to starvation times, have spurred a cottage industry aimed at reducing poverty and improving the diet of the nation's approximately 6.5 million children.

While Abukutsa-Onyango foresees the hot, arid lowlands being used for indigenous crops like bambara nuts, she is not averse to using the cool, damp highlands to grow cash crops. "For example, indigenous bambara nuts and pigeon pea yield relatively better in low fertility soils and with low rainfall, compared with beans. And this allows a diversified, sustainable production model that ensures nutritional security and prosperity."

About one thing, however, she is adamant: "I don't believe we can address the issues of nutrition security, poverty, and health in Kenya without relying on African indigenous crops. With a soaring food crisis, and maize harvests predicted to be 16 percent below former years as a result of changing Kenyan weather patterns, the only grains that could adequately replace maize in my opinion would be indigenous millets and sorghum, which are more drought tolerant."

Thus Abukutsa-Onyango's solution, which suggests harmony with nature rather than attempts to control it, may be the only way forward in a warming world—and not just for Africa but for the world.

Jeanne Roberts
Environmental writer, Minnesota
Source: See endnote 18.

produced for up to 15 months if pruned back at the end of the season. A typical farmer can harvest 10–20 bags of eggplant (30 kilograms each) every week throughout the seven-month growing season and earn $2,500 per hectare per year—almost twice the income possible from tomatoes. Growers of African eggplant allocated more land (0.76 hectares on average) to food crops and received higher estimated annual incomes ($2,041) than those who did not grow it (0.70 hectares and $1,692).[22]

Demand has also been rising steadily for African nightshade, another leafy green vegetable, especially in urban supermarkets, groceries, retail markets, and hotels, thanks to promotional activities by research institutes and NGOs in East Africa. African nightshade is very high in beta-carotene, a Vitamin A precursor. Growers traditionally obtain yields of about 3 tons per hectare—which compares dismally to potential yields of about 30 tons per hectare. Farmers have been trained to grow nightshade and have been linked to markets; the biggest constraint has been lack of seed supply systems. To keep up with increases in consumption and demand, the domestication and commercialization of these vegetables with the selection and introduction of *Solanum scubrum* lines have helped improve production. Seeds of some of these lines are already being commercialized by companies in East Africa as varieties called Giant Nightshade and medium-leaf Long Lasting.[23]

Vegetable cowpea is another indigenous vegetable in great demand but limited supply. Although sufficient genetic variation is available for successful development of cultivars for leaf production, the focus so far has mainly been on improving grain yields. But advances in breeding for resistance to and tolerance of stresses can be exploited in the selection process for cowpea as a leafy vegetable, helping farmers and consumers reap its nutritional benefits. Researchers have achieved some useful selections, such as "Tumaini" and "Vuli," which are now being commercialized by seed companies. And to help complete the circle, women farmers in the Kibera slum in Nairobi have received training from AVRDC to grow and sell seeds to rural farmers, increasing the women's incomes.[24]

But it is not enough just to know how to grow indigenous vegetables to raise incomes; people also need to know how to eat them. NGOs such as Slow Food International are working with children to reignite an interest in—and a taste for—indigenous vegetables, while research institutes, including AVRDC, are teaching consumers how to cook the different varieties. Often vegetables are cooked for so long that they lose most of their nutrients. To solve that problem, women are receiving training from research institutes and extension agents about how to improve the nutritional value of cooked foods.[25]

"Eating is believing," says Mel Oluoch, formerly of AVRDC. He notes that when people find out how much better food tastes—and how much less fuel and time it takes to cook—they do not need much convincing about alternative methods.[26]

An agricultural revolution that works for farmers, for businesses, and for the environment will involve more than just producing enough calories of rice, cassava, or wheat. It will also need to include amarynth, cowpea leaves, African nightshade, spiderwiki, and African eggplant—the vegetables that make those staples taste good.

Developing Innovations in School Cultivation

In Uganda, agriculture is often an option of last resort for young people—they are forced into farming if they do not do well in school or have enough money to go to university. As a result, many of them look down on farming and have come to despise agriculture. In addition, interest in and understanding of local foods and food culture in Uganda has dropped drastically.[1]

But in Uganda and other parts of sub-Saharan Africa, some students are not only learning about the importance of local foods but also learning to love agriculture. Thirty-one schools and more than 1,100 schoolchildren across the country are part of a project with Slow Food Mukono Convivium, a local chapter of Slow Food International that was "established to improve young people's relationship with agriculture and to develop innovative methods for long-lasting food sovereignty."[2]

Project DISC (for Developing Innovations in School Cultivation) was initiated in 2006 to excite young people about locally grown food in an effort to combat growing food shortages and to defend Uganda's culinary traditions.[3]

Teachers and volunteers help the children learn how to grow local crop varieties using traditional and environmentally sound methods. Because of their experiences growing, tasting, and cooking fruits and vegetables, the children not only begin to appreciate agriculture, they also learn about the importance of eating high-quality and fairly produced foods.[4]

In 2009 the project began collaborating with Slow Food International to develop 17 school gardens and to integrate a new taste and sensory program into the school curriculum. Over the school year, the project gained a lot of attention from local communities as well as nationwide. In fact, interest has been so high that some schools that want to join in have had to

be turned away. The staff consists mostly of volunteers who also have full-time jobs. In 2010, a total of 31 schools and communities were able to participate in Project DISC.[5]

The project leaders help each school create and care for its gardens. In areas designed to include innovations that can withstand an uncooperative climate, the children learn how to grow crops sustainably. For example, they use kitchen and *Mandala* (variety) gardens, double-dug and raised gardens, deep and drip irrigation using pots and plastic bottles, and a diversity of local varieties that are drought-tolerant.[6]

Through various interactive lessons, students are taught about nutrition and taste both during school and in extracurricular activities. The produce is taken directly from the garden and is incorporated into school meals; any extra crops are sold at the local market. And in some schools, gardens have been expanded so that jams and preserves can be prepared from the surplus to be sold as a fundraiser for the project.[7]

Volunteers and teachers cover a wide variety of topics so that the children come to understand the practical aspects of farming, including garden preparation, sustainable agriculture techniques, composting, and cooking. In addition to learning about the importance of eating local, nutritious foods, they can enjoy the tastes and textures of produce indigenous to Uganda.[8]

The teachers at DISC work to make sure that students appreciate local food and farming. And they have seen their hard work pay off. Students bring home their knowledge, starting gardens in their backyard and communities, choosing nutritious foods, and encouraging their family members to buy local produce. This change in attitude about food can have positive impacts on a community as the families start to put their money back into the local economy and to support local farmers.[9]

In addition to teaching the children about planting indigenous and traditional vegetables and fruit trees, DISC puts a big emphasis on food preparation and processing. If a person does not know how to grow, cook, or prepare food, they do not know how to eat. These lessons go far beyond those currently taught in the classroom. The students are excited when they learn what good, fresh food tastes like, and their eating habits actually change after being taught about nutrition. They continue to gain respect for farming and food production as a result.[10]

Improving nutrition is especially important for boarding school students, who eat all of their meals at school. These children come from all over Uganda. They just find food on the plate, says another volunteer, without any idea of where it comes from. And "this risks the future of cooking, since these children will get used to such lifestyle and not have local cooking skills." DISC tries to make them feel at home by growing crop varieties that are familiar to people from both the lowlands and the highlands.[11]

At both day and boarding schools, students work with school chefs to learn how to cook foods, giving them the opportunity to understand food production literally from farm to table.

Unlike most other schools in Uganda, DISC project schools get local fruits with their breakfast and can harvest their own desert at lunchtime.[12]

At the Annual Fruit and Juice Party, students, teachers, parents, and even representatives of the National Agricultural Advisory Services celebrate the success of DISC as they come together to enjoy the fruits prepared by the children right out of the garden. "Thanks to DISC, students no longer see agriculture as an option of last resort but rather as a way to make money, help their communities, and preserve biodiversity," said Nassaazi Jane, the head teacher of St. Balikuddembe Senior School, at the 2010 Fruit and Juice Party.[13]

—*Edward Mukiibi and Roger Serunjogi*
Project DISC

The One Acre Fund Puts Farmers First

After one growing season, Kenyan farmer Lydia Musila sold enough beans to build herself a new house. Rwandan farmers Gilbert and Edith started saving money from their bean harvests to send their first child to nursery school. Kenyan farmer Francis Mamati purchased three goats with his increased harvest income. One Acre Fund was founded in 2006 to serve small-holder farmers like Lydia, Gilbert, Edith, and Francis, helping provide rural farmers with the tools they need to feed their families and increase their incomes. The organization currently works with about 23,000 farmers in Kenya and Rwanda, and it plans to reach 50,000 farmers in 2011 and 1 million farmers by 2020.[1]

From the beginning, One Acre Fund talked to farmers to understand what they needed to succeed. The staff knew that farmers needed seed and fertilizer, but discovered that they also needed financing to purchase those inputs, as well as education on how to use them. And they needed access to a market to sell their crop after harvest.[2]

One Acre Fund offers a service model that addresses each of these needs. When farmers enroll with One Acre Fund, they join as part of a group of 6–12 farmers. They receive an in-kind loan of seed and fertilizer, which is guaranteed by the group members. One Acre Fund delivers the supplies to a market point within two kilometers of farmers' homes, and a field officer provides in-field training on land preparation, planting, fertilizer application, and weeding. During the growing season, the field officer monitors the fields. And then he trains the new members how to harvest and store their crops.

One Acre Fund also offers a harvest buyback program that farmers can participate in if they choose. Final loan repayment is several weeks after harvest—and 98 percent of the farmers repay their loans.[3]

Before they joined One Acre Fund, many of the participants in Kenya were harvesting 5 bags of maize from half an acre of land. After joining, their harvests typically increase to 12–15 bags of maize from the same half-acre of land—twice as much income from the same amount of land.[4]

Farmers use this additional income to feed their families, pay school fees, pay health care expenses, and buy livestock. Their long-term goals, however, are much bigger. At the first training session of the season, field officers ask farmers to write down what they hope to achieve if they have a good harvest. Some dreamed of building new houses, buying cars, or opening small businesses. One farmer, Martha Barasa, dreamed of buying a posha mill (to grind maize into flour). Another, Simon Munai, dreamed of opening a private school to educate the community's children.[5]

These dreams are the force that motivates One Acre Fund's innovation team to develop improvements to the core program model. As the organization strives to reach 1 million farmers in the next 10 years, it will continue to have an unflagging focus on customer service—building strong relationships and understanding what its farmers want and need. It seeks to contribute one thing to the Green Revolution in Africa: farmers first.[6]

—Stephanie Hanson
One Acre Fund

Drip irrigation in Niger

CHAPTER 4

Getting More Crop per Drop

Sandra L. Postel

Every farmer needs the right mix of sunshine, soil, seeds, nutrients, and water to work the magic on the land that is agriculture. The Green Revolution of recent decades brought the last three of these ingredients to millions of farmers and vast areas of the world's cropland. The combination of high-yielding seed varieties, fertilizer, and a doubling of world irrigated area led to a near tripling of the global grain harvest since 1960. By lifting the productivity of millions of hectares of cropland, this revolution not only enabled grain harvests to rise along with population, it spared substantial areas of forest and grassland from the plow.[1]

For all its benefits, however, the Green Revolution also came with some downsides. Among them is that it demanded vast quantities of water. Today, 70 percent of all the water withdrawn from rivers, lakes, and underground aquifers goes to irrigation. In many of the most important food-producing regions of China, India, Pakistan, and elsewhere, the use of water surpasses sustainable levels. Rivers are running dry, water tables are falling, lakes are shrinking, and wetlands are disappearing. Adding to these pressures on water, expanding cities and industries are now in keen competition with agriculture for finite supplies of water.[2]

Sandra Postel is Director of the Global Water Policy Project, which is based in New Mexico.

In addition, the off-the-shelf package of ingredients that constituted the Green Revolution was not appropriate for all regions and did not reach all farmers. Today enough grain is harvested to feed all the world's people, yet nearly 1 billion people remain chronically hungry and malnourished. About 60 percent of the food-insecure live in South Asia and sub-Saharan Africa—most of them on small farms. These farm families have neither the resources to make their land productive enough to meet their food needs nor the income to buy the food they need.[3]

For a great many of these small farmers, the missing ingredient is water. Today, thanks to a variety of innovative ways of making more of nature's water bounty available to crops when they need it, crop yields and family incomes are rising in some of the world's pockets of hunger, including in sub-Saharan Africa.

Water Vulnerabilities in Sub-Saharan Africa

Africa's water endowment is rich and varied but not easily accessible for conventional irrigation. Only 20 percent of the precipitation falling on land feeds rivers, streams, and underground aquifers, just a bit more than half the comparable figure for the world as a whole. The other 80 percent evaporates or is released by plants back to the atmosphere. And in the Sahel, the band of territory roughly from Senegal eastward to Ethiopia, this ratio of runoff-to-rainfall is scarcely 6 percent.[4]

With so little precipitation turning into what hydrologists call "blue water"—the water running in rivers and streams or held in lakes, ponds, and aquifers—there is much less water to tap for irrigation than there is in most other parts of the world. Combined with a lack of roads and infrastructure, as well as poor governance and chronic civil strife in many countries, these conditions have made irrigation difficult and expensive to develop. Today only 4 percent of the cultivated land in sub-Saharan Africa is equipped for irrigation, compared with 37 percent in Asia and 18 percent in the world as a whole. (See Figure 4–1.) Moreover, most of that irrigated land is in just four countries: Madagascar, Nigeria, South Africa, and Sudan.[5]

To make matters even more challenging, rainfall in the semiarid savannas and other drylands of sub-Saharan Africa is highly variable and unpredictable. In two out of three years, rain deficits occur during critical periods of the cropping season, greatly reducing that year's harvest. Once every decade, severe drought will lead to catastrophic crop failure—and deeper hunger. In 2009, famine stalked millions of people in the Horn of Africa as failed rains led to the worst food crisis in Ethiopia and Kenya in a quarter-century.[6]

With a large majority of livelihoods dependent on agriculture, and with agriculture dependent on fickle rains, both family and national incomes in some of the poorest African countries rise and fall with precipitation. In Niger, for example, where the majority of the 14.7 million residents earn less than $1 a day and where less than 1 percent of cultivated land is irrigated, yearly changes in annual economic growth show a remarkably close correlation with annual rainfall. (See Figure 4–2.) Nearly three quarters of Niger's people depend at least partially on livestock for meat, milk, and income, and droughts can decimate herds. In August 2010, when parts of Niger were gripped by their worst drought in nearly four decades, officials estimated that more than one third of the cattle in the Diffa region may have died. With climate scientists predicting that rainfall will decline in much of Africa in the decades ahead, food, income and economic security may suffer further.[7]

The silver lining in this otherwise bleak picture is that the biggest potential worldwide for gains in water productivity—for getting more crop per drop—is precisely in such low yielding rainfed agricultural areas. A large gap exists between the 0.5–2 tons per hectare that most farmers in sub-Saharan Africa produce and the yields that can be achieved under similar growing conditions. David Molden and his colleagues at the International Water Management Institute based in Colombo, Sri Lanka, estimate that three quarters of the world's additional food needs in 2050 could be met by increasing harvests on low-yielding farms to 80 percent of what high-yielding farms achieve on comparable land.[8]

Human-Powered Pumps to Obtain Water

As long as other ingredients are in sufficient supply, a crop's yield will increase linearly with the amount of water it takes in through its roots and then releases as vapor back to the atmosphere (the process known as transpiration). So innovative ways of channeling moisture into the root zones of crops will have a lot to do with filling this "yield gap" and meeting future food needs. Among the most promising methods in sub-Saharan Africa are on-farm practices that conserve moisture in soils, local harvesting and storage of rainfall to supplement soil moisture during the growing season, and access to affordable irrigation technologies that are specially designed for smallholder farmers. (See Table 4–1.) Only with a reliable and ample supply of water in the root zones of their fields can farmers confi-

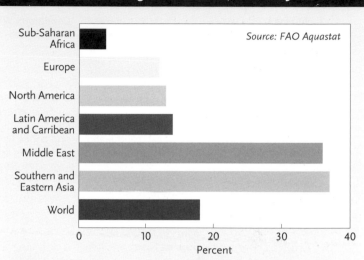

Figure 4–1. Percentage of Cultivated Land That is Irrigated, Selected Regions and World, circa 2005

Source: FAO Aquastat

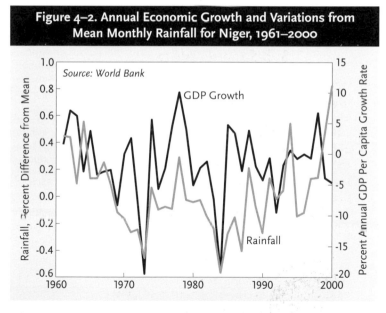

Figure 4–2. Annual Economic Growth and Variations from Mean Monthly Rainfall for Niger, 1961–2000

Source: World Bank

dently invest in higher-value seeds, fertilizers, and other yield-raising inputs, as well as plant higher-value crops to take to market.[9]

For more than 2.3 million poor farmers in the developing world—and some 250,000 in sub-Saharan Africa—this boost in farm pro-

Table 4–1. Selected Low-cost Innovations that Improve Water Access and Efficiency in Agriculture			
Technology or Practice	Example Locations	Conditions Where Appropriate	General Benefits
Manually operated (foot, hip, hand) pumps that extract water from surface and groundwater sources	Bangladesh, India, Burkina Faso, Ethiopia, Ghana, Mali, Malawi, Niger, Tanzania, Zambia	Shallow groundwater or surface water available; small farm plots; semi-arid zones or areas with distinct dry seasons	May offer entry point to irrigated agriculture by providing access to water (manual pumps) and ability to stretch scarce supplies (drip and micro-irrigation); reduce water-carrying burden and risk of crop failure; lift yields and allow diversification to higher-value crops for marketplace sales; increase income and food security
Micro-irrigation using bucket kits, shiftable drip systems, pitcher irrigation, and micro-sprinklers; solar-powered drip systems being piloted	Northwest, central and southern India; Nepal; Central Asia; China; Near East; semiarid regions in South America and sub-Saharan Africa; solar-powered pilots in Benin and Burkina Faso		
Fog water collection using mesh nets	Peru, Chile, Nepal, South Africa	Upland areas with frequent fog periods	Simple techniques make fresh water available for irrigation year-round, reduce groundwater extraction and the need to purchase water
Capturing surface runoff from "built" surfaces or rooftops in small channels, stabilization ponds, or small reservoirs	Beijing, China; Lima, Peru; Hyderabad, India; Ubuntu, South Africa	Rainfed, urban/peri-urban agriculture; rainfall runoff from greenhouses or other building structures	
On- and off-farm rainwater harvesting through terracing, stone bunds, vegetative barriers, check dams, recharge pits, and other methods	In low-lying areas: "fadama" in Nigeria; "dambos" in Malawi, Zambia, and Zimbabwe; "tassa" in Niger On sloping lands: "fanya-juu" in Kenya; "teras" in Sudan; vetiver contours in Mozambique, Zambia, and Zimbabwe	Where soil moisture is limiting factor to crop production and local, seasonal rains can be captured to fill soil-moisture deficit; where precipitation may result in topsoil erosion and rainfall runoff	Improve food security through effective soil and rainwater management; reclaim barren land, reduce deforestation by increasing per acre crop yields, retain soils and soil fertility and moisture; many methods build on indigenous practices

Source: See endnote 9. Examples compiled by Alexandra Tung, Worldwatch Institute.

ductivity, harvest reliability, and income has come from a modest human-powered water-lifting device called a treadle pump. In the original version, designed for Bangladeshi farmers by Norwegian engineer Gunnar Barnes, the operator pedals up and down on two poles (called treadles), which activates a cylinder that suctions water through a tubewell from depths of up to seven meters. For a total investment of $35, Bangladeshi farmers can irrigate 0.2 hectares (half an acre) during the dry season—enough to feed their families and even have some higher-value vegetables to take to market.[10]

Working with Barnes and Rangpur Dinajpur Rural Service, a northern Bangladeshi development organization originally sponsored by the Lutheran World Federation, the Denver-based non-profit International Development Enterprises (IDE) developed a highly successful marketing and promotion campaign to sell treadle pumps through Bangladesh's private sector. Sales rose rapidly, and today more than 1.5 million of these pumps dot the Bangladeshi countryside. IDE founder Paul Polak estimates that smallholder treadle pump investments of $37.5 million combined with donor investments of $12 million are generating net returns to Bangladeshi farmers totaling $150 million per year.[11]

Following on this success, a number of organizations have brought variations of the treadle pump into Africa. In 1998, the non-profit KickStart began marketing a line of MoneyMaker Pumps through its offices in Kenya, Tanzania, and Mali. Its most successful product, the Super MoneyMaker, is a foot-operated pressure pump that allows farmers to irrigate land situated several meters above their water source with "no more effort than a brisk walk." It can pump one liter of water per second, irrigate up to 0.8 hectares (2 acres), and typically costs farmers about $140 installed. A version suitable for irrigating smaller plots—the MoneyMaker hip pump—is available at less than half that price. Working closely with local organizations, KickStart has expanded its reach to Burkina Faso and Malawi. To date, an estimated 150,000 MoneyMaker pumps have been sold. These devices are generating $37 million a year in new profits and wages. In 2008, citing quality and cost reasons, KickStart shifted the manufacturing of the pump out of

Africa to China.[12]

Farmers in other parts of sub-Saharan Africa are benefiting from human-powered pumps as well. In the early 1990s, EnterpriseWorks/ VITA (which later merged with Relief International) introduced the treadle pump into Senegal and subsequently into Burkina Faso, Niger, and Mali. IDE has recently fashioned a new pressure treadle pump for Zambian farmers. In July 2009, after months of "listening exercises" to discern more precisely what farmers there needed and wanted, IDE introduced Mosi-O-Tunya, or "the pump that thunders"—a name adapted from the Tonga for Victoria Falls, "the falls that thunder." Manufactured locally and currently priced at $118, the new pump delivers 1.25 liters of water per second when operated at one stroke per second, a 25-percent increase over earlier versions. With many new markets yet to be tapped, the treadle pump in all its variations still has far to go to achieve its full potential to alleviate hunger and poverty.[13]

Affordable Micro-irrigation to Stretch Supplies

For many small farmers in Africa, stretching their limited water supplies may be just as crucial as gaining access to water. In response to this need, designers have developed a suite of low-cost, micro-irrigation technologies that are helping farmers make more effective use of locally scarce water supplies. These include a spectrum of inexpensive drip irrigation systems—from $5 bucket kits for home gardens to $25 drum kits for 100-square meter plots (about 400 plants) and $100 shiftable drip systems that can irrigate 0.2 hectares (half an acre), including plots on terraced hillsides.

As with drip systems used in wealthier farming regions, these low-cost systems deliver water through perforated pipes or tubes directly to the roots of plants. By increasing yields and reducing evaporation losses, drip systems often double water productivity. More than 600,000 of IDE's low-cost drip systems have been sold in India, Nepal, Zambia, and Zimbabwe.[14]

Because systems like small bucket irrigation lie so far outside the realm and image of "conventional" irrigation, they often go uncounted in the irrigation statistics reported to the United Nations and official government bodies. One study of informal bucket irrigation around the city of Kumasi, Ghana, for example, found that at least 11,900 hectares (29,400 acres) were irrigated this way. If this area were included in the official statistics, Ghana's irrigated area would increase by 38 percent. Though no formal accounting has been done, perhaps 8 million farmers till fields in Africa using this kind of informal irrigation.[15]

Smallholder micro-irrigation systems powered by solar photovoltaics are making their debut in West Africa. In two villages in the Kalalé district of northern Benin, the Solar Electric Light Fund (SELF) and its partners have introduced a solar-powered drip irrigation system that is improving nutrition and raising incomes for farmers in this pocket of deep poverty. (See Box 4–1.) With little rain falling during the six-month dry season, these villagers endure a long hunger season, with many children exhibiting distended stomachs, a telltale sign of malnutrition.[16]

One year after the solar-drip system's installation, an assessment by Stanford University researchers found that the villagers were eating three to five servings of vegetables per day. And with the income from market sales of tomatoes, okra, peppers, and other high-value crops, women were purchasing higher-protein foodstuffs for their families. Instead of carrying water, children were more often going to school. At a cost of about $18,000 to install the solar-drip system for a 0.5-hectare plot, plus $5,750 annually to maintain it, the Stanford team estimated a payback period for the system

of 2.3 years, assuming $10,000 in annual sales the first year and $16,000 thereafter. While financially out of reach for most poor farmers in Africa, if larger-scale local manufacturing and distribution can bring costs down over time and if reasonable access to credit is available, the benefits of these systems could spread more widely.[17]

More Effective Use of Rainfall

Irrigation is an obvious way to deliver water to crops in dry regions or seasons, but it is not the only way. More effective use and management of rainfall may offer the largest potential for improvement in crop production—especially in sub-Saharan Africa, where cereal yields average just 1 ton per hectare and more than 95 percent of cropland is watered only by rain. On these fields, only 15–30 percent of the rain that falls gets used productively by crops, and if the land is severely degraded, this share can drop to 5 percent. The remainder evaporates, percolates below the root zone, or runs off the field. As Johan Rockström of the Stockholm Environment Institute and his colleagues point out, crop failures commonly attributed to drought may be caused more by poor on-farm rainwater management than by a shortage of rainfall.[18]

So-called conservation farming practices can help capture, store, and make use of more rain that falls directly on a farmer's field—turning a larger share of rainwater into productive "green water" for crops. A host of such methods, both indigenous and introduced, have been implemented in sub-Saharan Africa. Much of their benefit is due to better management of the soil, the vessel for the plants' moisture and nutrients. Most small farmers in sub-Saharan Africa prepare their fields with hoes or animal-drawn plows, and they also remove and burn the crop residues from the previous harvest. These practices invert the soil and expose it to drying out from the sun and blowing away

Box 4–1. Solar Market Gardens: Increasing Access to Energy, Water, and Food

The Kalalé district of northern Benin in West Africa is home to 100,000 people, all of whom live off the grid. During the six-month dry season, from November through April, the region receives precious little rainfall. The land is parched, people are hungry, and malnutrition is widespread.

To help ease Kalalé's food crisis, the Solar Electric Light Fund (SELF), a Washington, D.C.-based nonprofit that delivers sustainable energy solutions to the developing world, teamed up with Dov Pasternak, a leading drip-irrigation expert with the International Crops Research Institute for the Semi-Arid Tropics, which is based in Niger. SELF decided that solar power would be a more sustainable, and ultimately cheaper, way to pump water to local crops than the diesel generators used previously.

In 2007, SELF installed three solar-powered drip-irrigation systems at women's farming collectives in two Kalalé villages, Dunkassa and Bessassi. The installations use SELF's Solar Market Garden concept, which combines solar pumping technology with drip irrigation for watering and fertilizing crops. The project is the first phase of a plan to electrify all 44 of Kalalé's villages.

By June 2009, visitors to the two villages could see a noticeable difference in the women, who had visibly filled out since 2006. Not only were they better fed and healthier, so were their families and the rest of the villagers, who now have year-round access to nutritious fruits and vegetables.

According to an assessment by Stanford University's Program on Food Security and the Environment, the Kalalé Solar Market Garden project "significantly augments both household income and nutritional intake" in the region. The study found that each garden supplies nearly two tons of fresh produce per month, about 20 percent of which is kept for home consumption. The rest is sold at markets, earning the women an extra $7.50 per week on average to pay for school fees, medical treatment, and overall economic development. The women are already starting to think about other income-generating schemes.

Phase II of the project, slated to launch in 2011, will involve "whole-village" electrification of Dunkassa and Bessassi. Solar power systems will generate electricity for the village's schools, clinics, homes, community centers, and street lights. SELF also plans to bring solar irrigation to other villages in Kalalé.

The Kalalé initiative shows that using solar energy and drip irrigation together is a cost-effective solution that can be replicated in many parts of sub-Saharan Africa, particularly areas that are poor in water resources but rich in sunlight. SELF's Solar Market Garden is simultaneously helping to combat climate change, improve food security, fight poverty, and empower women.

—Robert Freling
Solar Electric Light Fund

with the wind. By practicing soil-conserving tillage methods that leave the soil structure intact, moisture gets conserved in the root zone. Add in timely weeding to eliminate competition for that moisture, mulching to help keep the moisture in storage, and fertilizer to add nutrients to depleted soils, and a recipe for higher yields takes shape.[19]

Working with farmers on six experimental farms in Kenya, Ethiopia, Zambia, and Tanzania, researchers found yield gains of 20–120 percent for maize and 35–100 percent for tef (a staple grain of the Ethiopian diet) on farms using such soil- and water-conserving practices versus those using traditional methods. The best results were achieved when moisture conservation and spot fertilizer applications were combined, since often in these regions both water and nutrients are below optimal levels for crop production. On Ethiopian farms receiving both treatments, yields of tef were roughly double those on the conventional farms (1.1 ton per hectare compared with 0.5–0.7 tons). Five years after the trials were completed, the farmers involved in these experiments continued to practice the methods and spread the word to other farmers. Along with working side-by-side with the farmers, the researchers also partnered with local development organizations and extension services to increase the chances for broader adoption.[20]

Extra resilience can be added to drought-prone semiarid rainfed systems by supplementing farm conservation measures with small-scale irrigation. Typically this requires some method to harvest and store rainwater—such as channeling it into small surface ponds or promoting recharge of groundwater—and then applying that water to fields as necessary. For example, farmers in Malawi, Zambia, and Zimbabwe grow crops on seasonally waterlogged lands called dambos. Their crops get most of the moisture they need by tapping the underlying shallow groundwater through capillary action, but farmers supplement this natural supply with irrigation water lifted from shallow wells by buckets or hand-pumps. If used carefully in these fragile wetland areas, shallow treadle pumps and other small-scale irrigation devices could provide supplemental irrigation as well.[21]

Generations of farming under difficult conditions has spawned a host of ingenious, locally appropriate techniques that make productive use of the scarce resources available. Building on this indigenous knowledge can generate an expanded portfolio of productivity-enhancing methods—including mulching, terracing, planting vegetative barriers to retain soil and water, and constructing earthen dams and other structures to harvest rainwater for sup

plemental irrigation. A project in East Africa called Promoting Farmer Innovation, carried out from 1997 to 2000 in areas of water-limited rainfed cereal production, found a rich array of such indigenous practices. To cite one example: among many agricultural development specialists, vetiver grass has become the vegetative barrier of choice to promote soil and water conservation, but African farmers sometimes choose grasses more palatable to livestock so as to get both fodder and water conservation benefits from the vegetative barriers. If manure from the livestock is used to enhance the soil's fertility, this indigenous multipurpose farming system offers high production potential to build upon.[22]

Creative uses of information technology can also help poor farmers get more crop per drop of local rainfall. Satellite imagery is being used to track soil moisture content, helping farmers know when to irrigate. In Ugandan villages, farmers without computers are able to use the wealth of information on the Internet by calling in questions to a free telephone hotline called Question Box. They reach an operator who speaks their local language and who searches for the answers while the caller waits. A project of the California-based nonprofit Open Mind, Question Box enables poor farmers whose sole communication device may be a village phone to get real-time answers to questions about the weather, their crops, and many other issues.[23]

Many rural development experts lament the number of innovative soil and water conservation practices "on the shelf" that for one reason or another poor farmers have not adopted on a wide scale. While scientists tend to blame gaps between research and field extension, the bigger problem seems to be insufficient analysis of how farmers' socioeconomic conditions and risk perceptions influence their technology adoption decisions.[24]

Most poor farmers in sub-Saharan Africa face scarcities not only of water but of land, labor, and capital as well. Terraces and many other soil- and water-conserving technologies can require a great deal of labor to construct: 97 person-days for one hectare of rock embankments (or bunds), for example, and 279 person-days per hectare of stone dams. Spending time on this construction only makes sense if the net return exceeds other income-generating opportunities that could be pursued instead. Most farmers need a minimum rate of return of 50 percent to adopt a somewhat familiar method or technology and 100 percent rate of return for a new method. Thus some underwriting of early returns might help spread the adoption of conservation farming methods that carry long-term payoffs but short-term risks and opportunity costs.[25]

With no cookie-cutter approach akin to the Green Revolution package of seeds, fertilizer, and irrigation appropriate for most of sub-Saharan Africa, it is far more difficult to "scale up" these strategies and achieve widespread gains rapidly. So far there are few examples in the region of a concerted effort that has succeeded in building local markets and supply chains that enable innovative water management products to "take off"—as the treadle pump did in Bangladesh, for instance. But with more investment in research and development, partnerships with farmers and villages, entrepreneurial market development, extension services, seed money to pilot ideas, and financial incentives to launch projects, a larger transformation seems possible.

The hilly Machakos District in southern Kenya, nearly written off as a desertified wasteland a half-century ago, provides some idea of the possibilities. With funds from the Swedish International Development Agency, the Kenyan government worked with local groups of mostly women who practiced a terracing technique known as fanya-juu ("throw it upwards" in Kiswahili). The women basically dig a ditch, throw the soil up-slope to form an earthen wall along the contour, and plant on the bench terraces that form naturally. The terraces concentrate rainwater in the soil and control erosion. Field studies suggest yields of maize have increased by 50 percent.[26]

Though requiring 150–350 person-days per hectare, with this burden falling mostly to women, the terracing offered sufficient benefits to spread rapidly. Between the mid-1980s and early 1990s the women of Machakos built an average of 1,000 kilometers of terraces each year. Today, 70 percent of the cultivated land in the district reportedly is terraced. Besides producing greater harvests of staples, the terraces support production of higher-value cash crops. Green beans grown in Machakos are now sold in supermarkets in the United Kingdom.[27]

Looking Ahead

One strategy put forth for water-stressed countries is that they should import water indirectly through grain to help balance their water budgets and meet their food needs. On average it takes about 1,500 tons of water to produce one ton of grain, so it can make sense for water-scarce countries to import more of their staple foods and save their water for manufacturing and other higher-valued enterprises. But for poor, food-importing countries, this is a risky proposition. Most cannot afford the imports, and even if they can, the imported grains rarely make their way to the tables of the hungry. One of the most important lessons of the last half-century of global agriculture is that food security rarely trickles down to the very poor. Moreover, the food riots that erupted in Senegal, Mauritania, Haiti, and some half-dozen other countries as grain prices soared in 2007 and 2008 are likely a harbinger of what is to come. With global grain and oil markets increasingly uncertain, a degree of food self-sufficiency may be crucial to food security.[28]

Finally, it would seem that the industrial countries most responsible for the climate changes now under way have a moral obligation to assist the poor populations who will bear most of the consequences of climate change in preparing for, adapting to, and becoming more resilient to its effects. According to the Intergovernmental Panel on Climate Change, the Sahelian region of Africa has already experienced warmer and drier conditions that have shortened the crop-growing season and reduced harvests. By 2020, yields from rainfed agriculture in some sub-Saharan African countries could drop by half. Overall, within a decade between 75 million and 250 million people in Africa are projected to live in conditions of increased water stress due to climate change.[29]

The challenges loom large. It takes about 3,000 liters of water to meet one person's daily dietary needs—about 1 liter per calorie. Satisfying this dietary water requirement for all—in the face of rising population and consumption, persistent poverty, and global climate change—will take a commitment well beyond what has materialized to date.[30]

Rainwater Harvesting

There is an overdependence on rainfed agriculture in sub-Saharan Africa and not enough ways to deal with the effects of dry spells and droughts. As a result, grain yields are below one ton per hectare in most of the region. This has mistakenly been blamed on physical water scarcity. But it is not physical as much as it is economic. There is simply a lack of investments to both capture and boost water storage.[1]

Most sub Saharan African countries are currently using at most 5 percent of their rainwater potential. By recognizing and incorporating the greenwater—the water ignored in hydrological planning—it may be possible to improve the food insecurity situation while also protecting the environment.[2]

To help alleviate hunger and poverty, the Swedish International Development Cooperation Agency, through its Regional Soil Conservation Unit, helped establish the Southern and Eastern Africa Rainwater Network (SearNet) in 1998. SearNet consists of 12 national rainwater associations that work together to publicize rainwater harvesting information and innovations throughout the region. The network is hosted by the World Agroforestry Centre in Nairobi.[3]

In collaboration with Rwanda's Ministry of Agriculture and Animal Resources,the World Agroforestry Centre pioneered a method for upscaling trapezoidal-shaped ponds with off-stream runoff water conveyance mechanisms that facilitate the supply of water for irrigation and livestock development. The ponds can hold 120 cubic meters of water and are lined with a 0.8-millimeter plastic sheet. Inexpensive materials, including rope, a washer pump, and a siphon or easy-to-use treadle pump are used to bring the water up from the pond. As the pond costs around $800, farmers would need a sub-

sidy, a cost-sharing facility, or microfinancing to afford one. But the payoffs can be huge. Cost-benefit studies indicate that, with good management, farmers recover their investment costs in just two or three years.[4]

With access to more water, farmers are encouraged to plant vegetables such as kale, tomatoes, and onions as well as fruit trees, including mangoes and pawpaws, to boost production and improve nutrition. This innovation has spread across 10 districts in Rwanda: more than 400 ponds have been constructed and 800 more are in the pipeline.[5]

Rural women spend at least three to four hours a day collecting water from distant and often contaminated water sources for use in cooking. This is especially burdensome for girls who are in school; they have to wake up early in the morning, haul water, and then rush off to class. In the Kajiado District of Kenya, the U.N. Environment Programme (UNEP) and the World Agroforestry Centre have worked with Maasai women to build roof catchment ferro-cement tanks to provide domestic water for their households. Members of women's groups were encouraged to donate some of their own money so they could get matching funds from UNEP and the Centre. The women also provided local materials such as water, sand, and stones as well as labor for construction of the tanks.[6]

After initial training, 86 tanks were constructed. In addition, the women were encouraged to plant 100 trees for each tank built. The project is being upscaled on a rotational basis, with a target of each woman eventually having her own tank. Rotary International of Canada then adopted this community, and more than 200 tanks have been constructed using the same model. This has improved health, and the women have more time for other fund-raising activities.[7]

Farmers do not need expensive gadgets to find groundwater to help irrigate their crops. Green twigs, copper wires, and plumb bobs can be used to locate and determine the width and status of underground water bodies. Green twigs from *Croton megalocarpus* or *C. microstachys* tree species found in semiarid lands have been known to perform better than those from other tree species. The copper wire is used to determine the width of an underground water body, while the plumb helps estimate the depth. All in all, these tools have been used to map underground water bodies. A comparison with terrameters, the devices used by civil engineers in groundwater prospecting, has confirmed that these other tools are not only cheap (or free, for the twigs), but also accurate.[8]

In the western and Rift Valley regions of Kenya, water can be the entry point to rural development. Harnessing rain through water harvesting and conservation agriculture methods such as no-till farming and cover crops provides the basis for productive ventures that are crucial in helping to increase food self-sufficiency and improve rural economies. For annual crops, changes in yield are immediate. For perennial crops, it takes a few years before the impacts are realized. But with good agricultural husbandry, it is possible to realize positive returns when the availability of water or moisture is integrated with soil fertility management.

Water harvesting is more than just a matter of constructing ponds, dams, wells, or tanks, of course. It is a slow process of creating, of organizing communities to develop, maintain, and manage water-harvesting activities, of involving communities closely in every aspect of the project, and of setting up systems for using and sharing water sustainably and equitably. This is also precisely the reason why it has to be a matter of community involvement and participation.[9]

It is crucial, therefore, to create awareness and confidence among farmers and communities that water harvesting really works. The government should be a facilitator rather than an implementer. It has an important role to play in catalyzing the widespread practice of water harvesting. And the government could get scientific organizations to develop better designs of the systems. But the most important role for government is to provide financial incentives and grants for water harvesting in rural and urban areas.[10]

—*Maimbo Malesu*
World Agroforestry Centre

Students at their school garden outside the Community Innovation Centre in Kigoma, Rwanda

CHAPTER 5

Farmers Take the Lead in Research and Development

Brigid Letty, Qureish Noordin, Saidou Magagi, and Ann Waters-Bayer

Smallholder farmers in Africa, like those the world over, are relentless experimenters. On their own, without any external support, they have always created and tested possible solutions to the challenges they face. "I have been experimenting all along, as my father used to do," said Eddy Ouko, a Kenyan farmer. Building on this innovative capacity and encouraging farmers to drive the development of locally appropriate technologies are the keys to addressing the challenges that smallholders face.[1]

In Potshini in KwaZulu-Natal, South Africa, a farmer heard by chance about a new method of growing potatoes that involved burying the seed potatoes under a layer of mulch instead of beneath soil. He experimented with different materials for mulch and different depths of it in his attempts to obtain a satisfactory yield with much less work. Similarly, in Eastern

---

Brigid Letty is an agricultural development specialist and animal scientist at the Institute of Natural Resources in South Africa. **Qureish Noordin** is project coordinator for the Transboundary Water for Biodiversity and Human Health in the Mara River Basin Project at the Lake Victoria Basin Commission. **Saidou Magagi** is a crop scientist with the National Agricultural Research Institute of Niger. **Ann Waters-Bayer**, an agricultural sociologist, is with EcoCulture at the ETC Foundation in the Netherlands.

Tigray in Ethiopia, farmers noticed a plant that had been unintentionally introduced in sacks of grain brought into the area as food aid, and they explored how the new plant could be used. After informal trial-and-error experiments, they found that a solution made from its leaves kills ticks on livestock.[2]

Farmers in Kenya did their own investigations into the use of *Tithonia diversifolia* mixed with goat manure to make compost for growing maize and high-value crops. Eddy Ouko was one of the farmers involved: "When ICRAF [the World Agroforestry Centre] used to work in this area, they taught us how to use *Tithonia* for soil fertility improvement. When I recently got the dairy goats, I decided to experiment on my own. I decided to mix *Tithonia* with goat manure and make compost and then apply it to my crops. I could not believe my eyes the very good harvest I got from my *shamba* [field]."[3]

These are just three examples of informal farmer experimentation. Despite this evidence of farmers' ability to experiment and innovate, most agricultural scientists continue to do research on behalf of farmers rather than with them. Their results are passed on to farmers through extension workers and other development agents—that is, people working for organizations that aim to improve agricultural production and rural livelihoods. Many of the technologies developed by scientists and disseminated by development agents are not taken up by small-scale farmers, however. This is often because they were not sufficiently involved in the planning and in the research itself, so the results did not meet their needs.

Farmers and other community members, including local innovators, possess a wealth of knowledge and experience that, given the chance, could spur more community-owned development. Men and women farmers need to be in the forefront in development—identifying their needs, assets, and potential solutions and seeking answers to their own questions. Partnerships between development agents, scientists, and farmers can strengthen and build on farmer experimentation. This process of participatory innovation development sees farmers as the key actors driving the process, deciding when and how to draw in other people: development agents, scientists, business people, and so on. Fortunately, with scientists and extension workers starting to appreciate farmers' contributions to the development process, some institutions are starting to change the ways that they have traditionally functioned.

Supporting Farmer-led Innovation

Through a number of programs, development agents have played an active role in supporting and encouraging informal experimentation. Sometimes outsiders help farmers test and evaluate introduced technologies more systematically. For instance, the Kenya-based Muyafwa Development Program (a partnership between the Muyafwa Village Development Committee and World Neighbors, a U.S.-based nonprofit organization) has been involved in comparing the newly introduced orange-fleshed sweet potato with the existing indigenous variety. The villagers chose 10 farmers to conduct the trials and report back. One of these, Janet Wabwire of Muyafwa Village in Busia District, said: "We sat down as a group and discussed what we wanted to find out and agreed on production performance, size of tubers, pest attack, storability in the ground, ease of cooking, taste.... When we have the knowledge in experimentation, then nobody can cheat us as before, especially some of the seed companies. If they bring new seed, we are able to experiment and get our own answers. As a woman [experimenter], I get more respect in the community."[4]

Apart from seeking to ensure farmers a central place in partnerships for developing new technologies, facilitators of participatory research and development (R&D) also try to recognize and encourage local institutional innovations, such as the way people organize themselves in order to obtain resources. In Niger, partners involved in the Prolinnova (Promoting Local Innovation in Ecologically Oriented Agriculture and Natural Resource Management) network, when searching for innovations to support, decided to take a closer look at forms of local organization involving women. They encountered a group of women in the Aguié area who had transformed their traditional savings "merry-go-round" (called *adaché* in the Hausa language) into a new way of saving and sharing money. Normally, the members each make a monthly contribution, and every month a different member takes the whole amount of cash in the kitty for her own use.[5]

An *adaché* group of 20 women, after hearing that a nongovernmental organization (NGO) in another part of Niger was encouraging a system of "social credit," decided to try out something similar. Their new system consists of collecting a somewhat higher and more regular amount of savings from each member, giving loans to members who request them, and charging 10 percent interest on the loan. The group gives preference to the poorer women when deciding who should receive a loan. The women called their new system *asasu*, meaning "treasure" in Hausa. The Prolinnova partners are working together with this group and others to strengthen their capacities to manage funds in their savings-and-credit systems, make realistic plans to generate income, and organize themselves better so as to use the rotating funds in a more transparent and sustainable way.[6]

Some programs have led to changes in traditional gender roles, as Esther Omusi, treasurer of a community-level organization in Kenya, notes: "Things are starting to change in our community. Before, as a woman, I would not have dreamed of holding several

Sweet potatoes for sale at a market in Kerenge, Rwanda

important positions in society and people recognizing my work, including my innovation. It was difficult for men and fellow women to listen to my messages."[7]

In several countries in Africa and Asia, largely through the Prolinnova network, local innovation support funds are being piloted as a way to give small-scale farmers access to resources for the research they think is important and to stimulate farmer-led innovation processes. The funds are managed or co-managed by local grassroots organizations and are used to buy materials for farmers' experiments, pay for the services of a supporting specialist such as a technician or scientist, or obtain information from other farmers or specialists. Farmer-led local steering committees issue a call for proposals and, based on criteria developed by the community, select applications to be supported out of the fund. As explained by Joe Ouko of the Nyando Dairy Goats Farmers Group in western Kenya, "We call for proposals and vet them according to our own criteria and do the monitoring and follow-up. Of course, we partner with other organizations… but we take the lead role as farmers and thus determine our development agenda. Before, we use to be involved as mere spectators."[8]

A number of projects have shown that community-based research committees can be effective for farmer-led planning and decisionmaking about local innovation. For example, the national NGO AgriService Ethiopia has devoted several years to helping rural communities in various parts of the country establish their own community-based institutions and federations of such bodies. In the Amaro District of southern Ethiopia, where a local innovation support fund is being piloted, the community carried out its own appraisal of key problems and promising local solutions and decided what type of research should be supported through the fund. Farmer innovators are doing this research on behalf of their community.[9]

Similarly, in western Kenya, World Neighbors and the community-based organization Friends of Katuk Odeyo have taken steps to bring farmers together into a local research committee. Dorcas Wena, a local farmer and committee member explained: "We decided to organize ourselves in a research committee in order to be more effective and plan our research work the way we want it." Research committee chair Vincent Dudi continued: "Our work involves meeting with community members and brainstorming on issues affecting us and prioritizing the solutions, including research options. We then liaise with the appropriate partners and conduct the trials ourselves. The research committee makes a workplan on input distribution, laying out field trials and farmer training, follow up and

monitoring. We then call farmers for a field day to look at the different trials and plan for the dissemination work."[10]

Farmers Driving the Spread of Innovation

Farmers are taking the lead not only in local research but also in sharing the results of their experiments and investigations, from farmer to farmer. A number of initiatives have supported this. For example, Calistus Buluma, one of the volunteer extensionists associated with a program supported by World Neighbors in the Busia District of Kenya, explained that "each volunteer supports households near theirs so as to reduce the distances to be covered and also I understand my neighbors well, hence I can pass information to them easily." In South Africa, the Sivusimpilo Farmers Forum stimulates sharing between farmers in a number of neighboring villages. In Niger, farmer innovators in Takalafiya village organized "farmer open days" to present the results of their formal and informal experiments on using millet glumes as fertilizer in cassava production. Such forums are also important for giving recognition to outstanding men and women innovators.[11]

In Kenya, two exhibitions of farmer innovations were organized by Prolinnova-Kenya and PELUM (Participatory Ecological Land Use Management)-Kenya, one in Eastern and one in Western Province. These were one-day events where innovators exhibited and shared information about their innovations. "It is important for other community members and [local government] officers to value our work. We innovate on many issues including herbal medicine, soil fertility, agricultural equipment and many others that help the community at large. But hardly do we get recognized. Having such exchanges really helps," said farmer innovator Phillip Kilaki at one of these events.[12]

A number of organizations working with

smallholder farmers are also encouraging them to take the lead in documenting what they are doing. In Niger, for example, farmers are capturing and sharing information about their experiments using digital and video cameras, posters, and rural community radio. When farmers document their experiences and results themselves, they do this from a different perspective than scientists or development agents or journalists would. Since time immemorial, farmers have used traditional forms of recording and sharing information in songs, drawings, or stories. Now they are communicating information about their innovations and research findings not only verbally, during farmers' forums or workshops with scientists, but also in the form of photographs, videos, or PowerPoint files.[13]

Why Support Farmer-led Innovation?

Development approaches that support farmer-led joint innovation processes make a difference in at least three important ways. First, they lead to the development of innovations that meet the needs and suit the circumstances of local people and therefore lead to benefits such as higher production, greater food security, more income, fewer work requirements, and lower risks. In Tigray, Ethiopia, for example, farmers have developed drip irrigation systems and improved beehives, both using local materials. In southern Ethiopia, farmers have developed effective ways to deal with bacterial wilt in *enset*, a key problem in a crop that is a staple for millions of people in the region but that has been largely neglected by formal research. (See also Box 5–1.)[14]

Sometimes the product of one innovation process becomes the stepping-stone for further initiatives. For example, in the Muyafwa Development Program mentioned earlier, farmers have moved beyond experimentation and have joined to form common-interest groups that

multiply seed or planting materials of cassava, orange-fleshed sweet potatoes, soybeans, bush beans, and sorghum.[15]

Local innovations can also provide stimulating ideas for people working elsewhere under similar conditions. This does not mean simply "transfer of technology" but rather sharing of principles that can be tried out and adapted by other farmers. Farmers in one area might have developed a system of mulching using one type of material, for instance, and those in another area might try out the mulching principles using a completely different kind of material.

A second key, if indirect, impact is the strengthening of farmers' voices and leadership abilities that occurs through bolstering local institutions focused on farmer-led experimentation and innovation. For example, at the Science Week during the Annual General Assembly of the Forum on Agricultural Research in Africa held in South Africa in 2006, farmers presented innovations in the form of posters, printed materials, and videos they had made with the support of development agents. Scientific meetings and technology fairs, such as those held in Tigray Region in northern Ethiopia, where farmers were invited to present their innovations in market stalls, offer similar opportunities.[16]

Farmer innovators who have been recognized by people involved in research and development and who have engaged in joint experimentation with them have gained confidence to speak out about what they expect from research and advisory services. For example, Mawcha Gebremedhin, a woman innovator from Tigray who had defied customary norms and begun to do her own plowing using animal traction, spoke about her experiences to participants at an international workshop, including leading officials from the Ethiopian Ministry of Agriculture and the country portfolio manager from the International Fund for Agricultural Development.[17]

Third, the involvement of other R&D par-

Box 5–1. Sharing Innovations in Ethiopia

The smallholder farmers practicing agriculture in Ethiopia's highlands face numerous challenges, including decades of government neglect and severe ecological degradation. The destruction of the region's mountainous terrain seems irreversible. But there are signs that the environmental problems can be overcome—and livelihoods improved—when farmers and agricultural and natural resource professionals work together on activities that combine traditional knowledge with scientific approaches.

Since 1996, Ethiopia's Institute for Sustainable Development (ISD) has worked directly with farming communities and local agriculturalists in the semiarid and degraded areas of Tigray, the northernmost region of the country. As a result of these efforts, farmers are learning how to reduce their reliance on chemical fertilizers and pesticides, improve irrigation practices, and engage in farmer-to-farmer trainings—helping to scale up production in partnership with local agricultural experts.

To reduce their reliance on chemical fertilizers, farmers and experts in four communities were trained to make compost in pits and then apply it to their fields, most of which are less than a quarter hectare in size. In just two years, the farmers found that the compost was as effective as chemical fertilizer in increasing crop yields. Over the years, they found that the compost continued to improve soil fertility and raise crop yields, enabling them to stop purchasing the chemicals altogether. They equated the use of the chemical fertilizer with "bribing the soil," a practice they recognized as being unsustainable.

One of the challenges faced by ISD, and by many agriculture nongovernmental groups, is the mobility of local agricultural experts. In 2003, ISD changed its training strategy to involve both farmers and local experts. The farmers were charged with training 10 or more of their neighbors, and the local experts took responsibility for following up with the farmers and recording the impacts of compost use. Among the benefits of this approach have been a rapid scaling up of compost use throughout the region and a steady increase in overall food production.

One success story of local innovation is irrigation. Malede Abreha, a farmer-priest in Tigray, hoped to make his family's life more secure by finding water to irrigate his half-hectare plot during the long dry season. When he started digging in the dry, rocky area next to his homestead, his neighbors thought he was crazy and advised him to instead seek work as a day laborer in town. But he was convinced he would find water.

Abreha eventually did hit water, 12 meters down, and began planting fruit trees and vegetables. To lift the water from the well, he developed a pump that is easy to use and works quickly. Today his family grows a variety crops—vegetables, fruits, and even coffee—in their lush garden. They have increased their income, and Abreha has become a well-known local engineer. By sharing his innovations, he has helped transform the lives of many other families in the district, digging more than 10 wells for farmers and local institutions for a very small fee. When a neighbor asked Abreha to help him build a similar water-lifting device for his hand-dug well, it took only a week, compared with the eight months it took Abreha to develop his prototype.

Sue Edwards and Hailu Araya
Institute for Sustainable Development,
Ethiopia
Source: See endnote 14.

ticipants in recognizing and supporting farmer innovation—and peer reflection on these experiences—is leading to a rethinking of how institutions of research, development, and education operate. For example, many scientists in the National Agricultural Research Institute in

Malede Abreha and his handmade pump

Lessons for Development Practitioners

Processes that bring together different skills and sources of knowledge of many different kinds of people and organizations and that build on and enhance the creativity of farmers not only lead to new technologies or institutions that are more responsive to farmers' needs. They actually create a more vibrant and responsive innovation system composed of different kinds of partners who can work together to adapt to changing conditions of the farmers. Specific innovations serve only for certain situations and limited periods, so what needs to be strengthened and sustained is the innovative capacity of farmers and their partners in development.

To enter into true partnerships with farmers in agricultural R&D, the other parties need to recognize and stimulate the innovative capacity of farmers. Farmers, especially women, need to be able to claim the space to have their say when decisions are made in a democratic innovation system. It is therefore necessary to build the confidence and capacity of farmers to play a strong role in the joint innovation process. As Joe Ouko, Chair of the Nyando Dairy Goats Farmers Group in western Kenya, said: "When farmers are in the driving seat, we take full responsibility for our actions and it is much easier to mobilize community members to contribute towards development issues. We are empowered and discuss with researchers and other development agents as partners and they listen to us."[19]

Niger now use the participatory innovation development approach in some of their work. The Kenyan government has established an agricultural innovation fund managed by the Agricultural Sector Coordination Unit, and part of this is meant to support farmer innovation. Similarly, the Ministry of Agriculture in Ethiopia and the World Bank–supported Rural Capacity Building Project have remodeled the originally proposed Farmer Innovation Fund to work more along the lines of a local innovation support fund.[18]

Grain Trading in Zambia

Mike is a grain trader in Zambia. Like most local traders, he buys maize from farmers in rural areas and sells it to millers in urban areas such as Zambia's Copperbelt, a densely populated mining area. And sometimes he sells maize to traders from Lubumbashi, another mining area, just across the border in the Democratic Republic of Congo (DRC). Some years he imports maize from South Africa, if and when the local market demands it. In short, Mike is one of the key entrepreneurs in the food chain that links supply with demand.[1]

He watches how truckloads of maize cross the border at Kasumbalesa, the main border post between Zambia's Copperbelt Province and the DRC. To his surprise, all the maize comes from South Africa, by way of Zambia, to be sold in Lubumbashi. So why are South African farmers supplying produce for what is really the natural market for Zambian farmers?

Mike is about to experience firsthand something he knew about in abstract terms: agricultural trade barriers. To deal with DRC traders who come to Zambia to buy maize, he rented a warehouse near the border post. Before he begins selling from there, the local police tell him that he cannot trade maize at this location. Even though Mike only sells maize from his warehouse and does not export it himself, the police order him to close shop. Like many other countries in the region, Zambia does not allow free movement of food commodities across borders; closing Mike's shop demonstrates how the local authorities try to prevent illegal trade.

But what are the consequences of such a policy? For one, farmers in border areas cannot be sure of a market if the market in the DRC is denied to them by not allowing Mike or others to sell their maize there. Worse yet, the large milling companies in Lubumbashi have con-

tracts with South African suppliers, because Zambian suppliers are unreliable as a result of the export restrictions. And are export restrictions really necessary? When Zambia experienced national maize deficits, maize has always been imported from South Africa or other countries. It is more important to provide long-term incentives to farmers to grow maize. Such policies will result in increased maize production, will eliminate the need for export bans in the first place, and could make Zambia a breadbasket with the capacity to supply its neighbors.

Failure to increase food production and enhance food trade in Africa will have serious, if not catastrophic, consequences. The increasing demand in Africa's growing urban centers calls for more food, much of which can be grown by local producers—presenting a substantial agricultural development opportunity for Africa's farming community.

To address these trade barriers, the Common Market for Eastern and Southern Africa (COMESA), a regional economic community with 19 member states, has established the Alliance for Commodity Trade in Eastern and Southern Africa (ACTESA). Its mandate is to develop and implement programs that improve market access for farmers and traders. As a result of policy discussions led by ACTESA, issues of food commodity trade are now a fixed agenda item at Trade and Customs Technical Committee meetings, an important policymaking forum in the region. Backed by empirical evidence provided by Michigan State University, this policy development effort will help ACTESA and COMESA unleash the potential of regional trade in food commodities for the benefit of farmers and consumers.[2]

—*Jan Joost Nijhoff*
Ghana Country Office, World Bank

Louis Stippel/USAID

A farmer in Ghana waters his maize from shallow wells sited between the crops

CHAPTER 6

Africa's Soil Fertility Crisis and the Coming Famine

Roland Bunch

In Koboko Village in Malawi in September 2009, some 30 mothers and their children were gathering under a huge shade tree—the traditional site for the village's meetings. Gradually they squeezed together on an assortment of hand-woven mats and rough-hewn wooden chairs. The village chief and a few of his advisors faced the women, seated next to an outsider who was there to ask a series of questions. "What," the outsider began, "is the most important single problem that prevents you from having enough food to feed your children well?"[1]

Without even waiting for a village male authority to answer, one of the taller women spoke up: "Our soil is tired out. And it's getting worse every year." Almost before she had finished, four or five other women chimed in, all talking at once: "Yes, what she says is true." "Last year I harvested 35 bags of maize. But this year I only harvested 27, even though it rained well." "We no longer have any way to keep our fields fertile." "Our soil has become so hard that even when it rains, the water just runs off." When things died down again, the village chief, calmly and authoritatively, put

---

Roland Bunch is an agroecologist and the author of *Two Ears of Corn: A Guide to People-Centered Agricultural Improvement*, which has been published in 10 languages.

WWW.NOURISHINGTHEPLANET.ORG

his stamp of approval on the obvious consensus by voicing his heart-felt agreement.[2]

The visitor was surprised. Malawi, just five years earlier, had suffered one of Africa's worst droughts ever. People became so hungry that they were cooking up and eating the bark off of trees. Millions would have died if tons of emergency food had not been distributed throughout the country. Yet in this village, everyone concurred that soil fertility was an even greater problem than drought. The outsider asked why. The women explained that, sure, the droughts had been horrible. But droughts had only occurred a couple of times in more than a decade, whereas soil fertility was threatening to destroy their food supply permanently—forever.[3]

The women were absolutely unanimous, as were the men. They were adamant. And they were obviously scared. Even though they were among the planet's poorest people, they had never in their lives faced such a long-term and apparently insoluble threat to their survival.[4]

Over the next year, as part of two major studies, interviews were conducted with farmers from more than 75 villages in six African nations (Malawi and Zambia in Southern Africa, Kenya and Uganda in East Africa, and Mali and Niger in West Africa). With very few exceptions the same story was repeated everywhere. People no longer had any way of maintaining soil fertility. Harvests were crashing, dropping 15–25 percent a year. Most people expect that in five years they will harvest less than half what they get now. Yet they are already in desperate straits. Some villages now depend permanently on food aid. Whole villages are planning to uproot themselves and wander across the landscape looking for fertile land, a reasonable survival strategy back when Africa was not so full of people. But today, in most of Africa it is a strategy with very little chance of success.[5]

That Africa is facing a soil fertility crisis is no news to the well-informed. But that the tragedy

is rushing at us so quickly that tens of millions of people could starve within the next four or five years is big news indeed. The continent faces an imminent tragedy: a Great African Famine.

A Perfect Storm

The crisis is being brought on by a "perfect storm" of factors, all of which are simultaneously affecting the whole continent. But they will affect most severely Africa's subhumid and semiarid lowlands. These make up about a third of the continent's land area and are home to about one fifth of its rural population—some 200 million people.[6]

Four main factors are bringing on this perfect storm. First, animal manure has been widely used to fertilize Africa's soils for decades. But there is nowhere near enough. Population growth has reduced dramatically not only the amount of land each family can farm, but also each family's pastureland, to the point that many families have only two or three animals. Maintaining the fertility of enough land to feed a family requires about 15 healthy, well-fed cattle (and then only if the manure is managed well), making it impossible for animal manure to help much in maintaining Africa's soil fertility.[7]

The second method of maintaining soil fertility is the one that accomplished this job for millennia—fallowing the land. This involves setting land aside so the natural vegetation can grow back, replenishing the soil's organic matter over 10–15 years. But, again, population growth has dramatically reduced the size of each farmer's land, with the result that now most farmers have to crop all their land every year just to survive. Fallow periods for most African farmers dropped from 15 years in the 1970s to about 10 years in the 1980s and just 5 years in the 1990s. Today most farmers can fallow their land for at most 2 years, and many are unable to do it at all.[8]

Centuries of experience with fallowing tell us that African soils, without fallowing, will suffer losses in productivity until they produce next to nothing in just four or six years. That is what happened between fallow periods under virtually all slash-and-burn regimes.[9]

The third factor has been even more abrupt in bringing Africa's farmers to the edge of survival. The world has now used up all its cheap energy—thanks mostly to the wealthy nations. Petroleum that only nine years ago cost about $20 a barrel now costs around $80 a barrel. With economic recovery now quite likely, the price of petroleum is expected to continue climbing.[10]

The problem here is that most of the price of the nitrogen in a bag of fertilizer—and nitrogen is the element that African farmers most need—pays for the energy required to turn that nitrogen into fertilizer. Thus when energy prices rise, the price of the chemical fertilizer most needed in Africa also rises. And at today's prices, nitrogen-based fertilizer is no longer feasible for Africa's small-scale producers of basic grains. Farmers who spend $40 on chemical fertilizer will probably not increase their harvest of basic grains by even $35. As an investment, fertilizer no longer pays. So within the next year or two, the vast majority of Africa's subsistence farmers who use chemical fertilizer will have to give it up, which will cause a one-time drop in productivity of anywhere from 30 to 50 percent.[11]

The fourth factor is climate change. This has already brought the developing world an unprecedented irregularity of rains since about the 1970s. For centuries, farmers had planted their crops every June 24, for example, because they knew for sure the rainy season would start within a week or two. Now they have no idea whether the rains will start in May, June, July, or even August. This unpredictability is far more damaging to farmers' productivity than a 10- or 20-percent reduction in overall rainfall would be. It also affects soil fertility because not only do crops produce much less, so does the natural vegetation. Fallowing cannot accomplish much if the natural vegetation does not grow well.[12]

The combined impact of these four factors is that per-hectare food productivity has dropped precipitously over the last two or three years. And there is no way that Africa's farmers can solve that problem by using conventional agriculture based on chemical fertilizers.[13]

Of course, most of the rest of the developing world faces the same perfect storm. But in other areas the industrial sectors are large enough or macroeconomic growth is now vigorous enough that tens of millions of farmers will find work in the cities and towns. And in highland or humid areas of Africa, soils deteriorate less quickly. It is lowland subhumid and semiarid Africa that is suffering from by far the most rapid soil deterioration. These areas will therefore suffer the heaviest losses in human life.

Emerging Signs of a Crisis

In general, most people who spend time in Africa's villages, whether nationals and foreigners, only know what is happening in one or two countries or in certain areas of a single country. Many of them have noticed the soil fertility problem, but they haven't spoken up because they don't realize the same thing is occurring elsewhere. At the same time, people who work at the continental or regional level seldom get out to the villages or talk with farmers. They depend mostly on studies and statistics.

Dozens of studies and reports from Africa have warned that there could be serious problems of food shortages in the long run. About 265 million people are already short of food in sub-Saharan Africa, and it is widely recognized that the situation is getting worse. The worldwide agricultural research establishment, represented by the Consultative Group on

International Agricultural Research (CGIAR), has been warning for 10 or 15 years that Africa is suffering from a problem of soil deterioration, but they see it as developing much more gradually, over a decade or two. If the problem were fundamentally a lack of phosphorus or potassium, factors that the CGIAR people watch closely, the crisis would indeed be approaching much more gradually. But it is primarily the lack of organic matter that is destroying the productivity of Africa's soils—and the organic matter is being depleted much more quickly than phosphorus or potassium is.[14]

Hoeing in a field with drip irrigation, Niger

Nevertheless, some observers have recently begun noticing what may be harbingers of a very rapidly approaching famine. CARITAS International, a worldwide charity, reported in June 2010 that 8 million people in Niger were facing hunger, along with 2 million people in Chad, Mali, and Burkina Faso. Another major famine is taking place right now in Kenya and Ethiopia. "Droughts," which are often difficult to distinguish from soil fertility problems because depleted soil does not let rainfall penetrate it, have recently affected every country along the eastern coast of Africa—from Somalia and Ethiopia through Kenya, Uganda, Tanzania, Malawi, Zambia, Zimbabwe, Mozambique, and South Africa. Thus each of these droughts, rather than being remedied when the next rains fall, could be the cutting edge of the Great African Famine.[15]

Yet probably the best single authority on short-term food security in Africa, the Famine Early Warning Systems Network, apparently disagrees. Its most recent reports mention pockets of food insecurity, but in general it finds that there is little evidence through 2009 of a major decrease in African food production.[16]

Why the seeming contradiction? One factor could well explain why total production is maintaining itself while soil fertility is dropping rapidly: since soil fertility is dropping, farmers say, they are forced to farm more and more land in order to feed their families. Malian women report that they now plant two to three times as much land as they did 10 years ago in a desperate attempt to harvest the same amount of food. Thus total production remains the same while productivity per unit of land farmed is falling fast. The areas where malnutrition and famine have been spotted may well be the first ones where people can no longer plant twice the land they used to.

Thus the overall studies and statistics also seem to be pointing to a major, widespread famine—and soon.

Out in the villages a whole array of other factors point in the same direction. In virtually all the villages studied, the interviewers also visited farmers' fields and observed the fields along roads and highways. Productivity was also much lower than in the past. Another indication of trouble is that Africa's young men have realized there is no future out in the villages. There are very few of them left in rural areas.[17]

Traditional land tenure in much of Africa was based for millennia on the idea, strange to western ears, that everyone who needs land to grow food should have some. Yet in the last few years so many families and villages have abandoned the Sahel and moved south, to areas of better rainfall, that the receiving countries—Côte d'Ivoire, Ghana, Guinea, and Nigeria—no longer give them land to farm. Nigerian police now forcefully turn people back at the border.[18]

Across the Sahel, even many Fulani families, whose culture revolves around cattle and their care, no longer own any cattle because they had to sell or butcher them in order to survive. Throughout Mali, farmers 20 years ago routinely fallowed their land for 10–15 years. Now, as noted earlier, they cannot fallow it more than 2 years. If they do, farmers without any productive land will ask for permission to farm the fallowed fields, claiming that the owners must no longer need them. In some countries, fights over land have erupted, sometimes resulting in deaths.[19]

While a few of these phenomena have merely worsened over the last five years, several of them are unprecedented in the history of Africa. Something is afoot that never occurred on this continent before.

Options for Affected People

The villagers of Africa, as always, have a series of traditional coping mechanisms. One response to soil infertility has always been to move somewhere else. Whole villages would pick up and move to a new site where the soils were more fertile. But the population explosion has pushed people onto most previously unpopulated lands. Except for small bits of forest, very little land is left in the subhumid and semiarid areas that is not in use. Even the forests are rapidly being converted to farmland.

That farmers in Mali now pounce on any land that has been fallowed more than 2 years means there is virtually no land left on which to settle.

Another coping mechanism involves moving to the slums of the capital cities or large towns. But so many villagers have done this that wages for unskilled laborers in the cities are very low, and people can barely survive. Furthermore, since food prices will inevitably increase as food production falls, even many of today's slum-dwellers may no longer be able to survive there. Still other people will become environmental refugees—trying desperately to find leaky boats to Spain or Malta. And millions more are beginning to depend permanently on donated food.

If nothing major is done to prevent the next famine, the deaths from malnutrition and outright starvation could well reach into the tens of millions.

Four Proposed Solutions

The CGIAR system is recommending that the international community subsidize chemical fertilizers all over Africa. These could certainly mask the impact of infertile soils a while longer, if the fertilizers are heavily subsidized. (They are presently being subsidized by up to 75 percent in Malawi.) But cheap chemical fertilizers cannot solve the problem. They cannot repair soils bereft of organic matter.[20]

A further problem with this approach is that once poor farmers have access to cheap fertilizer, they abandon the use of most of their organic matter. Why lug dozens of smelly bags of animal manure out to the fields if one bag of fertilizer can seemingly do the same job? So the longer poor farmers use subsidized chemical fertilizer, the poorer their soils will become. And the harder it will be in the future to produce organic matter in the quantities necessary to improve them. In other words, cheap chemical fertilizer will act much the same as any efforts to try to maintain an economic boom. The longer the boom lasts, the greater is the crash when the subsidies end.

Furthermore, cheap chemical fertilizers act as a disincentive for farmers to look for the only solutions that can solve the problem sustainably. Thus by the time the world realizes that subsidizing chemical fertilizer is no long-term solution, Africa's drought-prone lowland soils will be too infertile to grow food, too hard to absorb water, and too full of noxious weeds like *Imperata* grass and *Striga* to produce anything at all. Furthermore, farmers will have lost precious years when they could have been trying out sustainable alternatives. When the fertilizer subsidies end, productivity will drop to virtually nothing. And the sustainable solutions will have become much more costly. Some places, like much of Niger and northwestern Uganda, have already reached this stage.[21]

When most people think of alternatives to chemical fertilizer, they immediately zero in on animal manure and compost, the second and third possible solutions. Both of these materials are very good at fertilizing the soil, and both should be used to the extent possible. But they each have their shortcomings when it comes to overcoming an extensive, continent-wide problem. In the case of animal manure, as noted earlier, there simply is nowhere near enough to solve the problem. Compost is certainly an excellent resource for growing high-value vegetables, fruits, and even rice. But for Africa's subsistence farmers, who mostly grow maize, sorghum, millet, and root crops such as cassava, traditional compost-making takes far too much labor. As with fertilizer, its costs unfortunately exceed the value of the increase it brings in yields.[22]

But there is a feasible solution to the Africa's soil fertility crisis—and one that could solve the problem in a highly sustainable manner in the near term. Furthermore, this solution is very inexpensive and brings a whole series of other social and environmental benefits. It is called "green manure/cover crops."[23]

A green manure/cover crop is any plant, whether a tree, bush, or vine, that is used by a farmer to, among other things, improve soil fertility or control weeds. These are thus quite different from the more traditional "green manures," which earned their name because they are plants cut down while they are still green and then are turned under, just as manure is. But when some agronomists and farmers began systematically working with green manure/cover crops in Brazil and Honduras during the 1970s, they realized that many tropical plants that could fertilize the soil also produce valuable high-protein leguminous grains. That meant that farmers would quite rightly resist destroying the plants before the grain was harvested. Furthermore, with the moisture and heat of the tropics, the plants decayed much faster, and earthworms or termites quickly buried the organic matter for them; burying these plants was, in most cases, both unnecessary and very expensive. Thus most farmers, after harvesting the seeds of these plants, cut down the rest and leave them on the soil surface.[24]

Green manure/cover crops also include crops such as cowpeas and scarlet runner beans any time these crops are also used to fertilize the soil, even though agronomists often classify these plants separately as "grain legumes." And within technical agriculture, trees are separated out as part of agroforestry systems. But the definition here of green manure/cover crops purposely includes trees. In fact, "dispersed trees" will form a major part of the solution to the Great African Famine.[25]

The Potential of Green Manure/Cover Crops

For some 5,000 years, fallowing restored, over and over again, the fertility of soils all across the tropics. As described earlier, farmers would not plant crops on land that had lost its productivity; in 10–15 years, the incipient forest or grassland would restore the fertility of the original plot of land. The natural vegetation would drop tons of leaves and branches on the ground and thereby replenish the organic matter that had been lost during farming. The farmers would then burn that down and begin planting crops once again. For thousands of years, these "slash-and-burn" systems produced no detectible deterioration in soil fertility.[26]

The world's temperate-area farmers used a similar process called green manuring. This system, described by writers as far back as the Roman Empire, was used right up until after World War II, when chemical fertilizers came into widespread use.

In other words, throughout the world and for most of human history, the principal method of maintaining soil fertility was always that of growing plants whose leaves would restore the fertility. Just because many farmers have used chemical fertilizers to maintain soil productivity for the last half-century does not mean that the method that kept humankind alive for millennia is no longer workable. Quite the contrary. There is far more proof from human history that the leaves of green manure/cover crops can maintain the earth's fertility sustainably than there is evidence that chemicals can do the same.

To avert another famine, the best thing to do is to have Africa's farmers imitate the method they used for millennia to successfully maintain their soil fertility. Farmers can grow plants and trees that can produce copious amounts of leaves and thereby rejuvenate the land. But today they do not have any land they can just let rest, so they will have to produce the necessary biomass on their farms and amid their crops. That is, they must grow trees, bushes, and creeping plants that can fertilize the soil or control weeds right along with their crops. Such systems are called "simultaneous fallows."

A tree planted in a maize crop, Kenya

©IFAD/Sahar Nirreh

To do this in lowland Africa, a three-tiered system is most often appropriate. Many plants and crops can be grown in the first tier—under the farmers' subsistence crops. These could include cowpeas, a nutritious group of beans that includes the "black-eyed pea," mung-beans, lablab beans, and jackbeans. Deciding which beans are best involves finding out whether they are already known and eaten in the area, how well they grow together with local crops, their market value, and how well they fertilize the soil.

Over a million farmers, mostly in Central and South America, now use green manure/cover crops. Increasingly, organizations in Africa and Asia have also begun working with these crops. More than 120 species are now known that are already used, or could be used, in Africa. With all this experience, it is possible to effectively choose which one or two species would work best in most situations.[27]

Tephrosia growing between crop rows, Cameroon

The second tier would be the farmers' traditional subsistence crops themselves. And then above the crops, farmers could grow a third tier—tree canopies. As long as this canopy is not too thick or too low to the ground, it can provide a light shade that will actually increase crop yields. This happens because crops in the lowland tropics suffer from too much heat at midday. As a result, if crops enjoy about a 15-percent shade, they will produce up to 50 percent more food than if they are out under the hot sun. Thus trees that either can be easily pruned, naturally have a sparse canopy, or have a canopy that is high enough that its shade moves across the field during the day can be grown in farmers' fields and will benefit the crops. Farming systems that include such trees spread across a field are called "dispersed trees" or "dispersed shade" systems.[28]

Apart from providing soil fertility and shade, dispersed tree systems have a number of other advantages for farmers. The shade keeps the soil moist longer, so in the subhumid and semiarid areas where the famine will hit hardest, these trees will help protect crops from droughts and lengthen the crops' growing season.

Agronomists and farmers will need to select the green manure/cover crop species that have as many extra potential benefits as possible:

- Green manure/cover crops can add up to 60 tons per hectare per year (green weight) of organic matter to the soil; the advantages of this include pumping nutrients up to the soil surface and improving the soil's water-holding capacity, nutrient content, nutrient balance, biodiversity, softness, penetrability, and acidity.[29]

- The biomass will add significant quantities of nitrogen to the farming system—precisely the nutrient that is most lacking in most of Africa's soils; nearly all the crops that would be used can fix more than 60 kilograms per hectare per year of pure nitrogen, and some can fix from 150 to 220 kilograms.[30]

- There are no transportation costs; farmers use the green manure/cover crops right where they produce them.

- Green manure/cover crops require no capital outlay whatsoever once the farmer has purchased the first handful of seed.

- These crops can also cut the labor required for weeding by up to 65 percent; since weeding is usually considered to be women's work in Africa, this could do more to decrease the workloads of Africa's women than any other single intervention inside or outside of agriculture.[31]

- Many green manure/cover crops can also reduce or eliminate the use of herbicides; others can act as nematicides or insecticides.

- The shade and soil cover provided, plus the increased infiltration and water-holding capacity due to the increased organic matter in the soil, decrease crops' vulnerability to

Trees for the Future/Michael Randall

drought; just the shade and green manuring from dispersed trees can nearly triple the moisture content of the soil during the dry season and give crops an additional 20 days of growing season.[32]

- After two to four years of heavy applications of organic matter from green manure/cover crops, farmers can switch to zero-till systems that retain very high levels of productivity and reduce soil erosion.
- Green manure/cover crops will also have a major positive impact on climate change: they will avoid the widespread use of nitrogen-based chemical fertilizers, which require huge amounts of fossil fuels to manufacture, and they will sequester thousands of tons of atmospheric carbon.[33]
- Dispersed trees act as nutrient and moisture pumps, reduce wind erosion, increase rainfall, act as windbreaks that also reduce water losses in crops, and slow down or reverse desertification; many green manure/cover crops also produce food, animal feed, or salable commodities that improve farmers' nutritional well-being and incomes, although any of these uses will to some extent reduce the amount of biomass being recycled into the soil.

By adopting the use of green manure/cover crops, Africa's subsistence farmers will not only be avoiding a great famine, they will be establishing whole new farming systems that reduce costs, reduce labor (especially for women), increase incomes, improve their families' nutrition, and build up rather than destroy the world's natural resources.[34]

Critics' Claims of Disadvantages of Green Manure/Cover Crops

People who advocate the use of conventional, chemically based agriculture like to point to a number of disadvantages of green manure/cover crop systems. First, they say that systems not based on chemicals inevitably require more labor and are incapable of producing high yields. Second, they claim that these systems will not work in semiarid areas. Both of these claims are just plain false, as tens of thousands of subsistence farmers around the world have proved.

Third, critics claim that low-chemical-input systems cannot supply the nutrients that crops need. But green manure/cover crops can supply all the nitrogen that crops need. They can also supply a fair amount of phosphorus by, for instance, trapping the soil blown every year during the Sahel's dry season by the "harmattan" winds. African soils can also gain phosphorus from the animal manure and urine that will still be applied to the fields. Very small amounts of rock phosphate or chemical phosphorus may still need to be applied to achieve absolute sustainability, but the cash cost of such applications would be one fifth to one tenth as much as a complete reliance on chemical fertilizer.[35]

A fourth criticism is that green manure/cover crop systems are knowledge-intensive and that a lot of time is needed to teach tens of millions of farmers about it. This is a valid point. But the time factor can be reduced tremendously by concentrating on just four or five crop species in each ecological zone, keeping the training as simple as possible, changing virtually nothing in people's present farming systems, and using native plants the villagers already know.

Furthermore, these systems will very likely spread spontaneously from one village to another. Near Bamenda, Cameroon, a villager tried growing tephrosia as an improved fallow crop. Eight years later, over a thousand farmers were using tephrosia as an improved fallow. The farmers had spread the news of the new technology among themselves. The same thing is likely to happen here because farmers are crying out for a solution to their soil fertility problem. They know what is coming, and they are genuinely worried.[36]

A Positive Note

The Dogon people inhabit a part of Africa that is most susceptible to drought. Yet several Dogon villages near Koro, Mali, have developed—on their own—a very simple green manure/cover crop system. First, they plant leguminous trees throughout their fields (including *Acacia albida* and several other acacias) and they trim all the trees' lower side branches each year just before the rains come, to fertilize the fields and regulate the shade.[37]

They also intercrop their subsistence millet crop with cowpeas, using a short-cycle variety so the cowpea produces its grain and is buried by the termites before the millet is harvested and the grazing animals are set free. They also grow several other food-producing green manure/cover crops, such as Bambara nuts, fonio, and peanuts, in rotation with their subsistence crops. And occasionally they invite Fulani herders to overnight their cattle in the Dogon fields, so their manure is added to the soil.[38]

As a result of these innovations, many of these Dogon farmers are now harvesting nearly two tons per hectare a year of millet—about three times the average achieved across the African Sahel in areas of similar rainfall. Furthermore, the yields are maintaining themselves, or even, in some cases, getting better as time goes by.[39]

These Dogon farmers live in one of the most drought-prone areas of Africa, where green manure/cover crops are most difficult to grow. Yet they aren't worried about a great famine in their future. They have already solved the problem.

New Cassava Varieties in Zanzibar

Millions of cassava farmers in eastern and central Africa are in distress from viral cassava diseases that are ravaging their crops. But farmers on the popular tourist island of Zanzibar are undergoing a quiet revolution using new disease-resistant and high-yielding varieties that were introduced three years ago.

The four varieties—Kizimbani, Mahonda, Kama, and Machui—have given cassava a new lease on life after the crop was devastated by the two main diseases in the region: brown streak disease and mosaic disease. These diseases cost Africa's cassava sector more than $1 billion in damages every year. Small-scale farmers bear most of the economic effects.[1]

Cassava mosaic disease first appeared in Uganda in the mid-1980s and spread rapidly in eastern and central Africa through the sharing of infected planting materials and via white flies. Scientists, governments, nongovernmental organizations, and farmers were able to bring the disease nearly under control through the development and deployment of resistant and tolerant varieties and widespread awareness-raising on ways to curb the mosaic's spread. Then the cassava brown streak struck. This disease had been around for much longer but only in the coastal low-altitude areas of eastern Africa and around Lake Malawi. In 2004 it started spreading rapidly to mid-altitude areas that were recovering from the mosaic.[2]

Haji Saleh, the head of Zanzibar's roots and tuber program under the Ministry of Agriculture, Livestock and Environment, says the first survey of cassava brown streak on the island in 1994 indicated that 20 percent of the crop had disease symptoms. In a follow-up survey in 2002, the disease was found everywhere. "All the local varieties grown by the farmers were susceptible. The farmer and authorities were

crying out for help," Saleh said.[3]

Heeding this call, Zanzibar crop scientists in collaboration with the International Institute of Tropical Agriculture (IITA) started a breeding program to develop varieties resistant to the two diseases. Their efforts paid off: after only four years, four new varieties were released in 2007.[4]

"Cassava is a very important staple in Zanzibar, where it comes in second after rice," Saleh said. "However, it is first in terms of acreage and production, with over 90 percent of farmers growing the crop. It is our food security crop as it grows in most of the agroecological zones, including in the dry parts of the island where other crops do not perform well. So when the diseases hit, they were very devastating to the island's food security."[5]

The research team started a rapid multiplication program, working with farmers to spread the improved varieties on the island and beyond. "We selected pilot farmers in each district to help," Saleh said. "We trained them on how to grow cassava to get good yields and maintain soil fertility, and on business skills, as they were to sell the planting material as a business."[6]

One farmer, Ramadhani Abdala Ame of Kianga village, participated in the on-farm trials using the improved varieties. During the trials, farmers helped the researchers select not only the best-performing varieties but also those that met farmer preferences and requirements for various uses of the crops. Ame said he had given up on cassava, which was suffering from "kensa ya mhogo," or "cancer of the cassava." Infected by the brown streak disease, the crop develops a dry rot in its roots—the most economically important part of the plant—which makes it useless for consumption.[7]

"The cassava looked good in the field, but when you harvested, the roots were rotten and

WWW.NOURISHINGTHEPLANET.ORG   **69** useless, with all your labor and efforts going down the drain," Ame said. He was given 40 cuttings of the four new varieties to test on his farm. "At that time, they did not have names, only numbers. I was amazed at their performance: the tubers were huge, and had no disease. I selected the two I liked best."[8]

Ame said the sale of cassava roots and planting materials has made a big difference in his life. He bought two cows, constructed a cowshed, and is now building a better brick and iron-sheet house for his family.[9]

Another pilot farmer, Suleiman John Ndebe of Machui village, had also given up on cassava after 10 years of bad harvests due to the "cancer" and other pests and diseases such as mealy bug and cassava green mite. But the varieties given to him at Kizimbani Research Station for testing excited him and motivated him to resume growing the crop.[10]

Ndebe says his involvement in the project has turned his life around. Farming for him is now a serious business. He estimates that he makes profits of between 50 and 100 percent from his cassava, depending on the season, and his income increased more than four times. "Before the training, I did not know agriculture was a business. I did not know whether I made a profit or a loss. Now, I know how much cassava I have planted, the cost of labor and manure, how much I expect to harvest, and how much profit I will make. I am now able to save some money in the bank and my life is less stressful."[11]

Yet there is still a big gap to fill before all the farmers on Zanzibar can enjoy the new cassava varieties. According to Salma Omar Mohamed, a research officer with Kizimbani Research Station, only some 8,000 farmers out of nearly 800,000 are currently growing the new varieties. She says the business model of distributing the planting materials has excluded poor farmers who could not afford the materials. Still, she was thankful for the strides made with funding from donors such as the Alliance for a Green Revolution in Africa, which supported the free distribution of planting materials to poor farmers under a voucher program.[12]

Mohamed hopes they can get more such support to spread the improved varieties to all the farmers on Zanzibar and to neighboring Pemba Island, where the disease is also prevalent and penetration of the new varieties is even lower.

Edward Kanju, a cassava breeder with IITA, says hope is also on the way for farmers in Kenya, mainland Tanzania, and Uganda, as 15 promising cassava varieties suitable for the climatic conditions of these areas are in the last testing stages. "With scientists and farmers working together," notes Kanju, "they can eliminate the diseases in the region, securing the food and livelihoods of over 200 million farmers in sub-Saharan Africa who depend on the crop."[13]

—Catherine Njuguna
International Institute of Tropical Agriculture

Hand-picked coffee beans in Uganda

CHAPTER 7

Safeguarding Local Food Biodiversity

Serena Milano

uinea-Bissau means rice. On average,
people there eat half a kilogram apiece
of rice a day, and if they have not
eaten rice, they will tell you they
haven't eaten. Until the 1960s, this small
country in western Africa between Senegal
and Guinea-Conakry produced enough rice to
export the surplus to its neighbors. Many different traditional varieties were cultivated.
Some, selected by the Balanta, the country's
main ethnic group, were (and still are) grown
in salty water using a very sophisticated technique called *arroz de bolagna*. The Balanta
regulated the inland waterways, which look like
rivers but are actually deep marine inlets, by
building earth-and-mangrove dikes and letting the seawater gradually run out from the
basins through drainage canals (made by posi-
tioning dugouts on the dike) and then filling
them with rainwater.[1]

Today the number of traditional rice varieties has declined and, more significant, so
has national production. Too little rice is grown
in Guinea to meet even domestic demand.
The deficit is covered by cheap rice imported
from Asia, particularly Thailand, which has
replaced local rice in people's food preferences. The rice is brought back by the ships

---

Serena Milano is the general secretary of Slow Food International's Foundation for Biodiversity.

that travel to the coasts of Asia with over 100,000 tons of Guinean cashews a year. Since the mid-1980s Guinea has focused on this crop while neglecting most others, undermining its food self-sufficiency. The cashew is now the country's real currency. Along Guinea-Bissau's roads there are endless lines of these trees. From May onward, everyone in the community picks the nuts, with women even abandoning the village vegetable gardens to help with the harvest. Cashew wine is made in every village and has brought with it a plague of alcoholism, common even among children.[2]

The case of Guinea is emblematic of what is happening in many other countries in Africa. Over the past few decades, traditional agriculture based on local diversity has given way to monoculture crops destined for export, including cashews, palm oil, and peanuts, and to more widespread use of chemical fertilizers and pesticides. This typically reduces biodiversity, threatens local economies, and undermines the autonomy and cultural identity of communities. Many farmers, nongovernmental organizations (NGOs), and scientists are questioning and resisting this trend, however. They are finding ways to restore both agricultural and cultural biodiversity in the field, at the market, and on dinner tables in Guinea-Bissau and all over Africa.

Preserving Wild Resources

Agriculture is linked to the environment. It cannot be treated as only an economic sector or rigidly subjected to the laws of demand and supply. Food production must also protect ecosystems and soil fertility, it must preserve wild resources, including forests, and it must protect the ocean, rivers, lakes, and groundwater supplies. When forests disappear, for example, so do the ecosystems that are fundamental to a country's hydrogeological equilibrium and the survival of communities. When the trees are lost, so too are many wild foods

and medicinal herbs essential to communities' diet and health. The same is true of waterways that become contaminated, destroying marine life and sources of food for local communities.

The southern highlands of Ethiopia are rich in biodiversity. The pothole-riddled road leading to the area winds tortuously up to 4,200 meters above sea level and must be navigated at a snail's pace. Visitors who reach the Sanetti Plateau, however, are welcomed by a vast stretch of heather covering the tableland like a quilt, its color shifting from white to lavender. This land is still home to the Ethiopian wolf, the only wolf native to sub-Saharan Africa. A keen observer might see one, red fur against the green-white of the plateau's vegetation, moving silently on the hunt for wild rabbits. The road continues toward Harenna and what remains of the equatorial forest. The forest hosts more than 700 plant species, but that number is steadily falling as a result of deforestation.[3]

One of these species is coffee, which flourishes wild in the permanent shade of huge trees. The variety is likely Arabica, but due to its varying physical traits it is impossible to define its characteristics with precision. In fact, its variability in this region helps protect it from disease. The people who live in the forest, among the poorest in Ethiopia, harvest and dry the beans, then sell them to traders who transport them to Djibouti and export them as second-grade coffee. The coffee gatherers receive very little for the beans, forcing them to focus on quantity rather than the quality processing that could help them get a higher price at market.[4]

Now, however, farmers are working with NGOs and commodity exchanges—including Slow Food International, ACDI/VOCA (an NGO working with farmers and businesses throughout Africa), and the Ethiopian Coffee Exchange—to learn how to protect wild coffee plants, fertilize them with organic compost, and process them to retain the qualities savored by coffee drinkers. Slow Food's project involves training communities to pick the berries only when ripe and to dry them carefully, using frames made from locally available materials. These sorts of innovations not only make coffee taste better, they help farmers earn more. If something is not economically viable, it cannot be sustainable, noted Joe Welsh, country representative for ACDI/VOCA.[5]

Similar challenges confront West African fishing communities. For small-scale fishers, making a living by harvesting the oceans is becoming increasingly difficult. After exhausting most of the fish stocks in their own seas, fishing fleets from Europe, China, Japan, and Russia have now found ideal conditions on the African coasts. Many governments are happy to grant fishing licenses, even if it means the depletion of fisheries, and the lack of regulations and controls means the foreign fleets can fish indiscriminately. Currently 9 million people make their living from small-scale fishing in Africa, but massive overfishing means coastal communities are disintegrating. In many cases, the fisherfolk are becoming workers in fish-processing factories run by foreign companies and are often forced to sell their boats at low prices.[6]

But in Senegal, next door to Guinea-Bissau, women's groups are finding alternatives to overfishing. Consider the *yeet*, for example, an endemic mollusk living in the shallow, sandy waters along Senegal's Saloum Delta. The *yeet* has been an important food source for the delta communities; the snail is extracted from its shiny shell, dried in the sun, and cooked in various dishes. But the once-abundant mollusk is now at risk of extinction; while it can grow up to 35 centimeters in length, the sizes and quantities of snails have decreased dramatically as demand from Japan has increased. Today most of the harvest is sold for export, leading to a reduction in an important local source of protein.[7]

Intervening in this situation is not simple. Ideally the sale of *yeet* to traders would be blocked or, even better, harvesting would be suspended to allow the mollusk to regenerate its stocks—which would remove the main source of income for the local people. On the other hand, diversifying the local economy and finding other sources of income, including harvesting and adding value to local fruits, can help the community. So women in three communities of the delta islands—Dionewar, Falia, and Niodior—are working to map the varieties of fruit available on the island, including *karkadè*, *pain de singe*, *ginger*, *tamarindo*, *ditakh*, and *new*. The women are not only collecting the fruit, they are also processing it into value-added products, such as juices and jam, that are then sold to businesses and residents.[8]

Ghanian farmer inspects cashew fruit on his farm

"In diversifying our activity, the first problem to be solved was the mobility of the women, who were dependent on being able to use the fishers' pirogues [dugouts]," says Seynabou Ndoye, vice president of Fénagie Pêche, a fishers' group, and president of the Slow Food chapter in Sèelal Dundin. "In the Saloum Delta one must move between islands and has to be able to reach dry land regularly in order to pick the fruit, transform them and sell them. The first part of this project has given us two pirogues that are directly managed by the three cooperatives of women. By using the pirogues we also manage to make a small profit but above all we are now able to achieve the most important part of our project: to start up a laboratory for processing in line with regulations, where we can collect fruit, process, and pack them."[9]

Growing Biodiversity in the Field

Diversification allows communities to manage production, keeping some of their produce for their own consumption and selling the rest. They have a greater variety of things to sell throughout the year, which in turn provides income year-round rather than just during traditional harvesting periods. It helps ensure the availability of food in every season and helps protect against the risks of climate change, predators, and epidemics of diseases that attack crops. (See Box 7–1.) Diversifying production also means being less vulnerable to the fluctuation of prices set by international markets.[10]

The Dogon, an African people living on Mali's Bandiagara Escarpment between Mopti and Timbuktu, have built a close relationship with their harsh but magnificent land. They have built their houses into the sides of the red rock cliffs here, digging into the sandstone and constructing low huts made of mud. And like many other communities in Mali, they raise a wide variety of vegetables and grains, saving and conserving seed from year to year and developing varieties that are adapted to the hot, dry conditions. Visitors are shown bags and small gourds containing the precious seeds, and the women describe their traditional dishes: millet and bean beignets, tò (millet porridge), fritters of shallot and wood sorrel, onion powder, baobab powder, acasà balls made from a paste of peanuts and sugar, millet couscous, and millet beer.[11]

Alongside the barrages (small dikes built in the 1980s that made more water available) the Dogon grow shallots—an excess of shallots, in fact. Many rot in the fields or sit unsold in warehouses. So farmers are now switching production on small plots to more traditional foods, including an area of fruit trees (mango, orange, banana, shea), one for grains (rice, corn, millet, fonio) and peanuts, and one for vegetables and legumes. These products—partly farmed and partly wild—and the Dogon's farm animals are used exclusively for family consumption. The more the production is diversified, the richer and more complete is the family diet, regardless of the availability of money or external factors that are out of their control, such as climate, water supply, and the status of international markets.[12]

This range of biodiversity, packed into a small area (all these crops can often be found in single-hectare plots), is a very precious resource. And so is the knowledge of the women, who transform the flowers, fruits, and leaves of every plant into seasonings and other value-added products. Their ingenuity has led to the marketing of Dogon condiments, known as somè. These spices include kamà, a powder made from sorrel leaves; pourkamà, made by grinding pellets of leaves from a local tree called nerè; djabà pounan, made by grinding dried shallot slightly sauteed in peanut oil; gangadjou, dried okra powder; oroupounnà, baobab-leaf powder; and wangue-somè, a mix of ground local chili, garlic, and salt. These powders form the base of Dogon cuisine and are used to make sauces for rice or couscous (made from millet or fonio) and to season soups, vegetables, and meat.[13]

People in every African country have refined their own techniques for transforming wild and cultivated resources into a variety of seasonings to spice up dishes, but these more

Box 7–1. Diversity in the Food System

During the 1970s, rice paddies from India to Indonesia were threatened by grassy-stunt virus. After a five-year search in which over 17,000 cultivated and wild rice samples were screened, a wild species *Oryza nivara*, growing near Gonda in Uttar Pradesh, was found that contained a single gene for resistance to a grassy-stunt virus strain. Today, resistant rice hybrids containing the wild Indian gene are grown across some 110,000 square kilometers of Asian rice fields. More recently, the cassava mosaic virus spread in Uganda in the 1990s, diminishing harvests by 70–100 percent. The brown streak virus then infected another 10 percent of the cassava crops in the region. Through three innovations, local research stations working with farmers developed improved disease-free cassava planting material and extended improved cultivation methods and post-harvest processing to large numbers of farmers.

These examples suggest one vital role of genetic diversity: maintaining a gene "tool kit" that can be tapped to counter various threats to crop production. Yet during the twentieth century, some 75 percent of the genetic diversity of agricultural crops was lost. Only about 150 plant species are now widely cultivated, of which just 3 supply almost 60 percent of calories derived from plants. The trend has been rapidly downward in many countries, and one result is dietary impoverishment. In 4 out of 10 countries recently surveyed, more than one third of children were stunted due to insufficient and poor-quality food, with deficiencies of key vitamins and minerals most common. Worldwide, 2 billion people suffer from iron-deficiency anemia, including three quarters of pregnant women in southwest Asia, half in Africa, one third in the Americas, and one quarter in Europe. Anemia causes 65,000 maternal deaths per year in Asia, and severe vitamin A deficiency affects 100–250 million children worldwide.

One key to reversing this trend is restoring biological diversity on farms. Rice paddies, for instance, were traditionally important sources of fish protein, and fish living in the paddies helped cycle nutrients and control pests. But many insecticides are toxic to fish, and their increased use since the 1960s eliminated beneficial fish from paddies. Pests and diseases thrive in monocultures because there is an abundance of food and few or no natural enemies to check their growth. In the end, pesticide resistance inevitably develops within populations and spreads rapidly unless farmers are able to use new products. Take the insecticides away, though, and the fish can be reintroduced. This was done in China's Jiangsu Province; the result was rapid growth of rice aquaculture, from about 5,000 hectares in 1994 to 117,000 hectares in 2001 of rice/fish, rice/crab, and rice/shrimp systems. Rice yields increased by 10–15 percent, but the greatest dividend was in protein: each mu (one fifteenth of a hectare) produced 50 kilograms of fish. Additional benefits included reduced insecticide use and measured reductions in malaria incidence owing to fish predation of mosquito larvae.

Biodiversity on farms often confers a range of benefits, including higher yields, lower odds of crop failure, and reduced weed risks, labor requirements, and erosion. Some remarkable synergies can be obtained, as shown by the use of legumes and grasses to attract and repel parasites and pests. This "push-pull" system was recently applied to maize in Kenya with remarkable results. Researchers found that fodder and soil conservation grasses (such as Napier grass and molasses grass) attract stem borers to lay eggs on the grass rather than on maize, while legumes such as

continued next page

Box 7–1 continued

Desmodium act as repellents, driving the stem borers away. *Desmodium* is also a potent nitrogen-fixer and releases root allelochemicals that help control the parasitic weed *Striga*. Napier grass also releases attractant chemicals at a high rate in the first hour of nightfall, just as the stem borer moths seek host plants for laying eggs; when the eggs hatch, 80 percent die, as the grass also produces a sticky sap that traps the larvae.

Introducing sustainable agriculture to very small landholdings has also returned promising results. Increasing on-farm diversity translates into increases in diversity of food consumed by households, including milk and animal products from dairy cows and fish protein from rice fields or fish ponds or from keeping poultry and pigs in home gardens. As production increases, so does domestic consumption, with direct benefit, in particular, for women and children's health. One approach has centred on the use of raised beds, which (after labor-intensive construction) result in better water-holding capacity and higher organic matter. These beds can be highly productive and diverse, as well as able to sustain vegetable growth during dry seasons when vegetables in markets are in short supply.

One FarmAfrica project in Kenya and Tanzania is focusing on the revival and extension of indigenous vegetables on small beds. With 500 small farmers organized into 20 groups, and on average 20 beds of amaranths, cowpeas, nightshades, spinach, kales, or cabbage cultivated per farmer (on half to a whole hectare), farmers have been able to obtain greater returns from markets as well as use 50 percent less fertilizer and 30 percent less pesticide than with conventional vegetables. Individual growers can harvest five to eight crops of amaranth and nightshade per year, generating an annual income of some $3,000–$4,500.

Rural people who integrate on-farm diversity and ecologically sound practices are eating more food and a greater diversity of it, which has a fundamental impact on health. This in turn allows adults to be more productive and children to attend school and concentrate on learning. Sustainable agricultural systems thus tend to have a positive effect on natural, social, and human capital, while unsustainable ones feed back to deplete these assets for future generations.

Jules Pretty, University of Essex
Adapted by Vanessa Arcara, Slow Food USA
Source: See endnote 10.

complex preparations are increasingly rare. Even in the most remote rural areas, families buy sodium-laden Maggi flavored stock cubes to season soups and other dishes. These brightly packaged cubes, along with powdered milk and bottles of Fanta and Coca Cola, are another sign of how traditional foods are being replaced with less-healthy alternatives. But now the Dogon are helping reverse this trend by reigniting an interest in and a taste for local seasonings, which are both less expensive and healthier. And the flavor is spreading beyond the local community.[14]

Mamadou Guindo, a Dogon community leader, is working to bring together producers to package and sell the seasonings at major food fairs in Europe, attracting the attention of renowned chefs, including Galdino Zara from the Veneto region of Italy and Matthieu Toucas from France. "Naturally, the *somè* are closely related to the Malinese kitchen," says Zara. "However, it is important that international chefs are introduced to their interesting and pleasing flavors and magnificent colors. Many cooks would be interested in using them in their creative recipes, bringing the Dogon culture to the world."[15]

While their market will remain primarily local, international interest is reinforcing the women's awareness of the importance of guarding their precious store of knowledge. (See Table 7–1.)[16]

Biodiversity and the Market

A link with the local land gives traditional products unique characteristics that distinguish them on the market and allow them to compete with imported industrial products

Table 7–1. Selected Endangered Foods in Africa and Efforts to Save Them

Food	Special Characteristics	Why Endangered	Efforts to Save
Wenchi volcano honey, Ethiopia	Bees collect pollen and nectar from local plants, including heather and eucalyptus, giving the honey an intense floral fragrance	Hard for farmers to manage the bees; lack of support and development in the area	Slow Food helping to increase eco-tourism in the area; GTZ promoting sustainable management of local natural resources; Italian Association of Beekeepers providing training and technical support for local beekeepers to improve product quality and packaging as well as access to markets
Zulu sheep or *Izimvu*, South Africa	Reared and used by Zulu people for hundreds of years; have high tolerance to both heat and drought; resistant to internal and external parasites	Crossbreeding with exotic breeds	Enaleni Farm, near Durban South Africa, is preserving this variety and tracking bloodlines
Mulet fish, Mauritania	Fish is a staple food for the Imraguen, an ethnic fishers' group; important source of income	Commercial fishing practices have increased instead of the more sustainable traditional methods; in 2006, Mauritania sold fishing rights to the EU in exchange for a reduction in public debts	Slow Food providing training for women to improve processing techniques and the quality of fish; improved products received EU sanitary approval, allowing them to be sold there
Mananara vanilla, Madagascar	Blossoms are pollinated by hand and the beans are processed locally	Slash-and-burn agriculture is common, which destroys the habitat for vanilla plants	The Biosphere Reserve of Mananara-Nord, created by UNESCO and ANGAP, is helping local farmers to improve cultivation and preparation; improve access to markets and autonomy of independent sellers at local markets; form cooperatives; and improve low-impact cultivation to conserve local environment

continued next page

	Table 7–1 continued		
Food	Special Characteristics	Why Endangered	Efforts to Save
Harenna forest wild coffee, Ethiopia	The only place in the world where wild coffee plants are cultivated for sale; beans are gathered by hand	Farmers lack access to markets and efficient, high-quality processing techniques	The Italian Cooperation for Development working with small farmers to improve selection of berries, improve post-harvest production, improve access to markets, and create a producers' association
Andasibe red rice, Madagasar	Native to Madagascar; more nutritious than introduced varieties	Yields less than exotic varieties; poor processing techniques mean rice is sold for a very low price	The Slow Food Andasibe Red Rice Presidium, along with a local farmers' federation, helping farmers to improve yields and processing and packaging techniques, as well as improve crop transport for local markets
Dogon *somè* (Dogon shallots), Mali	Unique sweetness and flavor; can be eaten fresh or dried; the flowers, fruit, and leaves of each plant can be made into a condiment called *somè*	Cultivated in a dry and harsh landscape; farmers lack resources to improve processing and access to markets	Slow Food International's Dogon Somè Presidium is helping farmers to improve land selection; improve processing; improve access to markets (local, regional, and international); adapt packaging to different local, regional, and international markets; and improve the supply chain

despite smaller and less constant supply. What the French call *terroir* and have so successfully done with wine, Ethiopians are seeking to do with honey.

An ancient Egyptian legend claims that Abyssinia (modern Ethiopia) is the homeland of honey and wax. While the historical evidence may be ambiguous, what is certain is that Ethiopia is Africa's biggest honey producer— at 24,600 tons a year. Some of that honey comes from the villages of Wukro and Wenchi. Wukro is located in the heart of the Tigray region, near the Eritrean border in the far north of the country, on a 2,000-meter high plateau. In this arid land, imposing mountains of red rock alternate with deep gorges. Wenchi, meanwhile, is just a few hours' drive from Addis Ababa, Ethiopia's capital. The road lead-

ing west out of the capital climbs up through pastureland and palm trees before arriving at the Wenchi volcano's great caldera. Inside the crater is a lake surrounded by dense vegetation of false banana, eucalyptus, heather, fir, and wild rose.[17]

Like their places of origin, the two honeys have very different characteristics. The Wenchi honey is amber-yellow and creamy with a very fine grain, marked by floral notes and hints of lightly toasted caramel. The Wukro honey is bright white with a delicate fragrance, a subtle sweetness, and a lingering aftertaste.[18]

In 2006, when Slow Food International first met with the producers, the honey was being made in large cylinders of woven bamboo hung from trees or tied to rocky crags. The beekeepers only collected the honey and knew very little about the organization of the hives. To extract the honey they used a large amount of smoke, killing most of the bees and giving the final product an unpleasant smoky flavor. The honey obtained from these hives contained impurities and was sold in combs along the road to passersby.[19]

But after training with other Ethiopian beekeepers as well as Italian ones, the Wenchi beekeepers learned not only better beekeeping methods but also how to process and sell their honey more efficiently. Over the last four years, the number of producers, the selling prices, and the quantity of honey produced and harvested have all increased. The honey is no longer sold anonymously but is now labeled with the name of its place of origin and the producers' association.[20]

In 2009, a national network of beekeeping communities was created based on the example of the two organizations in Wukro and Wenchi. The network is working now to catalog the specific characteristics of each honey and to enhance quality with different processing techniques. It is also working to promote the sale of the honey in the cities, particularly Addis Ababa, where it is common to find honeys adulterated with sugar and with no identity or link to the land. This effort is consistent with the notion that it is important to help small-scale producers organize themselves to sell directly, removing as many intermediaries as possible and guaranteeing them a better income. Both consumers and producers in Africa would be less vulnerable if they depended on the local market—flexible and close to the needs of the communities—rather than the international market, conditioned by speculation and external interests.[21]

Biodiversity and the Community

African supermarkets typically contain very few products that have been domestically produced. Instead, they sell products imported from Europe, the United States, Asia, and even South America: fresh and powdered milk, baguettes and mayonnaise, lettuce that has been flown thousands of kilometers. Even staples like rice or corn are sometimes imported and, incredibly, they usually cost less than the locally grown products. Yet the traditional products are almost always better from a nutritional perspective, as is the case with local grains like *fonio* in Senegal compared with white rice from Thailand. Meanwhile, poor-quality imported processed foods, heavy in salt, fat, and sugar, are unbalancing diets, particularly in the cities, and leading to health problems.

Encouraging the consumption of local products though education, promotion, and added value is a decisive step toward strengthening the economy of the communities and improving people's health and quality of life. The production and preparation of local food gives strength and cohesion to the community and consolidates and improves social relations, thanks to the associated collaboration, the daily exchange of goods, work, and knowledge, the cementing of solidarity between different groups and generations, and the bonding that occurs through feasts, rituals, and food provided for the elderly or pregnant women. The bonds thus created help prevent social conflicts, positively reinforce local identity (as a shared cultural fund and not as an ideological barrier toward anything foreign), and reduce the economic and cultural attraction to western consumption habits. To some extent, they can even reduce mass migration toward the cities or other countries.

There are communities all over Africa demonstrating some or all of the benefits of local food production. The vegetable gardens promoted by Slow Food in Uganda and Côte d'Ivoire, for instance, are farmed sustainably, using composting, natural treatments for pests, and rational water use. They are planted with local varieties (with seeds produced by the communities themselves), intercropping fruit trees, vegetables, and medicinal herbs. In Côte d'Ivoire, in the village of N'Ganon, a community of women is cultivating a seven-hectare vegetable plot. Some of the harvest goes to feed their families, some is donated to the school to feed the children, and the rest is sold at the local market.[22]

In Kenya, 12 school gardens are managed in collaboration with Slow Food convivia and the Network of Eco-Farming in Africa (NECOFA). One of these, in Elburgon in the district of Molo, has been named by the Kenyan Ministry of Agriculture as the best school garden in the country. The produce grown by the students is used for school meals, while any surplus is made available for families. The study program brings horticulture together with other subjects, using the plants to teach mathematics (measuring the plants' growth), biology (looking at life cycles), language (documenting the garden's development), history (choosing traditional foods), art (exploring the colors, shapes, and patterns of the plants), and nutrition (preparing dishes based on fresh produce). The schools organize trips and cultural exchanges; students from different ethnic communities meet to share their experiences, and together they eat food produced from the school gardens.[23]

One of Slow Food's key goals in 2011 is to launch 1,000 food gardens in 20 African countries. Numerous other NGOs and institutions are also working to promote the creation of community food gardens (including Lay Volunteers International Association in Italy; Cooperazione Internazionale, also in Italy; the African NECOFA; and the eThekwini Municipality in Durban). Thus, interesting partnerships are being formed to manage several specialized aspects of this project, such as the creation of seed banks, compost production, and the development of natural methods to overcome insect and weed infestations.[24]

Simply cultivating a vegetable plot can do so much: produce healthy and fresh food for the community, pass on knowledge from older to younger generations, and encourage an awareness of local products, the safeguarding of traditional recipes, the sustainable use of soil and water, and respect for the environment.

FROM THE FIELD

Threats to Animal Genetic Resources in Kenya

Over the years, pastoralists like the well-known Maasai in Kenya have been pushed out of their traditional grazing lands to drier and drier regions, places where it was easy to ignore them. But as the effects of climate change, hunger, drought, and the loss of biodiversity become more evident, it is increasingly hard to push livestock keepers' rights aside. Governments need to recognize that pastoralists are the best keepers of genetic diversity.[1]

Anikole cattle, for example, a breed indigenous to East Africa, are not only beautiful to look at. They are one of the "highest quality" breeds of cattle because they can survive in extremely harsh, dry conditions—something quite important as climate change takes a bigger hold on Africa.

People who raise cattle have a good sense of the challenges livestock keepers face all over Kenya. They are aware that climate change is likely responsible for the drought plaguing much of East Africa, killing thousands of livestock in recent months. They know that conflict with neighboring pastoral communities over water resources and access to land makes headlines in Kenyan newspapers. And they know that many policymakers would like to forget they exist, considering their nomadic lifestyle barbaric.[2]

Unfortunately, governments and agribusiness are increasingly promoting cross-breeding of native breed with exotic breeds—breeds that were designed to gain more weight and produce more milk. The problem, however, is that these newer breeds have a hard time adapting to sub-Saharan Africa's dry conditions, as well as the pests and diseases found there. As a result, pastoralists who adopt these breeds have to spend more on feed and inputs, like pesticides

and antibiotics to keep cattle healthy.

One of the most serious problems involves the introduction of mixed breeds of more exotic cattle during the drought. Livestock keepers began replacing their indigenous Zebu cattle with mixed breeds about 15 years ago, after missionaries introduced them to the community. While the new breeds were bigger and could potentially produce more meat or milk, they are not as hardy as native cattle that can travel long distances without much water.[3]

According to a community elder in Samburu, Kenya, the "old breeds could go 40 kilometers [for food and water] and come back," but the new breeds cannot tolerate the distance or the heat. This is one reason different pastoralist communities sometimes clash: when cattle cannot travel far for water, livestock keepers have to find it elsewhere, often at sites traditionally used by different communities. One pastoralist acknowledged that although they fight with other communities over resources, "they're just like us," trying to survive with very little support from the government or anyone else. The conflict has not only affected the raising of livestock, it has also forced schools to close and has displaced more people as they are driven off the land.[4]

These livestock keepers understand that the world is changing. They know that many of their children will not live the same kind of lives that their ancestors lived for centuries. Many will choose to go to the cities. But for some of these people, livestock is what they do best and what they have a passion for—and they believe they should be allowed to continue doing it.

—*Jacob Wanyama, Africa LIFE Network*
—*Danielle Nierenberg, Worldwatch Institute*

The Benefits of Solar Cookers in Senegal

More than half the people in the world burn wood and other biomass—including charcoal, agricultural waste, and animal dung—for cooking, boiling water, lighting, and heating. Sub-Saharan Africa has one of the highest rates of biomass fuel use in the world, with over 75 percent of the population in most countries there saying biomass fuel is their primary source of household energy.[1]

Cooking and heating with solid fuels on open fires or traditional stoves in poorly ventilated indoor environments can lead to high levels of indoor air pollution. According to the World Health Organization, 1.6 million people every year—or one person every 20 seconds—dies from the effects of inhaling smoke from wood and other biomass cooking fires. It is the biggest killer of children under five in the developing world and a key cause of respiratory infections, glaucoma, and lung cancer.[2]

The reliance on biomass also leads to deforestation and a high burden of time for collecting wood. Sometimes women and children spend up to four hours a day looking for fuel—time that could be better spent on other activities, such as going to school, in the case of young girls. And the use of animal dung further depletes the scarce sources of materials to replenish agricultural land.[3]

In Senegal, where biomass accounts for 57 percent of primary energy supply and where the forest area has declined by 7 percent between 1990 and 2005, Solar Household Energy Inc., or SHE, partnered with Abdoulaye Touré—a former teacher and a solar cooking trainer with over 20 years of experience—to implement a solar cooking project at six sites. The aim of the pilot project was to demonstrate the benefits of solar cooking in a region very dependent on biomass and to test cultural acceptance of the technology.[4]

In Ndekou, a small village northeast of Dakar, 20 women took part in the pilot project. Ndekou is a village of less than 50 families, all of whom rely on subsistence farming and seasonal work in Thies and Dakar. Women used the solar cookers for various dishes, ranging from meals for their families to cakes for sale and special meals for family members with diabetes. All families reported the benefits of using the solar cookers in terms of savings on cooking and heating needs.[5]

Fatou Gueye used the solar cooker to help triple her family's income. The custom during the planting season is for men to spend most of the day on their family plot clearing and tilling land, while women collect firewood, cook lunch, and deliver it to their husbands. Gueye took her solar cooker to the family plot and helped her husband, Cisse Ndiaye, clear and till their land while the device cooked their lunch. This not only freed her up from fetching wood and eventually following her husband to the plot, it also helped prepare the plot for planting much quicker than their neighbors could do. This gave Ndiaye more time in his day and allowed him to rent his labor to neighbors with larger plots, which is how they tripled their annual income during the planting season.[6]

—Marie-Ange Binagwaho
Zawadi Enterprises Inc.

Samburu woman deals with drought in Kenya

CHAPTER 8

Coping with Climate Change and Building Resilience

Agriculture may be the human endeavor most affected by climate change—more frequent droughts, flooding, and extreme heat take a huge toll on crops and livestock. Agriculture also holds the most promise—and the biggest payoffs for mitigating climate change—in the short term through practices that sequester carbon in soils and minimize dependence on fossil fuels.

In this chapter, David Lobell and Marshall Burke discuss the need for an agnostic approach to climate change, one that analyzes which kinds of agricultural innovations help farmers adapt to climate change—and which do not. They call for quick recognition of what needs to be scaled up, so that nations can move quickly to protect farmers and crops.

Farmers also need more tools at their disposal in the field, particularly in the Sahel. Chris Reij argues that planting trees is not enough to halt the spread of desertification in Niger, Mali, and other countries. Instead, farmer-managed regeneration programs may be the key for halting soil degradation while also sequestering more carbon in soils, improving farmers' incomes, and decreasing hunger.

In the final essay, Anna Lappé describes why the current industrial food system contributes to climate change and how more ecological options to farming—and eating—can help reduce greenhouse gas emissions.

—*Danielle Nierenberg and Brian Halweil*

An Agnostic Approach to Climate Adaptation

David Lobell and Marshall Burke

Today a farmer in Malawi is buying seed that promises to double his maize yields in dry years. A farmer in Benin is installing a drip irrigation system in her garden. And one in Kenya is signing up for a new weather-based insurance program and plans to buy a sack of fertilizer in the coming weeks.

Each of these events, along with countless others in Africa, represents a hopeful moment in poor farmers' lives, an innovation that could help boost their income and their health. And each represents a possible strategy in the race to adapt to a changing climate. But each also represents a big risk: the spending of scarce money on something that may not work well or, worse yet, not at all.

The stakes are clearly very high. The vast majority of Africans depend on agriculture for their livelihoods, and a host of new research suggests agricultural productivity across the continent could suffer greatly as a result of climate change. Even with aggressive efforts to limit climate change, there will be a pressing need for adaptation in agriculture.[1]

This fact has not been lost on policymakers, with recent climate talks resulting in pledges of hundreds of billions of dollars in adaptation funding for the developing world. These are big numbers. If the pledges are honored, they would roughly double the amount of development assistance currently flowing from wealthy countries to the developing world. And the potential for private-sector investment is even bigger.[2]

How should this money be spent? Should it go toward improving the drought-tolerant maize varieties purchased by the Malawian farmer? Should it help the farmer in Benin invest in drip irrigation, or the Kenyan farmer purchase crop insurance? Or should it be spent on all three? Or on something else entirely? Unfortunately, no one really knows, and any claim to the contrary should be greeted with caution. Our ignorance is in part a result of climate change itself: the climates that will be experienced in Africa and elsewhere in the world within a few decades will be large departures from anything else that has been experienced in human history, and these out-of-bounds changes complicate any attempt to extrapolate from past experience.[3]

So how does the world proceed in the face of this massive uncertainty? Initial project selection will inevitably combine past experience and future simulation with large amounts of guesswork—and acknowledging the role of this guesswork will be crucial. That is, we need to be adaptation agnostics, willing to be honest about what we do not know and ready to expend the effort to figure out what actually works.

What this means in practice is that a small portion of the adaptation funding should be devoted explicitly to understanding whether or not particular adaptation approaches are working. The standard of evidence in these project evaluations should be high. For instance, simply comparing the yields of farmers who bought drought-tolerant seeds with the yields of those who did not will not tell you much about the performance of drought-tolerant seeds. Maybe the farmers who bought the seeds were more

---

David Lobell is a professor in the Department of Environmental Earth System Science and Program on Food Security and Environment at Stanford University. **Marshall Burke** is a graduate student in the Department of Agricultural and Resource Economics at the University of California, Berkeley.

capable farmers to begin with, for example, or had better soil on their farms. Or maybe they were different in any number of other ways not observable to the researcher.

A better project design might look something like this. First, acknowledge up front that we do not know whether new seeds are any better than what farmers are already planting, even if we think they are. If the project has enough new seed to supply 500 farmers, make a list of 1,000 farmers and randomly offer half of them the opportunity to purchase the seed. Then compare the yields of the farmers that had the opportunity to buy the new seed (the "treatment" group) with the yields of those who did not (the "control" group). Assuming that a reasonable portion of the farmers who were offered the new seed actually purchased it, this comparison will provide a much more informative picture of how the drought-tolerant seeds perform; distributing the seeds randomly has effectively eliminated the confusing effects of other variables that cannot be observed (such as farmer ability). These "randomized controlled trials" are the foundation of medical research and are increasingly common in economics research, but mention of them is remarkably absent in the discussions over how to spend billions in climate change adaptation funding.[4]

At least two arguments are commonly made against investing in this kind of project evaluation. The first is that there is neither the time nor the money to spend on control groups. Some even suggest it is unethical to have control groups if you have an intervention that could save lives. In principle, if an intervention is absolutely known to work and has proved to be cost-effective, then yes, it should be scaled up as quickly as possible. But this is by far the exception rather than the rule. Most ideas have some champions who "know" it will work, some cynics who "know" it will not work, and many others who are not convinced either way. Only with data can these debates be settled, and continuing to spend adaptation funds on unproven projects could be diverting crucial funding from other projects with real benefits.

A second and more formidable objection is that not everything can be evaluated in a clear and immediate fashion. For example, investments in crop or soil research may take a decade or longer to bear fruit, and policy changes cannot be randomized within countries. For this reason, it is important not to put

Dried hibiscus at a market in Niger

Bernard Pollack

overly stringent requirements for evaluation on each and every type of project. But the risk of having too many resources in evaluation is still far less than the risk of having too little.

In the end, successful adaptation to climate change will not require that all innovations work. Most likely only a small fraction of them will. The key will be whether public and private investors can quickly recognize what works and scale it up. Any project being implemented and planned should therefore be able to answer one simple question: How will we know if it works?

Investing in Trees to Mitigate Climate Change

Chris Reij

The conventional response to environmental degradation in the Sahel has always been: "Let's plant trees." Governments, non-governmental organizations, and donor agencies all propose and implement tree planting campaigns and then report on the impressive numbers of seedlings raised or trees planted. One recent example is the proposal of African heads of state to plant a "Great Green Wall," 7,100 kilometers long and 15 kilometers wide, through the Sahara from Senegal to Djibouti. The project is now included in the strategic cooperation agreement between the African Union and the European Union. Another example is the Billion Tree campaign of the U.N. Environment Programme, which hopes to plant 12 billion trees.[5]

An important assumption behind these projects is that the Sahara is relentlessly moving southward, threatening to engulf land that is now cultivated. The planners assume a Green Wall will stop the desert's march south. This assumption is wrong. Consider the border between Niger and Nigeria: High on-farm tree densities in southern Niger, which effectively create a farmer version of a Green Wall about 80 kilometers wide, have not prevented land degradation in northern Nigeria, which has low on-farm tree densities.

Tree planting is important, but the harsh reality is that only 10–20 percent of planted trees survive more than two or three years, particularly in dryland conditions. Had all the trees planted in the Sahel since the droughts of the 1970s and 1980s survived, many parts of that region would be a lot greener today than they actually are. There are several reasons for the poor survival rates, including late planting and a lack of clarity about who owns the trees.[6]

There is no argument that more trees are indeed needed. So how might tree cover be increased more successfully, both on-farm and off-farm? The key may lie in "farmer-managed natural regeneration," which is about farmers protecting and managing woody species that regenerate spontaneously. The many successes of this strategy offer important lessons for governments and donor agencies that are serious about halting soil degradation in the Sahel.

Re-greening: Already Happening

In 2005 and 2006, a multidisciplinary research team from Niger undertook a study of long-term trends in agriculture and environment. The team identified changes that had occurred between 1975 and 2005 and studied the impacts of public and private investments in natural resource management.[7]

The biggest surprise they uncovered was evidence of large-scale on-farm re-greening. Earlier reports had mentioned that farmers in the Maradi region had protected and managed spontaneous regeneration of woody species on their cultivated fields. But none of the previous studies mentioned the scale of on-farm re-greening in southern Niger. Farmers in the densely populated parts of the Maradi and Zinder regions have protected and managed spontaneous regeneration of woody species on 5 million hectares (12.5 million acres). This makes the region home to the

Chris Reij is a senior sustainable land management specialist at the Centre for International Cooperation, VU University Amsterdam, and facilitator of African Re-greening Initiatives.

largest environmental transformation in the Sahel, if not in Africa.[8]

Moreover, the effort had a great many positive social and environmental impacts that are proving central to ensuring the sustainability of projects to regenerate deforested land. For example, trees reduce temperatures and wind speeds, and thus evaporation, as well as sequester carbon and increase biodiversity. They can produce both fodder for livestock as well as fruit and edible vitamin-rich leaves for people. Some species fix nitrogen and thereby enhance soil fertility. The social benefits include improved household food security (from more complex, productive, and drought-resistant farming systems) and thus less hunger, less poverty, and lower infant mortality, as well as sharply reduced firewood collection time for women. The trees have even radically reduced conflict between herders and farmers in the re-greened areas of Niger as the "resource cake" has expanded.

Preliminary studies have also shown that it is economically rational for farmers to invest in natural regeneration. A 2006 study—which did not even count all the benefits just mentioned—showed an internal rate of return on investment in re-greening of 31 percent over 20 years. In short, there are clearly many reasons to promote the development of agroforestry systems through natural regeneration, and not just in Niger. A recent report by the World Agroforestry Centre with case studies from Malawi, Zambia, and Niger mentions similar impacts.[9]

The numerous examples, big and small, of farmers protecting and managing spontaneous regeneration of woody species on their farms in the Sahel led to the creation of the Sahel Re-greening Initiative in 2007. This program, which seeks to increase the scale of existing successes, became operational in Burkina Faso and Mali in June 2009 and has since expanded to Niger and Ethiopia. The widening success in the Sahel and other regions in Africa led to the decision to broaden the program into what is now called African Re-greening Initiatives.[10]

African Re-greening Initiatives is not about creating a big conventional project with vast sums of money and well-defined but unrealistic quantitative targets, such as planting X trees over Y hectares in Z years. Instead, the initiative seeks to create a movement of organizations willing to promote different processes of re-greening. It is about putting as much responsibility as possible where it belongs: in the hands of the resource users.

Although there are many successes to build upon, a great deal remains to be done. Many parts of the Sahel, as well as other drylands around Africa, remain badly degraded. Given current levels of rural poverty and population growth rates, it is urgent to expand the scale of existing successes as quickly as possible. On-farm re-greening on a few thousand hectares will not be enough. The important question is, How to achieve scale as quickly as possible?

Tools for Scaling Up

African Re-greening Initiatives has identified 16 tools for scaling up activities to reverse desertification and land degradation, based on past or recent experience. The first tool is to select a partner organization in each country that has relevant experience in participatory natural resource management (preferably with farmer-managed natural regeneration) and develop a proposal.

The quality of partner organizations and their leadership is vitally important. Development is not about projects but about people. In Burkina Faso, for instance, the lead partner in re-greening is the Reseau MARP, which has its roots in an Oxfam-funded agroforestry project in the Yatenga region and is considered one of Africa's most successful soil and water conservation projects. The Reseau MARP is involving other nongovernmental groups in re-

Bernard Pollack

Niger: tree seedlings waiting to be planted

greening activities and is working to build a movement of organizations.[11]

The role of national re-greening coordinators is also vitally important. They should be individuals with convening power who have the ability to communicate at all levels, which means with ministers and policymakers as well as with farmers and extension agents.

The second key tool is identifying and analyzing existing successes in re-greening. The 2005–06 Niger study uncovered the scale of on-farm re-greening in densely populated parts of the country and inspired a search for re-greening successes in Burkina Faso and Mali. The search was based on carefully documenting the age of on-farm trees during field visits. (Once people are introduced to the concept of natural regeneration, they begin to discover examples of it during field visits. But if people don't know to look for it, they don't see it.)[12]

One of the interesting successes identified in this way is Ousséni Kindo, a farmer in the

Yatenga region of Burkina Faso, who has gone to great lengths to protect and manage on-farm re-greening on what was completely barren land in 1985. Kindo experiments with planting fruit trees like mango and avocado. In 1985 only one tree could be found on his fields. In 2001, he had 15 woody species, including 100 young baobabs (*Adansonia digitata*). Since then his on-farm trees have increased in number and diversity.[13]

Another important tool is field visits by regional and local policymakers, elected officials, and technicians to areas re-greened by farmers; alternatively, they can be introduced to these activities by involving them in re-greening initiatives. Decisions about development activities have been decentralized in recent years, so it is useful to involve regional and local decisionmakers in re-greening projects. For example, during its first year (2009–10) the Re-greening Initiative in Burkina Faso organized a field visit for 20 mayors and regional technicians to the young agroforestry parklands on the Seno plains in Mali, and it held meetings with more than 230 agents of technical services and 200 local elected decisionmakers.[14]

It is also important to identify re-greening champions among national policymakers and legislators, perhaps by showing PowerPoint presentations or documentaries or by bringing them to the field to visit farmers who have already transformed their production systems. SahelECO showed a documentary about a farmer study visit to Mali's prime minister during a fair in the capital, Bamako, and the minister of environment subsequently chaired the official launch of the initiative in Mali.[15]

The fourth tool is helping farmers learn from other farmers. SahelECO in Mali organized farmer-to-farmer visits for 526 farmers in 2009–10 (27 percent of whom were women) and then produced a documentary about one of the visits. Study visits take place both within countries and across national borders. For instance, World Vision Senegal brought a delegation of farmers to the Maradi region in Niger to learn about farmer-managed natural regeneration. The group also invited a farmer from Niger to Senegal to train farmers in managing natural regeneration of on-farm trees. Eighteen months after the start of its re-greening program, World Vision Senegal reported that farmers have protected and managed natural regeneration, as well as planted trees, on 21,000 hectares.[16]

Building village institutions responsible for tree management is the fifth tool. Many examples can be found of individual farmers protecting and managing on farm trees, but the project is easier when communities decide to work together. The technical aspects of re-greening are fairly simple; building the social capital is much more complex. In some cases traditional village or inter-village institutions exist that have responsibility for the management of trees on their land. The Barahogon around Bankass in Mali, an excellent example of a traditional institution for tree management, protects and manages trees in 21 villages. During the colonial period it lost this role to the forestry service, but it was revitalized by SahelECO (then SOS Sahel UK) after enactment of the 1994 forestry law. The law gave farmers rights to their on-farm trees. The Barahogon protects on-farm trees against illegal cutting.[17]

New local tree management institutions can also be built. The Project for the Promotion of Local Initiative for Development in Aguié of the International Fund for Agricultural Development (IFAD) is a good example. This project helped create village-level as well as inter-village-level institutions to protect and manage trees. At village level, decisions are made, for instance, about measures against illegal cutting, fines to be paid when livestock damages trees, how the trees will be exploited, which part of the proceeds of the sale of firewood will go to a community fund, and how this fund will be used. At the same time the

project supported the creation of inter-village platforms for discussion about all issues related to the protection and management of trees.[18]

The next tool involves technical training for land users (farmers as well as pastoralists) in pruning, tree management, and exploitation. Resource users get maximum economic and environmental benefits when they plant woody species that regenerate spontaneously after pruning. The training is simple, and farmers are quick to catch on. They determine the density of trees and bushes they want to have on their fields. As soon as they feel the density is too high, they reduce it. Tony Rinaudo of World Vision Australia, who catalyzed the process of re-greening in Niger in 1984 and 1985, recently offered training in farmer-managed natural regeneration in Niger, Ghana, Tigray (Ethiopia), and Myanmar.[19]

Rural and regional radio is an important tool for spreading messages about re-greening. After the new forestry law in Mali was approved in 1994, SahelECO realized that farmers in the region around Bankass knew little about it. Using radio, the group informed farmers of the law's contents, including their right to their on-farm trees. Farmers immediately understood that they could refuse access to woodcutters arriving on their fields with permits from the forestry service. From that moment on, the number of farmers protecting and managing natural regeneration on their fields increased exponentially.

Many small rural towns in the Sahel have their own radio station. Some broadcast to millions of people. For instance, "La Voix du Paysan" (The Voice of the Farmers) in Ouahigouya, Burkina Faso, reaches the many farmers in the northern and central part of the densely populated central plateau. In Mali, 23 rural radio stations have created an association; together they reach the majority of rural producers.[20]

Competitions can be organized within a village, between villages in a district, or between districts about achievements and innovations in re-greening. They can assess which farmer has done the best, who has been the most innovative, or which initiative engaged the most farmers. In 2009/2010, SahelECO (Mali) launched a competition for the best farmer re-greening efforts across 10 communes in which 228 farmers participated. In each commune the best 5 farmers were selected, and in June 2010 the 50 farmers selected all received a T-shirt during a public ceremony. The T-shirt included the logo "Reverdir le Sahel" (Re-greening the Sahel). Such small gifts are highly appreciated and boost the confidence of the farmers.[21]

The ninth tool is to develop an information and communications technology (ICT) program around re-greening. The World Wide Web Foundation has adopted African Re-greening Initiatives as its first project. The foundation held a workshop in Ouagadougou in February 2010 to begin designing an ICT project in support of re-greening. The project will link the Internet, mobile phones, and rural radio and was scheduled to start before the end of 2010. Almost every family in every village on the Central Plateau of Burkina Faso has access to a mobile phone. The system will be able to send short text messages in the local language to all 1.5 million telecom subscribers.[22]

Another tool is national policy dialogues and national policies and legislation. Re-greening initiatives are about developing grassroots movements, but national policies and legislation are crucial for inducing millions of farmers to invest in on-farm trees. Experience shows that farmers will protect and manage trees when they have de facto ownership of them, yet few countries give farmers such ownership. In 1985, trees in Niger were presumed to belong to the state; now farmers presume that they own their on-farm trees—a huge step forward.

It is difficult for a single organization to influence national policies and legislation. Partners in national re-greening initiatives need to build networks of organizations to develop a dialogue with policymakers and legislators.

The next tool is mainstreaming re-greening into national agricultural development projects. This can only be achieved through the full involvement of ministries of agriculture, as on-farm trees are part of rural production systems. Another approach is to open a dialogue with donor agencies. For instance, IFAD has an interesting track record in land rehabilitation in the Sahel and is currently supporting re-greening activities in Niger.[23]

Agroforestry systems produce multiple benefits for farmers, like improved soil fertility or increases in fodder. Farmer interest in developing on-farm re-greening can be further enhanced by exploring possibilities for increasing income by developing agroforestry value chains. Shea nut in West Africa is a well-known example of an agroforestry product often collected by women's groups and procured by national companies as well as by pharmaceutical industries.[24]

At present, data about the income that shea nuts generate for women are scarce. Due to improved marketing and promotion based on ICT, the 365 members of the Zantiébougou Women Shea Butter Producers Cooperative in Mali managed to double their sales between 2007 and 2009 to about $62,500. Even though reliable data about the value of agroforestry tree products used for household consumption and marketing are scarce, there is no doubt that they constitute an important source of income for smallholder famers.[25]

It is also important to explore possibilities for developing value chains for currently undervalued species. *Moringa oleifera* is an interesting example of a species that holds considerable potential for increasing farmer income as well as improving nutrition. More research to substantiate the multiple benefits of this tree would be useful.

The large-scale on-farm re-greening in Niger, Burkina Faso, and Mali has drawn considerable attention from international media, pointing to another important tool to tap. And they continue to be interested in this kind of positive story because it defies common perceptions regarding the Sahel. Several documentaries were made in 2010, which clearly show a transformation of production systems. The documentary "More People, More Trees," produced by the Center for International Cooperation at VU University Amsterdam, revisits project areas in Kenya and Burkina Faso covered 17 years ago and meets with the same farmers and the same project staff. It is a powerful story about regions that are significantly greener and farmers who have reaped the benefits of re-greening.[26]

"The Man Who Stopped the Desert," a one-hour documentary, tells the story of farmer-innovator Yacouba Sawadogo in Burkina Faso, who developed the improved traditional planting pits, or *zaï*, that have been used to rehabilitate tens of thousands of hectares of strongly degraded land. There is considerable scope for more documentaries about, for instance, the large-scale re-greening in Tigray, which is still largely unknown. Media interest helps create a more balanced picture about what has already been accomplished in the fight against land degradation in Africa's drylands.[27]

One important tool is to seek the long-term commitment (for at least 10 years) of all stakeholders to re-greening. It is critical to develop a movement of stakeholders willing to engage in a process of promoting re-greening and willing to mobilize their own funding. An IFAD-funded soil and water conservation project in Burkina Faso is a shining example. Operational since 1989, the project has rehabilitated tens of thousands of hectares of degraded land, which has also led to more on-farm trees. Many donor agencies stop inter-

ventions after a few years. Expanding re-greening requires above all a combination of flexibility, transparency, and minimum bureaucracy as well as a willingness to accept that it is impossible to predict where the process will be in 5 or 10 years.[28]

A Pomme du Sahel tree grows in a crops research institute, Niger

Systems for self-monitoring and self-evaluation by farmers are also tools that need to be developed. Experience in an action-research project on farmer innovation in Burkina Faso has shown that farmers are perfectly able to monitor and evaluate farm inputs and outputs. Even illiterate farmers managed to do so, by using symbols for different activities. The Reseau MARP will develop a similar simple system for farmers' monitoring of changes in vegetation due to the protection of on-farm natural regeneration. This will be complemented by the analysis of high-resolution satellite images in combination with field visits.[29]

The final tool identified by African Re-greening Initiatives is the development of research activities around re-greening. More and better quantitative data are needed about the socioeconomic and biophysical impacts of re-greening—on rural poverty reduction, on reducing wind speed and evaporation, on soil fertility, on food security, and so on. African Re-greening Initiatives is primarily about developing action on the ground, but it also seeks to promote impact research that may strengthen the case for re-greening and, if necessary, lead to adaptation of activities.

Maximizing the Benefits

Are the benefits of on-farm re-greening likely to last? The answer is yes, most likely, but a great deal will depend on whether farmers are given exclusive rights to their trees. With farmers thus enabled and given incentives, they will protect and manage their on-farm trees. This will not only bring multiple benefits to farmers, it will also produce environmental services for wider communities—all at minimal cost to governments and donors.

So the value of scaling up re-greening initiatives is clear. Peter Uvin has distinguished several forms of scaling up: quantitative, functional, political, and organizational. The tools identified by African Re-greening Initiatives fit well into one form or another that Uvin describes.[30]

Quantitative scaling up is about the horizontal spreading of an activity. The key challenge for all re-greening intiatives is to create conditions in which millions of resource users will invest in trees. The speed of re-greening is essential. How do we move from a few hundred or a few thousand hectares each year to tens of thousands of hectares or more each year?

Note that the process of re-greening in Niger began around 1985 and had reached about 5 million hectares in the period 2005–10. This means that on average about 200,000 hectares were added each year. Projects contributed to this by organizing study visits for farmers and project staff, but farmers who observed the benefits also adopted it spontaneously. (Not all farmers or communities who observe the benefits of re-greening do adopt the practice; for instance, conflicts at village level may delay or prevent adoption.)[31]

Functional scaling up is about increasing the scope of the action. It is possible to just promote techniques of re-greening, but it is better to also support the building of local institutions to protect and manage the growing stock of trees—one of the tools identified earlier. By also exploring opportunities for developing agroforestry value chains, it is possible to increase rural incomes further.

Political scaling up is about efforts to influence the political process and work with other stakeholder groups. As noted earlier, re-greening initiatives need to develop national policy dialogues to mainstream re-greening into national agricultural development projects and to adapt forestry laws in a way that induces farmers to invest in trees. It is also necessary to create support at regional and local levels from technicians and elected officials and to inform national and international media in order to get re-greening efforts by farmers on national and international policymakers' radar.

Last, organizational scaling up is about an expansion of the organization implementing the intervention or about the involvement of other existing institutions. As indicated, African Re-greening Initiatives is about creating a process and a movement of different stakeholders who jointly promote different forms of re-greening. The process of building such a movement has begun.

A final caveat: It should be attractive to governments and donor agencies to promote re-greening by farmers because it allows multiple impacts to be achieved at minimal cost, especially to governments. But some governments and donors may consider this a weakness; big loans or grants pay for project infrastructure and equipment and may enhance the careers of donor agency staff. Adapting policies and legislation to induce millions of resource users to invest in trees is less glamorous and pays lower short-term political dividends than trying to plant a Great Green Wall through the Sahara or than investing large funds in planting trees to expand the Atlantic rainforest in Brazil.

But by mobilizing national and international champions for re-greening, by building alliances among those willing to promote different forms of re-greening by farmers, by influencing public opinion, and by involving farmer organizations whenever and wherever possible, we can create a greener, cooler, wealthier, and healthier world.

The Climate Crisis on Our Plates

Anna Lappé

New Forest Farm is nestled in the Kickapoo Valley 130 kilometers west of Madison, Wisconsin. In the summer of 2008, the state—and much of the U.S. Midwest—was deluged with unseasonal downpours, and large tracts of farmland were flooded. The heavy rains and flooding caused $15 billion in damages and left 24 people dead across the Midwest. Wisconsin declared a state of emergency. Yet on a visit just weeks after the rainstorms had swept the region, Mark Shepard of New Forest Farm does not seem beaten down at all.[32]

Shepard is lounging on the porch of his newly constructed cider mill, powered by solar panels and a soon-to-be built windmill. His farm is bursting with life: undulating fields of bush cherries, Siberian peas, apricots, cherries, kiwis, autumn olives, mulberries, blueberries, rosehips and asparagus, hickory nuts and oak, apples and chestnuts, and more. He escaped devastation from the deluge, he says, not by luck but by savvy farming.

It is a kind of farming that created these resilient fields and that puts Shepard at the heart of a movement scattered from the verdant valleys of the U.S. Midwest to the outskirts of South Korea, from the foothills of the Himalaya to the plains of southern Brazil. It goes by many names, but it is fundamentally about following agroecological principles. Shepard and like-minded farmers around the world are proving that a sustainable and abundant food system need not rely on fossil fuels. They are also showing how these climate-friendlier farms can help the world adapt to the climate crisis at the same time. Extreme weather events like the floods that swamped Wisconsin are only going to be more common as the climate destabilizes because of ever-greater greenhouse gas (GHG) emissions, including those from the food and agriculture sector.

Eating the Sky

The climate crisis and its main drivers generally conjure up images of dirty coal-fired power plants or fuel-guzzling sports utility vehicles. Yet the food industry and agribusiness are among the biggest contributors to climate change. In many developing countries without significant heavy industry, agriculture is in fact the most important source of greenhouse gas emissions, largely because of its role in deforestation.[33]

Farming, especially industrial-scale pro-

Anna Lappé is a co-founder of the Small Planet Fund and author of *Diet for a Hot Planet: The Climate Crisis at the End of Your Fork and What You Can Do About It.*

duction of livestock on factory farms, is among the biggest drivers of deforestation. As forests are cleared, the trees release enormous amounts of carbon into the atmosphere along with other greenhouse gases, including methane and nitrous oxide. The loss of forests contributes more than 17 percent of human-made emissions of carbon dioxide. Globally, livestock production accounts for 18 percent of global emissions, according to the United Nations. New Zealand's ruminant livestock animals produce 85 percent of that country's emissions of methane—a greenhouse gas far more potent than carbon dioxide.[34]

Showing off organically grown corn in Madagascar

Greenhouse gas emissions from food occur at every step in the food chain: farming, processing, packaging, transportation, wholesale/retail, food service, household consumption, and waste. Account for all the direct and indirect emissions—including land use changes, the production of farm chemicals and synthetic fertilizer, and fossil fuel energy use throughout the supply chain—and the food system is responsible for as much as one third of global GHG emissions. These emissions can largely be traced back to a radical remaking of agriculture and food systems in the twentieth century, first in the industrial world and then in developing countries.[35]

But it does not have to be this way. Innovative farmers like Mark Shepard are showing the potential of sustainable farms to feed the world while not depleting its finite resources like fossil fuels and not exacerbating the climate crisis. Sustainable farmers use a variety of techniques and innovations to protect against weeds and pests and to boost soil fertility without relying on fossil fuels or synthetic pesticides. Some of these techniques include using cover crops, crop rotations, and beneficial insects. Farmers like Shepard are also beginning to generate their own energy—in his case, through wind turbines and solar panels. Small-scale methane digesters can also convert animal waste into usable energy.

Sustainable farming techniques build healthy soil, which benefits plant health and climate stability. In side-by-side field trials over 30 years, the U.S.-based Rodale Institute found that corn and soybeans raised with organic techniques stored more carbon in the soil year after year. In a review of these field trials, Cornell University professor David Pimentel found that the organic farming methods produced the same yields of corn and soybeans as did industrial farming, but they used 30 percent less energy, less water, and no synthetic pesticides. Based on these lessons, former Rodale Institute chief executive officer Timothy LaSalle estimates that if 434 million acres of cropland in the United States shifted to organic production, nearly 1.6 billion tons of carbon dioxide could be sequestered annually, "mitigating close to one quarter of the country's total fossil fuel emissions."[36]

These findings, and similar results from research around the world, are remarkable, for they point to the potential of agriculture to

©IFAD/Rindra Ramasomanana

help mitigate climate change. Furthermore, research shows that sustainable farms are also better able to withstand the climate instability triggered by the greenhouse effect. At Rodale, researchers found that the organic test fields did better during dry years, "thanks to improved water-holding capacity of the extra soil organic matter," says LaSalle.[37]

On a global scale, the shift away from petrochemicals in the food supply need not threaten food productivity. In one meta-study of yields from organic and industrial farms around the world, researchers from the University of Michigan found that introducing agroecological approaches in developing countries led to two to four times greater yields. Estimating the impact on global food supply if all production shifted to organic farming, the authors found an average yield increase for every single food category they investigated.[38]

In one of the largest studies of how agroecological practices affect productivity in the developing world, researchers at the University of Essex in the United Kingdom reviewed 286 projects in 57 countries, mostly in Africa. Of the 12.6 million farmers who were transitioning to sustainable agriculture, the researchers found an average yield increase of 79 percent on farms. A 2008 U.N. Conference on Trade and Development and U.N. Environment Programme report concluded that "organic agriculture can be more conducive to food security in Africa than most conventional production systems, and...is more likely to be sustainable in the long term."[39]

In the most comprehensive analysis of world agriculture to date, the International Assessment of Agricultural Knowledge, Science and Technology for Development (IAASTD) found that "reliance on resource-extractive industrial agriculture is risky and unsustainable, particularly in the face of worsening climate, energy, and water crises," according to Marcia Ishii-Eiteman, a lead author of the report.[40]

How Do We Get There

The IAASTD study, the University of Essex findings, the Rodale Institute's conclusions, and Mark Shepard's abundant fields all point in one direction: If we are to continue to feed the planet—and feed it well—in the face of global climate chaos, we should be radically rethinking the industrial food system. We can start with what is on our plates.

We can make food choices in line with a climate-friendly diet. We can choose to eat foods from sustainable farms, reduce consumption of highly processed foods, and cut back—or cut out—meat and dairy that comes from factory farms. We can also reach for local and regionally grown foods. (Even though transportation-related emissions are a relatively small segment of the overall impact of most food items, choosing to support regional farmers is an important part of building a resilient, biodiverse food system.)

But it is important not to stop there. At least for now, climate-friendly choices are unavailable in most communities, largely because agricultural policies in the United States and elsewhere have been providing incentives for industrial production for decades—at the cost of sustainable producers. U.S. industrial livestock producers receive billions of dollars in direct payments etched into the Farm Bill, the multi-billion-dollar policy that governs food and farming. From 1995 to 2006, the Farm Bill legislation paid nearly $3 billion in direct subsidies to large-scale livestock producers.[41]

Livestock producers benefit from the U.S. Farm Bill in indirect ways, too. Between 2003 and 2005, corn producers received $17.6 billion in subsidies, and soybean producers another $2 billion. Because feed costs usually account for 60 percent or more of the total cost of production for most factory farm operators, policies that enable grain and soy prices to fall below the cost of production are a boon to processors and retailers. And since 67 percent of U.S. corn and nearly all of the soybean meal are used for domestic or overseas livestock or fish feed, these commodity subsidies could also be seen as livestock industry subsidies.[42]

In total, these federal subsidies saved the factory livestock sector an estimated $35 billion between 1997 and 2005, according to researchers at Tufts University. Livestock industry lobbyists also succeeded in getting payments from the Farm Bill's Environmental Quality Incentives Program (EQIP) for concentrated animal feeding operations, even though the program was designed to help small-scale farmers reduce pollution. By 2007, factory farms were receiving as much as $125 million a year from this program alone.[43]

These are just some of the "perverse" farm policies that are providing incentives to further a food system that is contributing to the climate crisis. But the Farm Bill could instead encourage a shift away from fossil-fuel-dependent agriculture and toward an agricultural system that is part of mitigating the climate crisis. It could, for instance, provide:

• farmer education to facilitate the transition from chemical agriculture to organic farming;
• broader incentives for farmers who make the transition and financial support to subsidize the costs of organic certification (in 2009, the EQIP Organic Initiative set aside more than $35 million in assistance for certified and transitioning organic farmers);

• incentives and support for all farmers to build healthier, carbon-rich soil matter and to reduce the use of synthetic fertilizer;
• greater enforcement of environmental regulations for emissions-intensive factory farming and commodity crop production; and
• research dollars to explore how to reduce on-farm greenhouse gas emissions (currently only 2.6 percent of the U.S. Department of Agriculture's research budget goes toward organic approaches).[44]

The Farm Bill could also expand its programs that encourage consumption of fruits and vegetables and local foods instead of highly processed products. The WIC Farmers Market Nutrition Program, for example, operates in 45 states and provides up to $30 a year in vouchers to low-income children and to pregnant and post-partum women for redemption at farmers' markets. Reaching 2.2 million people, this program could be significantly expanded, fueling greater consumption of climate-friendly foods and fueling regional food systems.[45]

These are just a few of the policy changes that could help shift the food system. While speaking up for policy reform, individuals can help provide market demand for climate-friendly foods by following the principles of a climate-friendly diet.

Yes, we cannot change the world just by buying organically grown apples from the neighborhood farmers' market, but it's a start.

An Evergreen Revolution for Africa

The challenge facing African agriculture is immense. At least a doubling of yields over the coming decades is required to produce more food for a growing population while at the same time combating poverty and rehabilitating the fertility of degraded soils. The risks that come with climate change make this task even more daunting.[1]

But for hundreds of thousands of smallholder farms in Zambia, Malawi, Niger, and Burkina Faso, the future looks brighter. They have been shifting to farming systems that are restoring exhausted soils and are dramatically increasing food crop yields, household food security, and incomes.[2]

"In the past, I used to get about 10 bags of maize from my fields, now I get at least 25 bags," says Mary Sabuloni, whose farm is about an hour's drive southeast of Blantyre in Malawi. "In the past, we often went hungry, but now I can feed my family all year round."[3]

Sabuloni is just one of many Malawian farmers who have seen their maize yields increase and their soils improve since they began planting fertilizer trees. Average maize yields can at least double with such trees. An increase from one to two tons on a hectare of land provides an additional kilogram of grain for 200 days for a family of five.[4]

For decades, scientists have evaluated various nitrogen-fixing trees and shrubs, such as *Sesbania*, *Gliricidia*, *Tephrosia*, and *Faidherbia*, which farmers can plant to improve soil fertility. These plants draw nitrogen from the air and transfer it to the soil through their roots and leaf litter and when their pruned leaves and other biomass are incorporated into the soil.[5]

Mariko Majoni in the village of Jiya in southern Malawi used to get 30–40 bags of maize from his land when he could afford mineral fertilizers. After the money ran out, he got just 6–9 bags. But in 2006, after establishing and attending to his fertilizer trees, his land yielded 70 bags of maize. "My soil is now very rich and much better at retaining water," Majoni says, adding that he has enough maize for himself and his family and plenty left over to sell.[6]

By combining the integration of trees in farming systems (agroforestry) with the principles of conservation farming, the concept of Evergreen Agriculture is emerging as an affordable and accessible science-based way to take better care of the land and increase smallholder food production. Conservation farming involves three basic principles: disturbing the soil as little as possible (that is, minimum or zero tillage), keeping the soil covered with organic material such as crop residues, and rotating and diversifying crops, especially making use of leguminous species that replenish soil nutrients. Currently about 100 million hectares of land around the world are being managed by these principles.[7]

With Evergreen Agriculture—as with most forms of agroforestry—trees offer multiple benefits to farmer livelihoods, including sources of green fertilizer to build healthier soils and enhance crop production, along with trees for fruits, medicines, livestock fodder, timber, and fuelwood.[8]

There are additional environmental benefits in the form of shade and shelter, erosion control, watershed protection, carbon sequestration, and increased biodiversity. If smallholder farmers improve the productivity of their land sustainably, this reduces the need for further agricultural expansion. The increased adoption of agroforestry also means many forest goods and services can be produced on the farm. If carbon markets become accessible to smallholder farmers in the future, the result will be an even greater number of trees in agricultural landscapes worldwide.[9]

Faidherbia albida is a unique fertilizer tree that could be the cornerstone of Evergreen Agriculture in the future. Indigenous to Africa, the tree is a natural component of farming systems across many parts of the continent. *Faidherbia* exhibits the trait of reverse leaf phenology, which means that it sheds its nitrogen-rich leaves during the early rainy season and remains dormant throughout the crop-growing period. The leaves regrow when the dry season begins. This makes these trees highly compatible with food crops, because they do not compete with them for light, nutrients, or water during the growing season. Only the tree's bare branches spread overhead while the food crops grow to maturity.

In Zambia, more than 160,000 farmers have extended their conservation farming practices to include the cultivation of food crops within agroforests of *Faidherbia* trees over an area of 300,000 hectares. And for good reason; maize grown in the vicinity of these trees is more productive and the health of the soils is improved.[10]

Maize production is the foundation of agriculture in Zambia and the basis for the country's food supply, yet the average yield of maize is only 1.1 tons per hectare. In the 2008 growing season, Zambia's Conservation Farming Unit observed that unfertilized maize yields in the vicinity of *Faidherbia* trees averaged 4.1 tons per hectare, compared with 1.3 tons nearby but beyond the tree canopy.[11]

Similar promising results have emerged from Malawi, where maize yields were increased up to 280 percent in the zone under the canopy of *Faidherbia* trees compared with the zone outside the tree canopy. And in Niger, over 4.8 million hectares of *Faidherbia*-dominated agroforests are currently enriching millet and sorghum production.[12]

Tembo Chanyenga from the Forestry Research Institute of Malawi says he can foresee a time when farming families will be able to eat fruit every morning for breakfast. "The landscape will be much richer in trees than it is now, and the soils more fertile," he says.[13]

A broad alliance is emerging of governments, international donors, research institutions, and international and local development partners committed to expanding this innovative approach to farming across Africa. Science-based solutions that build on the best of local knowledge and practices, and that are truly accessible and affordable, are the only way to ensure agricultural growth that combats extreme poverty.[14]

—*Dennis Garrity*
World Agroforestry Centre, Nairobi

A village woman in Zimbabwe takes corn from the communal storage area for that day's use

CHAPTER 9

Post-Harvest Losses: A Neglected Field

Tristram Stuart

Nearly every bug, fungus, bird, and rodent on the planet wants to get its metaphorical hands on the produce of cultivation. Since the origins of long-term food storage more than 10 millennia ago, humans have worked to avoid this. Today rich nations luxuriate in a wealth of food storage technologies and expertise that have reduced to a bare minimum the accidental loss of crops after harvest. An arsenal of preventative measures is at the disposal of agribusinesses to prevent food from spoiling before it reaches the market—from refrigerated storage, pasteurization and preservation facilities, drying equipment, climate-controlled storage units, transport infrastructure, chemicals that inhibit sprouting, and plant breeds designed to extend shelf life to professional know-how developed over decades with the backing of governments, academic institutions, and some of the world's largest companies.

All this may ironically have contributed to the cornucopian abundance that has fostered a culture in which staggering levels of "deliberate" food waste are now accepted or even institutionalized. Waste is now an unfortu-

---

Tristram Stuart is a historian and food activist. This chapter is based on his book *Waste: Uncovering the Global Food Scandal.*

nate—and unnecessary—corollary to wealthy nations' burgeoning food supplies. Throwing away cosmetically "imperfect" produce on farms, discarding edible fish at sea, disposing of breadcrusts in sandwich factories, overordering stock for supermarkets, and purchasing or cooking too much in the home are all examples of a profligate negligence toward food. But none of this should distract from the fact that modern food supply systems have made monumental achievements in avoiding accidental "post-harvest" losses between the farm and the market. Under optimal weather conditions in rich countries today, staple grain crops such as wheat can be harvested with losses as low as 0.07 percent.[1]

©IFAD/Roberto Faidutti

Collecting sun-dried mango slices in Guinea

Crop storage in poorer countries, in contrast, remains woefully inadequate—leading to phenomenal levels of waste in the very countries where food is needed most. The developing world is still crippled by many of the logistical storage problems that rich nations defeated decades or even centuries ago. Farmers and traders lose significant proportions of their crops to the ravages of nature, and tackling this problem should be a top priority as the

threat to global food security becomes a critical international issue.

The Green Revolution in the 1960s and 1970s brought new crop strains, machinery, pesticides, fertilizers, and other chemicals to world agriculture, and these boosted yields dramatically. Western corporations have made a fortune exporting their hi-tech agricultural solutions. What has been left out to a very large extent is the simpler stuff of grain stores, drying equipment, fruit crates, refrigeration, and other essentials of post-harvest technology. These offer less in the way of corporate profits, but they could yield greater benefits for overall food availability. Expensive high-yielding strains have even sometimes been part of the problem: traditional varieties were adapted to the environments in which they were grown and stored, having a lower moisture content in ripe grain and thicker husks that are resistant to rodents, insects, and molds, which meant they could survive in storage until the following season's planting. Today agricultural scientists, development workers, and farmers all realize it is not enough to just grow food. Crops need to be stored, preserved, and transported more efficiently.[2]

Uncountable Mounds of Waste

The neglect of post-harvest losses is one of the anomalies of world agriculture. In 1981 the U.N. Food and Agriculture Organization (FAO) suggested that reducing post-harvest losses "draws its importance not only from a moral obligation to avoid waste, but also because…it requires fewer resources and applies less pressure to the environment in maintaining the quantity and quality of food than through increased production." But despite the World Food Conference declaring it a development priority in 1974, and a

U.N. resolution the following year that called for a 50-percent reduction in post-harvest losses over the following decade, this still remains a vastly underfunded dimension of the development process.[3]

Foreign aid dedicated to improving developing-world agriculture has fallen globally from 20 percent of official development assistance in the early 1980s to 3 or 4 percent by 2007. And only 5 percent of investment in research and the promotion of agricultural improvement is directed at reducing post-harvest losses. As FAO declared, "It is distressing to note that so much time is being devoted to the culture of the plant, so much money spent on irrigation, fertilization and crop protection measures, only to be wasted about a week after harvest."[4]

Published figures on the exact levels of waste have usually been based on outdated estimates, and very few precise studies have actually been made—which is a symptom of the neglect this issue has received. Reliability of data is also often questionable because figures are sometimes manipulated—either to exaggerate losses in order to encourage aid donors to part with their money or, in contrast, to minimize them so as to avoid political embarrassment. Still, according to official estimates, in 1993 China lost 15 percent of its grain harvest; up to 11 percent of the nation's rice was destroyed because peasants stored it in poorly maintained buildings. In Vietnam, similarly, 10–25 percent of rice is normally lost, and in extreme conditions this can rise to 40–80 percent. Across Asia, post-harvest losses of rice average around 13 percent, while in Brazil and Bangladesh losses are recorded at 22 and 20 percent respectively. (See also Box 9–1.)[5]

Agronomist Vaclav Smil estimates that if all low-income countries are losing grain at a rate of 15 percent, their annual post-harvest losses amount to 150 million tons of cereals. That is six times as much as FAO says would be needed to meet the needs of all the hungry people in the developing world. Experts suggest that it should be possible to bring developing-world post-harvest losses of cereals and tubers down to just 4 percent.[6]

When grain is stored in bad conditions, even the salvaged portion, while edible, will be nutritionally degraded; levels of amino acids such as lysine can fall by up to 40 percent in storage, as can thiamine and carotene. Raw statistics on food losses therefore underestimate deficiencies in available nutrition.[7]

In 2008, *Homo sapiens* became a majority urban species. Food therefore now has to travel further from farms to mouths. A farmer who was once producing only for the local village may now be trucking produce to cities hundreds or even thousands of kilometers away, requiring technology and know-how that farmers and traders are not always familiar with. Many economies have recently liberalized trade, partly because of pressure from the World Bank, and consequently grain storage—which used to be a state concern in many countries—is now being run by private traders who often lack expertise or incentives to preserve the quality of the grain. Many of these problems can be solved merely through the dissemination of knowledge.

Supplying the newly populated, rapidly growing cities with plenty of quality food is essential if widespread social turmoil is to be avoided. In the past, food shortages in urban areas have helped to trigger numerous revolutions: Paris in 1789, for example, several European cities in 1848, and Russia in 1917. The food riots of 2008 in Burkina Faso, Cameroon, Côte d'Ivoire, Egypt, Haiti, Indonesia, Madagascar, and Senegal are no exception.

Food Waste in Africa

In sub-Saharan Africa—where child malnourishment has increased during the last 30 years by over 75 percent, meaning 12.9 million mal-

Box 9–1. Food Waste in Asia

Sri Lanka reportedly loses fruit and vegetables at an annual rate of 40–60 percent, or 270,000 tons, with a value of approximately 9 billion Sri Lankan rupees ($100 million). In the main produce market in the capital city of Colombo alone, where thousands cannot afford to buy enough fresh food for a proper diet, the Municipal Council discards some 11 tons of fruit and vegetables every day. Three quarters of the nation's fruit and vegetable post-harvest losses, argues the Sri Lankan Institute of Post-Harvest Technology, could be eliminated through relatively simple measures. At present, a great deal of the country's abundant supplies of fruit are thrown into polysacks and trundled on bumpy roads in the tropical heat many miles to market, by which time much of the farmer's hard work has been reduced to a sweet and sticky mess. Reusable wooden or plastic crates in which fruit and vegetables can be carefully stacked at the point of harvest—as is done in affluent nations—would help solve this problem.

Likewise, much could be achieved through education—for example, teaching farmers the right moment to pick fruit in order to maximize its shelf life. The exact position on the stem at which to pluck particular fruit can also have a significant impact on susceptibility to decay. In markets, cooling systems can involve nothing more complicated than shade and water. Adopting new methods such as these can make a huge difference. In recent years a variety of projects in Sri Lanka have cut waste levels from 30 to 6 percent and increased farm incomes by up to 23,000 rupees ($256) per hectare. Despite this good work, efforts in

Sri Lanka are chronically underfunded; even the government, which is subsidizing reusable plastic crates for fruit farmers, can only afford to support a fraction of the number required.

Pakistan and India face many of the same problems, but on a much larger scale. India is the third-largest agricultural producer in the world, growing 41 percent of the world's mangoes, 30 percent of its cauliflower, 23 percent of its bananas, and 36 percent of its green peas. And it is the third-largest cereal producer, with 204 million tons of food grain each year. With an annual output of 90 billion liters, it extracts more milk from more cows than any other country. And yet it has only a 1–1.5 percent share in global food trade and only processes around 2 percent of its produce, in contrast to some industrial countries that process 60–70 percent. Estimates suggest that 35–40 percent of its fruit and vegetables go to waste. In 2008, P. K. Mishra of the Department of Agriculture claimed an even higher figure: 72 percent losses.

The problem is illustrated by the prevalent method of harvesting mangoes in South Asia: using a stick and a locally made bag can cause a lot of fruit to fall to the ground; it could be improved by using a blade or crook to cut the fruit free. A bruise incurred at this stage may not be visible within a day or so of harvesting, but it soon becomes a broken defense mechanism that lets in an army of insects, fungi, and bacteria. In Pakistan alone, it is estimated that more than 1 billion rupees' worth of mangoes are wrecked each year; half of this could be avoided by better harvesting techniques.

Source: See endnote 5.

nourished children—even rudimentary measures to prevent post-harvest losses are still lacking. One study in 2009 uncovered widespread damage to harvested cereals in Zambia. Maize is Zambia's most important staple, pro-

viding 68 percent of the population's food calories and 76 percent of the income of smallholder farms. Maize shortages in this country have contributed to chronic malnutrition and famine, and yet resources aimed at post-harvest infrastructure to protect this most valuable crop from the region's high heat and humidity have so far been meager.[8]

In the study, 96 percent of stored maize samples were found to contain toxic fuminosins, which result from the growth of mold. A fifth of the samples also contained up to 10 times the government's recommended safe limit of aflatoxins, produced by *Aspergillus* fungi, which inhibit growth in children and livestock and cause cancer. In several African countries, a shocking 98 percent of people have aflatoxin in their blood in concentrations sometimes many times higher than those allowed by regulations in the European Union and the United States. This is caused almost exclusively by consuming moldy food.[9]

Weevils were also found in all the Zambian maize samples, which, in combination with the larger grain borer, eat the grain and themselves become vectors of destructive fungi. Even state-run grain stores were found to exceed the government's safe limits of mycotoxins. The problem comes down to the simple lack of facilities for storing grain so that it remains dry and free from vermin infestations.[10]

The study found that "nearly all farmers' storage facilities were in a poor state, conducive for insect infestation and fungal contamination." Storage structures commonly used are made with poles and woven twigs, or simply polypropylene bags stored in the farmers' homes. Ambayeba Muimba Kankolongo, a co-author of the study, says that "providing to farmers good quality grain storage facilities and training of farmers to increase their awareness on the issue will considerably improve grain quality."[11]

Even without the introduction of capital-intensive western-style grain stores, there is a great deal that smallholders can be helped to do to prevent such dramatic damage to their harvests. Smoke, mechanical means of cleaning stores, and chemical insecticides can be used to reduce the risk of infestation and are

practices often omitted on Zambia's small farms. There are even notable disparities in the performance of different types of local structure, with better results coming from bamboo structures or when bags are used in combination with a secondary container such as a steel drum surrounded by mud or bricks.[12]

In its *National Agricultural Policy 2004–2015*, Zambia's Ministry of Agriculture drew attention to the fact that the nation's post-harvest losses currently "compromise the ability of the agriculture sector to benefit from its full potential and, hence, make a significant dent on the country's poverty levels." It announced its hope that "post harvest crop losses will be reduced from the current high of 30 percent to less than 10 percent by 2015." This would be achieved, it promised, by designing and promoting "appropriate on-farm transportation, processing and storage structures especially for small-scale farmers to minimize or prevent post harvest losses."[13]

Progress is slow, but donor organizations have been helping to implement the government's plans. German agencies have been helping Zambian farmers build improved grain stores from locally available materials, and the results indicate that these inhibit or completely eliminate mold growth. Cereal losses are particularly damaging because cereals supply the staple calories for most people in the world. But the level of waste in perishable foods is often far higher.[14]

Dairy produce is highly susceptible to waste owing to a lack of technology such as refrigeration and pasteurization on farms and in markets. In Zambia, the Japanese government, Care International, and the U.S. Agency for International Development, in collaboration with local businesses and stakeholders, have helped establish rural milk collection centers. Smallholder cattle producers who had never engaged in milk trade can now deliver their surplus milk to the collection centers, which are equipped with cooling facilities that allow the milk to be sold on the market to processors and ultimately to create a self-sustaining business that increases farmers' income and the availability of locally produced milk.[15]

In East Africa and the Near East alone, milk losses amounted to $90 million in 2004; in Uganda they account for 27 percent of all milk produced. Provision of modest levels of training and some equipment has the potential to raise income for farmers and improve local diets, and it would remove the need to import dairy products into the region: dairy imports in the developing world as a whole increased by 43 percent between 1998 and 2001, which FAO claims is "unnecessary and could be reduced by the simple expediency of post-harvest loss reduction."[16]

Projects elsewhere in Africa have also demonstrated the cost-effectiveness of measures to prevent the waste and degradation of harvested crops. One community project in Guinea achieved dramatic reductions in aflatoxin exposure in subsistence farming communities by instigating a set of simple, affordable procedures to prevent fungal growth on stored groundnuts, an important food crop in the region. Farmers were shown how to sort groundnuts by hand, eliminating any that were moldy or damaged. Instead of being dried on the ground, which can be a source of humidity, groundnuts were dried in the sun on locally produced natural-fiber mats. Farmers learned how to judge the completeness of sun drying: shake the kernels to listen for the free movement of the dried nuts. Rather than using plastic or other synthetic bags for storage, which promotes humidity, natural-fiber jute bags were used and were stored on wooden pallets rather than on earthen floors, and insecticide was sprinkled under the pallets to kill pests.[17]

The results of the program were reported in *The Lancet* and showed that in villages following these straightforward post-harvest measures, aflatoxin exposure was more than halved

and the proportion of individuals whose blood was completely free from aflatoxins was 10 times greater than in control villages where farmers were left to follow their normal practices. The cost of all the post-harvest procedures combined came to $50 per farmer, a large sum in a country where average annual income is $1,100, but costs could almost certainly be brought down and should be set against the very substantial gains in terms of health, nutrition, and farm income.[18]

Saving Food

Western nations use preservatives—including propionic, sorbic, and benzoic acids and, more recently, antioxidants such as propyl paraben and reserveratrol—to protect stored crops, and these may become increasingly viable measures in the developing world. But even without recourse to these modern synthetic chemicals—which are often expensive, of poor quality, and unavailable in rural parts of the developing world—the use of commonly available low-cost "natural" alternatives could be promoted. Recent research has suggested that a traditional African medicine extracted from the dried roots of *Securidaca longepedunculata*, for example, is effective at deterring insect pests from stored grain, and in correct doses in laboratory conditions it was responsible for 100 percent mortality of adult pest species. Such findings should give hope to development agencies and national governments keen to use local resources to promote rural enterprises at the same time as bolstering food security.[19]

The "lowest-hanging fruit" of all in terms of quick cost-effective savings is, appropriately, in the fruit and vegetable sectors. Waste of these valuable foodstuffs occurs even where people are not getting anything like enough of them to eat. Fruit and vegetables not only supply vital micronutrients, they make the predominantly herbivorous diet of many of the world's poor more palatable and enjoyable. The African staples cassava and yams have a short shelf life, and there is little tradition of transforming them into more stable products like flour, so they rot in the barns of the hungry.[20]

The sweet potato—the seventh most important food crop in the world and one rich in B-carotene, a precursor of vitamin A—has a high water content, which means that it is naturally more prone to decay than dried cereals. In ideal conditions in rich countries, sweet potatoes can be stored for up to one year, whereas in sub-Saharan Africa as much as 79 percent of a stored tuber crop can be lost. Nevertheless, careful design of storage systems, including measures such as taking the stems off the tops of the potatoes, has been shown to improve recovery of the crop by up to 48 percent. Recent work has helped to identify the exact point in the crop's maturity (at 105 days) that it is best to harvest the tubers to maximize productivity, nutritional quality, storage properties, and consumer acceptability. So improving food availability and reducing waste can often be a matter of directing resources to training farmers in best practices, without even the need for capital expenditure.[21]

Changing the way African farmers harvest tubers can help them feed their families while at the same time opening up new opportunities to capitalize on the growing demand for fresh produce in urban centers. Stringent cosmetic standards laid down by retailers catering for urban consumers present a hurdle that many subsistence farmers are not accustomed to; here again, training can play a critical role in increasing farm revenues. African farmers often have no dedicated storage facilities and instead traditionally keep potatoes on earthen floors in their mud and thatched huts. There the potatoes can be exposed to sunlight, which can lead to significant losses due to greening and sprouting, especially when doors are regularly opened and closed during the day.

Partially degraded crops such as these are still used by small-scale African farmers for household consumption or for sale locally at reduced prices, but they are not salable on commercial markets and thus represent a loss of potential income. Cold storage of tubers as practiced by large-scale growers worldwide may not be an appropriate or affordable technology for these farmers, so a viable alternative is to leave crops in the ground for longer periods after maturity, and to harvest them in batches sequentially rather than all at once. This can help distribute farm labor inputs and income as well as helping to meet the quality standards for commercial sales.

One study in South Africa compared losses from traditional harvests stored in farmers' stores with sequential harvesting, leaving potatoes in the ground for up to six weeks after maturity. In the best instances, sequential harvesting cut wastage from 37 percent of the harvest down to just 11 percent—a 71-percent reduction in losses. On average throughout the year, 8 percent of the entire crop was saved through sequential harvesting.[22]

Emerging economies are now investing heavily in the kind of cold storage supply chains used in the West, despite the high energy requirements. The Indian government's 2009–10 budget allocated incentives and capital subsidies for the establishment of warehousing and cold storage facilities, though industry lobby groups are still pressing for further financial stimuli, and not without an element of self-interested scaremongering. The Associated Chamber of Commerce and Industry, which provides a forum for dialogue between business and government in India, claims that the country needs to increase its cold storage capacity by one third, or an additional 10 million tons, in order to save the 40 percent of fruit and vegetable harvests that it claims goes to waste each year post-harvest.[23]

A less energy-intensive and therefore arguably more appropriate method of preservation in tropical and subtropical regions is to use the abundant solar heat available to dry a greater proportion of locally grown fruits. An innovative project in West Africa dried mangoes to a moisture content of around 10 percent in a greenhouse solar dryer. The dehydrated mangoes retained their provitamin A carotenoids for over six months, and the organizers ambitiously estimated that by saving the 100,000 tons of mangoes that go to waste in the region after harvest each year, this system could increase dietary vitamin A supply in the region 27,000-fold.[24]

By drying waste bananas, a new food waste organization, A Taste of Freedom, has developed a product that can be eaten as a confectionary or rolled into sheets to form a sweet, natural wrapping for other foods, suitable both for export and for domestic consumption. Such innovative preparation techniques of already popular foodstuffs have a good chance of being received favorably by consumers and can boost local economies.[25]

Fermentation is another low-input, locally appropriate food preservation method. In Africa, kefir is an acidic, mildly alcoholic dairy beverage produced by the fermentation of milk with a grain-like starter culture. It is arguably a method of preservation that is more feasible for some producers than pasteurization and refrigerated supply chains. Recent work in South Africa has focused on methods of commercializing this unique beverage.[26]

Biotechnology may have disproportionately dominated recent agricultural spending, sometimes to the exclusion of investment in the proven efficacy of basic post-harvest and storage infrastructure. But it could have an important role to play in preserving food. One technology transfer partnership involving the International Potato Center and Belgian experts at Bayer Crop Science aims to redress the fact that almost all genetically modified crops commercially available so far have been for large-scale agriculture rather than for the subsistence crops of the world's poorer farmers. In central and eastern Africa, average yields of sweet potato are a meager 4.17 tons per hectare, well below the potential of 50 tons. The partners' efforts to engineer a genetically modified sweet potato strain capable of withstanding weevils and viral diseases, which are responsible for between 50 and100 percent of crop losses among poor farmers in the region, could be an invaluable boon to farmers and could benefit the food security of millions.[27]

Helping Farmers Feed the World

Some attempts to solve the problems faced by developing-world farmers have failed, but those that were well designed and executed have transformed rural societies. The microcredit facilities of Grameen Bank, for example, have helped villagers invest in rural enterprises, and similar low-interest loans have been directed at building infrastructure that reduces post-harvest losses. The Village Community Granaries scheme in Madagascar helped 27,000 small farmers store 80,000 tons of paddy rice, increasing output by 50 percent. In Benin, beans were placed in hermetically sealed storage containers, which meant that insect larvae infestations were asphyxiated; yams were stored in houses on stilts to help control humidity.[28]

In rural Nigeria, major losses in cassava occur during traditional methods of harvesting (14 percent), handling (9 percent), and processing (23 percent). But in the 1990s the International Institute of Tropical Agriculture invested in village processing centers in Nigeria that more than halved the losses in processing and cut labor hours by 70 percent. In the wake of the 2008 food crisis, the government of the Philippines—one of the countries worst hit by rice price rises—announced heavy new investment in rice-drying machines to address the losses of 25–50 percent (by value, taking into account losses in quantity and quality) suffered by Southeast Asian rice growers.

In Timor, the United Nations has funded local blacksmiths to construct hundreds of small grain silos and given training to farmers and householders—all in an attempt to save food that is already being produced.[29]

During the mid-1980s, the United Nations helped 9 percent of Pakistani farmers in non-irrigated areas invest in metal grain storage containers in order to replace jute bags and mud constructions, and this cut the farmers' storage losses by up to 70 percent. Simultaneous projects aimed at eliminating rat infestations boosted yields by 10–20 percent. But a vast proportion of farmers continue to use suboptimal methods of grain storage and are still at the mercy of moths, rodents, and mold.[30]

Appalling though it is, in some way it is actually encouraging that millions of tons of food currently go to waste unnecessarily through the indifference of the affluent and the accidental post-harvest losses in developing countries. It means that much more food could be made available comparatively easily. As Figure 9–1 illustrates, when food travels from farm to table, it loses a total of 1,800 kilocalories post-harvest and as animal feed before ever leaving the field. After adding losses and waste due to processing, distribution, and household handling, the total losses amount to 2,600 kilocalories, leaving only 2,000 kilocalories available per person for consumption. If the world needs to bring more grain onto the world market, the vast pit of spoiled grain in developing countries would be a sensible place to begin foraging. The developing world would benefit from investment in agricultural technologies to prevent accidental losses, while the industrial world should rein in its profligacy. These distinct measures to address two very different kinds of waste could help improve the lives of the poor.[31]

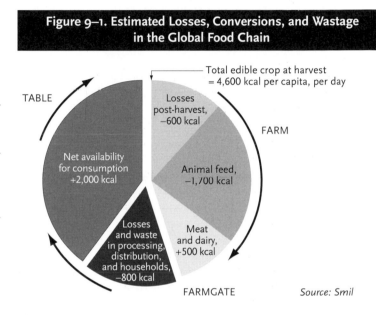

Figure 9–1. Estimated Losses, Conversions, and Wastage in the Global Food Chain

Total edible crop at harvest = 4,600 kcal per capita, per day

TABLE

Losses post-harvest, –600 kcal

FARM

Net availability for consumption +2,000 kcal

Animal feed, –1,700 kcal

Losses and waste in processing, distribution, and households, –800 kcal

Meat and dairy, +500 kcal

FARMGATE

Source: Smil

It is more sustainable to increase available food by reducing waste than by chopping down virgin forests to increase cultivable land—which is the principal method by which food production is being made to increase globally. International aid agencies, governments, and individual donors as well as food corporations and consumers both in affluent countries and in the developing world can help make more food available without having to chop down a single extra tree.

Turning the Catch of the Day into Better Livelihoods

Outside Banjul, capital of The Gambia, a group of women stand roadside offering oysters for 15 dalasis a cup—about 55¢ for some 75 pieces of oyster meat. Local women have been harvesting oysters from the nearby extensive mangrove wetlands for decades. Much of the harvesting is done in Tanbi National Park, a wetland of international importance.[1]

Although the mangroves remain healthy, the oyster harvesters have witnessed the effects of increased pressure on the oyster population first hand. The oysters today are smaller and harder to find than just 10 years ago. Even with the increased effort this involves, more women are harvesting today than in the past. They rely on oysters for their livelihoods, and they contribute to food security in a country heavily dependent on seafood for protein.

In 2007 a group of oyster harvesters organized themselves into a producer association called TRY Women's Oyster Harvesting Association. Membership grew rapidly—from 14 women in one village to 500 harvesters from 15 communities in Greater Banjul today. This growth was no small feat. Although the women are all Jola, a minority ethnic group, they come from different sects with distinct languages and heritages. Through TRY, they have been able to put aside these differences, making decisions by consensus and collectively setting priorities.[2]

In fall 2009, TRY became linked with Ba Nafaa, the Sustainable Fisheries Project funded by the U.S. Agency for International Development. Ba Nafaa has helped TRY expand the scope of its mission and has worked to create a sustainable co-management plan for the oyster fishery that respects the needs of harvesters, consumers, and the environment.[3]

Working with Ba Nafaa, the women have collectively agreed to practices that may be diffi-

cult in the short run but pay off over time. Traditionally oysters are harvested during the dry season, with the wet months of July through December closed. In 2010, the members agreed to extend the closed season until March. When harvesting resumed, the women saw the benefits immediately—a marked increase in the size of oysters harvested. In addition, each community agreed to close one tributary in their territory for the entire year to encourage regeneration of the oyster population there.[4]

The women are also adopting practices to ensure that Tanbi remains a healthy ecosystem. They have learned, for example, that cutting roots with machetes to collect any attached oysters damages the ecosystem's capacity to support oysters and fish nurseries. They are sharing these lessons with other Gambians through short plays on harvesting techniques. They are also helping the Department of Parks and Wildlife Management police the wetlands by reporting any illegal fuelwood harvesting they see.[5]

One of TRY's first accomplishments was to raise the price of oysters from 10 to 15 dalasis per cup. One of the big goals is to see the price grow exponentially by opening new markets in the high-end retail outlets serving tourists. This would be greatly aided if there were a permanent market for harvesters, who now rely on customers stopping by the side of the road or at temporary markets in Greater Banjul. Eventually the harvesters could develop an export market to the United States or Europe, which could yield prices high enough to create living wages for them. In the meantime, the oyster harvesters can still be found selling their catch along the road outside of Banjul—and working together to improve their situation.

—Christi Zaleski
Gambia-Senegal Sustainable Fisheries Project

Fruit vendors in a market in Antananarivo, Madagascar

CHAPTER 10

Feeding the Cities

Nancy Karanja and Mary Njenga

When Alice Wairimu arrived in Nairobi, Kenya, in 1987, she joined a stream of other migrants moving to the cities—a stream that over the last 50 years has rendered sub-Saharan Africa almost completely unrecognizable. Her story is not unusual. She settled at Kawangware, one of the low- to middle-income settlements in the city, and started selling chickens. She later married Michael Macharia, who lived in the Kibera slum. He bought his wife five cows, which she tended until one was stolen during political unrest in 2007 and they were forced to sell the other four to pay hospital bills. The couple also tried wastewater farming on a piece of land that belonged to a government institution, which repossessed it in 2010. They drew on their meager savings to rent land in the same vicinity and are continuing to practice urban agriculture there.[1]

For Alice Wairimu, Michael Macharia, and millions of others, urban agriculture has become a lifeline in a time of upheaval and profound change. The appearance and staggering growth of Nairobi and other sprawling cities—annual urban growth rates in the region are approaching 5 percent—are presenting new challenges to their inhabitants as well as to

Nancy Karanja and **Mary Njenga** are researchers at Urban Harvest, based in Nairobi, Kenya.

governments, nongovernmental organizations (NGOs), and the world at large. Food security, a perennial issue, is in many ways magnified by the growth of these cities.[2]

In the cities of developing countries, the contrast between rich and poor is dramatic and visually striking. Big houses surrounded by landscaped gardens and with access to infrastructure and other services to ensure comfort and security are literally right next door to slums. The people in these slum communities, such as Kibera in Nairobi and Jamestown in Ghana, struggle for adequate shelter and basic services such as water and sanitation. They are vulnerable to crime and to food insecurity; poverty and malnutrition tend to go hand in hand. Food purchases absorb as much as 80 percent of the money spent by poor urban households, and the urban poor are often hungrier and at a greater disadvantage than their rural counterparts because they have to purchase most of their food. And millions of slum dwellers live under the constant threat of eviction because of a lack of land tenure; technically most are squatters, setting up homes, businesses, and farms on unused government land. Much of this land is considered uninhabitable or problematic to develop because it is located in wetlands or on steep slopes.[3]

These are formidable challenges. But they have stimulated some innovative and promising solutions, including a resurgence in the cultivation of food for consumption and sale within the urban environment. All across sub-Saharan Africa and throughout the developing world, communities are creating locally adapted urban agricultural systems to address critical issues of nutrition, gender equality, income, and food security. (See Table 10–1.)[4]

In many of these cities, urban agriculture has a long, if interrupted, history of increasing food security and reducing hunger among vulnerable populations. Surveys conducted in the late 1990s in 24 cities, mainly in Africa and Asia, showed that people involved in growing some of their food accounted for anything from an important minority to a large majority of all households. The surveys also showed that people in poor households practicing urban agriculture ate more meals and had more balanced diets than other people. Data from Kampala, Uganda, in the 1990s suggest that children in farming households were better nourished than those in non-farming households.[5]

Growing their own food also enables people to save money that they might have used to purchase food. And by growing their own food, city-dwellers gain an important source of employment and income that can be spent on school fees, clothes, and household necessities. A survey in Lome, Togo, for instance, showed that market gardeners earned 10 times the monthly minimum wage of other people.[6]

The food supplied by urban agriculture in cities is worth tens of millions of dollars a year and is quite substantial. In terms of livestock, for example, 250,000 chickens and 45,000 sheep and goats were reared in Nairobi in 2004 and 42 million liters of cow milk were produced. In the late 1990s, cow milk produced each year in Dar es Salaam, Tanzania, was estimated to be worth more than $10 million. In Zimbabwe's capital, Harare, urban agriculture was valued at $25 million in 2003 and involved more than 9,000 hectares of land. It was estimated that there were anywhere from 50,000 to 168,000 urban cattle in Kampala in 2004, of which 73 percent were high-yielding cattle.[7]

Cities are becoming centers of development interventions and planning strategies that aim to alleviate hunger, poverty, and inequality in order to promote sustainability. By offering ways to address several of the region's pressing needs, including food insecurity, income generation, community building, waste disposal, and the status of women, urban agriculture in sub-Saharan Africa is a potentially important part of this movement.

Table 10–1. Innovations That Nourish Cities

Innovation, Location	Description
Vertical Farm, Urban Harvest, Nairobi, Kenya	Gardens grown in sacks full of dirt and poked with holes. In Kibera in Nairobi, more than 1,000 farmers—mostly women—are using these gardens to feed their families and improve their income.
Tire Garden, ECHO Farms and throughout sub-Saharan Africa	Old tires cut in half and converted into lightweight and easily portable planters provide urban farmers with small gardens without soil. Farmers use the wall of the tire for support and then fill it with trash to create stability for plant roots. Organic or commercial.
Rooftop Garden, Eagle Street Rooftop Farm, New York City	In Brooklyn, New York, Eagle Street Rooftop farms is growing fresh produce to sell at local markets and to local restaurants on top of an old warehouse. Local volunteers can come on weekends to help care for the garden and learn techniques for creating small urban gardens of their own on their window sills, fire escapes, and roofs.
Platform Garden, ECHO Farms and throughout sub-Saharan Africa	Platform gardens help urban farmers who have access to space but not dirt. By using compost, trash, and either organic or chemical fertilizer, farmers can use platform gardens to better manage soil quality, protect crops from flooding, and avoid pests.
Community Supported Agriculture, Harvest of Hope, South Africa	Harvest of Hope works with over 50 community and institutional gardens outside Cape Town, South Africa, to help them become sustainable. Once the gardens are growing enough to create a surplus, the excess is sold to Harvest of Hope, which delivers the produce in boxes to local city schools. The program provides an income for peri-urban farmers and fresh produce for urban students.

Source: See endnote 4.

Growing Food, Increasing Security

Urban agriculture already contributes substantially to food security in many cities, both as an important component of urban food systems in general and as a means for vulnerable groups to address their own particular food insecurities. (See Figure 10–1.) An estimated 800 million people are engaged in urban agriculture worldwide, producing 15–20 percent of the world's food. Of these urban farmers, 200 million produce food for markets and employ 150 million people. It is estimated that by 2020, some 35–40 million Africans living in cities will depend on urban agriculture to meet their food requirements.

This could provide some residents with up to 40 percent of their recommended daily allowance of calories and 30 percent of their protein needs.[8]

Growing food in cities has some advantages over rural farming, including proximity to markets, low transportation costs, and reduction in post-harvest losses because of reduced time between harvests. In times of conflict or other unrest, urban agriculture often keeps people fed when food supplies from the countryside are interrupted. In Nairobi in 2008, for example, unrest after the national elections cut off transportation and the movement of goods and services, including food, into the city. But people there did not go

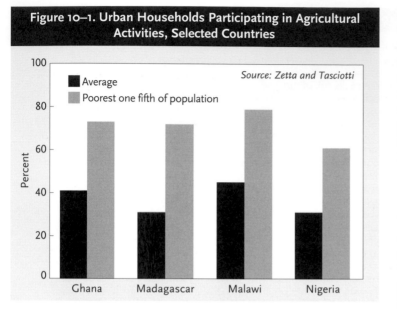

Figure 10–1. Urban Households Participating in Agricultural Activities, Selected Countries

learned, share information on market opportunities and inputs such as planting materials, and strengthen social bonds and the community. Where conditions reflect destitution, hope has thrived alongside vegetables produced by these women living in the slum. They currently have 10,000 vertical gardens.[10]

Building Community

Urban agriculture brings city dwellers together and helps generate social interaction. "Self-help" groups of young people, women, and vulnerable people, including the elderly, meet as a result of their involvement in urban agriculture, giving them the opportunity to organize and share information and skills. This helps improve individual well-being while providing a voice that otherwise would not be heard. These groups are also important avenues through which their members obtain technical skills and market opportunities. Through these groups, farmers exercise their sense of self-determination and dignity in the face of hardship.

hungry, as supplies of vegetables and other food were available from within the city boundaries and nearby areas. "The vegetable gardens along Ngo'ng river valley and around Nairobi dam saved our families from starvation during the political crisis of 2008," said Mary Mutola, a wastewater farmer from Kibera slums. This experience won the attention of the International Red Cross, which then provided farmers in Kibera with vegetable seeds to use in gardens.[9]

Growing vegetables in vertical basket gardens, though an old practice in Kibera, one of the largest slums on Earth, became very popular during the crisis. The vertical gardens are made of recycled sacks or biodegradable cement bags that are filled with soil mixed with livestock manure. Leafy vegetables and herbs such as coriander and spring onions are sown at the top and sides of the bags to optimize yield in limited spaces. NGOs such as the French group Solidarites have provided technical assistance and material support to the urban farmers in Kibera as well as self-help groups. The women are able to teach each other lessons they have

Another form of community building in cities takes place through school gardens and extension schools. Students acquire practical knowledge about how food is cultivated and harvested, as well as other important traits such as leadership, social organization, and responsibility. Because schools typically have access to land, water, and buildings, they have been used as agents of urban agriculture extension and seed production. The city council of Kampala, for example, has opened a number of extension schools to give training as well as technical and material support to the city's urban farmers, and many primary schools have gardens to teach students about urban farming and nutrition. Other examples exist throughout sub-Saharan Africa, tackling issues like community development, the impact of AIDS, and food security.[11]

Raising Women's Status

The majority of urban farmers around the world are women. They are often in charge of obtaining food for their families, and they tend to predominate in subsistence farming. (Men play a greater role in urban food production for commercial purposes.) Sometimes this is achieved by means of kitchen gardens and urban agriculture plots, sometimes by food the women grow on farms in rural areas and near the cities. Women try their best to sustain their families in often-difficult circumstances, which is why, in a very real sense, they end up feeding the cities and need institutional support.[12]

"I am a very happy women as I have been able to purchase a farm in my rural home using the income I have earned from urban agriculture here in Nairobi," said Mary Mutola, a farmer in Kibera. She added that the income she had received through the sale of vegetables had improved her kitchen and sitting room, and now she has a comfortable room that is welcoming to visitors. Mutola helps with research work on urban farmers in Kibera, which earns her the respect of other farmers and in turn helps her get them involved in household surveys, group discussions, and workshops.[13]

Another urban farmer, Eunice Ambani, who belongs to the same group of farmers as Mutola, feels quite empowered as she is able to meet her family's expenditures on food, clothing, and shelter. She supports destitute children in Kibera, an activity that brings her joy and satisfaction. Her family eats whatever she thinks is good for their health, and her choice does not depend on the amount of money she has, as happens for many other women in her neighborhood. Jane Okaka is a single, HIV-positive mother in Kenya. She was introduced to urban agriculture through an Urban Harvest project and after two years had this to say: "Besides taking antiretroviral drugs, the traditional vegetables made me stronger every day. I sold the surplus vegetables and the money I earned was spent on recommended foods like eggs and white meat and other needs for my children."[14]

Improving the Environment

In addition to enhancing food security and women's status, urban farming can help improve environmental quality in at least two ways. (See also Box 10–1.)[15]

First, most cities in developing countries must deal with pollution and waste disposal from farming and industry. The urban poor are often adept at waste recycling and compost production on a limited scale in many towns. A study of urban food production in Kenya, for instance, identified widespread use of organic inputs by urban farmers. In fact, wastewater reuse for urban agriculture is a widespread practice with a long tradition in many countries. In China, Egypt, India, Lebanon, Mexico, Morocco, Peru, and Vietnam, wastewater has been a source of crop nutrients for many decades. At least 2 million hectares in developing countries are irrigated with raw sewage or partially treated wastewater, and at least 10 percent of the world consumes wastewater-irrigated produce.[16]

In sub-Saharan Africa, millions of tons of waste of all types are produced annually, including 730,000 tons in Nairobi, 646,780 tons in Dar es Salaam, 313,900 tons in Kumasi, and 765,040 tons in Accra. Over 60 percent of these cities' solid waste is biodegradable material that, if recovered, could be used as livestock feed or to make compost, thereby generating income and employment for poor urban dwellers and

Box 10–1. Pushing the Limits of Urban Agriculture

As a growing number of people in cities around the world turn to urban gardens for their food and sometimes a source of income, important challenges remain to be addressed, such as air, water, and soil pollution that can undermine people's health and improper management of urban waste waters, solid wastes, and livestock wastes. In response, the International Development Research Centre (IDRC) and its partners have supported evidence-based policy development and technical innovations in several countries, including Jordan and Uganda.

Jordan is one of the 10 most water-scarce countries in the world. Three quarters of its people live in cities and towns where there is barely enough water to drink. A 2001 census of Amman found that 40 percent of the population used gray water (water that has been used for household purposes, such as bathing, laundry, or food preparation) to some extent to irrigate their gardens. Some 50,000 households practiced various forms of food production, but largely using fresh water. Several projects funded by IDRC and the Inter-Islamic Network on Water Resources Development have explored new technologies to expand safe and acceptable household use of gray water for

agriculture in order to curb freshwater use and help produce more food for the poor.

Researchers tested different low-cost technologies, settling on a system that uses four plastic barrels that hold 50–220 liters. The system was piloted in a few households in the small town of Tafila. Initial water savings were at least 15 percent, and there were other cost savings as well, as septic tanks required less-frequent emptying. Crop yields (of olives and eggplants, for example) also improved, meaning that the cost of units could be recovered quickly. Benefits ultimately outweighed costs by a ratio of five to one over the 10-year life span of the units. One unit was installed at a local mosque to irrigate landscaping and trees around it; another, at the local girls' school, collected waste water from the drinking faucet system and sent it to the olive trees in the school garden. Gray water from the treatment units meets the World Health Organization's standard for restricted irrigation, which means it is fit for irrigating trees and crops that must be cooked before they are eaten.

The Jordanian Ministry of Planning was so impressed that in 2002 it supported the construction of 689 systems in 91 communities across the country. The Ministry of Social

saving farmers from the expense of artificial fertilizers.[17]

Second, urban farming in the form of agroforestry can also benefit local environments. The trees often provide shade for livestock and supply fruits and nuts. Agroforestry products can include charcoal, timber, and seedlings, all of which can be sold in local markets. Trees can also act as windbreaks (helping to decrease erosion and stabilize soils), improve air and water quality, provide places for outdoor leisure, conserve biodiversity, and be a source of shade under which artifacts are displayed for sale.

Environmental services provided by urban forests include the reduction of air pollution and storm water mitigation, which greatly contribute to the sustainability of the urban centers. Moreover, trees and other vegetation act as sinks for carbon dioxide in the atmosphere, thus contributing to reduction of greenhouse gases. Researchers, policymakers, and urban planners have accepted urban forestry management as one important strategy to improve urban living and working environments. In China, for example, research projects and education programs have been initiated to better plan for urban forests.[18]

Box 10–1 continued

Development has become involved, offering training for the poor in various skills need to use the technology. Many of Jordan's thirsty neighbors have also become interested, and gray water reuse projects are under way in Lebanon, Syria, the West Bank, and Gaza.

A follow-on IDRC grant in 2004 supported the scaling up and improvement in design and construction of the technology in Jordan's Karak governate. More than 110 households saw a significant reduction in their need for additional domestic water supply in the summer months. A late 2006 survey revealed that a majority considered their gray water systems as personal possessions and would encourage relatives and friends to use gray water.

In Kampala, Uganda, cattle raising within the city limits has been legal since 2004, the year the municipal council adopted a train of ordinances legalizing agricultural activities in the city. This was the result of long and patient work by the Kampala Urban Food Security, Agriculture, and Livestock Coordinating Committee (KUFSALCC), which was created by nongovernmental organizations; the municipal council; the Ministry of Agriculture, Animal Industry, and Fisheries; Makerere University; the National Agricultural Research Organization; and the Consultative Group on International Agricultural Research. Members helped educate and lobby municipal authorities on the need to modify the city's existing farming regulations. Most critics had focused on negative health impacts while ignoring the health benefits.

KUFSALCC showed that it was possible to control roaming cattle without banning them entirely. It has also investigated health hazards, including zoonoses, risks caused by pollutants, food security and nutrition issues, and vegetable irrigation with wastewaters. In pursuit of crucial support from elected officials, Councillor Winnie Makumbi spearheaded a public review of agricultural reforms first proposed by municipal authorities in 1998. KUFSALCC then convinced the Council to allow stakeholders to contribute to the drafting of the new ordinances. User-friendly versions of the new ordinances in local languages were prepared. KUFSALCC has been asked to pilot-test the ordinances to assess challenges of implementing the new rules.

—Luc J. A. Mougeot
International Development
Research Center, Canada
Source: See endnote 15.

Policies for Urban Agriculture

Most cities ignored urban agriculture until recently, giving it little policy attention or perhaps only allowing it as a temporary use of land. But today farming in the city is increasingly being recognized for its contribution to reducing poverty and hunger, as a source of local food production, and as a component of sustainable urban development. In 2007 the American Planning Association adopted a policy that encourages its members to help build "stronger, sustainable, and more self-reliant" local food systems.[19]

In Argentina, policy support for urban agriculture appeared as a response to its 2001 economic crisis. With the country's economy in shambles, the million-plus citizens of Rosario had to adapt to survive, and many began cultivating available plots of land throughout the city to ensure a steady supply of food for themselves and their families. Local authorities recognized the value of this practice and started to make public lands available for farming. The city also provided many of the urban farmers with tools, seeds, and other essential supplies.[20]

Acknowledging "the stark reality…that

hunger, food insecurity, and poor nutrition are pressing health issues, even in a city as rich and vibrant as San Francisco," Mayor Gavin Newsom in July 2009 asked all municipal departments to conduct an audit of land under their jurisdiction to create an inventory of land suitable for gardening. This was part of the first-ever city-wide food policy, which was based in part on the recommendations of the San Francisco Urban-Rural Roundtable, a group of urban and rural stakeholders that had been meeting for nine months. The group also recommended that a trade mission be established that could bring regional food growers together with local restaurants and food purchasers. And it suggested that philanthropic funds could be used to help residents who use food stamps to shop at local farmers markets.[21]

Kale and spinach in a garden in Kibera, Kenya

Bernard Pollack

This movement toward an urban food policy can be observed in other regions as well. A Ministers' Conference on Urban and Peri-urban Agriculture in East and Southern Africa was staged in 2003, for example. From that meeting came the Harare Declaration on urban and peri-urban agriculture, signed by all the participating nations, which called for promotion of a shared vision of urban and peri-urban agriculture that takes into account the specific needs and conditions in the region.[22]

Kampala can already boast guidelines and a department of urban agriculture within its city council that is to institutionalize the practice. In Kenya, the 2009 National Land Policy has a section on urban agriculture and forestry, and a national urban agriculture policy is also under development.[23]

The Future of Farming the Cities

In short, urban agriculture is here to stay, and it seems likely not only to help feed city dwellers but also to serve as an important driver of growth in the agriculture sector. But greater political recognition of urban agricultural practices is needed in order for the practice to become more sustainable, productive, and inclusive.

Urban agriculture needs to be integrated into urban land use planning procedures and policy measures in order to manage it and address any potential risks. Policies related to this should be aimed at poverty reduction, local economic development, environmental management, integration of disadvantaged groups, and promotion of participatory governance and democratic cities. To protect the interests of the low-income urban farmers who rely on informal access to land for subsistence agriculture, local governments need to undertake localized land use planning and guarantee adequate compensation for the loss of access to land.[24]

Similarly, activities that interact with urban farming systems, including nutrient cycling involving compost making and manure handling, need to be integrated in urban policies. Developing such a well-orchestrated and integrated strategy will require financial, human, and social capital. Thus urban agriculture should be included in urban development and land use plans and be regulated by municipalities.[25]

The key challenge for cities now is to integrate the ideas of designers and planners with the needs and wishes of farmers and consumers to establish designs that sustainably harness little used resources and to catalyze participatory and citizen-driven models for the creation of sustainable neighborhoods.

Women and young people also need a greater voice in decisions about urban agriculture. Deliberate efforts should be made to recognize women as independent actors and beneficiaries, whether the farming is for subsistence or for market. Policymakers seeking to support urban agriculture must recognize the real value of women's contribution and confront the facts that men's and women's needs are different, that public policies and projects have different effects on men and women, and that access to and control over resources are restricted by sociocultural, economic, and institutional configurations. Policies must address these inequalities. In these ways, cities can contribute to reducing hunger and alleviating poverty while conserving the urban ecosystem for generations to come.

Promoting Safer Wastewater Irrigation in West Africa

In Ghana and surrounding areas, polluted stream water is often used to irrigate vegetable crops. The problem is that the water often contains biological and chemical substances that are harmful to human health. Fortunately, there are ways to overcome this problem—even in parts of sub-Saharan Africa where conventional wastewater treatment has only limited coverage.[1]

The International Water Management Institute has initiated several projects to improve public health in Ghana, working with the Ministry of Food and Agriculture, two national universities, and a variety of other stakeholders, including growers. These projects focus on "non-treatment" or "post-treatment" interventions, such as promoting safer irrigation practices and the effective washing of vegetables.[2]

A main emphasis of the Ministry's new agricultural extension policy is innovative ways to make technologies more accessible to farmers. To help with this process, the Consultative Group on International Agricultural Research's Knowledge Sharing in Research project looked for ways to bring together researchers and extension staff, two groups that often do not reach out to each other. The project staff worked in three cities with large urban open spaces used for vegetable farming: Accra, Kumasi, and Tamale. Here, the only available water source for irrigation is local streams contaminated by sewage waste from surrounding households.[3]

Collaborating with vegetable farmers, traders, and street-food kitchen staff, the research partners developed and tested some 15 "good practices" to enhance food safety—examining their efficacy in controlling germs, their cost, and their "adoption potential." If practices that enhance food safety cost more or require more labor than current practices, it can be hard to persuade farmers to adopt them. Most consumers are not willing to pay more for safer crops that are more expensive to produce, as most are not aware of the health risks of unsafe practices.[4]

The researchers used perception studies and social marketing methods to analyze how best to present their recommendations and "sell" the need for change. Student researchers worked for several weeks in street-food restaurants to learn firsthand the daily routines and constraints related to hygiene and food safety. They documented risk-awareness factors and cultural habits and tried to identify the best entry points for interventions. At the same time, researchers and farmers explored together the options for safer water fetching and irrigation. They found that improved land tenure was a strong incentive for adopting new practices—indicating that policy, practice, and food safety are closely linked.[5]

The recommended practices were then summarized in videos designed for use by trainers and extension staff. Some of the videos were produced with farmers and food vendors, who helped with the scripts and the filming. As a result, they are more realistic and convey messages in ways that match local perceptions.[6]

After identifying a range of possible best practices, project staff organized "World Cafés"—focus groups where people feel comfortable enough to express their opinions in small groups—to get feedback on the findings before finalizing any recommendations. Once the café participants verified a set of best practices, these were translated into audiovisual materials and tested in perception studies. Perception studies are critical to ensure that messages are conveyed in culturally appropriate ways. (For example, the researchers' symbol for a magnifying glass, to "see" otherwise invisible pathogens, was too often identified as a frying pan and had to be changed.)[7]

The materials were pretested with farmers before being printed out. The responses were positive, with one participant observing: "When we go to collect water from the dugout, we used to walk into it. But now we know that disease-causing germs settle in the ponds. So we no longer walk into them, but fetch water from standing on a plank of wood."

Given their relatively small numbers and close proximity, urban farmers in Ghana and elsewhere can easily be reached through training workshops and extension officers. But where farmers are more remote, or where the target group (such as street-food vendors) is too big for localized events, radio can be an effective channel of communication. The use of radios across Africa has grown tremendously over the last decade and has proved to be an effective way of reaching farmers in their own languages. For the Knowledge Sharing in Research project, the program "Radio Justice," based in Tamale, was selected because it broadcasts in the Dagbani and Gonja languages and covers almost all of northern Ghana, where vegetable farmers are more difficult to reach.[8]

A food-safety radio program was broadcast in two sessions with two different panels, including agricultural extension officers, farmers, traders, university experts, and street-food vendors. Listeners could participate by calling in during the program. The show proved to be an effective strategy because it provided relevant information about the local agroecological and cultural context and it helped researchers understand how farmers and food vendors discuss their problems in the community. As one vegetable trader in Tamale put it: "When buying vegetables on farm, I used to wash them with the local stream water. But I stopped after listening to the [radio] program. I have also informed some of my colleagues…and believe that…such radio programs could play a key role in public education for improved health."[9]

To show the authorities how farmers and street-food vendors are taking health issues seriously, representatives from other stakeholder groups were invited to join a "road show" event. Participants were taken on a bus tour, starting from a farm where wastewater is used, through the market, and ending at street restaurants where the vegetables are most commonly sold. At each stop, participants learned firsthand about health threats and risk reduction methods. Although the road show required careful planning and facilitation, the method dissolved the traditional separation between active teachers and passive learners. By sharing their knowledge of good practices, participants become trainers, champions, and mediators.[10]

The road show also provided a common platform for communication among different groups. Farmers, vegetable sellers, and caterers or food vendors who rarely meet city authorities were able to discuss issues related to their livelihoods. As the Metropolitan Director of the Ministry of Food and Agriculture put it: "All stakeholders have now seen the practical situation on the ground and understand the part they have to play and that it is a joint responsibility and not solely for any one individual or group of people."[11]

These examples show that for agricultural research to truly benefit countries where the links between research and extension are weak, the publication of scientific papers needs to be accompanied by innovative and effective options—such as world cafés, participatory radio programs, and road shows. These options can facilitate the adoption of appropriate practices, and, in this case, increase the productive use of water.

—*Pay Drechsel*
International Water Management Institute

An Agricultural Answer to Nature's Call

It's hard to believe, but an estimated 2.6 billion people in the developing world still lack access to basic sanitation services. This presents a significant hygiene risk, especially in densely populated urban areas and slums, where contaminated drinking water can spread disease rapidly. Every year, some 1.5 million children die from diarrhea caused by poor sanitation and hygiene.[1]

It is in these crowded cities, too, that food security is weakened by the lack of clean, nutrient-rich soil as well as growing space available for local families.

But there is an inexpensive solution to both problems. A recent innovation, called the Peepoo, is a disposable bag that can be used once as a toilet and then buried in the ground. Urea crystals in the bag kill off disease-producing pathogens and break down the waste into fertilizer, simultaneously eliminating the sanitation risk and providing a benefit for urban gardens. After successful test runs in Kenya and India, the bags were being mass-produced in 2010 and sold for 2–3¢ each, making them more accessible to those who will benefit from them the most.[2]

In post-earthquake Haiti, where many poor and homeless residents are forced to live in garbage heaps and to relieve themselves wherever they can find privacy, SOIL/SOL—a non-profit working to improve soil and convert waste into a resource—is partnering with Oxfam to build indoor dry toilets for 25 families as well as four public dry toilets. The project will establish a waste composting site to convert dry waste into fertilizer and nutrient-rich soil that can then be used to grow vegetables in rooftop gardens and backyards.[3]

In Malawi, Stacia and Kristof Nordin's permaculture project uses a composting toilet to fertilize the crops. Although these units can be expensive to purchase and install, one company (Rigel Technology) manufactures a toilet that costs just $30 and separates solid from fluid waste, converting it into fertilizer. The Indian non-profit Sulabh International also promotes community units that convert methane from waste into biogas for cooking.[4]

On a larger scale, wetlands outside of Kolkata (Calcutta), India, process some 600 million liters of raw sewage delivered from the city every day in 300 fish ponds. These wetlands produce 13,000 tons of fish annually for consumption by the city's 12 million inhabitants. They also serve as an environmentally sound waste treatment center, with hyacinths, algal blooms, and fish disposing of the waste, while also providing a home for migrating birds and an important source of local food for the population of Kolkata.[5]

Aside from cost and installation, the main obstacles to using human waste to fertilize crops are cultural and behavioral. UNICEF notes in an online case study that a government-run program in India provided 33 families in the village of Bahtarai with latrines near their houses. But most villagers still preferred to use the fields as toilets, as they have been accustomed to doing their whole lives. "It is not enough just to construct the toilets," said Gaurav Dwivedi, Collector and Bilaspur District Magistrate. "We have to change the thinking of people so that they are amenable to using the toilets."[6]

—*Molly Theobald*
Worldwatch Institute

Women farmers of a Ghanian cooperative process palm fruits for their oil

CHAPTER 11

Harnessing the Knowledge and Skills of Women Farmers

Dianne Forte, Royce Gloria Androa, and Marie-Ange Binagwaho

"It is a problem of invisibility, nobody knows we are there." With these words, Imodale Caulker-Burnett, who lives in the United States but returns to her village in Sierra Leone for three months every year, summarizes the challenges confronting rural communities in Africa and especially women farmers. She founded Lesana, a community development organization in her village, Mambo, because she believes that women who leave the village must become ambassadors for those who remain. They must make the women visible to policymakers. This visibility is as important as productive inputs and markets for women, who as primary household food producers strive to move from subsistence to effective contributors to the end of hunger on this continent.[1]

Up to 75 percent of agricultural producers in Africa are women. Yet even as they are the guardians of food and nutritional security, they are disproportionately found among the 51

Dianne Forte is a Washington-based management consultant with 22 years experience managing programs in Africa. **Royce Gloria Androa** is a senior partner at Reach Your Destiny Consult Ltd. in Uganda, with 26 years experience in agricultural extension in Uganda. **Marie-Ange Binagwaho** is the owner of Zawadi Enterprises, Inc.

percent of Africans who are the absolute poor—people living on less than $1.25 a day. In 2009, hunger increased in Africa, the region with the highest prevalence of hunger in the world. The United Nations set a goal in 2000 of cutting global hunger in half by 2015. Clearly this goal will not be met without a revolution in the way decisionmakers think of women as agricultural producers and their connections to markets. Yet there are wildly successful strategies that have moved women from absolute poverty to successful players in global markets—some in as little as six years.[2]

These innovative strategies have several things in common, such as paying attention to how women obtain and relate to information, credit, and technology and how to increase their participation in formal economic life. They address the needs of poor women food producers on three levels: as market-oriented smallholders, as subsistence farmers, and as farm laborers—and all in terms of property rights, social services, insurance, and other social protections. Furthermore, these strategies incorporate changes in information technology and communications, creative new linkages within and across markets, women-centered credit programs, agricultural extension services, and media messaging—all while building on the knowledge and skills of women farmers. The result is increased nutritional and food security and access to markets on fair terms.[3]

Women Pursuing the World Market

Shea butter gave Mawoubé of Sokode, Togo, a bicycle and her dream of becoming a doctor. Shea butter—known as woman's gold or *karite*, which is Dioula for life—also brought the women of Mawoubé's village access to water, health care, and an education for their children. Shea butter production and trade opened a window through which the poorest women on the planet had access to global markets.[4]

Shea grows in only one place: a 500-kilo-meter band of the Sahel that encompasses 19 countries, including Burkina Faso, Guinea, Mali, Senegal, Togo, and Uganda. Like diamonds, it is naturally occurring. And like diamonds, shea is sought after by consumers of western luxury goods. But unlike diamonds, shea is controlled by women. And it is used and valued by those who control its harvesting and processing. Shea nuts provide four times more vitamin C per ounce than an orange and have traditional uses that include fuel for lamps, oil for cooking, repellent against mosquitoes, soap, healing for ailments, and balm for the dead. The shea tree is so precious that it is rarely cut down for firewood.[5]

The key to realizing Mawoubé's dream was the link between the shea nut crop and the global fair trade and organic ("ethical") markets for beauty products—a link made possible by concerned people who provided resources and made the communities visible. The shea butter success story hinges on a business model that shortens the distance between farmer and final consumer.

The value chain starts with local women's cooperatives in Africa. These organizations allow producers to realize better economies of scale and to connect with international nongovernmental organizations (NGOs), national governments, and U.N. agencies. Jointly, they created a network to provide market information, access to better technology, and the support needed for policy changes (for instance, to secure land title for women). At the other end of the chain, fair trade organizations and socially responsible firms pay fair prices for the shea butter and invest in the local communities. Often crucial to this "virtuous circle" are Africans such as Imodale Caulker-Burnett and Olowo –n'djo Tchala, who emigrated but maintain their roots in the village, providing visibility for and connections to local producers. (See Box 11–1.)[6]

Companies such as L'Occitane, Body Shop, Origins, and L'Oreal all buy shea butter directly

Box 11–1. Social Capital Investments: An Innovation to End Poverty

Mawoubé is a rare phenomenon in Togo: the oldest of eight children, she is 14 years old and is in the correct grade for her age. She lives 5 kilometers from the high school. To get to school, Mawoubé rides a bike. She was one of the first recipients of one of 3,000 bicycles provided by the Agbanga Association's U.S. affiliate, Alaffia. Early pregnancy had been common in the villages around Mawoubé's hometown of Sokodé because the girls often had to trade sex for a ride to school. But there have been no pregnancies among the 3,000 bicycle recipients.

The bicycle project is one of Alaffia's investments in the community. Rose Hyde, product developer for Alaffia's products, insists that the company is not an ethical beauty retailer. Alaffia, instead, is a social capital concept. This Togolese company keeps more than 100 rural women who own it happy, healthy, and empowered. Alaffia was founded by Olowo-n'djo Tchala, who saw his

mother earning $1 for 30 hours of work—the rate paid for about 4 kilograms of shea nuts, which yields about 1 kilogram of butter.

Upon graduating from the University of California, Davis, Tchala supported the Sokodé women as they formed the Agbanga Karite Women's Fair Trade Shea Butter Cooperative. Women working there earn $4 a day making the shea butter whose products are marketed by Alaffia Sustainable Skincare. Alaffia USA formulates Agbanga's shea butter into finished products that are sold directly to outlets such as Whole Foods. The company pays all overhead costs of production in Togo (taxes, transportation, shipping, and custom fees) and then returns a minimum of 10 per cent of sales to the community for empowerment projects. Since 2003, Alaffia USA has returned $1.25 million to community development initiatives such as the bicycle for education project.

Source: See endnote 6.

from women's producer organizations like Burkina Faso's Association Songtaab-Yalgre and Ghana's Ideal Woman Shea Butter Producers and Pickers Association. Buyers such as L'Occitane have invested in women's groups, facilitated ethical fair trade certification, and enabled the women producers to compete in international fair trade markets.

Here is one example of how these relationships get started. In 1998, a poor, rural Burkinabe woman, Fatou Ouedraogo, organized *karite* traditional nut gatherers into the Association Songtaab-Yalgre. UNIFEM, the U.N. fund for women, worked with Burkina Faso's Minister of Women's Advancement to establish the group's relationship with L'Occitane and a network of other international organizations that provided training, technology, standardization, and fair prices. This added $7 million to Burkina Faso's income in 2001

alone, making shea butter the third highest national income earner after cotton and livestock. By 2004, the Association Songtaab-Yalgre had become a union of over 150 associations with 3,100 members. Six years later, women who had been illiterate, isolated, and invisible are producing a regular newsletter on a computer.[7]

In a country such as Burkina Faso where women are disinherited from their land upon the death of a husband, where 92 percent of women are illiterate, and where over 85 percent of rural women depend on subsistence agriculture—moving from $1 to $4 a day is a milestone. To do so within the space of six years is a significant achievement that reflects the effectiveness of fair terms of trade as well as having connections to a source of "social capital" that enabled visibility and provided valuable remittances.[8]

Shea butter production coincided with growing demand in richer countries for hand-crafted, organic products in health, craft, and beauty markets, creating an unprecedented opportunity for landless rural women. Yet it is worth noting that the fair trade market buys only about 10 percent of the shea produced. The main buyers are a handful of global chocolate manufacturers, which are increasingly replacing cocoa butter with shea fat in their chocolate. The typical smallholder shea producer growing for the chocolate market has no share in the value added further down the production chain, nor any share of the profits from marketing.[9]

As women compete in traditional markets, in addition to the tremendous structural barriers of global standards and a lack of access to credit and information, as they try to rise above $1 a day they find themselves at odds with global corporations' demand for the cheapest labor. As Marilyn Carr and Martha Chen observe in the *International Labour Review*, "The very factors which led to women's 'inclusion' in the global economy in the first place now have them trapped in downwardly mobile positions."[10]

While agricultural liberalization policies pursued by African governments in the 1990s benefited people with greater power, information, access to land, financial assets, and markets, women's access to international markets remains precarious except in the few instances where supporting agencies play an active role. Economist Jeffrey Sachs points out that "extreme poverty is almost always synonymous with extreme isolation, especially rural isolation." Mechanisms that provide information to women on a wide scale are necessary.[11]

Extension Services Aimed at Women

Rural extension workers are critical to the "word of mouth" approach through which women get their information. Extension services are an important way of using local knowledge, bridging traditional and formal agricultural methods, and supporting women farmers through women extension workers. Unfortunately, women have been excluded from many of these programs, whether as service providers or recipients. Lower levels of investment in women result in lower levels of literacy compared with men and fewer trained female agricultural extension workers. In Uganda, only 15–30 percent of the students enrolled in agricultural training colleges are women.[12]

When extension programs invest in women farmers and women extension workers, the payoff can be huge. Women receive an education, raise yields, increase their incomes, raise the nutritional status of the household, and contribute to the improvement of their communities. (See also Box 11–2.)[13]

In an April 2010 assessment of potential income-generating activities in four Karimojong settlements in northeastern Uganda, 1,135 individuals were interviewed. Women identified quick-maturing seeds and drought-resistant crops such as sorghum, cassava, maize, potatoes, cowpeas, groundnuts, sunflower, and vegetables as priority crops. They also wanted better farming tools, such as slashers, hand hoes, wheelbarrows, watering cans, and ox plows to plow larger fields. The women noted that they needed water for livestock and crops and also better environmental management, including more planting of local indigenous trees, improved fruit tree seedlings, and fast-growing trees for firewood and building poles. Keeping and selling livestock was an important activity for empowering and increasing the income of these women farmers.[14]

The women in these communities also said they needed better post-harvest technologies, including grinding mills for cereals such as cassava, sorghum, and millet, as well as simple oil presses for extracting oil from sunflower and simsim. Some women requested storage infrastructure, such as "grain banks," to hold crops

Box 11–2. Engaging Cocoa-Growing Communities to Support Women's Empowerment

Community engagement is the cornerstone for any successful and sustainable program and can lead the way to women's empowerment. The nonprofit World Cocoa Foundation (WCF) works to promote social and economic development and environmental stewardship in cocoa-growing communities around the world. WCF funds two innovative programs to help women find ways to improve their livelihoods: Video Viewing Clubs and Family Support Scholarships.

In West Africa's cocoa-producing regions, farmer training activities are typically led by community-based facilitators who have learned how to educate their peers—male and female cocoa farmers—on production and post-harvest techniques. Participating farmers learn how to develop a better-quality and therefore more valuable crop. A study by the International Institute of Tropical Agriculture's Sustainable Tree Crops Programme (STCP) found low female involvement in the training, however, because most women were at home taking care of their children, collecting fuel and water, and growing food. In some cases, their husbands did not allow them to go to the training.

STCP worked to create a convenient and comfortable learning environment for women by using videos to provide similar training exercises. Participants in these Video Viewing Clubs are expected to share the knowledge they gain with two other cocoa farmers, ensuring that the lessons reach a greater number of farmers in the community. Since 2006, nearly 1,600 farmers in Côte d'Ivoire and Ghana have received cocoa production training directly through the Video Viewing Clubs.

Other ways to reach women farmers go beyond agricultural training and support the community as a whole. The WCF program Empowering Cocoa Households (ECHOES), for example, strives to improve the lives and

livelihoods of the next generation of farmers through vocational training, education, and leadership development. In many West African cocoa-growing regions, school-related expenses are too high for parents to pay. As a result, ECHOES developed the Family Support Scholarship program, a three-tiered program implemented through Winrock International that is designed to help mothers keep their children in school while improving their existing enterprises. The first component of funds goes directly to the school to pay the children's annual expenses. After the mother completes a business training course, she receives the remaining two thirds to invest in her business. In the following two years, the increased profits she makes are put toward the children's school-related expenses.

ECHOES fully engages communities in the development and ownership of the Family Support Scholarships by encouraging community-based selection committees, which review the applications and identify who will receive the scholarships. Since 2007, committees in Côte d'Ivoire and Ghana have awarded scholarships to more than 250 households. One recipient, Sopi Akissi from Côte d'Ivoire, was able to add new products to her food-vending business and increase her monthly profit. The extra revenue enabled her to join a community savings group, where she could qualify for a loan and then purchase a freezer to further diversify the items she sells. "I have no problem taking care of the house expenses," Akissi said. "Same for the schooling of my children, including one who will start university this year."

—*Cat Alliston*
World Cocoa Foundation
Source: See endnote 13.

against periods of scarcity. Cereal banking brings good income and ensures household food security, but without adequate training on post-harvest handling processes to manage moisture content, storage pests, and diseases, the stored produce can all be lost to spoilage.[15]

Senegalese women process cashew fruit

The women stressed the need for capital to meet startup costs. Few women have access to such money. Ugandan female extension workers like Susan Ocokoru and Janet Asege mobilize revenue through village-level savings and credit schemes. Such associations can be very powerful: extension workers find it easier and more cost-effective to support and train women farmers who are organized into groups that have a common interest, such as vegetable growers, cassava processors, or produce buying and selling groups. The extension workers serve as a link between rural women's indigenous knowledge and new technology and resources. For example, they have introduced women's groups in Uganda to coolbot technology, which uses solar energy and an

inverter to reduce temperatures and prolong the shelf life of vegetables in stores made of reed, mud, and grass thatch.[16]

Working in groups unites women and strengthens their voices so that they are heard by development partners, policymakers, and other actors in the market. Empowerment can be measured through women's increased participation in group activities and trade fairs. The women prefer to be trained by female extension workers like Ocokoru and Asege because they feel women understand each other better.

Extension services contribute directly to higher productivity. In turn, higher productivity means improved household food security, more diversity in household diets, increased income through greater surplus production, and more economic resilience through more diverse farming. One study in Uganda showed that deliberately planting crops with the intention to grow and sell a surplus was a new idea to many farmers, and simple techniques such as increased spacing between banana plants, planting in rows rather than "broadcasting" seeds, and using manure fertilizers reportedly dramatically increased yields.[17]

Women appreciated that the Ugandan government's National Agricultural Advisory Services (NAADS) had included them, given them seed, and taught them as well as their husbands. Some people who had little formal education appreciated that through NAADS they were gaining useful knowledge; some even claimed to have learned some writing skills from their groups and from attending training seminars where writing is expected. Farmers also appreciated that some participants had gained leadership skills.[18]

Microcredit to Fight Poverty

Microcredit and microfinance institutions have been very popular tools in the struggle for poverty alleviation since the mid-1970s. The industry has flourished, with an emphasis on lending to women and lending for even the smallest business ventures. The success of microloans did not automatically translate to an increase in access to credit for the rural poor, however, mainly because of the challenges of lending in rural rather than urban areas. Lending very small amounts in sparsely populated areas where transportation infrastructure is poor, where the distance between clients is great, and where operations are much riskier than small-scale services for urban populations is not easy.

Nonetheless, in the last 10–15 years there has been a resurgence in rural financing led by microfinance institutions. Unfortunately, the increase in microlending for agriculture has benefited male farmers far more than female ones in spite of the fact that women greatly outnumber men in agriculture.[19]

According to the U.N. Food and Agriculture Organization, only 10 percent of credit allowances are extended to women in the sub-Saharan African countries where information is available. This is because they lack property rights and are discriminated against in customary law, making it difficult for women to provide collateral against loans. Lack of access to credit hampers poor women farmers' access to technology and to the market. In Senegal, rural women spend up to 13 hours a day on household chores such as fuelwood collection, water collection, and food preparation. For these women, access to credit would help them obtain time saving technologies such as fuel-efficient stoves and grain processing machines, as well as transportation to get goods to market. In the absence of effective government policies, market groups and some individuals have taken local actions to help women.[20]

In Malawi, as in the examples described earlier, educated women returning to rural areas have been an important source of ideas on how women farmers can get access to credit and other agricultural services. Dinnah Kapiza is an agrodealer in Mponela, Malawi, 60 kilo-

meters north of the capital, Lilongwe. She is a former primary school teacher who moved to Mponela in 1998 when she and her husband, also a teacher, retired. Her work there has evolved from selling seeds out of her small clothing shop in 2002 to owning four shops in rural Malawi that sell inputs to small-scale farmers and buy their produce.[21]

After some training in business management, input quality control, recordkeeping, and stock management skills through the Rural Agricultural Input Supply Expansion Program implemented by the international development group CNFA, Kapiza started Tisaiwale Trading out of her clothing shop. She got the backing of the CNFA credit guarantee, which allowed her to stock inputs on credit. Today, Tisaiwale Trading provides extension services through demonstration plots and field days. The company helps farmers test their soil to see which type of fertilizer suits their area, and it offers free advice on product handling and usage.[22]

As an agrodealer, Dinnah Kapiza has not only brought farming inputs and extension services closer to the 3,000 farmers she works with, she has also used her capacity to deal with volume to help the most vulnerable farmers around Mponela: women farmers, specifically widows. In 2009 Kapiza organized two groups of women. One group of widows, called Chiyembekezo (Hope), has 50 members. A second group, Kanananji, has 43 women. Both groups were introduced to the MicroLoan Foundation, where Kanananji sought loans for inputs for maize and groundnut production. The loans were easier to obtain because Kapiza guaranteed both groups that she would purchase their produce.[23]

For Dinnah Kapiza, helping to form these groups and introducing them to microfinance institutions where her reputation and promise to purchase their goods is accepted as collateral is not only good community service but also expands her customer base. "The

Kanananji group was formed in May of last year after the women approached me for agricultural inputs on credit but at the time I was not able to accommodate them, hence I decided to link them to a microfinance company and guaranteed to purchase their stock. Their first loan was for $71 for each member and their second loan was for $94 for each member." [24]

The Kanananji group used their first loan to purchase agricultural inputs for the winter season. They planted on fields averaging a quarter of an acre; they produced enough to provide for their families and used the remaining loan money to purchase inputs to make cakes, clothes, and other low-input items for sale. They then used those revenues to service their loan. All 43 women paid their loans back in full and had enough revenue to buy inputs for the next season. They each planted soy, maize, and tobacco. The tobacco has already been harvested and the proceeds used to service their second loan. Dinnah Kapiza expects to purchase the excess soy and maize harvest produced by the group. [25]

The success of the Kanananji group in obtaining and servicing multiple loans did not go unnoticed in Mponela, and by May 2010 three more women's groups had formed and were in negotiations with Kapiza and the MicroLoan Foundation. [26]

Impact of New Technologies

Recent studies show that innovations in knowledge creation, management, and communication are helping to level the playing field for women. Special agricultural programming via radio has been particularly well adapted to the needs of low-resource women farmers. No innovation has surpassed the impact of the mobile phone in the past decade, however, nor holds as many possibilities of reaching as many rural women. Intermedia's June 2010 report on media use, information flows, and communication in Ghana and Kenya con-

cluded that media environments are not gender-neutral. Women in these countries are less likely than men to use media regularly. [27]

As noted earlier, women depend on word of mouth as their main source of information. When they do use media, African women have overwhelmingly used radio. But mobile phones are increasingly becoming the new "word of mouth" for rural women. The level of mobile phone use is approaching that of radios. For the whole of Africa, mobile phone subscribers skyrocketed from 1 million in 1996 to an estimated 278 million in 2007. [28]

A 2009 study of 110 small to medium-sized rural agricultural households in Uganda found that 33 of the 54 women in the study had acquired mobile phones since 2007. The study concluded that farm group membership is associated with knowledge transfer and that women who belonged to farmer organizations acquired the means, the information, and the motivation to acquire new technology such as the mobile phone. The phones also help women in cooperatives to more efficiently coordinate access to inputs, market prices, or financial information such as microfinance loan guidelines and household or business remittances. Women farmers most commonly use mobile phones to obtain help in emergencies, such as calling a veterinarian for advice in caring for a sick animal. [29]

The Uganda study provides an example of how mobile phones—which have quickly become a critically important tool for commerce in Africa—are breaking rural women's isolation, providing them with access to information and literally enabling them to bypass the grid. Seemingly insurmountable structural barriers have traditionally kept rural women from obtaining vital services. This includes the high costs of traditional finance, their low level of financial literacy, and the lack of products designed specifically to meet smallholders' and small-scale traders' needs. Remittances are the largest form of investment in women's rural enterprises. Yet methods to transfer money cheaply and reliably from urban to rural households were unavailable until recently. Also missing was the ability to connect women's rural small and medium-sized enterprises to national banks and international credit.[30]

NetHope, an information and communication technology organization of 29 international NGOs, indicates that rural women finally have a chance to get access to mainstream banking. Innovative mobile technology such as Kenya's M-Pesa is able to bring banking services to poor rural women. And the mobile phone is only the first wave. Access to other technologies, such as the Internet, which still remains largely outside the reach of rural communities, is promising a boon to women as new fiber optic lines materialize and as groups such as the German development agency GTZ working in rural Zimbabwe make connectivity available to rural communities. This is a vital intervention, as the average cost of a digital subscriber line in Africa is $366 a month, compared with India's cost of between $6 and $44 a month. In wireless-dependent Africa, vertical information and communication technology businesses proliferate with a backbone network of as little as 1 percent fiber optic cable, whereas in broadband-intensive countries, about 40 percent fiber optic cable use is more typical.[31]

While it remains true that rural women need low-technology time-saving and energy-saving devices to ease their back-breaking triple burden, their connection to markets depends on high-technology innovations. The International Fund for Agriculture and Development describes innovation as "a process that adds value or solves a problem in new ways"—and that is exactly what the mobile phone does for rural women.[32]

Poor rural women in Africa finally will have a chance to overcome infrastructural barriers to information and markets through emerging digitalization, access to fair terms of trade, and international institutional and personal linkages. Policymakers have an unprecedented opportunity to ensure that these women are included in the changes ahead.

Women have been excluded long enough. Empowering women empowers communities: their children do better and their communities do better, building hope for a better present and future. If policymakers are not deliberate about including women, if they do not respect what women know, if they are not prepared to fight for women's rights in the context of traditions and laws that marginalize women, then their development programs will do poorly or fail outright. Women deserve better, and so does Africa. The ideas are there and so are the technologies. What is needed is a vision that gives women their voice and that supports their right to make decisions and to control their economic activities. The possibilities are enormous, waiting only for the vision and the will to improve women's lives.

Using Theater to Help Women Farmers

After decades of stagnation in agricultural yield and little or no investment in rural economies, African countries are beginning to give priority to the development of agricultural production and markets. Rural development and agricultural productivity now feature prominently on the agendas of national governments and regional bodies. Continent-wide plans and investments through programs like the Common Africa Agriculture Development Programme and the Alliance for a Green Revolution in Africa are encouraging and guiding national efforts. And international donors also recognize the need to invest in agricultural development, as evidenced most clearly by the 2008 *World Development Report* of the World Bank.[1]

The Food, Agriculture and Natural Resources Policy Analysis Network (FANRPAN) is a multi-stakeholder, multinational network based in Pretoria, South Africa, that supports the development of better food, agriculture, and natural resources policies—with a vision of a food-secure Africa. The network has more than 670 members—including universities, farmers' organizations, businesses, government agencies, and civil society organizations involved in food, agriculture, and natural resource policy in 13 African countries. The organization lives up to its name by linking farmers, businesses, academia, researchers, donors, and national and regional governments.[2]

In July 2009, recognizing the critical role that women farmers play in ensuring household food security, FANRPAN launched Women Accessing Realigned Markets (WARM), a three-year pilot project working to strengthen women farmers' ability to advocate for appropriate agricultural policies and programs in Mozambique and Malawi. The goal is to assist women farmers to gain access to tools, such as credit

and better seeds, that will allow them to farm more successfully—and to do this by ensuring that local and national policies and services address their needs.[3]

In Africa, most rural farmers are women. According to the U.N. Food and Agriculture Organization, women in sub-Saharan African countries constitute 75 percent of the agricultural workers and provide 60–80 percent of the labor to produce food for household consumption and sale. They are also responsible for 100 percent of the processing of basic foodstuffs, 80 percent of food storage and transport from field to village, 90 percent of the hoeing and weeding work, and 60 percent of the harvesting and marketing activities. Thus women farmers bear more than half of the responsibility for agricultural labor. But their agricultural productivity and access to markets is generally very low. Consequently, women-headed rural households tend to be poorer and more food-insecure than those headed by men.[4]

Women in Africa are often excluded from decisionmaking, lacking a seat at the table in local governance. As a result, the needs of women farmers are often not reflected in local and national agricultural policies. Women are often marginalized in business relations and have minimal control over access to factors of production such as land, inputs such as seed and fertilizer, credit, and technology. Due to a combination of logistical, cultural, and economic factors, they are often not able to benefit fully from development programs and services. By empowering women farmers to advocate for their concerns, the WARM project hopes to ensure that women farmers have what they need to increase their income and provide for their families.[5]

The WARM project uses theater for policy

advocacy to engage women farmers, community leaders, service providers, and policymakers, to encourage community participation, and to research the needs of women farmers. Popular theater personalities travel to communities in Mozambique and Malawi and stage performances using scripts based on FANRPAN's research. After each performance, women, men, young people, and local leaders are encouraged to participate in facilitated dialogues. These give all community members—especially women—a chance to openly talk about the challenges they are facing without being culturally incorrect. More important, they allow women to tell development organizations what they really need—not the other way around.

FANRPAN developed "The Winds of Change" script based on the results of some input subsidy research studies done in Malawi in 2006–09. The play explores challenges rural women face in obtaining farming inputs. It focuses on Nkonkoni, a village headman, who dominates and gives his family and friends preferential access to subsidized farming inputs distributed by government and development agencies. His long-standing practice is to distribute seeds and fertilizer to his cronies, depriving women—among them widows struggling to support their families alone—so much that some have not farmed in three years. But Nkonkoni is eventually challenged by one desperate widow, by the area's newly-elected Member of Parliament, and by his own wife. The conflict over distribution of the inputs highlights the power dynamics as they are played out in the village: between men and women, old and young, urban and rural.[6]

The play was performed for the first time during the 2009 FANRPAN Regional Policy Dialogue in Maputo, Mozambique, to more than 250 delegates from over 22 African countries, representing farmers' organizations, government departments, civil society organizations, research institutions, development partners, and regional economic communities. Following the performance, the audience was asked to join in discussing the main issues that arose during the play.[7]

Linda Nghatsane, a woman farmer and member of the Nelspruit Agricultural Development Association in South Africa, said: "Farmers know what they want." Decisions about agriculture should be made in the outdoors, she noted, under trees and with the people whose livelihood it is to farm—not by those with suits in boardrooms. She stressed that policymakers need to engage in dialogues with farmers to better understand their challenges and wants instead of dictating what they should do.[8]

Ngatshane was supported by former Zambian Deputy Minister of Agriculture and Co-operatives Chance Kabaghe, who said "a farmer knows what he or she wants, but you always have someone at the headquarters deciding to give the farmer what he/she does not want." He called on governments to come up with policies that allow farmers to get access to markets beyond their borders, as this will allow smallholder farmers to take advantage of competitive markets. Cecilia Makota, a Zambian farmer, confirmed that in 2008 she more than quadrupled her income from agriculture after she started selling maize across the border in Zimbabwe.[9]

Obed Dlamini, former Prime Minister of Swaziland and currently a member of Liqoqo, the King's advisory council, applauded the innovative use of theater to amplify women farmers' voices, calling it "a simple but effective method." The WARM project seeks to leverage FANRPAN's experience as a regional multistakeholder policy research network to bridge the divide between women farmers, researchers, and agricultural policy processes. FANRPAN is partnering with other stakeholders—regional and national farmers' organizations, national research institutions, universities, community-based groups, and national and regional policymakers—to ensure that farmers have access to markets, extension services, better seeds, adequate fertilizer, and other important resources.[10]

—Sithembile Ndema
Food, Agriculture and Natural Resources
Policy Analysis Network

What Is an Appropriate Technology?

At the launch of his new book *Science and Innovation for Development* in January 2010, Gordon Conway said: "It doesn't matter where the technology comes from, it matters that it is appropriate." Too often international development researchers, policymakers, and practitioners get caught up in the source of a technology, and use this to measure whether it will be successful. The way a technology is designed, the country it comes from, and the type of institution that produced it are not as important as whether the product is appropriate.[1]

An appropriate technology is accessible, affordable, easy to use and maintain, and effective—and it meets a real need. A rice seed, for example, that has been bred or engineered to mature faster can be appropriate anywhere the variety thrives. Local farmers will usually want to buy this seed—whether it comes from local seed saving efforts or the International Rice Research Institute.

Many scientists and policymakers in industrial countries also often say that you cannot apply different types of technology to the same problem. In fact, this is often exactly what is needed. In drought-prone areas, farmers need "traditional" water conservation techniques and planting methods such as the *zai* system in West Africa, where they use small holes filled with manure and the extensive underground termite tunnels that result to both capture water and recycle soil nutrients.

But they can also use "intermediate" technologies, such as drip irrigation, as well as existing and upcoming "new platform" technologies, such as cereal varieties genetically modified to survive and even prosper in drought conditions. Farmers should have access to all types of solutions. In fact, farmers are often best positioned to choose the optimal combination for their own fields and to innovate as conditions change.

A telling example of the strong bias that some hold for particular sources of technology was revealed at a recent plant biotechnology conference. Some presenters introduced the methods they had been working on to control the parasitic weed *Striga*. On one side was the biological systems approach: intercropping maize with plants that suppress *Striga*. The other side advocated a technological solution: breeding resistance to the herbicide that kills the weed into the maize seeds themselves, so that the seeds can be dipped into the herbicide. The treated maize seeds kill the parasitic seeds in the ground, allowing the maize to grow and the environmental impact to be minimized.[2]

Both systems have drawbacks—more labor and skilled management needed for biological control, and higher research costs and risk of resistance developing for the seed modification approach. So why not use both?

Instead, the two sides argued. And when another presenter suggested using more conventional herbicides in Africa, it was met with immediate derision, due partly to the source of the herbicides (U.S. manufacturers). Most did not consider the fact that conventional herbicides, if applied in an educated and selective manner, may be a great tool for poor farmers.

But this may be changing. As Jeff Waage, coauthor of *Science and Innovation for Development*, stated: "Between the extremes of a technological 'silver bullet' approach to development science, and the belief that local and intermediate technologies are the only legitimate approach, there is emerging today a new community of scientists dedicated to an inclusive view of appropriate science for development."[3]

—*Sara Delaney*
Imperial College, London

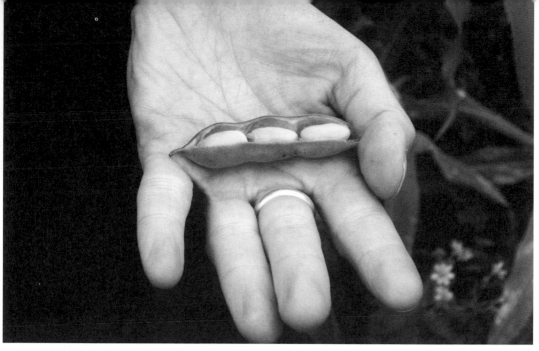

Broad beans in Ethiopia

CHAPTER 12

Investing in Africa's Land: Crisis and Opportunity

Andrew Rice

Robert Zeigler, an eminent American botanist, flew to Saudi Arabia in March 2009 for a series of high-level discussions about the future of the kingdom's food supply. Saudi leaders were nervous. Heavily dependent on imports, they had seen the price of rice and wheat, their dietary staples, fluctuate violently on the world market over the previous three years, at one point doubling in just a few months. The Saudis, rich in oil money but poor in arable land, were groping for a strategy to ensure that they could continue to meet the appetites of a growing population, and they wanted Zeigler's expertise.[1]

There are basically two ways to increase the supply of food: find new fields to plant or invent ways to multiply the yield from existing ones. Zeigler runs the International Rice Research Institute (IRRI), which is devoted to the latter course, using science to expand the size of harvests. During the so-called Green Revolution of the 1960s, IRRI's laboratory developed "miracle rice," a high-yielding strain that has been credited with

---

Andrew Rice is the author of *The Teeth May Smile but the Heart Does Not Forget: Murder and Memory in Uganda*. This chapter is based on an article he published in 2009 in the *New York Times Magazine*, "Is There Such a Thing as Agro-Imperialism?"

saving millions of people from famine. Zeigler went to Saudi Arabia hoping that the wealthy kingdom might offer money for the basic research that leads to such technological breakthroughs. Instead, to his surprise, he discovered that the Saudis wanted to attack the problem from the opposite direction. They were looking for land.

Saudi government officials, bankers, and agribusiness executives told an IRRI delegation led by Zeigler that they intended to spend billions of dollars to establish plantations to produce rice and other staple crops in African nations like Mali, Senegal, Sudan, and Ethiopia. Zeigler was flabbergasted, not only by the scale of the projects but also by the audacity of their setting. Africa, the world's most famished continent, cannot currently feed itself, let alone foreign markets.[2]

Robert Zeigler was catching a glimpse of an emerging test of the world's food resources, one that has begun to take shape over the last few years, largely outside the bounds of international scrutiny. A variety of factors—some transitory, like the spike in food prices, and others intractable, like global population growth and water scarcity—have created a market for farmland, as rich but resource-deprived nations in the Middle East, Asia, and elsewhere seek to "outsource" their food production to places where fields are cheap and abundant. Because much of the world's arable land is already in use—almost 90 percent, according to one estimate, if you take out forests and fragile ecosystems—the search has led to the countries so far least touched by development. One of Earth's last large reserves of underused land is the billion-acre Guinea savanna zone, a crescent-shaped swath that runs east across Africa all the way to Ethiopia and southward to Congo and Angola. According to a study co-sponsored by the U.N. Food and Agriculture Organization (FAO) and the World Bank, only 10 percent of the zone's arable land is currently cropped.[3]

Foreign investors—some of them representing governments, others private interests—are promising to construct infrastructure, bring new technologies such as improved seeds, create jobs, and boost the productivity of underused land so that it not only feeds overseas markets but also feeds more Africans. (More than a third of the continent's population is malnourished.) They have found that impoverished governments are often only too welcoming, offering land at giveaway prices. A few transactions have received significant publicity, like Kenya's deal to lease nearly 100,000 acres to the Qatari government in return for financing a new port, or South Korea's agreement to develop almost 400 square miles in Tanzania. But many other land deals, of nearly unprecedented size, have been sealed with little fanfare.[4]

Yet even as proponents of the investments extol their potential benefits for agricultural advancement in sub-Saharan Africa, some critics are raising an alarm, decrying the investments as "land grabs." They say that the transactions taking place are exploitative, and they predict that the outcome will not be development but a litany of dire possible consequences: xenophobia, riots, coups, and more hunger. "This is quite serious and quite dangerous," said Alexandra Spieldoch of the Institute for Agriculture and Trade Policy. "What's at stake is the direction of international development, food security, and control over resources."[5]

More recently, and perhaps in response to highly publicized controversial land deals, the focus has shifted to alternative business models as a meeting point for involved parties. A 2010 report commissioned by a number of intergovernmental agencies, including FAO, assessed in great detail these community-investor partnerships. While the results were mixed, building an understanding of what makes for a successful collaboration is paramount as the demand for land becomes more intense.[6]

Ethiopia's Land Rush

Ethiopia might seem an unlikely hotbed of agricultural investment. To most of the world, the country is defined by images of famine: about a million people died there during the drought of the mid-1980s, and today about four times that many depend on emergency food aid. But according to the World Bank, as much as three quarters of Ethiopia's arable land is not under cultivation, and agronomists say that with substantial capital expenditure, much of it could become bountiful. Since the world food crisis, Prime Minister Meles Zenawi, a former Marxist rebel who has turned into a champion of private capital, has publicly said he is "very eager" to attract foreign farm investors by offering them what the government describes as "virgin land." An Ethiopian agriculture ministry official told Reuters in 2009 that he has identified more than 7 million acres ripe for investment.[7]

The government's pliant attitude and Ethiopia's convenient location have made this country an ideal target for Middle Eastern investors, including Sheikh Mohammed Al Amoudi, a Saudi Arabia–based oil-and-construction billionaire who was born in Ethiopia and maintains a close relationship with Zenawi's regime. Not long ago, a newly formed Al Amoudi company, Saudi Star Agricultural Development, announced its plans to obtain the rights to more than a million acres—a land mass the size of Delaware—in the apparent hope of capitalizing on the Saudi government's initiative to subsidize overseas staple-crop production.[8]

Al Amoudi's plans raise a recurring question surrounding investment in food production: who will reap the benefits? Since the Green Revolution helped nations like India and China, scientists and policymakers have been trying to achieve similar productivity increases in sub-Saharan Africa. President Barack Obama—who in a passage of his inaugural speech that addressed the world's poor said "we pledge to work alongside you to make your farms flourish"—has made food security issues a foreign policy priority. Yet despite decades of research and millions in grants, the international community of specialists who concern themselves with feeding the planet have little to show for their African efforts.[9]

Advocates of private investment say that it is time to try another approach. "Africa is the final frontier," says Susan Payne, the chief executive of Emergent Asset Management, which is in the process of investing several hundred million dollars into commercial farms around the continent through its new African Agricultural Land Fund. Thus far, most established financial firms have been wary of investments in the developing world. Payne believes that they are missing a golden opportunity: Africa may be known for decrepit infrastructure and corrupt governments—problems that are being steadily alleviated, Payne argues—but land and labor come so cheaply there that she calculates the risks are worthwhile.[10]

Within the international aid community, which has watched the nascent expansion of agricultural investment in Africa with some trepidation, there has been much talk of using subtle tools, such as nonbinding codes of conduct, to encourage "win-win" investments. But in Ethiopia, foreign investors are not waiting for instructions. A supervisor at Mohammed Al Amoudi's farm near Lake Ziway, where dozens of laborers plant corn and onions in fields dotted with massive sycamore, said that the 2,000-acre enterprise currently produces food for the local market but that there were plans to irrigate with water from the lake and to shift the focus to exports.[11]

Workers here do not get paid much—just around nine birr each day, or around 75¢—but Al Amoudi's defenders say that is the going rate for farm labor in Ethiopia. They argue that his investments are creating jobs, improving the productivity of dormant land, and bringing economic development to rural communities. Ethiopian journalists and opposition figures, however, have questioned the economic benefits of the deals, as well as Al Amoudi's cozy relationship with the ruling party.[12]

Explosive Potentials

By far the most powerful opposition surrounds the issue of land rights—a problem of historic proportions in Ethiopia. Just down the road from the farm on Lake Ziway there is a modest village. Its residents tell a resentful story. Decades ago, they say, during the rule of a Communist dictatorship in Ethiopia, the land was confiscated from them. After that dictatorship was overthrown, Al Amoudi took over the farm in a government privatization deal, over the futile objections of the displaced locals. The billionaire might consider the land his, but the villagers have long memories, and they angrily maintain that they are its rightful owners.[13]

Throughout Africa, the politics of land is linked to the grim reality of hunger. Famines, typically produced by some combination of weather, pestilence, and bad governance, break out with merciless randomness, unleashing calamity and reshaping history. Every country has its unique dynamics. Under the present regime in Ethiopia, private ownership of land is banned, and every farmer, foreign or domestic, works the fields under a licensing arrangement with the government. This land tenure policy has made it possible for a one-party state to hand over huge tracts to investors at nominal rents, in secrecy, without the bother of a legal process.[14]

Ethiopia's government denies that anyone is being displaced, saying that the land is unused—an assertion many experts doubt. "One thing that is very clear, that seems to have escaped the attention of most investors, is that this is not simply empty land," says Michael Taylor, a policy specialist at the International Land Coalition. If land in Africa has not been planted, he says, it is probably for a reason. Maybe it's used to graze livestock or deliberately left fallow to prevent nutrient depletion and erosion.[15]

Of course, there have been scrambles for African land before. But it was not until October 2008, when the international advocacy group GRAIN compiled a long list of such deals into a polemical report entitled *Seized!*, that experts really began to talk about a serious trend. Although deals were being brokered in disparate locales like Australia, Kazakhstan, Ukraine, and Vietnam, the most controversial field of investment was clearly Africa. (See Table 12–1.) Within a month, GRAIN's warnings seemed to be vindicated when the *Financial Times* broke news that the South Korean conglomerate Daewoo Logistics had signed an agreement to take over about half of Madagascar's arable land, paying nothing, with the intention of growing corn and palm oil for export. Popular protests broke out, helping to mobilize opposition to Madagascar's already unpopular president, who was overthrown in a coup in March 2009.[16]

But there's more than one side to the argument. Development economists and African governments say that if a country like Ethiopia is ever going to feed itself, let alone wean itself from foreign aid, which totaled $2.4 billion in 2007, it will have to find some way of increasing the productivity of its agriculture.[17]

Traditionally, the model for feeding hungry people in countries like Ethiopia has involved shipping in surpluses from the rest of the world in times of emergency, but governments that are trying to attract investment say that the new farms could provide a lasting, noncharitable solution. Whatever the long-term justification, however, it looks bad politically for countries like Kenya and Ethiopia to be letting foreign investors use their land at a time when their people face the specter of mass starvation.

Table 12–1. Selected Proposed and Completed Foreign Investments in Land in Africa

Investor	Host Country	Details of Arrangement
Various companies	Mali	Already approved land deals include a joint 10,000-hectare project between Petrotech and AgroMali to produce biodiesel feedstock from jatropha seeds for Europe, the United States, and Egypt. Additional long-term leases for outside investors to help develop more than 160,000 hectares of land. (Reported December 2009)
Ruchi Soy Industries	Ethiopia	A leading edible oil processor, Ruchi Soy, signed a memorandum of understanding with the Ethiopian government to cultivate soybeans and install a processing unit in Gambella and Benishangul Gumuz. The deal includes 25,000 hectares (with the possibility of expanding to 50,000 hectares) and the lease basis is 25 years. (Announced January 2010)
Trans4mation Agric-Tech Ltd. (U.K.)	Nigeria	T4M signed a 25-year contract to grow and process rice and cassava, in a large-scale commercial and mechanized way, on 30,000 hectares of land in the Niger delta. (Reported in 2008)
Saudi Arabia	Sierra Leone	Sierra Leone and Saudi Arabia signed a Memorandum of Understanding for Saudi investment in the production of rice for home consumption and export. (Reported December 2009)
Foras International Investment Co. (Saudi Arabia)	Sudan	The investment arm of the Islamic Chamber of Commerce and Industry launched its first project to ensure food security: the Al-Faihaa Integrated agricultural project, in Sudan's Sennar state. The seven-year project has an estimated investment of $200 million and covers about 126,000 hectares. (Reported January 2010)
South Korea (private sector)	Sudan	As of the end of 2008, the Sudanese government had committed 690,000 hectares of land for South Koreans to grow wheat for export back home. (Reported February 2010)

continued next page

A Lasting Appetite

Some experts, echoing Thomas Robert Malthus, the nineteenth-century prophet of overpopulation and famine, warn that humanity is on the verge of outgrowing its food supply. Others believe that the world will always be able to invent new ways of increasing productivity, especially if we increase agricultural investment sectors. FAO has made just such a proposal, calling Africa a "sleeping giant" of agriculture, while the World Bank, reversing decades of de-emphasis, has recently been talking up farming's potential for leading economic growth. The Bank estimates that "GDP growth originating in agriculture is at least twice as effective in reducing poverty" as development in other sectors.[18]

Yet agriculture has historically been a tiny item in foreign aid budgets. For years, governments, private foundations, and donor institutions like the World Bank have been urging African governments to fill the spending gap with private investment. Now, at the very moment a world food crisis has come along, creating the perhaps fleeting possibility of an influx of capital into African agriculture, some of those same organizations are sending con-

Table 12–1 continued		
Investor	**Host Country**	**Details of Arrangement**
HADCO (Saudi Arabia)	Sudan	To acquire more than 10,000 hectares north of Khartoum for production of wheat and corn for export, Saudi agribusiness firm Hail Agricultural Development Company (HADCO) committed $45.3 million, while the state-owned Saudi Industrial Development Fund promised about 60 percent of the project costs. (Reported February 2009)
Chongqing Seep Corp (China)	Tanzania, Nigeria	In 2008, China's Chongqing Seed Corp announced it had selected 300 hectares of land for production of hybrid rice in Tanzania. Plans were to hire local farmers to produce and export the harvest to China. Chongqing began similar projects in Nigeria and Laos in 2006. (Reported May 2008)
China (private sector)	Uganda	Uganda leased 4,046 hectares to be farmed by 400 Chinese farmers using imported Chinese seeds. The project is overseen by Liu Jianjun, head of the China–Africa Business Council, and the farmers grow corn and other crops. (Reported April 2008)
United States, United Arab Emirates	Zambia	Agriculture Minister Brian Chituwo indicated Zambia had a surplus of prime farmland and expressed no hesitation about making deals with companies from the United States and the United Arab Emirates who expressed interest in establishing large farms to grow sugar and grains (including for ethanol production), as well as with a Dubai company that wants to grow rice or wheat. (Reported June 2009)

Source: See endnote 16.

flicting messages. FAO, for instance, cosponsored a report calling for a major expansion of commercial agriculture in Africa, but the organization's Director-General has simultaneously been warning of the "neocolonial" dangers of land deals.[19]

In theory, investments could yield immense payoffs. In a country like Ethiopia, farmers put in backbreaking effort, but they yield about a third as much wheat per acre as do farmers in Europe, China, or Chile. Even modest interventions could start to close this gap. With the addition of advanced implements, improved seeds, and fertilizer, the wheat yield in the Great Rift region's rich clay soil can double. Ethiopia, like all of Africa, is full of such opportunities—situations that, with wise investment, could be turned to fill both stomachs

and wallets. The key, say many experts, is including Africans in the process of their own development. "You...propose to go and invest in a county you don't know anything about and you don't want to speak to the local people?" Chido Makunike, a Zimbabwean-born commercial farmer said at a conference on the land acquisition phenomenon in May 2009. "I don't get it—I do not understand from a purely business perspective how that can make sense. Agriculture and farming are risky enough as it is."[20]

Makunike makes a crucial point: uneven business deals are not just morally objectionable and detrimental to the interests of poor farmers—they are also bad business. When Madagascar's president was overthrown, the South Korean conglomerate that had struck the land deal saw its investment plans go up in smoke, and it endured an onslaught of negative publicity. Hoping to avoid such embarrassments, last year the prime minister of Japan—a country that imports more food than it produces—began pushing for an international code of conduct to govern land investments. FAO has recently held a series of regional meetings in an attempt to create what they call voluntary guidelines for good governance when it comes to land.[21]

Of course, the problematic word is "voluntary." If Ethiopia and Saudi Arabia, both ruled by opaque and authoritarian governments, decide they want to cut a land deal, what can international organizations do, other than frown? And what right do they have to take stronger action? When representatives of U.N. agencies and nongovernmental organizations, many of them from nations with a long history of large-scale agribusiness, come forth with lectures about proper investment, developing nations can be forgiven for detecting a whiff of paternalism. So, can anything be done? There are no one-size-fits-all solutions, but devising reforms that answer a few simple questions could go a long way toward assuring that agricultural investments are channeled to mutual benefit.

First, who owns what? Most experts agree that, before land changes hands, it is crucial to determine who in fact owns it in the first place—a thorny problem in developing nations, where much land is held under undocumented customary systems. Studies show that when land is legally titled, its economic productivity improves. An assessment of a 1984 initiative that issued 8.5 million titles over 5 million hectares in Thailand, for instance, found that after 16 years the land was yielding larger harvests, selling at higher prices, and giving its owners greater access to credit. At a recent World Bank

conference on the issue of land rights, speakers emphasized that even rudimentary steps, like making maps that delineate property ownership, would go a long way toward ensuring the interests of smallholders.[22]

A farmer in Mozambique shares information on selecting the best seed for the next planting season

Second, who calls the shots? Much of the international community's effort on the issue of private investment in agriculture has been directed toward encouraging local consultation by both government and investors before deals are struck. In theory, almost everyone agrees with the principle that people living where agricultural investment is directed should give their free prior and informed consent. In practice, however, deciding what constitutes consent, and how it is obtained, has been easier said than done. Take the case of Mozambique. It farms only about 4 million of its 34 million hectares of arable land, and not long ago its government declared that it was open for foreign investment. It instituted a policy of consultation with local communities. But the meetings turned out to be flawed, scant on information, and dominated by local chiefs to the exclusion of small stakeholders and women. There was an enormous amount of confusion, some of it deliberate. Some parcels were "sold" three times to different sets of investors. The system was eventually overwhelmed by chaos and demand; after receiving proposals totaling 13 million hectares, the government imposed a hasty moratorium to prevent "another Zimbabwe."[23]

And third, who is going to pay? There is general agreement that investment in agriculture needs to increase in the world's poorest nations. This includes funding for physical infrastructure, agricultural education, and research, which has declined in half of all African nations over the last 10 years. Yet during the global recession, many donor nations have found their foreign aid budgets sharply constricted. But there's hope. Africa's economies have done relatively well compared with their First World peers—the International Monetary Fund was forecasting that gross domestic product growth in sub-Saharan Africa would rise to nearly 6 percent in 2010—and that makes the continent an increasingly attractive field for private investment.[24]

In addition, there are many ways to invest in farming without removing the African farmers. David Hallam, an FAO trade expert, has suggested a model in which large-scale commercial farms, owned by international investors, operate in "a symbiotic relationship" with smallholders who sell them their harvests and receive payments, credit, and technical assistance in return. Another idea, which has mixed but promising results in nations like Zambia, is the "outgrower" model, in which smallholders handle all the production, and a larger company packages their goods and sells them, either domestically or overseas. In Ethiopia's Rift Valley region, one such a cooperative scheme involves a group of around 300 Ethiopians, working plots of 4–10 acres. During the European winter, they grow green beans for the Dutch market. The rest of the year, they cultivate corn and other crops for local consumption. The land has been irrigated with the help of a nonprofit organization and an Ethiopian commercial farmer named Tsegaye Abebe, who brings all the produce to market.[25]

A group of farmers in this cooperative said that the arrangement, while not perfect, was beneficial in the most crucial respect: they were not toiling for someone else. They had heard rumors that foreign investors were eyeing Ethiopian land. Imam Gemedo Tilago, a 78-year-old cloaked in a white cotton shawl, shook his finger, vowing that Allah would not allow the community to remain passive. But that was a problem for the future, and the farmers had more grounded concerns. Driving down the rural paths that led to this farm, it was evident that the earth was parched, and the cattle were showing their ribs through their dull brown hides. The worried farmers said that this year, the seasonal rains were late in coming to the Rift Valley. If they did not arrive soon, there'd be hunger.[26]

Better Food Storage

No farmer wants the fruits—and vegetables—of his or her labor to go to waste. But in some parts of sub-Saharan Africa, where more than 265 million people are hungry, more than a quarter of the food that is produced is going bad before it can be eaten because of poor harvest or storage techniques, severe weather, or disease and pests. Annual post-harvest losses for cereal grains, roots and tuber crops, fruits, vegetables, meat, milk, and fish amount to some 100 million tons, or $48 million worth of food.[1]

Ziyelesa Banda is one of the peasant farmers in Mambwe district of Zambia's Eastern Province who for many years has had to deal with termites and other pests destroying crops. On one hectare, farmers produce between 2.5 tons and 2.8 tons of maize annually, but termites destroy about 20 percent of the harvest. Banda also has to deal with the cassava mosaic virus.[2]

Sunduzwayo Banda, an agricultural extension officer, estimated that $260 is lost per year out of the almost $760 he anticipates earning from the sale of the harvest. In a country where most people live on less than $1 a day, that loss is monumental.[3]

Ziyelesa Banda and other farmers stand to benefit from technology being developed by the National Institute for Scientific Research and Industrial Relations (NISIR) and other research institutions. "Here at NISIR, we want to start producing a pesticide [by] working with Mindeco small mines, which produces talc powder," said Ray Handema, the Institute's acting executive director. The mines are paying for NISIR to find out how effective the talc powder is as a pesticide. With laboratory work complete, NISIR is now beginning field tests. Handema said that with Zambia importing most of its pesticides, NISIR intends to "find a local solution to local problems" by using locally produce materials with technology developed in Zambia.[4]

The Community Markets for Conservation, which services a network of farmers in the Eastern Province of Zambia, has begun acquiring grain bags from GrainPro, Inc. of the Philippines to protect maize from weevils and grain borers. "Through its pesticide-free hermetic storage technology, post-harvest losses of grains, seeds, and high-value crops, particularly in hot, humid climates, are prevented," noted Daniel Tesfaye Haileselassie, GrainPro's Africa Sales & Marketing Manager. "GrainPro's patented Cocoons—flexible hermetic enclosures—allow safe storage of such crops as rice, corn, and wheat and such high-value crops as coffee, cocoa, and peanuts for very long periods of time, preventing damage from insects, rodents, and molds. Seed storage to preserve germination capability using hermetic storage is another big 'win' and is now used in a rapidly growing number of countries."[5]

Another option for protecting crops is storage bags like those developed by Purdue University, called Purdue Improved Cowpea Storage (PICS). These are hermetically sealed to prevent contamination from oxygen and pests and, according to Purdue president Martin C. Jischke, "the method is simple, safe, inexpensive, and very effective." In western Africa, cow peas provide protein to millions of people. Unlike maize, cow peas are indigenous to the region and have adapted to local growing conditions, making them an ideal source of food.[6]

In addition to preserving an important seasonal crop year-round, the PICS bags also save farmers money on expensive pesticides. With support from the Bill & Melinda Gates Foundation, the PICS project hopes to reach 28,000 villages in Benin, Burkina Faso, Cameroon, Chad, Ghana, Mali, Niger, Nigeria, Senegal, and Togo by 2011.[7]

"Most food goes to waste because we have no processing facilities," Ray Handema of NISIR said. But mangoes, papaya, tomatoes, and other fruit can be preserved by dehydration using low-cost driers. Groundnut and sweet potatoes can be boiled and dried to help make them last longer. NISIR is also making lemonade drink as a way of packaging lemons, and it is making wine from wild fruits like masuku and mpundu.[8]

Processing foods can also help farmers make a more appealing product. In Kenya, the Mazingira Institute is training communities how to process foods to preserve them longer and make them more appetizing to consumers. The institute helped Esther Mjoki Maifa of Nairobi, for example, capitalize on a growing interest among Kenyans for natural healthy products by training her to process groundnuts without any preserves or chemicals. It takes her about one day to produce 50 kilograms of groundnuts, and she sells jars for about $2.50–$3.50 each. Maifa is hoping to eventually make enough money from her products to purchase her own nut grinding machine.[9]

Pasteurization, along with other processing methods, can also help prolong the shelf life—and value—of foods. Unpasteurized milk can spoil easily, so pasteurization—which requires the milk to be heated to a specific point, thereby killing pathogenic bacteria—is critical. But as with refrigeration, most farmers do not have access to the facilities they need to process and produce a higher-quality milk product.

In Kenya, Uganda, and Rwanda, the East Africa Dairy Development (EADD) project is helping livestock farmers improve the processing and preservation of milk in order to produce longer-lasting products that are also better tasting and safer for the consumer. EADD encourages farmers to join cooperatives, giving them access to group-owned and -run refrigerated milk collection centers and significantly reducing the financial burden. The milk is sent to a processing facility and then to market, where it will receive a higher price than unpasteurized milk.[10]

Improved local food production and markets would protect local economies while also improving access to food and reducing waste. When Iceland's volcano erupted in April 2010 and grounded all flights in Europe, piles of gourmet produce and cut flowers—some of Kenya's chief exports—rotted in limbo. Meant to be shipped to upscale grocery stores throughout Europe, lilies, roses, carnations, carrots, onions, baby sweet corn, and sugar snap peas went bad in heaps, on the vine, and in the ground because airport warehouses were already full and there was no local market for this expensive produce.[11]

As food prices continue to rise worldwide, reducing food waste will be a critical element in alleviating global hunger and poverty. Even small steps such as improved storage, growing vegetables in backyards, and simple processing techniques can reduce waste significantly.

—*Benedict Tembo, Zambia Daily Mail*
—*Molly Theobald, Worldwatch Institute*

Bernard Pollack

Peanuts for sale at the Grand Marche outside Niamey, Niger

CHAPTER 13

The Missing Links:
Going Beyond Production

Samuel Fromartz

When people talk about African agriculture, food surpluses are not usually the focus of discussion. Invariably, the more familiar topics are famine, starvation, deforestation, and the vast inability of a continent to feed itself, which is brought home by the latest food crisis.

That's why the headlines in Lusaka, Zambia, in May 2010, were so surprising, announcing a stunning bumper crop of maize. On the back of fertilizer subsidies and propitious rains, production by the nation's 800,000 maize farmers had rocketed 48 percent to the high-est level in 22 years. This boom came after a 31-percent rise the previous year. Now speculation was mounting about a crash in maize prices, especially during the dry June-August period. "A tidal wave of maize will be hitting the market," predicted Rob Munro, a senior market development advisor for the U.S. Agency for International Development (AID) in Lusaka.[1]

In the cities, the focus was on the price of mealie meal, the porridge-like staple made from ground maize, and whether millers would pass on savings or fatten their profit margins.

Samuel Fromartz is the author of *Organic, Inc.*, a food blogger, and a contributor to the *Washington Post* Food Section.

The government was fretting about what to do with all this food. Zambia had a 600,000-ton surplus from the 2009 harvest, some of which was still sitting in warehouses. And now on top of that, it would reap a 1.1 million–ton surplus for 2010. Exports were uncertain, because of sporadic trade restrictions. Plus, the crop was uncompetitive with South African maize, the low-cost producer in the region.[2]

Zambia was growing so much food that the food itself had become an issue. Yet, it was also an unequivocal success. Zambian farmers had produced more than enough maize and done so without genetically modified crops or even, for the most part, irrigation and mechanized farm equipment. But further development raised a number of questions: If farmers actually modernized and improved their yields, would the surplus be even greater, dwarfing any political ability to deal with this bounty? And why were people still facing chronic hunger and childhood stunting in a country where the food was in oversupply?

Food Security from the Ground Up

In a way, Zambia's situation provides the perfect case study of a value chain—that is, all the steps it takes to produce food and bring it to market. (See Box 13–1.) Too often, the issue of food security gets reduced to a sound bite to "feed 9 billion by 2050" that in turn is wrapped around a new and possibly genetically modified seed. But while magic bullets are enticing, they are far from a comprehensive solution. Indeed they amount to a simplistic, even misguided, approach if divorced from the larger context of agriculture: where and how the farmer gets seed and inputs and how much he or she pays for them; whether there is ample labor and equipment; whether timely extension advice is available; whether there are viable markets to sell the crop; whether prices are transparent; and whether, at the end of the day, the farmers have made enough money

to buy food and send their kids to school, and perhaps even to lift themselves out of poverty. A seed and a sound bite do not address these problems, nor will the single-minded aim of more production without attention to these details, as the case of Zambia shows.[3]

These issues come into focus rumbling down a potted dirt road in Mkushi, in the heart of Zambia's maize belt about three hours northwest of Lusaka. Advisers from AID's PROFIT (Production, Finance, and Technology) Program are headed out to the "bush" to meet with farmers. This innovative $17-million "private-sector development program" launched in 2005 sought to work with existing businesses to jump-start smallholder agriculture. It did so by first making inputs available to the farmers—not by a handout but by explaining to input dealers that the small farmer was a valuable and viable market. Then they sought to open new channels for the farmers to sell to, since the odds were so often stacked against small farmers in traditional distribution channels. In 2009, PROFIT estimated, the projects generated more than $14 million in earnings for the 150,000 farmers who participated in some way.[4]

In the bush outside Mkushi, thatched-hut villages are surrounded by maize fields that farmers work by hand. Much larger "commercial farms," with huge mechanical booms irrigating maize and wheat crops, stretch into the distance alongside the dirt road—no different than a corn field in Iowa. Many of the commercial farmers immigrated from Zimbabwe after their lands were appropriated; they are doing quite well in the investor-friendly Zambian climate. These modern commercial farms (about 700–800 of them), along with the top 4 percent of smallholder farmers, grow about half of the nation's maize.[5]

They are in a wholly different realm from the vast majority of Zambia's small-scale farmers, who work with hoes, oxen, or, if they are lucky, a tractor. These 750,000 farmers grow

Box 13–1. A Better Deal

Matooke, or green bananas, are Uganda's top food crop, but the traditional means of distribution benefits neither the farmer nor the wholesaler. Buyers set up in farming towns, then hire "bicycle boys" who make the rounds gathering bananas from farmers. The farmers generally have little knowledge of the market and a great deal of distrust of the traders.

With such robust banana demand, Techno-Serve, a U.S.-based nongovernmental group, thought the crop might generate income for the farmers if the problems in the market could be addressed. This was just one of many recent attempts in Africa to improve the value chain by connecting farmers with input dealers, building transparency into sales, using mobile technology to deliver pricing and market data, arranging microfinance loans—and improving transactions for buyers and sellers.

TechnoServe first encouraged Ugandan banana farmers to form business groups, which would buy inputs, offer technical advice to farmers, and also sell their crop. Group rep-

resentatives met with banana buyers, discussing pricing structures, product requirements, and distribution points.

By aggregating farmers, transaction costs declined dramatically. "The price farmers receive has improved by about 70 percent," said Eratus Kibugu, Uganda Country Director for Technoserve. "The buyer is able to pass on his savings because he's no longer losing money from inefficiencies built into the marketing chain."

About 20,000 farmers now participate in the Uganda banana project. TechnoServe also engaged a bank lender to provide microfinance loans after the farmers sought to expand their farms. The loans average a few hundred dollars, and repayment rates have been 97 percent.

In Kenya, vegetable and horticultural farmers had a similar problem. The prices they received from traders were far lower than in the wholesale market in Nairobi, where their

continued next page

the remaining 50 percent of the maize crop. Because they lack irrigation, smallholder farmers plant maize in November just before the rains arrive and then harvest the crop in April when the rainy season ends. For the dry winter months, little field work is done unless the farmer has managed to set up an irrigation system. Treadle pumps, the foot-operated pumps that can channel water from streams or wells, are popular with those who want to diversify into vegetable crops during the winter. The abundant sunny days and mild climate of the winter months are perfect for high-value crops like tomatoes. But without a water source, or the cash to buy a pump, the farmers sell maize and then wait for the rains to return in the spring. That's why 35 percent of these small farmers are net buyers of food during the year.[6]

As in other regions of Africa, the end of the harvest marks a tricky time for these farmers, since they slowly consume the portion of the crop they have saved or buy food with the money they've made on crop sales. By December, food stocks and money typically run low. "The farmers run out of food and then they have to work hard in the fields, with very little to eat," Mabvuto Chisi, PROFIT's business adviser in Mkushi, points out. "December to March are the hardest months, because they are working and waiting for the harvest in April." This is doubly tough for women in single-parent households, who account for about one-in-five agricultural households.[7]

Down a long dirt road in the countryside, many women walk on the side of the road carrying goods and babies. Children in school uniforms carry hand hoes, ready to work in the

Box 13–1 continued

product eventually ended up. A venture known as DrumNet now links the farmers to the market, so that they can make better decisions and more advantageous sales. DrumNet plans to offer a range of for-fee services over the Internet, including market linkages, real-time prices, coordination of produce transport, and group purchase of farm inputs.

Cell phones have also played an important role across Africa in providing market data and even transaction capabilities, often by text messages, which are cheaper than voice calls. In Niger, mobile phone use for market information has cut the variation in regional grain prices by 20 percent. It also reduced traders' search costs by 50 percent and provided information so that farmers could plan in response to grain surpluses and shortages. E-soko, a mobile phone company in Africa, offers yet another example, since it provides price data from 300 markets and can track specific commodities. The data can also be uploaded to the Web so that farmers can

see market information over time.

Another technological innovation, brought to Uganda by the Grameen Foundation in June 2009, is the Google Trader. With a grant from the Bill and Melinda Gates Foundation, this technology connects farmers with the larger market through an online "bulletin board." In addition, an application called Farmer's Friend provides farmers with regional weather forecasts and information on livestock and crop pest and disease control, as well as planting and storage tips.

In another example, the Zambia National Farmers Union, supported by the International Fund for Agricultural Development, provides market prices and traders' contact information through text messaging and a Web site. It currently has 30,000 clients who compare and negotiate prices and then arrange for transactions. The project will soon be expanded to the Democratic Republic of Congo.

—*Samuel Fromartz and Abigail Massey*
Source: See endnote 3.

fields. Occasionally someone rides by on a bicycle. A few have strapped bags of maize to their bicycles or carry them by hand. Children who look as young as five balance a sack of maize on their heads. These bags weigh about 50 kilograms (110 pounds) when full, though the ones children carry are smaller.

The farmers haul the maize to drop-off points on the side of the road, where the bags are piled high. Trucks come to haul the crop away, and the farmers go home with whatever they can get from these grain dealers, usually about 20,000–25,000 kwacha ($4–5) a bag. Often the price is cut because of perceived inferior quality—too many broken kernels, dirty maize, and so on. A farmer who grows one hectare (2.5 acres) of maize that yields about 1.7 tons ends up with about 34 bags of maize. That earns around $170 before

expenses for fertilizer, seed, or the bags themselves. And that is only if the entire crop is sold, which it isn't, because some is held back for food and seed. Two hectares (five acres) of maize is the outer limit for a farmer working alone, which means a fairly meager income even in a good year. Many do not have the luxury of picking when to sell or whom to sell to; they are desperate and need to sell to eat. So they take whatever price they can get. Griping about unfair transactions is common, but there is little alternative.[8]

Along the road, farmers' markets are bustling, stocked with bulbous eggplants and giant sweet potatoes, tomatoes, and cucumbers. While these rural areas are poor, lacking running water, paved roads, and any sign of electricity (aside from cell phones), no one appears to be starving. "Here, everyone can get at least one meal a day," says Wilson Mwape, a farm equipment dealer traveling with the AID team, who grew up in the Mkushi area. In the maize belt, people are getting by, so the issue then becomes, how can they improve their lot rather than live hand to mouth? Raising yield is part of the equation, since it will translate into higher productivity. But it is not just yield, because massive production could send prices tumbling. That is what appeared to be happening in 2010, when the amount of land planted increased by a fifth, maize yields shot up 22 percent, and the amount of corn actually harvested rather than abandoned in fields rose as well. (See Figures 13–1 and 13–2.) So how might a farmer navigate this boom-and-bust world?[9]

Justine Chiyesu, an "emerging farmer" who represents perhaps 4 percent of Zambia's farmers—a small but notable commercial group—provides an answer. He lives in the village of Chikupiloi, about 60 kilometers from Mkushi, deep in the bush, in a brick house with a tin roof that is a step up from the thatched huts of his neighbors. He has two cell phones, one of which frequently chimes in a low voice, "boss, you have a text message." He sports an Armani blazer. Despite these signs of success, there is no electricity in his village (solar chargers are used for cell phones). There is only a one-room schoolhouse, and most of his neighbors still harvest grain by hand, pounding the dried corn husk

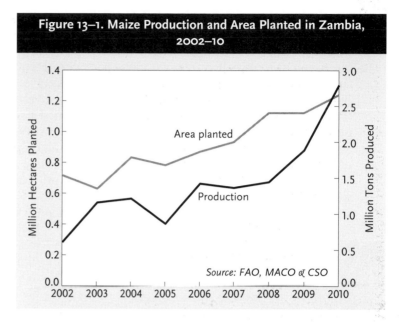

Figure 13–1. Maize Production and Area Planted in Zambia, 2002–10

Source: FAO, MACO & CSO

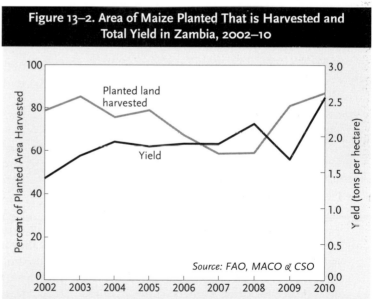

Figure 13–2. Area of Maize Planted That is Harvested and Total Yield in Zambia, 2002–10

Source: FAO, MACO & CSO

with a stick over a wood grate to release the kernels. Chiyesu has a mechanical threshing machine and is looking to buy a new one, which is why the equipment dealer, Mwape, is traveling with the AID workers. In many ways, Chiyesu is living in two worlds: among the small farmers, but no longer one of them.[10]

His trajectory is remarkable, considering that he just started farming a few years earlier. He began with two hectares, working the land with a hand hoe and an ox-drawn plow. But there were limits. "My family is just too small, so two hectares was just too much to do manually," he said. "When I started weeding, by the time I reached the end of the field, the maize would be taken over by the weeds." The first year, he harvested 54 bags of maize, yielding 1.3 tons per hectare, about average for a small farmer.[11]

A farmer contemplates his stunted maize during a 2006 drought in Southern Province, Zambia

When he heard, through the PROFIT program, about an opportunity to become a local agent for an input company, he jumped at the chance. He could raise his yields but also act as a dealer for other farmers in the area. He trained in applying the chemicals correctly, then strapped a sprayer on his back and doused the weeds in his fields with herbicide. With twice as much land and the aid of these inputs, he more than tripled his yield to 4.3 tons per hectare . He expanded over the next few years to 37 hectares and currently had a labor force

of eight full-time workers and more than 30 seasonal workers.[12]

Since he did not have a bank account until very recently, he had managed by stuffing millions of kwacha (tens of thousands of dollars) into bags, piling clothes on top to hide the cash. He was earning money not just from input sales and farming but also from trading for his neighbors. Since the smallholder farmers selling their maize by the side of the road are price-takers, the price they take is not very good—$4–5 a bag. Chiyesu realized there was not much profit selling to intermediaries, who then sold to the mills in town, so he went directly to the mills on his own. Acting as a dealer for 200–300 farmers in his village, he would get about double the roadside price, which he passed on to the farmers after transportation costs and a small commission.[13]

Chiyesu also acted as an agent for commercial farms in the region, since he had connections to the truckers and millers. When asked which was the better business, trading maize or growing it, he says farming. If he grows the maize himself and sells it direct to the mill, he keeps all the profit—from growing and from selling. He eventually wants to expand to 50 hectares and build a mill in town.[14]

This sounded a lot like "vertical integration," and while he did not appear to know the term, he had embraced the concept thoroughly. He wants to own every piece of the supply chain so that he can keep all the profits rather than losing slices to the input seller, the grain dealer, the trucker, and the mill. And that's when it becomes clear: he is an African entrepreneur.

In terms of the maize glut, one strategy to avoid the price crash would be to sell after the tsunami of maize hit the market and prices recovered. But Chiyesu has other plans: "I'm going to sell now," he says. He wants to get out before prices crash, rather than waiting for them to recover. (There is no futures market in Zambia). But he also has the flexibility to take a lower price, if he has to, because he is so much more productive than the typical smallholder farmer. At four to five tons of maize per hectare, he can manage as prices fall, because he is producing so much relative to his costs; most farmers reaping one or two tons a hectare would not be so lucky. They would still sell for whatever price they could get, with little if any reward for their labor.[15]

In this way, the glut sends two conflicting market signals to farmers: plant less because the odds of making money are so bad, or plant more and become far more productive to make up on volume what you lose on price.

Costs and Benefits

But if Chiyesu's model looks like the best strategy, it also has its costs in a nation that is losing about 1 percent of its forestlands per year. With approval from his tribal chief, he razed forest to expand his farm, then planted corn upon corn with fertilizers and herbicides. This looked like a strategy to exhaust his soil if it continued, but he plans eventually on adding a rotation of soybeans or ground nuts to keep the soil productive. Yet for a farmer with an abundance of forest, it is not difficult to see his other option: till more virgin land and farm extensively as well as intensively.[16]

It could be worse, however. At least Chiyesu is following conservation farming practices, such as leaving maize stalks to decay in the field to build up humus rather than burning them, which is the common practice. He also uses methods to minimize soil tillage and thus avoid soil erosion. If the goal is to raise yield and income, it is hard to see a more direct path, for the use of fertilizers and conservation farming raises yield. But he is in the minority. Most farmers till the soil and eventually end up with infertile hardpan, which means abandoning

fields and razing more forests for agriculture.

As for inputs, dealers never considered the smallholders a market, because the farmers are so spread out. Instead, the dealers focused almost exclusively on selling to the large commercial farms. PROFIT sought to change that by building the village-level dealer network starting in 2006. Within three years it had over 1,500 agents, like Chiyesu, reaching 56,000 farmers. "Once you tap into this market the potential is huge," says Lytton Zulu, the managing director of agrochemical dealer CropServe, which is active in this program. Sales, most of it hybrid seed but also of herbicides, shot up to over a million dollars. In essence, PROFIT fostered a new market for the agro-suppliers, who in turn brought their technology and knowledge into the countryside.[17]

Is there an alternative to these chemical inputs? There does not appear to be one readily accessible to Chiyesu. No agroecological extension agents, for example. In fact, "organic" never comes up in discussions among farmers and advisers in Zambia. In stores, there is little apparent local demand, and without that, there is no incentive to spread practical knowledge about alternative agricultural methods.

This is a major challenge for agroecological advocates in Africa: what is the incentive to spread these methods, which are knowledge-intensive and do not involve the sale of an input? In contrast, agrochemical companies have every incentive to spread their methods, for Africa is a new and growing market.

That said, there are hybrid maize seeds that require fewer inputs, cassava that requires little fertilizer, and mixed farming that integrates animals into fields. In the latter method, cattle graze lightly on maize stalks after harvest, so they can deposit manure and raise soil fertility. Another promising approach promoted by conservation farming advocates is to expand plantings of the nitrogen-fixing *msangu* (*Faidherbia albida*) tree, which has a reverse phenology. That is, it grows leaves in the dry season, when the fields are dormant, then sheds them in the rainy season when maize is growing, allowing sunlight to reach the crop. Because *msangu* fixes nitrogen in the soil, it boosts fertility. The tree increases yields by 250–400 percent and acts as a carbon sink, with the potential of generating carbon credits for Zambian farmers.[18]

The question about each of these methods is not which is "best" in an absolute sense, but what method is best suited and viable, given the reality faced by the farmer. For Chiyesu, inputs were the clearest way to raise productivity and income, regardless of the "external costs" in the form of pesticide exposure or forest degradation.[19]

For all Chiyesu's success, it could not have been achieved without a tractor. A tractor gave him a means of cultivating his own fields and it was also crucial in his village, for he was the only one out of several hundred farmers who had managed to buy one. By offering tillage services, it became a means for other farmers to be more productive as well. In this way, Chiyesu's success generated income throughout the village. Recognizing this potential, a partnership of multilateral aid agencies has tried to jump-start a tractor loan program in Zambia, which is evident in Chongwe in the Central Province, where a farmer has received one.

Help from Outside

"Look for the Dunavant office," James Luhana, an adviser for AID's PROFIT says after driving for hours on dirt roads. Dunavant, a U.S. company, buys cotton from Zambia, but there is no "office" in the village—just a dirt-floor hut with a small Dunavant sign and a solar-powered laptop where an administrator keeps records. The farmer Luhana meets had patiently waited for much of the day. So Luhana gets right to work. The task: to create

a profit/loss statement so the farmer can qualify for a private-sector loan. In a somewhat complicated arrangement, he has already gotten the tractor and the loan from the group, but the loan portfolio is going to be taken over by a bank, which needs a financial statement. So in the shade of an open-air thatched hut, Luhana fills in the statement: costs for fertilizer, seed, diesel, and inputs, and sales and yield per hectare, all by month. Amazingly, the farmer has all the figures in his head. After three hours, the profit statement and balance sheet are completed and Luhana gets back in his truck and drives five hours to Lusaka. A laptop, spreadsheet, and portable printer would have done wonders for this process, but no matter—a day later, the loan is approved. (See Box 13–2 for another Dunavant joint project to help farmers.)[20]

The loans were launched as part of the Purchase for Progress initiative of the World Food Programme (WFP). The WFP bought food supplies locally, avoiding humanitarian food imports that do so much to stifle local agriculture. By identifying emerging farmers and financing rural tractor sales, the WFP was spurring agricultural development aligned with its local purchasing goals. In the $150,000 loan program, the WFP has financed 10 tractors; Dunavant, eager to get tractors into fields in order to increase cotton production, has financed 10 more. The three-year loans have been a success, and the first farmer paid his loan back in 12 months, encouraging the private-sector lenders to join in. As such, it was an example of how multilateral agencies could spur a private-sector initiative, which would then take on a momentum of its own.[21]

The group behind these loans—which also includes the International Finance Corporation and PROFIT—knew that getting tractors to farmers and producing food is not the only issue. So is selling the food in the Zambian market. So the WFP began getting its humanitarian food supplies from a nascent grain

Box 13–2. Phone Banking

Enos Banda may be the hardest working farmer in Malawi—and the one with the biggest smile. He supports his family—five children in all—by farming. But Enos is missing out on small-scale farming's biggest change in decades. Just over the border in the noisy town of Chipata, Zambia, Mobile Transactions and the cotton giant Dunavant launched a new payment system that will have cotton farmers receiving electronic credit instead of cash.

Using mobile banking technology, 100 cotton farmers are getting paid through their personal accounts on their mobile phones. And around these farmers stretches a web of shops and businesses accepting that form of payment for farming inputs and implements. Schools are ready to accept electronic payments for children's fees as well.

Farmers using cell phones is not all that revolutionary on its own. But it will be. There is a growing network of rural financial access and liquidity that will allow a wide array of new services to be created—with rural Zambians front and center. This network will allow farmers to make interest-earning deposits, create raw data needed for feasible crop insurance models, provide information on patterns of farmer spending that is needed for profitable agricultural loan packages, enhance disbursement and repayment abilities to extend the reach of agro-financing, and forge new and more trusting relationships between farmers and businesses—the bedrock of new commercial engagements.

Back in Malawi, Enos Banda knows little of these exciting possibilities. But he may soon. There are many reasons to get rural mobile money networks into Malawi as soon as possible. For starters, the country has a population density 10 times that of Zambia, making a financial network easier to construct. The existing mobile phone networks mirror those in Zambia, so any changes to existing technology will be relatively simple and straightforward. Agricultural production covers almost every square meter of Malawi, so the relevance of opening up new agro-finance avenues is huge. And there is just as much possibility to systemically change the financial support of the agriculture industry as there is in Zambia.

This is where a savvy donor or investor could create real change. Mobile Transactions, the technology company pioneering a rural money network in Zambia, and other companies like it are still in their infancy. The effort and capital required for mobile banking to firmly establish itself in Zambia are large, and even more is needed for it to go international. But the models are there. The technology is there. The expertise is there and growing daily. This is the perfect place for those with resources and vision to accelerate real change for rural farmers like Enos Banda.

—*Graham Lettner*
Mobile Transactions, Lusaka, Zambia
Source: See endnote 20.

exchange in Lusaka, called Zamace, which opened in 2007. The exchange has a daily trading session and warehouses in grain-producing regions, which could certify the quality of the crop. No longer would farmers need to sell to whomever comes down the road; they could actually sell at a chosen price on the exchange, as long as their crop is of high enough quality to be accepted at a certified warehouse.

The WFP, for example, put out a tender for the grain it wanted to buy, then let dealers on the exchange post their asking prices. During the trading session, the price could fall if a dealer chose to lower it; when the trading session closed, the WFP would take the lowest price. This cut the cost of their food programs, but it also added transparency missing from the more informal roadside deals—and reduced the number of brokers in the middle. Plus, farmers could decide whether to sell or to hold off in hopes of a better price later.

"Right now it's more of a theoretical model," says Rob Munro of AID's PROFIT Program. The exchange is still too small to influence pricing on a widespread basis, though with the legitimacy brought by the WFP, it is growing. Turnover on the exchange grew by 127 percent in 2009 to $19.3 million, but trade was still half the expected levels. For the near term, smallholder farmers really do not have much in the way of an alternative to the roadside dealers, and they will not unless the exchange reaches critical mass.[22]

The farmers' prospects are further clouded by the government's Food Reserve Agency (FRA), which bought maize at a premium price. The FRA stored the grain, then sold a portion of it, which is why in the face of the looming 2010 surplus it still had maize sitting around from 2009. What farmers hoped for was a government purchase at the higher price, yet only a fraction of farmers managed to get it. Looked at this way, Zambia spent millions on fertilizer subsidies to produce the bumper crop, then spent millions again to try and mop up the excess, and then millions more storing the grain in warehouses, where a portion of the crop rotted. The end result was that no one, save the traders on Zamace who handled a sliver of the trade, really knew what the transparent market price was. And that too was whipsawed by government purchases and the imposition of trade restrictions. For farmers, the FRA price acted as a perceived "floor price," even though it had little relation to the market and produced one clear effect: the vast majority of farmers who failed to secure an FRA contract would feel cheated by the remainder of the market.[23]

So what is the alternative? If the government ends fertilizer subsidies, production will plummet and incomes will fall, or perhaps farmers will shift to less input-intensive crops like cassava. Or maybe the government could put more money into basic infrastructure, like roads, rail, and water, which in turn could cut transaction costs (as well as have social benefits). The net result would be a more competitive maize crop. PROFIT and its team put its hopes in this market model, which would lead farmers to become competitive with low-price maize in Southern Africa. But by the time that approach runs its course, a lot of farmers will likely be off the land. They would not all be able to boost their yields the way Justine Chiyesu has. After all, he is an "emerging farmer"—an outlier among the top 4 percent, not a smallholder trying to live on one or two hectares.[24]

In the meantime, the maize boom means falling prices and income for farmers. In Zambia, as in Africa, a boom in production alone does not solve smallholders' impoverishment. Production is the first consideration when it comes to farming and feeding people, but it is certainly not the last. Nor is it one to be pursued on its own.

Churches Moving Beyond Hunger Relief

Churches and other faith-based aid groups working in Africa have a long and mostly admirable history of working to alleviate hunger. Too often, however, these groups have focused their relief solely on food aid and have stopped short of addressing hunger's underlying causes. Doling out sacks of Nebraska wheat during famines or giving farmers yearly gifts of petro-fertilizers and "miracle" seeds may alleviate hunger in the short term, but it perpetuates African farmers' dependence on outside benevolence. And it does little to improve the long-term resiliency of the land.

Today a number of churches and Christian development organizations with long tenures in Africa are gaining attention with approaches to hunger that are more holistic, ones that look for answers from farmers themselves.

Peter Cunningham, an Australian agricultural missionary who has worked for nine years with Serving in Mission in Niger, is well aware of approaches to hunger that do not work. "There have been countless project interventions and millions of dollars spent in Niger over the last 30 years," he says, "all aimed at reducing poverty, all with little or no lasting benefits at the village farm level. Adoption has not continued when the project ended or left."[1]

Working alongside small farmers, Cunningham sought instead an agroecological approach that would be both regionally adapted and culturally specific. That meant starting with the Sahel's original ecosystem. "In zones where God created the ecosystem as a savannah—trees, grasses, and herbs—then we should follow that pattern with trees. If large areas of productive land once had trees and were cleared, then we should go back to having trees with annual crops inter-planted between them," says Cunningham.[2]

Following the pattern with trees is an idea Cunningham and local Niger farmers have developed into an agroforestry project they call Sowing Seeds of Change in the Sahel. In addition to indigenous trees, this project features edible acacia trees from Australia. The acacias, which add nitrogen to the soil, serve to "nurse" annual crops and other trees, which are planted in alleys in between. The seeds, high in protein, can be eaten by both people and livestock. Acacias confirm the Hausa proverb: The one who plants trees will never be hungry.[3]

The success of this agroforestry model has been immediate and impressive, with yields two to three times higher than traditional farming methods. Rather than a rigid system, it is more of a template, easily adaptable to each region. Could it be duplicated in other parts of Africa? Cunningham thinks so. To spread this idea he has turned to ECHO, the Educational Concerns for Hunger Organization.[4]

The mission of this nondenominational Christian organization is to "equip people with resources and skills to reduce hunger and improve the lives of the poor." Its primary role is to collect ideas that help impoverished farmers and disseminate that knowledge to poor farmers via agricultural missionaries and development workers.[5]

Over the past 30 years ECHO has become a storehouse of agroecological and appropriate technology wisdom from the tropical and sub-tropical regions of the world. On ECHO's 50-acre model farm in Fort Myers, Florida, there are six ecosystems represented—everything from a tropical monsoon area to an urban rooftop garden. In each zone a host of region-specific "best practices" are on display.[6]

ECHO acknowledges that poor farmers have a wealth of agricultural knowledge. The group does not presume to "teach" people how to farm. Rather, it works to make small farmers more effective at growing crops under harsh conditions. It does this in a number of ways: monthly papers called ECHO Technical Notes, which can be downloaded free from the Web site; an extensive tropical seed bank, with free, trial packets of seed available to international development workers, community leaders, and missionaries; and a Technical Response Unit of experts who answer questions from the field.[7]

Stan Doerr, ECHO's CEO, hopes that despite the challenges of climate change and drought, Africa's small farmers can not only feed themselves but even thrive. "I would maintain that Africa has more natural resources than any place in the world: human intelligence, land, water, minerals. Africa is extremely blessed in those areas. It's just a matter of using them more effectively."[8]

While Doerr and his colleagues help increase that effectiveness by spreading knowledge, perhaps the biggest untapped potential for promoting sustainable agricultural development in Africa lies with African churches. The church is often the largest nongovernmental organization around; as such, it has the infrastructure and resources to teach sustainable agriculture.[9]

Take, for example, the Episcopal Church of Sudan (ECS). After a decades-long genocidal war during which food production all but ceased and people came to rely heavily on food aid, the ECS has launched a series of agricultural initiatives to help returning war refugees reacquire lost farming skills. Robin Denney, who did part of her training at ECHO, is an American agricultural consultant whom ECS invited to join the diocesan staff. Over the next few years she will train agricultural officers in 11 dioceses who will then work on behalf of the church as extension agents in their region. "Part of the essence of being a worker in the church," Denney says, "is that you go and live among the people; in doing so you learn a lot about their struggles, about what works and what doesn't."[10]

In addition to hiring Denney, ECS has also begun incorporating agricultural training into the curriculum at its theological colleges. Ellen Davis, professor of Old Testament at Duke Divinity School, is working with her Sudanese counterparts to develop the curriculum. Since the peace accords were signed in 2005, Davis has regularly traveled to Renk Theological College in southern Sudan, where she teaches courses in biblical Hebrew.[11]

The combination of classes in scriptural study and sustainable agricultural development is one Davis believes should be duplicated at seminaries across sub-Saharan Africa. It is part of what she calls "a holistic model of theological education." Seminary graduates, she says, are going to be the best-educated people in their local communities, are trusted disseminators of knowledge, and therefore have the ability to teach sustainable agriculture that can bring about lasting change at the community level.[12]

And in a region long plagued by conflict, ECS's role in promoting agriculture is leading to more than just food security and soil-building. As one Sudanese man told Davis, "Agriculture is peace-building. It is an alternative to war."[13]

Planting trees in the Sahel, sharing sustainable agriculture ideas with needy farmers, enlisting seminarians and church members in agricultural work—each is an example of how faith-based groups and churches are moving far beyond aid-based hunger relief in Africa. They are working to create vibrant small farms and communities where hunger is not an option, where the land is resilient in good years and bad, where the abundance of creation does not depend on yearly gifts from outsiders.

They might say they are working toward a vision of peace the biblical writers called *shalom*, where people live in harmony with each other and with the land. As Martin Price, founder of ECHO, points out, "Eliminating hunger and malnutrition is only the first step. There is just so much more to life than not being hungry."[14]

—Fred Bahnson
Farmer, writer, and 2009–10 Food and Society Fellow at the Institute for Agriculture and Trade Policy

Cattle seek shade in Botswana

CHAPTER 14

Improving Food Production from Livestock

Mario Herrero, with Susan MacMillan, Nancy Johnson, Polly Ericksen, Alan Duncan, Delia Grace, and Philip K. Thornton

Livestock herders and small-scale farmers who mix crop production with raising livestock are facing big challenges. Over the next 25 years, the growing populations and cities in the developing world will demand more and more animal-source foods—milk, meat, and eggs. At the same time, water scarcity, changes in climate, and new technologies are likely to drive big changes in small-scale farming. These smallholder systems are feeding most of the world's poor today. And they will become increasingly important to global food security in the future.[1]

The world needs livestock food systems to meet the nutritional, economic, and environmental needs of a billion poor people. To this end, we must find ways to increase milk, meat, and egg production without hurting the environment. At the same time, the most vulnerable groups of livestock producers—including nomadic herders like the Maasai in Kenya and the Fulani in Niger—need help in coping with the increasing droughts, temperatures, and extreme weather events likely to occur due to

Mario Herrero is a senior researcher at the International Livestock Research Institute in Nairobi, Kenya. **Susan MacMillan**, **Nancy Johnson**, **Polly Ericksen**, **Alan Duncan**, **Delia Grace**, and **Philip K. Thornton** are senior scientists at the Institute.

climate change. A wide array of mechanisms—from better feeding strategies to healthier animals to new ways of coping with climate change—can help. Our challenge and that of the world's small-scale livestock keepers is to make full use of these mechanisms and to continue bringing new options on stream, so that livestock enterprises increasingly reduce human and environmental poverty alike.

Why Livestock Matter

Farm animals are an ancient, vital, renewable natural resource. Throughout the developing world, up to 1 billion people rely on farm animals for their livelihoods. Livestock sustain most forms of agricultural intensification—from the Sahelian rangelands of West Africa to the mixed smallholdings in the highlands of East Africa to highly intensified rice production in Asia. And livestock production today is becoming agriculture's most economically important subsector (see Table 14–1), with demand for animal foods in developing countries projected to double over the next 20 years.[2]

In herding societies, which largely live off ruminant animals raised on lands too marginal to support crop production, milk is a food staple. In mixed crop-and-livestock production systems, which remain the backbone of agriculture in developing countries, the high nutrient density of milk, meat, and eggs means that even small quantities of these foods make an important contribution to the nutrition of households subsisting largely on starchy grains.

Livestock are not just a source of meat, milk, or eggs in poor communities, however. For many rural people, livestock are above all an asset—like land, a house, or a bank account. Surplus income is used to buy animals, which are kept and sold to meet household expenses—with sales of smaller animals (chickens, goats, sheep) covering routine expenses and those of larger stock (cattle, water buffalo, camels) used for big investments or for coping

with a medical or other crisis. Typically, what spurs even poor farmers to increase their livestock productivity is not an ambition to produce more food for themselves but rather better access to agricultural markets, where they can sell more of their livestock and livestock products.

But things are changing—and changing fast in many regions. An ever-rising demand for livestock foods in the developing world as incomes rise and people move to cities is creating booming livestock markets. Technical and institutional changes in the non-livestock agriculture sector will reduce people's reliance on livestock for their subsistence. Stronger financial institutions will reduce the need to store capital in livestock. More mechanized tillage operations will leave more feed for livestock producing milk and meat. Greater access to inorganic fertilizers could reduce the need for farmyard manure. Improvements in rural infrastructure, such as better roads and mobile phone connections, will bring markets closer to producers.

These changes will speed the intensification of livestock production in developing countries. Feeding strategies will increasingly focus on the production of milk and meat rather than the other functions of livestock, but this will depend on location. More regular and higher-quality feeds will be given to fewer, more productive animals. More animals on farms will be confined in stalls rather than allowed to graze freely on communal lands. Breeding strategies will combine the hardy traits of native livestock with the higher productivity of exotic animals. And more-specialized livestock producers will emerge to form commercial dairies and feedlots.

These developments will take more time in some places than others. But as they unfold, livestock technologies, policies, and investments aim either to enhance a benefit of livestock development—such as food, nutritional, economic, or environmental security—or to min-

Table 14–1. Livestock, Livelihoods, and the Environment

Sector or Resource	Contribution or Impact
Production	Developing countries produce 50 percent of the world's beef, 41 percent of the milk, 72 percent of the lamb, 59 percent of the pork, and 53 percent of the poultry. Mixed crop/livestock systems also produce close to 50 percent of the global cereal. Growth in the industrial pig and poultry sectors will account for 70 percent of production in South America and Asia. These systems will create the need for more grain as feed (which will account for more than 40 percent of global cereal use in 2050).
Value of production	Milk has the highest value of production of all commodities globally. Apart from rice (which is second), meat from cattle, pigs, and poultry is next in order of importance. In the least developed countries, the industry has around $1.4 trillion in livestock assets, excluding the value of infrastructure or land.
Greenhouse gases (GHGs)	Livestock contribute 18 percent of global GHG emissions (25–30 percent of the methane and the nitrous oxide and 30–35 percent of the carbon dioxide).
Carbon sequestration	Due to the area occupied, rangelands can be a global sink of a roughly similar size to forests. However, there is a real need to research how this large potential can be tapped through technologies and policies.
Water	Some 31 percent of global water use for agriculture goes to livestock, but with projected demand for livestock products, agricultural water use may need to double due to the increased need for feed production. Rangelands could be the source of significant regional increases in water productivity.
Nutrients	Globally, manure contributes 14 percent of the nitrogen, 25 percent of the phosphorus, and 40 percent of the potassium of nutrient inputs to agricultural soils.
Deforestation	Extensive cattle enterprises have been responsible for 65–80 percent of the deforestation of the Amazon. Some 400,000–600,000 hectares of forest a year are also cleared for growing crops, like soybeans, mostly to feed pigs and poultry in industrial systems and to provide a high protein source for concentrates of dairy cattle. However, this is changing due to enforcement and incentives by the Brazilian government for farmers and the retail sector.

Source: See endnote 2

imize a problem caused by livestock production—such as pollution of water sources with manure or emission of greenhouse gases. The increasing levels of livestock produced to meet the growing demand for products in developing regions need not increase the sector's environmental "hoofprint" at proportionately high levels. As production systems intensify, for example, and become more efficient, less feed will be needed to produce a given unit of livestock product. On the other hand, the future is likely to involve more livestock production in urban areas and higher concentrations of livestock in dairies and feedlots, which will bring with them pollution problems in terms of the disposal of animal excreta.

It is also important to remember that any modifications to a livestock-based food sys-

Cattle being herded toward a communal dipping facility in Surubu town, Tanzania

tem will affect outcomes beyond the environment. Improving feed, for instance, will not only lower greenhouse gas emissions but also, because it is usually more expensive, may increase the cost of livestock products.

Better Feeding Strategies

Feed is often cited as the primary constraint to improving livestock production in smallholder systems. This assumes that smallholders in developing countries, like larger farmers in industrial nations, keep livestock primarily for their meat and milk. But, as noted earlier, small-scale farmers may equally value livestock as a means of saving money, as traction for plowing or transporting goods, as a source of manure for fertilizing cropland, or as a source of milk for household consumption. Viewed in these terms, the widespread livestock herder practice of keeping many rather than a few

animals and the smallholder practice of maintaining livestock on minimal feed that cannot produce a marketable surplus of meat and milk are entirely rational. The Maasai of East Africa, for example, follow this strategy—cows are seen as walking banks that are sold for sending children to school, for marriages, and in times of crisis. For centuries, pastoralist peoples have traveled with their animals—cattle, goats, even camels—along well-established migration routes in East Africa. But that is changing due to conflict, water shortages, shrinking regional and international borders, and expanding crop production.[3]

The multiple functions of livestock in developing countries are usually supported by "opportunistic" feeding strategies, making use of whatever feed livestock keepers have at hand. These include the stalks, leaves, and other wastes of crops after their grain has been harvested; such crop residues play a key role in feeding farm animals throughout the developing world. Green fodder, not usually grown specifically for livestock feeding, is also used, along with thinnings from arable crops and material cut from roadsides. And grazing ruminant animals on communal lands is widely practiced. The little supplementary concentrate feed that is provided to smallholder stock is typically given to dairy cows and to other animals whose productivity depends on the better nutrition.

In Gomma District, in western Ethiopia, however, women have increased the productivity of their small animals by setting up and running sheep fattening cycles. Larger numbers of healthier animals are fetching higher prices when they (or their related products) are sold in markets. Farmers are using the increased income to expand and increase the number of animals in the fattening program and to purchase agricultural inputs like seeds, fertilizer, and farm tools. Household items, especially food, are also more accessible. And they can pay for their children's education. Households are making a profit of 2,250–4,500 birr ($167–333) annually from the sale of fattened animals. Women in particular are benefiting, as they are traditionally responsible for fattening up the small-animal stock.[4]

In India, where feed shortages are common, farmers are trying to improve the quality of their feed to produce more milk with fewer animals—and indirectly reduce GHG emissions. A. K. Singh, a farmer in Andhra Pradesh, makes a living by keeping just three buffalo. He uses both the milk and the manure they produce. He takes good care of them, feeding them mostly on grass, sorghum stover, and brans. Each buffalo used to produce about 5 liters of milk a day until he started feeding them on stover from varieties of sorghum bred to produce both large amounts of grain (for human food) and more-nutritious stalks and other crop residues (for animal feed). Using this better feed doubled the amount of milk his buffalo produced. With his income from milk increased by 50 percent and with the sale of one animal, he was able to enroll another of his children in school. At the same time, the better feeding regime reduced by 30 percent the amount of methane (a potent greenhouse gas) his animals produced for each kilogram of milk. Stover (fodder) is the main source of feed for buffalo in India. Research centers and crop breeding companies have recognized the value of developing such crops for feed as well as food.[5]

Better feeding strategies for livestock in developing countries will come about largely through the application of existing nutritional principles. With livestock diets currently dominated by crop residues and other low-quality feeds, more energy-rich diets will have to be found to support higher levels of milk and meat production. There is likely to be greater use of milling byproducts, oilcakes, and other agro-industrial byproducts combined more effectively with basal diets to enhance the animals' use of the feed. Crop residues will be chopped and made into feed blocks for easy transport and marketing. As demand for high-value livestock products continues to increase, the practice of growing crops specifically for animal feed will become economically competitive in certain areas. Better methods of processing and conserving feeds will allow them to be transported over longer distances. And there will be greater movements of feed from rural to urban producers.

Much of the knowledge about improved feeding practices already exists. The slow uptake of improved feeding practices has been mainly due to costs, including heavy labor requirements. Persistent attempts to promote feeding technologies in the smallholder livestock sector have failed to understand this.

Healthier Animals

The presence of animal disease in tropical countries greatly hinders trade in animals and animal products. Despite recent attempts at liberalization, sanitary and phytosanitary regulations still allow importing countries to take a precautionary "if in doubt, keep it out" approach. This denies livestock-rich but poor countries an opportunity to trade their way out of poverty while doing nothing to prevent unpredictable shocks from hitting some of the world's poorest nations.[6]

More than 70 percent of emerging diseases are zoonotic—that is, transmissible between people and livestock. In ecosystems that are relatively stable and whole, such as highly diversified smallholder agricultural systems, the coevolution of pathogens and their hosts (people and livestock) and vectors (ticks and tsetse flies) favors relatively low levels of pathogenicity and disease. But with increasing human incursions, agricultural and otherwise, into relatively virgin ecosystems, pathogens are encountering new hosts, with the result that new diseases are emerging, some of which, like HIV/AIDS, have the potential to harm public health in incalculable ways.[7]

While intensive agriculture can produce cheap products, it also introduces new health risks for both animals and people. In particular, it selects pathogens hard to detect in animal populations (such as *Campylobacter* spp. in poultry or *Escherichia coli* in cattle) or that can survive conventional treatment (through the evolution of genetic resistance to antibiotics). The wide geographic scale and large volumes of modern consolidated food distribution systems mean that food-borne diseases can spread rapidly and affect large numbers of people greatly removed from the origin of the food.

Among the most important and successful animal health innovations of all time is the development of curative drugs for animal illnesses (such as antimicrobials, parasiticides, and acaricides). Official veterinary policies at national and global levels stipulate that health treatments be given only under the oversight of a veterinarian, with the result that many veterinary drugs have reached remote users not because of policies but in spite of them. In most poor countries, which have tens of millions of livestock and livestock keepers and only a few hundred veterinarians, informal and quasi-formal drug distribution systems have blossomed.[8]

This disconnect between veterinary policy and reality in poor countries makes it difficult for all those who are unofficially treating animals to get information on how to do this properly. The consequent improper treatments are a main reason that resistance to drugs is fast evolving in the organisms causing livestock diseases. Integrated disease control, which reduces reliance on therapeutic regimes by combining different methods of controlling disease, has succeeded where the scale and profitability of farming justify high managerial and technical inputs. The development of teams of community-based animal health workers is a promising innovation for many poor livestock-keeping communities.[9]

Vaccines are the most cost-effective way of controlling most animal as well as human diseases. Among key innovations in vaccine development over the last few decades are DIVA vaccines; as the name indicates, these allow disease control officers to "differentiate infected from vaccinated animals." This makes vaccination a much more attractive control option than culling animals, which is increasingly as unpopular in rich countries as it is unaffordable in poor ones. Development of thermostable vaccines was the key to the recent eradication of rinderpest and is helping to control Newcastle disease in village poultry. (See Box 14–1.)[10]

At the same time, health communities are shifting from technology-based solutions, which address the proximate causes of disease (such as lack of vaccines), to more holistic approaches, which focus more on the interconnections among human, animal, and environmental health. The convergence of these disciplines in "One Medicine–One Health" or "EcoHealth" approaches is likely to have profound implications for veterinary as well as medical care in the twenty-first century.

In some cases, traditional knowledge has improved disease surveillance. For example, Somali and Maasai herder early warning systems in East Africa were key in identifying the risk factors and symptoms of Rift Valley fever in an outbreak in 2006 and 2007. Rift Valley fever is an acute viral zoonosis spread by mosquitoes. It primarily affects domestic livestock such as cattle, camels, sheep, and goats, but it can also infect and kill people, especially those handling infected animals. In the 1970s, explosive outbreaks occurred among people throughout Africa, the Indian Ocean states, and the Arabian Peninsula. Epidemics in Egypt in 1977/78 and in Kenya in 1997/98 each killed several hundred people. Another outbreak in Kenya in 2006/07 killed more than 100 people.[11]

Box 14–1. Controlling Newcastle Disease in Poultry in Mozambique

Newcastle disease, which can wipe out entire flocks of chickens and can spread from farm to farm, is especially devastating for rural farmers in sub-Saharan Africa. Vaccines for Newcastle used to be hard to come by in Africa. They were imported and usually expensive, putting them out of reach of small farmers. And even when they were available, they required refrigeration, which is not common in many rural villages.

Today, however, thanks to the work of the International Rural Poultry Center of the Kyeema Foundation in Mozambique, villages have access not only to vaccines but also to locally trained community vaccinators (or para-vets) who can help spot and treat Newcastle and other poultry diseases before they spread. With help from a grant from the Australian government's overseas aid program, Kyeema developed a thermostable vaccine that does not need to be refrigerated and is easier for rural farmers to administer to their birds.

Vaccinations take place three times a year and farmers are taught—with cleverly designed flip-charts and posters—how to apply the vaccines with eyedroppers. The community vaccinators try to link the control of Newcastle with efforts to address avian influenza because the symptoms of the two diseases—coughing, diarrhea, lethargy, runny eyes, mortality—are often similar. Community leaders help Kyeema identify people who are well respected in the community to be community vaccinators. Typically, women are chosen: not only do they tend to stay in the villages more than men, but the money they earn usually does much more to help the family because they use it to buy food or school-books for their children. Because more birds are surviving thanks to the vaccinations, Kyeema is also working with farmers to build better housing for their poultry and to find additional sources of feed.

—*Danielle Nierenberg*
Source: See endnote 10.

Somali pastoralists of northeastern Kenya accurately assessed the likelihood of the 2006/07 outbreak based on their assessments of key risk factors, and they did so long before veterinary and public health interventions began. They are particularly able to predict not only the symptoms of Rift Valley fever in their animals but also the likelihood of an outbreak of the disease. Indeed, observations by local communities in risk-prone areas were often more timely and definitive than the global early warning systems in use during the 2006/07 outbreak. Maasai herders of northern Tanzania accurately recognized symptoms such as high abortion rates as indicating the presence of the infection in their herds. These examples point out the important role that livestock keepers can play in early warning and veterinary surveillance.[12]

Coping with Climate Change

The impacts of livestock production on climate change have been discussed widely in the general as well as the scientific press. Yet each of the estimated 1 billion people who rely on small-scale livestock enterprises has a tiny environmental footprint compared with people in industrial countries. Set against the vital contributions that livestock make to the livelihoods of the poor, the greenhouse gases their animals produce are modest.[13]

The changing climate is already affecting the livelihoods and well-being of livestock keepers in developing countries, who face increasing water and feed scarcity, losses of livestock genetic diversity, and changing disease threats. As climate changes, climate variability is likely to increase—with more-frequent droughts and floods putting at greater risk the food, economic, and environmental security of livestock communities practicing both pastoral and mixed crop-livestock production. The complicated trade-offs between desires to conserve water and other natural resources, to reduce GHG emissions, and to help poor people enhance their livelihoods and food security are even more complex when the possibility of increased biofuel production is included.

Kenyan farmer with her healthy cow

The two main options for dealing with agriculturally related climate change are finding ways to reduce or mitigate emissions of greenhouse gases from agricultural production and helping farmers adapt to the changing climatic conditions. Adaptation options range from the technological (such as the use of drought-tolerant crops) and the behavioral (changes in diets) to the managerial (different farm management practices) and the policy-related (such as developing markets and infrastructure to ensure supplies of more-appropriate inputs and fairer producer prices). Some farmers are using seasonal weather forecasts to help them plan

their agricultural cycles. Others are buying livestock insurance that is "weather-indexed."[14]

Insurance is something of a holy grail for those working with African livestock, particularly for pastoralists who could use it both as a hedge against drought—a threat that will become more common in some regions as the climate changes—and to increase their earning potential. Fortunately, thousands of herders in Kenya's arid and drought-stricken north can now purchase insurance policies for their livestock, based on a new program that anticipates whether drought will put their camels, cows, goats, and sheep at risk of starvation. This "index-based" livestock insurance program uses satellite imagery of grass and other vegetation to determine potential losses of forage and to issue payouts to herders when drought is expected to occur. Insuring livestock of pastoral families had long had been considered impossible due to the formidable challenges of verifying deaths of animals that regularly are moved over vast tracts of land in search of food. This system works because getting compensation does not require verifying that an animal is actually dead. Payments kick in when the satellite images, available practically in real time, indicate that forage has become so scarce that animals are likely to perish. Droughts are frequent in the region—there have been 28 in the last 100 years and 4 in the past decade alone—and the losses they inflict on herders can quickly push pastoralist families into poverty.[15]

In some regions, opportunities are arising for farmers both to mitigate their greenhouse gas emissions and to adapt to climate change. Management practices that increase the photosynthetic input of carbon or slow the return of stored carbon to carbon dioxide via respiration, fire, or erosion help sequester carbon. More effective storage and management of manure can help reduce GHG emissions and increase the efficacy of the manure when applied to crops. Payments to livestock herders and others for the environmental services they provide, such as maintaining populations of wild animals and other forms of biodiversity or storing carbon, represent major opportunities to help poor households diversify their livelihoods and increase their income.

Conclusion

The speed of global changes in human demographics, technology, resource use, public perceptions, and other factors mean that food production systems, including livestock, will inevitably change too. There are good examples around the world of creative ways to adapt to the pace of these changes in a sus-

tainable manner. Whether strategies focus on diversification of income, sustainable intensification or expansion, or a mix of these, stories of success often combine a mixture of local entrepreneurship with public- and private-sector support for sound policy and investments in technology development, infrastructure, services, and market development. In some sectors, such as the smallholder dairy sector in Kenya and increasingly in other parts of East Africa, these factors have combined to create an enabling environment for increasing milk production in the region. Farmers now have access to better cows, feeds, and veterinary services, which together with national policy support have enabled incomes, food provision, and informal milk markets to flourish in the region.

Small-Scale Livestock Production in Rwanda

Recovery is a word heard a lot in Rwanda. From public service announcements on television to billboards—this is the motto for a place that just 15 years ago was torn apart by genocide. More than 1 million people were murdered in 1994, as ethnic strife turned neighbor against neighbor in one of the bloodiest civil wars in history.[1]

"Heifer is helping a recovery process," explained Dr. Dennis Karamuzi, a veterinarian and the programs manager for Heifer International Rwanda. In 2000, Heifer started working in Rwanda in a community in the Gicumbi District, about an hour outside of the capital, Kigali. This district is making a comeback now, thanks in part to Heifer International.[2]

The group's start in Rwanda was a little rocky. At first, the community was suspicious: Heifer was giving farmers "very expensive cows," says Holimdintwoli Cyprien, one of the farmers trained to raise dairy cows. Many community members thought this was a plot by the government to have local farmers raise livestock that would then be taken away.[3]

Heifer introduced a South African dairy breed known for its high milk production because, according to Karamuzi, "no stock of good [dairy cow] genes" was left in the country after the genocide; livestock had been killed and farm fields burned. In addition, he said, these animals help prove "that even poor farmers can take care of high-producing cows."[4]

These animals do more than just provide milk—an important source of protein and income to families. They also provide manure, which is a source of fertilizer for crops and is now providing biogas for cooking to households as part of a National Biogas Program.[5]

Helen Bahikwe began working with Heifer International in 2002. She now has five cows—and an excess of manure. With a government subsidy, Bahikwe built a biogas collection tank that lets her use the methane from decomposing manure to cook for her family. She no longer has to collect or buy firewood, saving both time and money and protecting the environment. The fuel also burns cleaner, eliminating the smoke that comes from other sources of fuel.[6]

Holindintwali Cyprien has not always been a farmer. After the genocide, he and his wife, Donatilla, were school teachers, making about $50 monthly. Living in a small house of mud, without electricity or running water, they were saving to buy a cow to help increase their income. But when Heifer International started working in Rwanda, the Cypriens were chosen as one of the first 93 farmers to be Heifer partners. Along with the gift of a cow, the family received training and support from Heifer project coordinators.[7]

They have used their gift not only to increase their income—they now make anywhere from $300 to $600 per month—but also to improve the family's living conditions and nutrition. In addition to growing elephant grass and other fodder for the five cows they currently own, the Cypriens are also growing vegetables and keeping chickens. They have built a brick house and have electricity and are earning income by renting their other house.[8]

Today Cyprien is making plans to teach again—this time teaching other farmers. And in 2008 the government instituted the One Cow Per Poor Household Program, which aims to give the 257,000 poorest households in the country training and support to raise milk for home consumption. Heifer International, says Dr. Karamuzi, is also building an exit strategy by connecting farmers to cooperatives, which can organize and train farmers themselves.[9]

—Jim DeVries, Heifer International
—Danielle Nierenberg, Worldwatch Institute

Eggplant harvest from the Bakau Women's Garden Project in Bunjul, The Gambia

CHAPTER 15

A Road Map for Nourishing the Planet

Throughout this book, we have discussed the diversity of innovations that exist to help alleviate hunger and poverty in the places where these problems are most acute. From participatory plant breeding techniques and rainwater harvesting to making sure that crops do not spoil before they get to market, the chapters have highlighted ways to nourish both people and the planet.

These on-the-ground innovations, however, do not exist in a vacuum. They depend on other innovations—including innovations that help us understand the connections between all parts of the food system; innovations that guide us in evaluating how well a particular practice or policy work; and innovations in institutional, governance, and policy reform that protect farmers, food sovereignty, and the fundamental human right to food. The experts we have gathered for this final chapter include some of the world's leading thinkers, scientists, and advocates in agricultural development.

—*Danielle Nierenberg and Brian Halweil*

WWW.NOURISHINGTHEPLANET.ORG

165

Innovations in Understanding Complex Systems

Hans R. Herren

In the last 50 years the gross world product has exploded from roughly $7 trillion per year to nearly $60 trillion. This staggering expansion has had disastrous effects on natural resources, both renewable and nonrenewable. By 2003, for instance, some 27 percent of the world's marine fisheries had already collapsed. Oil production is declining in most countries and is expected to reach its peak within a few decades, if not sooner. Water is becoming scarce, and water stress is projected to increase; within 20 years supplies will be adequate to satisfy only 60 percent of world demand. Rates of species extinction have far exceeded background rates for decades.[1]

These gloomy facts are all too familiar. What is less well known is that agriculture is one of the major culprits in this scenario. Agriculture today accounts for 70 percent of water withdrawals and 15 percent of greenhouse gas emissions—with nearly 75 percent of that emitted by developing countries. An additional 11 percent of total emissions are caused by the destruction of 13 million hectares of forest each year, largely by agricultural encroachment. Global population, now approaching 7 billion, is expected to jump another 35–40 percent by 2050. This additional population, and further economic growth, will add up to sharply higher global demand for food, feed, and fiber and to higher meat consumption.[2]

Agriculture as we know it today is in trouble. The challenges and uncertainties it faces require a paradigm shift that will have to take into account the complexity of "agri" and "culture"—the tangled intersection of farm-

ing and human social and political systems.

Agriculture's complexity arises from several sources. First, farming itself is complicated in ways that nonfarmers can hardly grasp: a successful farmer must understand crop characteristics, weather and microclimate, soil types and fertility, pests and disease threats, field rotation schemes, livestock/crop interactions, market demand, and a host of other factors. Sustainable farming is knowledge-intensive, requiring more research and the merging of innovations with farmers' knowledge.

Second, sustainable agriculture is more complex because it does not take place in an economic vacuum; food production is only one facet of an intricate socioeconomic system. For example, agriculture is facilitated by a proper social context, where knowledge and skills are broadly available, and by a thriving economic setting, where financial resources and risk management systems are available. At the same time, strong and sustainable agriculture is essential for harmonic socioeconomic development, providing income and resources to the most vulnerable households.

And third, food production is embedded in and also reshapes the natural environment. Farming often begins, or has begun, with forest clearing. But if it is done in harmony with the environment, it also provides essential ecosystem services beyond food, feed, and fiber, such as carbon sequestration in soil, clean water and air, natural pest control, and pollination.

Past attempts to identify effective agricultural policies in isolation from the broader ecological context or without properly recog-

Hans R. Herren is president of the Millennium Institute in Arlington, Virginia. Andrea M. Bassi and Matteo Pedercini of the Institute also contributed to this article.

nizing the strong linkages with other sectors have had unintended consequences and poor outcomes. To succeed in tinkering with changes in the agriculture sector, researchers and policymakers simply must think and analyze it in complex systems terms.[3]

Fortunately, there are ways to do this systematically, using computer models that have proved extremely useful. In particular, system dynamics models make it possible to represent agricultural development as a process involving many social, economic, and environmental factors, and then to ask lots of "What if?" questions. By doing this systematically, it is possible to compare different policies across various scenarios.

For example, using a system dynamics model to compare the use of organic and chemical fertilizers reveals that transitioning to organic fertilizers can lead to higher soil quality and yields as well as lower water consumption and more carbon sequestration in the soil—thus potentially playing a lead role in curbing the rise of atmospheric carbon dioxide concentrations. At the same time, it can show that as oil and fossil fuel prices increase in the future, chemical fertilizers are likely to become less competitive, especially for farmers in developing countries. As a consequence, over a medium- to long-term horizon, more-sustainable practices present real economic and ecological advantages.

The transition from current conventional and traditional agriculture to ecological agriculture requires better management of key resources such as soil, biodiversity, and water, supplemented with research and extension services. These practices increase productivity, create employment, and mitigate emissions.[4]

Managing this transition will take money and time. In particular, new and synergistic investments in the agriculture, water, and forestry sectors will be needed. Agricultural investments should be split among four areas:
• reduction of pre-harvest losses, currently

estimated to reach about 30 percent of total crop production;
• reduction of post-harvest food losses through better storage and processing in rural areas;
• agriculture management practices for increased farm productivity by making the transition to organic, conservation, and agroecology farming (at an average cost of $85–100 per hectare); and
• research, development, capacity, and skill building for sustainable agriculture.[5]

Investing in these areas will have considerable impacts within the sector and across sectors (for example, by supporting economic growth and employment, improving nutrition, and reducing negative externalities such as energy consumption and carbon emissions).[6]

A critical difference between this investment strategy and business-as-usual (BAU) strategies is their effects on natural resource stocks. The ecological agriculture and green economy scenarios demonstrate why economic development and natural resource exploitation should not be considered analogous. The modeling results indicate that, using a global average, green scenarios in the medium to long term assure greater food availability (measured as per capita calories per day). While they result in slower economic growth due to conservation of natural resources and low carbon production in the short term, they are more sustainable with faster growth over the long term. In this respect, the green scenarios show more resilience: they lower emissions, reducing dependence on fossil fuels, and emphasize efficient and sustainable use of natural resources, curbing global warming and resource depletion.

Investing in BAU development, on the other hand, accelerates consumption, which stimulates economic growth in the short and medium term but extends and worsens current trends of natural resource depletion. And the long-term trend is frightening. Once natural resource stocks start to decline severely (such as soil fertility, fish, forests, and fossil fuels), the economy and employment begin to suffer because of reduced production, higher energy prices, and growing emissions. Additional consequences may include massive migration driven by resource shortages (water, for example), accelerated climate change, and considerably higher rates of extinction.

In the green simulations, total agricultural production (including agricultural products, livestock, fish, and forestry products) increases compared with BAU scenarios. Employment, including both direct and indirect jobs, grows considerably even though the total harvested area remains about the same or even declines, due to higher yields. A reduced demand for land indicates positive synergies between ecological agriculture investments and forest management (through increasing yields and better soil quality, driven by larger forestland and the use of organic fertilizers). Investments in improving water efficiency allow a reduction of agricultural water demand per hectare, offsetting the effects of increasing water stress on yields. It is worth noting that emissions from chemical fertilizer use, deforestation, and harvested land decline greatly relative to BAU.

Finally, it is reasonable to expect that green scenarios would see the introduction and major expansion of second-generation biofuels. Up to 25 percent of agricultural and forestry residues are estimated to be readily available for production. Combined with the use of marginal lands, this resource could create as many as a few million jobs by 2030 and effectively support the transition beyond oil. One caveat in this scenario is the long-term maintenance of soil fertility through "re-investing" all pos-sible crop and biofuel production residues as organic fertilizers. Additional research is needed to guide biofuel development toward sustainability, if at all.[7]

It is well past the time to take a systemic and long-term view of the shape of agriculture in a sustainable future. There are no longer any excuses, as tools are now available to help inform new agricultural research and development (R&D) policies. Most countries will miss the deadline of 2015 for all the Millennium Development Goals agreed to in 2000, many of which have strong synergistic links with agriculture, the environment, and society. Firm and effective action is strongly needed to change the present agricultural paradigm.[8]

The actions required will vary from place to place, as agriculture depends heavily on local environments, people, and other factors. This is where tools that assess agricultural systems within the wider context of the environment, society, and the economy come in handy. Playing out "What if?" development policy scenarios with all interested stakeholders will allow visualization and discussion leading to common understanding and agreement on a way forward, with a grasp of the intended and unintended consequences of given policy choices. If we are going to spend billions of dollars reinventing agriculture—and it is clear that we must—then we must also invest in rural infrastructures and institutions beyond agriculture. We must eliminate perverse subsidies in favor of rewards for sound agricultural practices and we must change consumption patterns. That is the only way to ensure the difference between business as usual and business as unusual.

Innovations in Evaluating Agricultural Development Projects

Charles Benbrook

It is striking how few of the development success stories described in this book depended to any significant degree on cutting-edge scientific and technical breakthroughs. Indeed, access to simple, low-cost, durable, easy-to-maintain tools and techniques to accomplish everyday tasks is a far more common ingredient in successful projects than cutting-edge technologies or system changes made possible by science breakthroughs.

Virtually everyone in the development community recognizes the need for objective, sober analysis of the roots of food insecurity, as well as for research and development in food production, handling, storage, marketing, and policy. But far too little attention is directed at probing the kind of analysis, research, and technology applications that will most cost-effectively promote sustainable agricultural and economic development. This needs to change—and quickly.

Given the gravity of today's food security challenges, coupled with the growing fragility of the people and ecosystems in heavily populated areas vulnerable to drought, floods, fire, tsunamis, and earthquakes, the world community needs to exploit science and technology more than ever, but in different ways and with greater discipline than in the recent past. (See Box 15–1.)[9]

The lack of consensus and clarity on the surest path toward greater food and economic security, and deep-set mistrust among stakeholders and intended beneficiaries, cries out for transparent and independent assessment of the impacts of development projects and strategies. The search in this volume for essential elements in successful and sustained initiatives is a good first step, but agricultural development must go viral and spread more quickly—or risk falling down the always expanding list of global priorities.

A critical step in sharpening project oversight and benefit assessment is agreeing on a set of performance parameters and evaluation criteria against which a given technology, practice, system, or project can be evaluated. Six "first principles" are suggested for consideration as new evaluation methods are developed and deployed:

- Promote biodiversity.
- Work within natural limits.
- Target solutions at the root of problems.
- Incrementally improve soil quality and productivity.
- Preserve capacity to innovate.
- Favor self-sustaining solutions.[10]

Even with these principles in hand, the majority of successful development initiatives require several things to happen in a logical, incremental sequence. The right things done at the wrong time often lead to disappointing results.

Improving the fertility and productivity of worn-out soils is probably the single most universal challenge standing in the way of sustainable, home-grown food security in Africa and parts of Asia. Several projects have achieved rapid and dramatic results by making fertilizers available to farmers via a variety of infrastructure investments and subsidy schemes. The euphoria triggered by early successes often

Charles Benbrook is chief scientist at The Organic Center, which is based in Boulder, Colorado.

Box 15–1. Agricultural R&D: New Public-Private Sector Dynamics

Until recently, governments, universities, multilateral organizations, and other public institutions have set priorities and paid for most science and technology development in the area of agriculture and food systems. The private sector accepted a significant degree of dependence on and guidance from public institutions in pursuing food system R&D.

The transition to private-sector dominance of agricultural R&D began in the 1970s, accelerated in the 1980s as the profit potential of genetic engineering came into focus, and was essentially complete by the turn of the century. In 1986, total public plus private-sector research investments in production agriculture were about $3.33 billion in the United States, with 54 percent from the public sector and 46 percent private.

By 2009, Monsanto was spending $980 million on worldwide agricultural R&D and Syngenta invested $960 million. Other leading seed-pesticide companies invested at least $4 billion, and another $3 billion or more was spent by other agricultural input industries (farm machinery, animal health,

irrigation, precision farming, and so on), for a total private-sector investment of not less than $9 billion. As total public agricultural R&D spending in the United States was approximately $3.5 billion that year, the public's share of total R&D fell from 54 percent in 1986 to around 28 percent in 2009, and the private sector's share rose from 46 to 72 percent.

In this same period, significant reductions occurred in public funding for agricultural research, development, and training programs, driving public institutions to the private sector in search of funds, hat in hand—sometimes at some significant cost in terms of independence and the integrity of science.

Private companies are bound by law in most countries to maximize economic returns to their investors. It is a stretch for a major corporation to deliver the customary profit margin and return to investment and intellectual property when the company is a partner in a development project serving the needs of small-scale farmers in poor regions of the world.

Source: See endnote 9.

creates demand for "more of the same," leading to a continuation of subsidies and progressively higher rates of fertilizer use. Farmers are often sold on the notion that they can grow high-yield cash crops every year, as long as they invest enough in the inputs to support the higher yields.[11]

This "new religion" can push interest in agroecological approaches to the back burner and bring on a new generation of pest, soil, and plant health problems triggered by excessive or imbalanced nutrients. For example, when too much nitrogen is applied, the excess will usually stimulate a flush of soil microbes that consume organic material in the soil. As a result, soil quality declines despite the infusion of fertilizer inputs.[12]

Research suggests that it will take 5–10 years of focused, intensive effort in most regions of Africa to increase soil organic matter levels enough to markedly increase water intake and holding capacity as well as soil fertility levels. But as soil health is incrementally restored, reliance on fertilizers shipped into the region can decline, and more of the nutrients supporting plant development can come from the farm and the region. Shifting reliance to essentially home-grown fertility is one of the best ways to increase the share of crop income that stays on the farm.[13]

Much of today's acrimony in the agricultural development arena can be traced to people, organizations, and companies with an agenda of their own, elements of which have been repackaged and offered as the surest path to progress. The debate over the proper role and uses of genetic engineering (GE) versus agroecological systems in production agriculture is particularly contentious. The debate is also fundamentally important because it will shape the direction and impacts of development assistance and agricultural policy reform for the foreseeable future and hence will help determine whether the world becomes more or less food-secure. Over time, street fighting among development stakeholders could undermine political support needed to ramp up and sustain funding for development assistance programs.

Some people argue today for blending or merging competing approaches to agricultural development, in the hope that a hybrid system will perform better than either approach. While attractive in the abstract, merging systems that are fundamentally different is generally a bad idea and will produce erratic and disappointing results.[14]

Instead, development agencies and funders should invest in a diversity of approaches and strategies, giving each a fair chance to demonstrate whether and how they can contribute to wider margins of food security on an affordable and sustained basis. Rigorous project evaluation drawing on widely accepted performance parameters derived from first principles like those just described should then be used to identify the most promising and cost-effective approaches.

Agroecological and organic farming principles and genetic engineering both have potential to contribute to more productive, safer, and sustainable farming systems. But the former is likely to do so with greater impact and more cost-effectively than the latter because, in general, the sort of management-based solutions embedded in agroecological and organic farming systems are designed to build soil quality and promote plant and animal health.

An agroecological system can build soil quality sufficiently to increase sustainable yield goals by 50 percent or more and with relatively few inputs from outside the region—and it can do so in about the time it takes to develop, test, and introduce a GE crop cultivar. Genetic engineering of crop cultivars has the potential in most cases to add a few percent and occasionally 10 percent yield potential to an otherwise well-adapted conventional crop variety. But that increment of yield potential will require other inputs on an annual basis, and the transformed variety will likely not prove as robust under some environmental conditions because of the unanticipated impacts of the genetic transformation on crop physiology and/or response to stress.[15]

It is worth noting as well that any future GE plant variety will do better in a field in which degraded soils have been restored through adherence to soil-building agroecological practices. Likewise, any family managing a small, agroecological crop-livestock farm will benefit from a new, genetically engineered animal vaccine that prevents a recurring disease. But these examples of how agroecological and GE approaches can augment each other should pale in comparison to the profound differences between them.

GE technology and input-intensive systems generally focus one intervention on one problem, with the goal of keeping in check the damage caused by pests or problems arising from imbalances in a farming system. Historically, the inputs and new technologies introduced to keep yields high and rising have created other problems such as resistance to herbicides or collateral damage to nontarget organisms, like fish and bees. Western societies have been able and willing to contain and deal with such collateral damage through complex and costly regulatory programs and ongoing research and surveillance. Is it realistic to expect African and Asian countries to do the same?

Input-intensive systems also tend to erode economic sustainability at the farm-family level

A rice cultivar developed in Uganda for increased yield

the combination of herbicide-tolerant soybeans and no-till planting systems. While highly productive in terms of crop income per hour of labor invested, these farms do very little to enhance the economic well-being of resource-limited people living where the crops are grown. Income is generated that flows, like the crops, outside the region.

Fortunately, there are other models for development and agricultural production that lead to fundamentally different outcomes. As several chapters in this book show, the economic and nutritional needs of resource-poor farmers can best be met with diverse, value-added systems that draw on local knowledge, skills, resources, and biodiversity. When such systems evolve in step with a diverse mix of enterprises, coupled with supportive policies and targeted investments in infrastructure, real opportunities will emerge to promote food security through systems that tend to limit and spread risks.

by increasing crop yields and production costs but lowering net farm income per hectare, at least in most years. For several decades North American farmers have simply farmed more hectares in order to sustain family income in the face of incrementally lower net returns per hectare. A handful of farmers in Latin America have followed suit, building operations spanning tens of thousands of hectares through

Innovations in Institutions to Support People and the Planet

Marcia Ishii-Eiteman

We find ourselves poised today on the threshold of the potential collapse of vital ecosystem functions on which people and the planet depend. At the same time, we are seeing intolerable levels of poverty, with nearly 1 billion people going hungry every day as a result.

With agriculture facing converging global crises of climate change, water scarcity, and diminishing fossil fuel supplies, alongside severe social and economic crises on the farm and an epidemic of land grabs, a rapid and decisive reorientation toward ecological sus-

Marcia Ishii-Eiteman is a senior scientist at the Pesticide Action Network North America and one of the authors of the International Assessment of Agricultural Knowledge, Science and Technology for Development.

tainability and equity is imperative.[16]

Fortunately, we have the capacity to produce adequate supplies of healthy food while building ecological resilience, assuring social equity, and cooling the planet. But doing so at a global scale requires deep-seated political commitment and resolve, informed by a clear understanding of the root causes of poverty and hunger and a willingness to change course. This in turn requires policymakers to grapple honestly with the political economy of hunger and the political ecology of a food system in crisis.

The most comprehensive evaluation of global agriculture to date, the United Nations–led International Assessment of Agricultural Knowledge, Science and Technology for Development (IAASTD), did that, and more. Written by over 400 scientists and development experts from more than 80 countries, and endorsed by 58 governments, the report concluded, "Business as usual is not an option." It found that industrial agricultural technologies and practices—and the political, economic, and institutional arrangements supporting them—have increased crop yields at times but at enormous cost to public health, the environment, social and gender equity, and the very foundations of food security.[17]

The landmark report detailed the dire results of these technologies and practices: the few have benefited at the expense of the many, the natural resource base on which human survival depends has been severely degraded, there are unprecedented levels of greenhouse gas emissions associated with industrial agriculture, and a continuation of these agricultural practices now threatens water, energy, food, and climate security.[18]

The IAASTD also warned that growing market concentration in the food and agribusiness industries, vertical integration of the food system, the speed with which trade liberalization has taken place in many regions, and corporate influence over public policy, research,

and extension have had largely negative consequences for the poorest countries, their environments, and the health and livelihoods of their people. The reality is that in too many countries the rural poor simply cannot afford the price of food grown at home, particularly when those prices are driven up by the effects of food aid, dumping, and financial speculation. So, what needs to change?[19]

To scale up the remarkable successes presented in *State of the World 2011* and achieve equitable and sustainable development in the twenty-first century requires a major redirection of institutional and policy support and investments. As described in the IAASTD, this requires not only investing in biodiverse ecological farming practices but also establishing new institutions and creating an enabling policy environment to support the food and livelihood security of small-scale farmers and rural communities. It also requires freeing farmers to use their own skills and knowledge to do what they know how to do, and supporting them where additional information, collaborative efforts, or policy and market interventions are needed.[20]

As some have argued, the advances demonstrated by farmers practicing ecological agriculture have not come about because of supportive national policies. Rather, they have happened largely in their absence and in spite of massive pressure to abandon such efforts exerted by, for example, global market forces and neoliberal trade agendas that favor large-scale resource-extractive commodity production. The good news is that with a concerted and coordinated effort on the part of policymakers, working in close collaboration with all members of civil society, much more can be achieved. Broad-based participatory planning could lead, for example, to the establishment of a coherent national framework to guide a country-wide transition toward agroecological production.[21]

Supporting farmers means providing political support for the establishment of farmers', women's, indigenous, workers', and other community-based organizations, such as the Network of Farmers' and Agricultural Producers' Organisations of West Africa, the Chilean Asociación Nacional de Mujeres Rurales e Indígenas (National Association of Rural and Indigenous Women), the Bangladesh Agricultural Farm Labor Federation, and the National Federation of Fishworkers in Sri Lanka. These groups and many others have key roles to play in strengthening farmers' social and economic well-being, particularly where collective action increases political power, protects farmers' rights, and reduces the risks and costs of getting access to desirable markets.[22]

Supporting rural communities also means ensuring that peasant farmers have secure access to and control over land, water, seeds, markets, and capital, while increasing public investments in health, education, and infrastructure in rural areas. Revision of intellectual property (IP) laws toward a more equitable system that recognizes farmers' rights to save, use, exchange, and sell seed can begin to address some of the threats to livelihoods posed by current IP regimes that tend to favor large corporations as patent holders. In addition, the establishment of flexible and fair regional and global trade arrangements is a fundamental policy shift that must occur to enable farmers and developing countries in particular to meet their basic food and livelihood security needs.

Thus, ultimately what is required today is nothing less than the democratization of the global food system. A fully functioning food democracy requires food literacy of its members—that is, people need to understand not just the origins of the food they consume but the social, political, and cultural context of its producers and everyone involved in the distribution of that food.[23]

In practical terms, rebalancing power in the food system involves both revitalizing local and regional food systems and curtailing the concentration of power and excesses of influence in the globalized system. Progress toward the former can be accomplished through democratic local and state food policy councils that enable broad public participation in setting food policies, as found in Canada, India, the Netherlands, the United Kingdom, and the United States. Farmers' parliaments can collectively determine natural resource and agricultural management practices at the community level, as happens in Rajasthan, India. And urban and peri-urban agricultural projects can be encouraged, as they already are in cities in Brazil, China, Cuba, Ghana, Kenya, India, Uganda, Venezuela, and Vietnam.[24]

But communities acting on their own cannot redefine the global structures, institutions, and market forces that all too often favor short-term financial gain by powerful interests over the long-term well-being of the vulnerable and poor and the ecosystem functions on which life on the planet depends. Thus national and international intervention is necessary.

Financial incentives—such as credit lines, crop insurance, income tax exemptions, green procurement policies, and payments for ecosystem services—can encourage farmers' conversions toward environmentally sustainable practices, while taxes on health and environmental harms can raise revenues for environmental conservation while discouraging reliance on chemical inputs, fossil fuels, and water- or energy-intensive production.

Strong moral leadership from national governments and international bodies is needed to halt the current epidemic of land grabs and to establish and enforce high environmental and social justice standards. National engagement is required in global arenas to strengthen international environmental agreements and treaties, revise international laws of ownership and access, and ensure that national efforts to protect the public good are not undermined by a narrow interpretation of trade rules. In domestic arenas, public policy intervention is increasingly sought to reverse trends in corporate concentration in the food and agricultural industry, enforce anti-monopoly and fair competition policy, and ensure that public research agendas serve the public good.[25]

Finally, social movements around the world are calling for a rights-based approach to food—and a growing number of governments, including Brazil, Ecuador, Malawi, and Nepal, are taking just such an approach. Protecting, respecting, and fulfilling the right to food through equitable and environmentally sustainable development must become a defining goal for the twenty-first century. The IAASTD provides us with a comprehensive array of some of the best and most promising ways to implement a rights-based approach to the fair governance of food and agricultural systems, consistent with sound ecological and social knowledge and thus grounded in the principles of food sovereignty.[26]

Innovations in Governance

Anuradha Mittal

Agriculture is the world's largest industry, employing more than 1 billion people and generating at least a trillion dollars' worth of food annually. Yet nearly a billion people remain hungry, even while agriculture's destructive impacts on climate and biodiversity continue to expand.[27]

A humanitarian and ecological crisis of this proportion necessitates a questioning of the current industrial agricultural system. In 2008 an alarming increase in the number of hungry people triggered numerous high-level conferences on food security. Lofty commitments and pledges were made promising aid and change. Two years later, not much has changed.

The problem lies in this key fallacy: World hunger continues to be framed as a crisis of supply and demand that should be addressed mainly by improving agricultural output and development. This has resulted in undue emphasis on technological solutions such as genetic engineering and increased use of chemical inputs to boost production, while ignoring issues of governance and accountability related to aid commitments, public spending, public/private partnerships, and policy recommendations of international financial institutions and donor countries.

To ward off the charge that this framing of the issue ignores the structural causes of food insecurity, and to build acceptance for technology-based solutions, the talk now is about the need for investment in all approaches to end hunger—agroecological, chemical-intensive, and genetic engineering. Bill Gates, co-chair and trustee of the Bill and Melinda Gates Foundation, which is a major player in agriculture through the Alliance for a Green Revolution in Africa, contended in a speech at the 2009 World Food Prize Symposium that both productivity and sustainability in agriculture are needed to launch a comprehensive program to help poor farmers.[28]

But this attempt at reconciliation ignores the fact that most agricultural investment today is going into technical solutions that concentrate power in the hands of a few while missing the social and environmental potential of

---

Anuradha Mittal is executive director of the Oakland Institute in California.

others. More important, it overlooks the key point that genetic engineering—the human manipulation of an organism's genetic material in a way that does not occur naturally, which carries poorly studied environmental and health risks as well as problematic IP laws—has predictably thrived because of the creation of a favorable environment made possible by several actors. These include public/private partnerships, like the research partnership for developing transgenic SPFMV-resistant sweet potato between the Kenya Agricultural Research Institute (KARI), Monsanto, the Agricultural Biotechnology Support Program (ABSP) of the U.S. Agency for International Development (AID), and the Mid-American Consortium. This partnership, while focused on sweet potato, has helped influence the establishment of national biosafety structures, the preparation and submission of biosafety permit applications, laboratory and field biosafety evaluation of genetically modified crops, and intellectual property rights (IPR) protection and technology transfer mechanisms. Agroecological innovations did not benefit from protected IPR and had to rely on the financially strapped public sector for their development. The partnerships have also allowed the biotechnology industry to mine public agricultural colleges and land grant universities for scientific research while seeking academic backing for technology.

Another boost has come from philanthropic institutions, including the Rockefeller Foundation and the Gates Foundation, whose financial power has advanced an agricultural system that has come under criticism from many civil society and farmer groups for undermining a farmer-led, low-input approach. The Gates Foundation, for instance, has spent millions of dollars on the development of GE "nutritious" cassava, bananas, rice, and sorghum. It awarded a $21.2-million five-year grant in 2009 to the International Potato Center to produce high-yielding, stress-tolerant varieties of sweet potato and nearly

$1.4 million for three years to Centro Internacional de Agricultura Tropical in 2010 to support efforts aimed at accelerating breeding of cassava for greater productivity, disease resistance, and other traits. And in partnership with the Rockefeller Foundation and the Syngenta Foundation, it is funding the Insect Resistant Maize for Africa Project at the Kenya Agricultural Research Institute. Nearly 80 percent of Gates Foundation funding in Kenya is directed toward biotechnology, and over $100 million in grants are to organizations connected to Monsanto.[29]

Another key player that has helped advance GE in global agriculture is the U.S. Agency for International Development. One of its major projects, initially managed by Michigan State University and now by Cornell, is the Agricultural Biotechnology Support Program, which includes private-sector partners such as Monsanto, Alpha Seed, and Bayer. One example of an ABSP project was the Southern Africa Regional Biosafety Programme, with the stated objective of providing the "regulatory foundation to support field testing of genetically engineered products." AID has also supported the development of insect-resistant eggplant varieties in India, where they were to be released and then transferred to the Philippines and Bangladesh, despite widespread resistance that eventually led to a moratorium on its release in India.[30]

While the discourse of "increased investment in agriculture" is used to pave the way for a technical revolution in agriculture, U.N. Special Rapporteur on the Right to Food Olivier de Schutter has noted, like many before him, that the issue is not merely one of increasing budget allocations to agriculture but rather choosing from different models of agricultural development, which may have different impacts and benefit various groups differently. Alternatives that would meet the needs of the hungry, smallholder farmers, and the environment abound at local, national, and regional levels.

Belo Horizonte in Brazil, for example, is recognized as a world pioneer in governance for food security. In 1993 the city set out a policy framework that committed it to the concept of food sovereignty: the right of peoples to define their own food and agricultural policies, to protect and regulate their production and trade in such a manner as to secure sustainable development, to determine the degree of their autonomy, and to eliminate dumping in their markets.[31]

Citizens' right to food was actively realized through several innovative programs, including a council of citizen, labor, business, and church representatives to advise in the design and implementation of a new food system; participatory budgeting; "Direct from the Country" farmer produce stands in busy downtown areas; markets that provide food at about two thirds of the market price; "People's Restaurants" that daily serve 12,000 or more people using mostly locally grown food for the equivalent of less than 50¢ a meal; and extensive community and school gardens as well as nutrition classes. Federal funds, used to buy whole food mostly from local growers, also subsidize school lunches.[32]

Thanks partly to these programs, in just a decade Belo Horizonte has cut its infant death rate—widely used as evidence of hunger—by more than half. Today these initiatives benefit almost 40 percent of the city's population for about a penny per day per person.[33]

There are also examples of action at national levels to protect the livelihoods of farmers and food security. For instance, in Indonesia, after achieving self-sufficiency in rice in 1984 the government liberalized its agricultural markets in the 1990s and drastically reduced public support to its farmers. By 1998, the tables had turned and the country was the world's

Locally grown melons for sale in Nouakchott, Mauritania

largest importer of rice and largest recipient of international food aid. The government reversed its liberalization policy in 2002 and curbed imports of rice while encouraging domestic production through higher tariffs. Indonesia was self-sufficient in rice once again in 2004. In 2008, when rice prices skyrocketed in international markets, Indonesia's public policy allowed the country to keep rice prices stable, ensuring access to food for the country's poor and vulnerable.[34]

For an example at the regional level, the Economic Community of West African States (ECOWAS) makes an interesting case. In May 2008, at the peak of the food price crisis, ECOWAS launched the "offensive for food production to combat hunger." The strategy—rapid and sustainable increase of staple food production, value chain organization, and regional market integration and regulation, along with safety nets—is intended to implement the common agricultural policy that was prepared in 2005 but never implemented. The strategy also sets up an ECOWAS commission to support member states in developing agricultural investment programs and partnerships for coordinated implementation.

ECOWAS has already mobilized $900 million in supporting funds. This integration strategy is also catching on in East Africa and Southeast Asia.[35]

To address concerns around increasing productivity and improving livelihoods, there are also examples that demonstrate a low-input, farmer and environmentally friendly way forward. For instance, to address significant limitations on grain productivity and food security, researchers from the Rothamsted Research Station in the United Kingdom and the International Center of Insect Physiology and Ecology have worked in East Africa to develop an effective ecologically based pest management solution for stem borers. Stem borer losses in this region average 20–40 percent and reach as high as 80 percent in some areas. Losses to *striga* can be even greater, with 30–100 percent losses recorded in many areas. When the two pests occur together, farmers frequently lose their entire grain crop. Economic losses from stem borers and *striga* weeds amount to about $7 billion annually.[36]

A "push-pull" intercropping technology has emerged for managing stem borers and *striga* weed while increasing animal forage and enhancing soil quality and fertility. From initial experimental trials to on-farm experimentation and widespread project implementation, the push-pull selective intercropping strategy has proved highly successful. A seven-year agronomic and cost-benefit study of push-pull technology in six districts in western Kenya revealed that it consistently delivered significantly higher maize grain yields when compared with maize-bean intercrops and maize monoculture systems. The study's cost-benefit analysis showed that in all but one of the districts the push-pull systems outperformed maize-bean and maize monoculture systems economically, despite initial variable and labor costs being higher in the first year.[37]

One useful tool to achieve some of the needed shifts in models of agricultural development that are needed is an ombudsman—an independent authority with the power to mediate between an institution and the people it is meant to serve. An example is the Office of the Compliance Advisor/Ombudsman (CAO), a recourse mechanism for the International Finance Corporation (IFC) and the Multilateral Investment Guarantee Agency (MIGA), the private-sector lending arms of the World Bank Group. CAO works to address the concerns of individuals or communities affected by IFC/MIGA projects, to enhance the social and environmental outcomes of these projects, and to foster greater public accountability of IFC and MIGA.[38]

For example, in response to a complaint filed by nongovernmental organizations, a 2009 CAO audit found that IFC funding of the Wilmar Group, an Indonesian plantation developer, violated the institution's own procedures by allowing commercial concerns to trump environmental and social standards. This led to a suspension of IFC funding of the oil palm sector pending the development of safeguards to ensure that lending does not cause social or environmental harm. A similar governance structure, which provides communities recourse and helps address their grievances, could be useful in guiding major foundation and aid agency funding in the realm of agriculture.[39]

Social audits are another valuable tool for ensuring that funders and corporations are supporting truly sustainable agriculture. The goal is careful assessments of the social and environmental effects of economic actions. For example, since 1989 the ice cream company Ben & Jerry's has completed and published an annual Social and Environmental Assessment Report. This details the company's progress on social mission goals (such as fair trade ingredient conversion, implementation of sustainable dairy programs, and greenhouse gas reductions) and includes a comprehensive review of social and environmental impacts, written with input from department heads. What makes the report legitimate is its audit by an independent third party and its use for internal stakeholder education, external communications, and tracking and planning by management and directors. This public and transparent tracking of social, economic, and environmental footprints through independent audits leaves little room for "green-washing" and public relations opportunism.[40]

There is growing recognition that to successfully address world hunger, which is rooted in poverty and environmental degradation, intervention and a paradigm shift are required that would recognize agriculture as being fundamental to the well-being of all people—both in terms of access to safe and nutritious food and as the foundation of healthy communities, cultures, and the environment. More important, agriculture needs to be seen as a struggle to ensure the human right to food for all. This requires that the emphasis shift from finding silver bullet solutions to hunger to identifying the true causes of hunger so they can be dealt with effectively.

Innovations in Policy Reform

Alexandra Spieldoch

The remarkable news is that after years of neglect, governments are reinvesting in agriculture and giving priority to small-scale producers. They are recognizing the important role of women, infrastructure, safety nets, and local markets, and they are rightfully reviewing ways to improve emergency food assistance, financial markets, and market linkages. They are claiming support for a stronger United Nations and for more-coordinated and effective responses to the food crisis. All of this holds great potential for eradicating hunger.

Leaders are taking important steps to improve the global food system at a time when change is greatly needed. In 2008 a high-level task force came out with the Comprehensive Framework for Action (CFA), which represents a general road map for governments to engage in food and agricultural policy reform. At the U.N. World Food Summit in 2009, governments affirmed the role of the Committee on World Food Security of the U.N. Food and Agriculture Organization (FAO), strengthening its mandate and using the CFA as a guideline for content. In 2009, the World Bank launched the Global Agriculture and Food Security Program, also referred to as the food security trust fund, to set up lending programs for developing countries. In June 2010, the fund identified five countries to receive the first round of food security support. And in the United States, in 2010 the Obama administration launched its Feed the Future initiative, which focuses on food security, health, and gender as top priorities for international development.[41]

Despite all these positive steps, a major concern still is that a large chunk of investment is being earmarked to increase global supply, to expand the role of agribusiness in guiding

Alexandra Spieldoch is Coordinator of the Network of Women Ministers and Leaders in Agriculture within Women Organizing for Change in Agriculture & Natural Resource Management.

new markets, and to expand trade. In this context, some donors are putting too much emphasis on increasing supply for an international food market rather than the kind of investment that will reinvigorate local markets and smallholder producers.

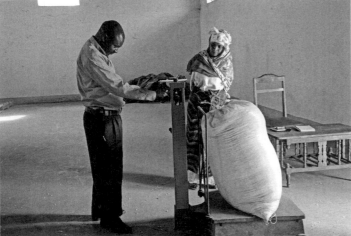

A farmer watches her maize being weighed into a cooperative warehouse, Tanzania

The U.N. statement in 1999 on the right to food maintains that "the roots of the problem of hunger and malnutrition are not lack of food but lack of access to available food, inter alia because of poverty, by large segments of the population." The fact that access and distribution—not supply—are contributing most to hunger is an important distinction. Daryll Ray from the Agricultural Policy Analysis Center at the University of Tennessee reported in early 2010 that increasing production does not correlate with reducing hunger. From 1980 to 2009, the production of barley, corn, millet, oats, rice, rye, sorghum, and wheat increased by nearly 55 percent and that of seven oilseeds increased by almost 189 percent, for a total of some 67 percent for 15 crops. Meanwhile, hunger also increased and countries' food self-sufficiency declined in that same period.[42]

Clearly, global markets have a crucial role to play in contributing to food security. But markets are not self-correcting, and they need certain controls so as to reduce their potential to do harm. During the 2008 price crisis, countries lacking productive capacity were too dependent on the global food market and lacked the proper controls to curb speculation and price volatility, leading to the huge spike in the number of hungry people.

Thinking ahead, policymakers need to take the appropriate steps to guarantee that markets are monitored more closely. Protectionist measures are often dismissed by the most entrenched free-market ideologues. Yet some protections make good sense and should be part of the policy reform that is being proposed for food and agriculture. In the mix of reforms being proposed and implemented, governments do not have to reinvent the wheel. They can begin by reviewing either existing initiatives or those that have been proposed to achieve food security and sustainable development in different regions and communities.

Since 2003, for example, developing countries—including African nations—have sought protections through Special Safeguard Mechanisms such as higher tariffs that would block food imports being able to flood their domestic markets. They have also tried to exempt certain foods from tariff reductions through a list of Special Products. While these provisions will not solve all market discrepancies, they are important tools that give countries more room to invest in and protect their own domestic production to meet food security goals. For example, import surges in sugar and dairy undermined production in Kenya; the same is true with poultry, rice, and vegetable oils in Cameroon, with maize, sugar, and milk in Malawi, and with rice in Indonesia and Nepal.[43]

In one case, poultry imports increased in Cameroon by 300 percent between 1999 and 2004. Not surprisingly, 92 percent of domestic poultry producers left the sector as they were unable to make a living with the cheap flood of birds into the country. There are different reasons for this trend. One major factor is that during those years, Cameroon reduced its import tariffs to less than 25 percent; this led to poultry imports increasing by close to six times in that time period. When Cameroon raised its tariffs to 42 percent in 2004 and restricted a certain number of imports, the local poultry industry saw some improvement as domestic producers were able to receive a higher price.[44]

Given excessive speculation in 2008 and predictions that prices will continue to rise as much as 40 percent in the next decade, governments should be thinking about markets differently. In June 2010, President Obama signed the Wall Street Reform and Consumer Protection Act. Americans hope that this will restrict excessive speculation on agriculture commodity futures markets and mandate public and regulated exchanges. The legislation is an important step to ending market manipulation. The Institute for Agriculture and Trade Policy points out that "greater transparency and tougher position limits in the U.S. will also benefit many developing countries that rely on agricultural exports as they will benefit from greater price predictability and stability in the global market."[45]

Governments can also support stable markets by investing in production and infrastructure for food reserves at varying levels; these can serve to restore confidence in markets and contribute to food security on the ground. They can help farmers store their produce so that it does not go to waste, gain access to credit by using their crop inventory as collateral, and meet the food security needs of their communities. Small-scale farmers, including women, local communities, and culturally appropriate foods can and should be given priority in reserves programs.

In terms of regional initiatives, warehouse and warehouse receipting programs are being set up in Africa with support from the World Food Programme, the East Africa Grain Council (EAGC), and the U.S. Agency for International Development. The EAGC has launched three certified warehouses (mostly for maize) in Kenya. The Southern African Development Community has a regional food reserves facility. In Asia, the ASEAN + 3 East Asia Emergency Rice Reserve has been set up to respond to shocks and food scarcity in that region. At the global level, some commentators are also proposing an international mechanism through virtual reserves or some global governance body to monitor stock levels and prices. Strengthening the Food Aid Convention will also be important to help countries get culturally appropriate food when they need it.[46]

As for investment, large investment deals to outsource food and fuel, sometimes referred to as "land grabs," are occurring without proper regulations and processes in place to protect people's rights and the environment. In September 2010, the World Bank released a report that highlights the need for more yield output in Africa but also continues to raise concerns about how investment can undermine land rights and marginalize small-scale producers. Principles on Responsible Agricultural Investment have also been drafted by the World Bank Group, FAO, the International Fund for Agricultural Development, and the U.N. Conference on Trade and Development. Conceptually, they would help guide investors so that existing rights to land and associated national resources are recognized and respected, food security is strengthened, and investment is transparent, accountable, and subject to environmental review and human rights impact assessments.[47]

But in order for this kind of investment—

or for that matter, any investment—to be successful, mandatory codes of conduct are necessary to hold corporations accountable to broader social and environmental goals. These should include provisions to ensure that land rights and land reform laws are protected, that corporations are properly taxed and a certain percentage of money stays in the community, that they invest in needed infrastructure (such as schools, hospitals, and roads), that small-scale producers benefit, that production does not harm the environment, that labor rights are protected, and that corporate dealings are publicly discussed, monitored, and changed as needed to achieve the hoped-for results. Without these safeguards, and certainly a few more, land deals will remain precarious at best and devastating at worst.

Developing countries need the kind of investments that would help them move away from their dependence on export-led growth and international markets for overall food supply (particularly risky in times of high prices) and instead toward the priorities of small-scale producers, a less intensive approach to agriculture, and sounder food security policies in line with the right to food. In 2009 FAO released a guide to conducting a "right to food" assessment, which can help countries identify the hungry and the poor, conduct an assessment of legal, policy, and institutional frameworks, develop a national food security plan, set responsibilities and obligations, monitor progress, and establish legal recourse.[48]

Reference to the right to food already exists in 24 constitutions as well as in different national policies, food security institutions, and courts. The U.N. Special Rapporteur on the Right to Food has reviewed right-to-food initiatives under way in Brazil, India, Mozambique, Nepal, and South Africa, among others. The results are encouraging and embrace a mix of approaches, including legal reform and participatory processes for creating sound domestic and foreign policy. And while the results may be mixed or perhaps not as fast as some would wish, the initiatives set important precedents for achieving the right to food.[49]

For instance, Ecuador passed a framework law in 2009 to implement its commitment to the right to food, which includes provisions to give small-scale farmers access to capital and resources, public participation in decision-making processes, and protection for indigenous peoples, among others. In another example, Brazil's Fome Zero (Zero Hunger Strategy) supports the right to food through emergency assistance, increased access and supply to basic food, and income generation. One noted program within the Fome Zero is the school feeding program that provides free meals to schoolchildren. A minimum of 30 percent of the food purchased under the school feeding program must come from small family farms in Brazil. Another program provides cash transfers to poor families to help increase their buying power for food.[50]

There is much to celebrate in terms of the new attention to food and agriculture. The challenge now is to shape it so that it benefits real people on the ground. Because agriculture is at the heart of international development, it must stay at the forefront of the world community's radar. There is no time like the present to get the proper global framework in place.

Notes

State of the World: A Year in Review

October 2009. World Bank, "Uganda Registers First Forestry Project in Africa to Reduce Global Warming Emission," press release (Washington, DC: 6 October 2009); Norwegian Nobel Committee, "The Nobel Peace Prize for 2009," press release (Oslo: 9 October 2009); "China's Lead Smelters Poison Hundreds of Children," *Environment News Service*, 14 October 2009; Pew Research Center for The People and The Press, "Modest Support for 'Cap And Trade' Policy. Fewer Americans See Solid Evidence of Global Warming," press release (Washington, DC: 22 October 2009).

November 2009. K. L. Smith et al., "Climate, Carbon Cycling, and Deep-ocean Ecosystems," *Proceedings of the National Academy of Sciences*, vol. 106 (2009), pp. 19211–18; U.S. Environmental Protection Agency (EPA), "EPA Study Reveals Widespread Contamination of Fish in US Lakes and Reservoirs," press release (Washington, DC: 10 November 2009); WWF, "Data Shows Illegal Ivory Trade on Rise," press release (Cambridge, U.K.: 16 November 2009); U.N. Food and Agriculture Organization, "Renewed Commitment to End Hunger," press release (Rome: 16 November 2009); "China Unveils Emissions Targets Ahead of Copenhagen," *BBC News*, 26 November 2009.

December 2009. Slow Food International, "Terra Madre Day: A Thousand Ways to Celebrate," *Slow Food Time*, December 2009; U.N. High Commissioner for Refugees, "Climate Change Could Become the Biggest Driver of Displacement: UNHCR Chief," press release (Copenhagen: 16 December 2009); "Copenhagen Accord" (Copenhagen: 18 December 2009), available at www.denmark.dk/NR/rdonlyres/C41B62AB-4688-4ACE-BB7B-F6D2C8AAEC20/0/copenhagen_accord.pdf.

January 2010. District Department of the Environment, "Fenty Administration Begins 'Skip the Bag, Save the River' Education Campaign," press release (Washington, DC: 16 November 2009); Commonwealth of Massachusetts, Executive Office of Energy and Environmental Affairs, "Patrick Administration Releases Final Blueprint for Managing Development in State Waters," press release (Boston: 4 January 2010); Lester R. Brown, "U.S. Car Fleet Shrank by Four Million in 2009—After a Century of Growth, U.S. Fleet Entering Era of Decline," *Plan B Update* (Washington, DC: Earth Policy Institute, 6 January 2010); "Prius Hybrid Tops Japan's Car Sales in 2009," *ClimateWire*, 11 January 2010; Simon Romero and Marc Lacey, "Fierce Quake Devastates Haitian Capital," *New York Times*, 12 January 2010; "Haiti's Earthquake Death Toll Revised to at Least 250,000," *Daily Telegraph* (U.K.), 22 April 2010.

February 2010. U.N. Environment Programme (UNEP), "UN Wildlife Conference Enhances Intergovernmental Cooperation to Safeguard Sharks," press release (Bonn: 12 February 2010); "Smallholders, Rural Producers Key to Slashing Global Hunger and Poverty—Ban," *UN News Service*, 17 February 2010; Conservation International, "Primates in Peril," press release (Bristol, U.K.: 18 February 2010); Mekong River Commission, "Drought Conditions Cause Low Mekong Water Flow," press release (Vientiane: 26 February 2010).

March 2010. Booz & Company, "A New Source of Power, the Potential for Renewable Energy in the MENA Region," press release (Abu Dhabi: 14 March 2010); Arctic Species Trend Index, "High Arctic Species on Thin Ice," press release (Whitehorse, Canada: 17 March 2010); Tyler Hamilton, "CO2-eating Algae Turns Cement Maker Green," *Toronto Star*, 18 March 2010; Clifford Coonan, "More than 50 Million Hit by Drought in South of China," *Irish Times*, 22 March 2010; Michael Renner, "Auto Industry in Turmoil, but Chinese Production Surges," *Vital Signs Online* (Washington, DC: Worldwatch Institute, 11 February 2010).

April 2010. Bo Elberling, Hanne H. Christiansen, and Birger U. Hansen, "High Nitrous Oxide Production from Thawing Permafrost," *Nature Geoscience*, vol. 3 (2010), pp. 332–35; Jeffrey Gettleman, "With Flights Grounded, Kenya's Produce Wilts," *New York Times*, 19 April 2010; Jeremy Clarke and Antony Gitonga, "Volcano Disrupts African Rose Exports," *Reuters*, 20 April 2010; Campbell Robertson, "Search Continues After Oil Rig Blast," *New York Times*, 20 April 2010; Campbell Robertson and Clifford Krauss, "Gulf Spill Is the Largest of Its Kind, Scientists Say," *New York Times*, 2 August 2010; Cape Wind, "Cape Wind Approved by Federal Government as America's First Offshore Wind Farm; Project Will Add Clean Energy Jobs for Region," press release (Boston: 28 April 2010).

May 2010. Nitin Sethi, "CFL Bulb Scheme Will Be World's Biggest Carbon Credit Project," *Times of India*, 1 May 2010; EPA, "EPA Sets Thresholds for Greenhouse Gas Permitting Requirements/Small Businesses and Farms Will Be Shielded," press release (Washington, DC: 13 May 2010); Timothy R. McClanahan, "Effects of Fisheries Closures and Gear Restrictions on Fishing Income in a Kenyan Coral Reef," *Conservation Biology*, 21 May 2010; "REDD+ Partnership" (Oslo: 27 May 2010); World Resources Institute, "Global Alliance Launched to Curb Trade in Illegal Wood," press release (Washington, DC: 26 May 2010).

June 2010. European Environment Agency, "Climate Change: Commissioner Hedegaard Welcomes Fall in EU Greenhouse Gas Emissions for Fifth Year Running," press release (Brussels: 2 June 2010); Sarah H. Olson et al., "Deforestation and Malaria in Mâncio Lima County, Brazil," *Emerging Infectious Diseases*, July 2010; Maplecroft, "New Maplecroft Index Rates Pakistan and Egypt Among Nations Facing 'Extreme' Water Security Risks," press release (Bath, U.K.: 24 June 2010); Paul Gipe, "Italy Surpasses USA in Solar PV," *GreenEnergyTimes.org*, 28 June 2010.

July 2010. WWF, "Russia to Create New National Parks and Reserves Nearly Size of Switzerland," press release (Gland, Switzerland: 6 July 2010); UNEP, "Global Trends in Green Energy 2009: New Power Capacity from Renewable Sources Tops Fossil Fuels Again in US, Europe," press release (Nairobi: 15 July 2010); U.S. National Oceanic and Atmospheric Administration, "NOAA: June, April to June, and Year-to-Date Global Temperatures are Warmest on Record," press release (Washington, DC: 15 July 2010); Amie Ferris-Rotman and Aleksandras Budrys, "Russia Swelters in Heatwave, Many Crops Destroyed," *Reuters*, 16 July 2010; "General Assembly Declares Access to Clean Water and Sanitation Is a Human Right," *UN News Service*, 28 July 2010; UNESCO, "List of World Heritage in Danger: World Heritage Committee Inscribes the Tombs of Buganda Kings (Uganda) and Removes Galapagos Islands (Ecuador)," press release (Paris: 29 July 2010).

August 2010. Panthera, "Myanmar Officially Designates World's Largest Tiger Reserve in the Hukaung Valley," press release (Hukaung Valley, Myanmar: 3 August 2010); University of Delaware, "Greenland Glacier Calves Island 4 Times the Size of Manhattan, UD Scientist Reports," press release (Newark, DE: 6 August 2010); "Pakistan's Flooding Sweeps South," *BBC News*, 6 August 2010; Nathanial Gronewold and ClimateWire, "Is the Flooding in Pakistan a Climate Change Disaster?" *ScientificAmerican.com*, 18 August 2010; International Economic Platform for Renewable Energies, "Economic Crisis Will Slow Global CO2 Emissions," press release (Münster, Germany: 31 August 2010); Tim Cocks, "Drought Tolerant Maize to Hugely Benefit Africa: Study," *Reuters*, 25 August 2010.

September 2010. International Water Management Institute, "In a Changing Climate, Erratic Rainfall Poses Growing Threat to Rural Poor, Justifying Bigger Investment in Water Storage, New Report Says," press release (Stockholm: 6 September 2010); Conservation International, "Shell Shock: The Catastrophic Decline of the World's Freshwater Turtles," press release (Washington, DC: 10 September 2010); FAO, "925 Million in Chronic Hunger Worldwide," press release (Rome: 14 September 2010); Allan Dowd, "World Pays High Price for Overfishing, Studies Say," *Reuters*, 14 September 2010; "Global Fisheries Research Finds Promise and Peril: While Industry Contributes $240B Annually, Overfishing Takes Toll on People and Revenue," *ScienceDaily.com*, 14 September 2010; Vattenfall, "Vattenfall Inaugurates World's Largest Offshore Wind Farm," press release (London: 23 September 2010).

Chapter 1. Charting a New Path to Eliminating Hunger

1.   Christine Zaleski, e-mail to Danielle Nierenberg, 27 August 2010; Christine Zaleski, "Turning the Catch of the Day into Improved Livelihoods for the Whole Community," *Nourishing the Planet Blog*, 12 July 2010.

2.   Zaleski, "Turning the Catch of the Day," op. cit. note 1.

3.   U.N. Food and Agriculture Organization (FAO), "925 Million in Chronic Hunger Worldwide," press release (Rome: 14 September 2010). Box 1–1 from the following: FAO, op. cit. this note; Ghana from Sara J. Scherr and Courtney Wallace, "Rural Landscapes and Livelihood in Africa: Sustainable Development in the Context of Climate Change and Competing Demands on Rural Lands and Ecosystems," Issue Paper for Dialogue towards a Shared Action Framework for Agriculture, Food Security and Climate Change in Africa, Eco-Agriculture Partners, and World Wildlife Fund, Washington, DC, 6–9 July 2010, p. 4; FAO, "Global Hunger Declining, But Still Unacceptably High," Policy Brief (Rome: 14 September 2010); FAO, "Food Security Statistics by Country," at www.fao.org/economic/ess/food-securitystatistics/food-security-statistics-by-country/en; World Health Organization, *Children: Reducing Mortal-*

ity Fact Sheet (Geneva: November 2009); International Food Policy Research Institute (IFPRI), "2009 Global Hunger Index Calls Attention to Gender Inequality," press release (Washington DC: 14 October 2009); Shaohua Chen and Martin Ravallion, *The Developing World Is Poorer Than We Thought, But No Less Successful in the Fight against Poverty* (Washington, DC: Development Research Working Group, World Bank, 2008), p. 4; UN HABITAT, *State of the World's Cities 2010/2011: Bridging the Urban Divide* (London: Earthscan, 2010), p. 28; U.S. Agency for International Development, "USAID's Office of Food for Peace 2009 Statistics," press release (Washington, DC: 10 January 2010); trends in agricultural development funding from U.N. Department of Economic and Social Affairs, *Trends in Sustainable Development 2008–2009: Agriculture, Rural Development, Land, Desertification, and Drought* (New York: United Nations, 2008); African national agricultural budgets from U.N. Department of Economic and Social Affairs, Division for Sustainable Development, "Summary Report of Multi-Stakeholder Dialogue on Implementing Sustainable Development," 1 February 2010, New York; grain imports from Stacey Rosen et al., *Food Security Assessment, 2007 GFA- 19* (Washington, DC: Economic Research Service, U.S. Department of Agriculture (USDA), 2007); Figure from FAO, "Hunger Statistics," at www.fao.org/hunger/en, and from FAO, "Hunger," at www.fao.org/hunger/hunger-home/en.

4.   FAO, Fisheries and Aquaculture Department, *The State of World Fisheries and Aquaculture 2008* (Rome: 2009), p. 4.

5.   International Assessment of Agricultural Knowledge, Science and Technology for Development (IAASTD), *Agriculture at a Crossroads, Synthesis Report* (Washington, DC: Island Press, 2009); Figure 1–1 from FAO, *FAO Food Price Index* (2010).

6.   World Bank, *World Development Report 2008: Agriculture for Development* (Washington, DC: 2007).

7.   FAO, "Global Hunger Declining," op. cit. note 3.

8.   W. Makumba et al., "The Long-Term Effects of a *Gliricidia*-Maize Intercropping System in

Southern Malawi, on *Gliricidia* and Maize Yields, and Soil Properties," *Agriculture, Ecosystems & Environment*, August 2006, pp. 85–92; D. Garrity and L. Verchot, *Meeting the Challenges of Climate Change and Poverty through Agroforestry* (Nairobi: World Agroforestry Centre, 2008); storage of cowpeas from Purdue University, "Gates Foundation Funds Purdue Effort to Protect Food, Enhance African Economy," press release (Seattle, WA: 6 July 2007).

9.   Chris Reij, Gray Tappan, and Melinda Smale, *Agroenvironmental Transformation in the Sahel: Another Kind of "Green Revolution,"* IFPRI Discussion Paper (Washington, DC: IFPRI, 2009).

10. Consultative Group on International Agricultural Research, *Financial Report 2008* (Washington, DC: 2008).

11. Data on research expenditures from Board on Agriculture, *Investing in Research: A Proposal to Strengthen the Agricultural, Food, and Environmental System* (Washington, DC: National Research Council, 1989), "Appendix B: Private Sector Research Activities and Prospects." Totals exclude Forest Service and Economic Research Service research and development and do not count research by the food processing industry.

12. R. Bunch, "Adoption of Green Manure and Cover Crops," *LEISA Magazine*, vol. 19, no. 4 (2003), pp. 16–18; see Chapter 6 for interviews with farmers and information on soil exhaustion and fertilizer subsidies.

13. Johan Rockström et al., "Managing Water in Rainfed Agriculture–The Need for a Paradigm Shift," *Agricultural Water Management*, April 2010, pp. 543–50; see Chapter 4 for MoneyMaker and other pumps.

14. See Chapter 4; Johan Rockström et al., "Conservation Farming Strategies in East and Southern Africa: Yields and Rain Water Productivity from On-farm Action Research," *Soil & Tillage Research*, April 2009, pp. 23–32.

15. Soil Association, *Telling Porkies: The Big Fat Lie About Doubling Food Production* (Bristol, U.K.: 2010), p. 3.

16. Stockholm International Water Institute, *Saving Water: From Field to Fork—Curbing Losses and Wastage in the Food Chain* (Stockholm: 2008); see Chapter 9 for low-cost fixes.

17. See Chapter 13 for information on Justine Chiyesu.

18. Forum for Agricultural Research in Africa, *Framework for African Agricultural Productivity* (Accra: 2006); "Rural Landscapes and Livelihoods in Africa: Sustainable Development in the Context of Climate Change and Competing Demands on Rural Lands and Ecosystems," draft Discussion Paper for Dialogue towards a Shared Action Framework for Agriculture, Food Security and Climate Change in Africa, Bellagio, Italy, 6–9 July 2010.

19. People depending on urban agriculture from Alice Hovorka, Henk de Zeeuw, and Mary Njenga, *Women Feeding Cities: Mainstreaming Gender in Urban Agriculture and Food Security* (Warwickshire, U.K.: Practical Action Publishing Ltd, 2009); see also Chapter 10.

20. Developing Innovations in School Cultivation, at projectdiscnews.blogspot.com, viewed 12 May 2010.

21. Number of hungry children in the United States from Mark Nord, Margaret Andrews, and Steven Carlson, *Household Food Security in the United States, 2008*, Economic Research Report No. 83 (Washington, DC: USDA, November 2009), p. 15; USDA, Food and Nutrition Service, "National School Lunch Program," program fact sheet, at www.fns.usda.gov/cnd/Lunch/About Lunch/NSLPFactSheet.pdf, updated September 2010; World Food Programme, *Feed Minds, Change Lives: School Feeding, the Millennium Development Goals and Girls' Empowerment* (Rome: 2010).

22. See Chapter 7.

23. Via Campesina, at viacampesina.org/en, viewed 27 September 2010; Global Crop Diversity Trust, at www.croptrust.org, viewed 27 September 2010. Table 1–1 from the following: world population total and share that is urban from FAO, "Global Issue: World Hunger and Poverty Facts and Statistics 2010," www.worldhunger.org/articles/

Learn/world%20hunger%20facts%202002.htm; population in sub-Saharan Africa, world urban population, share of sub-Saharan Africa that is urban, and average ages from United Nations, *World Population Prospects: The 2008 Revision* (New York: 2008); arable land from FAO, *FAOSTAT Statistical Database*, at faostat.fao.org; share of world food production that is smallholder from Development Fund/Utviklingsfondet, *Norway, A Viable Food Future* (Oslo: 2010), p. 7; share of sub-Saharan African food production that is smallholder from Eric Holt-Giménez, "From Food Crisis to Food Sovereignty: The Challenge of Social Movements," *Monthly Review*, July-August 2009, p. 145; urban population in sub-Saharan Africa from UN HABITAT, "Urban Indicators," at www.unhabitat.org/stats; hungry populations from FAO, "Global Hunger Declining," op. cit. note 3; underweight children from UNICEF, *The State of the World's Children 2009* (New York: December 2008), p. 23; percentage underweight from UNICEF, *The State of the World's Children 2008* (New York: December 2007); per capita added value output of agriculture from Forum for Agricultural Research in Africa, *Framework for African Agricultural Productivity* (Accra, Ghana: June 2006), p. 8.

24. Restriction to U.S. grown crops from U.S. Government Accountability Office, *International Food Assistance: Local and Regional Procurement Can Enhance the Efficiency of U.S. Food Aid, but Challenges May Constrain its Implementation* (Washington, DC: 2009); Barack Obama, Remarks at the Millennium Development Goals Summit, United Nations, New York, 22 September 2010; World Food Programme, "P4P Overview," at www.wfp.org/node/18711, viewed 12 May 2010.

25. Sara J. Scherr and Sajal Sthapit, *Mitigating Climate Change Through Food and Land Use*, Worldwatch Report 179 (Washington, DC: Worldwatch Institute, 2009), pp. 5, 9; World Agroforestry Centre, *Creating an Evergreen Agriculture in Africa for Food Security and Environmental Resilience* (Nairobi: 2009), p. 23; Scherr and Wallace, op. cit. note 3, p. 33.

26. See Chapter 8.

27. Ellen Gustafson, "Obesity + Hunger = 1 Global Food Issue," TEDxEast Talk, May 2010.

28. IAASTD, *Agriculture at a Crossroads: The Global Report* (Washington, DC: Island Press, 2009).

Measuring Success in Agricultural Development

1. P. B. R. Hazell, "Transforming Agriculture: The Green Revolution in Asia," in D. J. Spielman and R. Pandya-Lorch, eds., *Millions Fed: Proven Successes in Agricultural Development* (Washington, DC: International Food Policy Research Institute, 2009), pp. 25–32.

2. J. W. Bruce and Z. Li, "Crossing the River while Feeling the Rocks: Land-Tenure Reform in China," in Spielman and Pandya-Lorch, op. cit. note 1, pp. 131–38.

3. O. Erenstein, "Leaving the Plow Behind: Zero-Tillage Rice-Wheat Cultivation in the Indo-Gangetic Plains," in Spielman and Pandya-Lorch, op. cit. note 1, pp. 65–70.

4. C. Reij, G. Tappan, and M. Smale, "Re-Greening the Sahel: Farmer-Led Innovation in Burkina Faso and Niger," in Spielman and Pandya-Lorch, op. cit. note 1, pp. 53–58.

5. P. Roeder and K. Rich, "Conquering the Cattle Plague: The Global Effort to Eradicate Rinderpest," in Spielman and Pandya-Lorch, op. cit. note 1, pp. 109–16.

Chapter 2. Moving Ecoagriculture into the Mainstream

1. Kijabe Environmental Volunteers 2008, at tdesigns.free.fr/kenvo/index.html.

2. Millennium Ecosystem Assessment, *Ecosystems and Human Well-being: Synthesis* (Washington, DC: Island Press, 2005); Z. G. Bai et al., *Global Assessment of Land Degradation and Improvement. 1. Identification by Remote Sensing* (Wageningen, Netherlands: ISRIC–World Soil Information, 2008); Intergovernmental Panel on Climate Change (IPCC), *Climate Change 2007: Impacts, Adaptation and Vulnerability* (Cambridge, U.K.: Cambridge University Press, 2007).

3. J. A. McNeely and S. J. Scherr, *Ecoagriculture: Strategies to Feed the World and Save Wild Biodi-*

versity (Washington, DC: Island Press, 2003); S. J. Scherr and J. A. McNeely, "Biodiversity Conservation and Agricultural Sustainability: Towards a New Paradigm of 'Ecoagriculture' Landscapes," *Philosophical Transactions of the Royal Society B*, 12 February 2008, pp. 477–94.

4. Robert Watson from International Assessment of Agricultural Knowledge, Science and Technology (IAASTD), "Inter-Governmental Report Aims to Set New Agenda for Global Food Production," press release (London: 31 March 2008); Figure 2–1 prepared by Molly Phemister, adapted from O. P. Rupela et al., "Evaluation of Crop Production Systems based on Locally Available Biological Inputs," in N. T. Uphoff et al., eds., *Biological Approaches to Sustainable Soil Systems* (Boca Raton, FL: CRC Press, 2006), Figure 35.1.

5. M. Altieri, "Biodiversity and Biocontrol: Lessons from Insect Pest Management," *Advances in Plant Pathology*, vol. 11 (1995), pp. 191–209; S. R. Gliessman, *Agroecosystem Sustainability: Developing Practical Strategies* (Boca Raton, FL: CRC Press, 2001); N. Uphoff, *Agroecological Innovations: Increasing Food Production with Participatory Development* (London: Earthscan, 2002); McNeely and Scherr, op. cit. note 3; N. Uphoff et al., "Understanding the Functioning and Management of Soil Systems," in Uphoff et al., op. cit. note 4, pp. 3–13.

6. J. Thompson et al., "Biodiversity in Agroecosystems," in S. J. Scherr and J. A. McNeely, *Farming with Nature* (Washington, DC: Island Press, 2007); H. H. Koepf, B. D. Pettersson, and S. Wolfgang, *Biodynamic Agriculture: An Introduction* (Hudson, NY: Anthroposophic Press, 1976); B. Mollison and R. M. Slay, *Introduction to Permaculture* (Tyalgum, Australia: Tagari Publishers, 1991); J. G. Bene, H. W. Beall, and A. Côté, *Trees, Food and People: Land Management in the Tropics* (Ottawa: International Development Research Centre, 1977). Box 2–1 from the following: H. Willer and L. Kilcher, eds., *The World of Organic Agriculture—Statistics and Emerging Trends 2009* (Bonn, Frick, and Geneva: International Federation of Organic Agriculture Movements (IFOAM), Research Institute of Organic Agriculture, and International Trade Center, 2009); P. A. Oduol et al., "Adoption and Impact of Agro-

forestry Technologies on Rural Livelihoods in Southern Africa," presented at the Second National Agroforestry and Environment Workshop, Mbeya, Tanzania, 14–17 March 2006 (Maputo, Mozambique: World Agroforestry Centre (ICRAF), 2006); ICRAF, *Creating an Evergreen Agriculture in Africa* (Nairobi: 2009); P. R. Hobbs, K. Sayre, and R. Gupta, "The Role of Conservation Agriculture in Sustainable Agriculture," *Philosophical Transactions of the Royal Society B*, 12 February 2008, pp. 543–55; evergreen agriculture from W. Makumba et al., "The Long-Term Effects of a *Gliricidia*-Maize Intercropping System in Southern Malawi, on *Gliricidia* and Maize Yields, and Soil Properties," *Agriculture, Ecosystems & Environment*, August 2006, pp. 85–92, and from ICRAF, *Creating an Evergreen Agriculture*, op. cit. this note.

7. McNeely and Scherr, op. cit. note 3; J. Milder et al., "Landscape Approaches to Achieving Food Production, Natural Resource Conservation, and the Millennium Development Goals," in F. A. J. DeClerck , J. C. Ingram, and C. R. del Rio, *Integrating Ecology into Poverty Alleviation and International Development Efforts* (New York: Springer, in press). Figure 2–2 prepared by Molly Phemister, adapted from photographs of the Kijabe, Kenya, landscape.

8. Figure 2–3 prepared by Molly Phemister, adapted from ISRIC–World Soil Information, "Green Water Credits," Policy Brief, Wageningen, Netherlands, undated, Figure 2.

9. G. Schroth and M. S. S. DaMota, "Tropical Agroforestry," in Scherr and McNeely, op. cit. note 6, pp. 103–20; G. Schroth and M. S. S. DaMota, "Conservation of a Forest Landscape and Traditional Livelihoods in an Area of High Land Use Pressure in the Central Amazon," at www.landscape measures.org/?p=77.

10. C. L. Neely and J. Butterfield, "Holistic Management of African Rangelands," *Leisa Magazine*, vol. 20, no. 4 (2004), pp. 26–28.

11. EcoAgriculture Partners, "Sustainable Tea Production in Kericho, Kenya," *Ecoagriculture Snapshots*, Washington, DC.

12. J. Pretty, "Can Sustainable Agriculture Feed Africa? New Evidence on Progress, Processes and Impacts," *Environment, Development, and Sustainability*, vol. 1, nos. 3–4 (1999), pp. 253–74; L. E. Buck et al., "Scientific Assessment of Ecoagriculture Systems," in Scherr and McNeely, op. cit. note 6; Schroth and DaMota, op. cit. note 9; R. R. B. Leakey, "Domesticating and Marketing Novel Crops," in Scherr and McNeely, op. cit. note 6.

13. Africare, Oxfam America, and WWF-ICRISAT Project, "More Rice for People, More Water for the Planet," WWF-ICRISAT Project, Hyderabad, India, 2010, pp. 2, 8, 28; N. T. Uphoff, "Increasing Water Savings While Increasing Rice Yields with the System of Rice Intensification," in P. K. Aggrawal et al., eds., *Science, Technology and Trade for Peace and Prosperity*, Proceedings of the 26th International Rice Congress, 9–12 October 2006, New Delhi (Los Banos, Philippines: International Rice Research Institute), pp. 353–65; Siddimallaiah from Africare, Oxfam America, and WWF-ICRISAT Project, op. cit. this note.

14. National Academy of Sciences, *Toward Sustainable Agricultural Systems in the 21st Century* (Washington, DC: 2010); IAASTD, *Agriculture at a Crossroads: Global Report* (Washington, DC: Island Press, 2008).

15. International Development Association, "Restoring China's Loess Plateau," at go.worldbank.org/RGXNXF4A00; EcoAgriculture Partners, "Paying for Silvopastoral Systems in Matiguás, Nicaragua," *Ecoagriculture Snapshots*, No. 12, Washington, DC.

16. L. E. Buck and S. J. Scherr, "Building Innovation Systems for Managing Complex Landscapes," in K. M. Moore, ed., *The Sciences and Art of Adaptive Management: Innovating for Sustainable Agriculture and Natural Resources Management* (Ankeny, IA: Soil and Water Conservation Society, 2009); Landscape Measures Resource Center, at treadwell.cce.cornell.edu/ecoag1a; Kevin Kamp from L. E. Buck et al., EcoAgriculture Partners' Landscape Measures Initiative Toward a Proof of Concept, Planning Workshop, Washington, DC, 12 May 2009.

17. K. D. Warner, *Agroecology in Action: Extending Alternative Agriculture Through Social Networks* (Cambridge, MA: The MIT Press, 2007); M. A. Altieri and C. I. Nicholl, "Scaling up Agroecological Approaches for Food Sovereignty in Latin America," *Development*, vol. 51 (2008), pp. 472–80; G. Rundgren, ed., *Building Trust in Organic* (Bonn: IFOAM, Germany, 2007).

18. S. Franzel et al., "Scaling Up the Impact of Agroforestry: Lessons from Three Sites in Africa and Asia," *Agroforestry Systems*, vol. 61–62, no. 1–3 (2004), pp. 329–44; EcoAgriculture Partners, "The Community Knowledge Service," Washington, DC, 2008.

19. African Wildlife Foundation, "The African Heartlands," at www.awf.org/section/heartlands; The Ibero-American Model Forest Network, at www.bosquesmodelo.net/new/english/index.html.

20. Milder et al. op. cit. note 7.

21. Mars, Inc., "Cocoa Sustainability," at www.mars.com/global/assets/documents; Nestlé, "Water and Environmental Sustainability," at www2.nestle.com/CSV/WaterAndEnvironmental Sustainability.

22. *Propuesta de Estrategia Centroamericana de Desarrollo Territorial (ECADERT)* (San Jose, Costa Rica: 2009), at pesacentroamerica.org/pesa_ca/prupuesta_ecadert.pdf; TerrAfrica, at www.terrafrica.org.

23. Yale University and Center for International Earth Science Information Network, *Environmental Performance Index* (New Haven, CT: 2008).

24. U.N. Food and Agriculture Organization, *FAOSTAT Statistical Database*, at faostat.fao.org/default.aspx.

25. L. Brussaard et al., "Reconciling Biodiversity Conservation and Food Security: Scientific Challenges for a New Agriculture," *Current Opinion in Environmental Sustainability*, May 2010, pp. 34–42; R. E. Green et al., "Farming and the Fate of Wild Nature," *Science*, 28 January 2005, pp. 550–55.

26. U.N. Environment Programme, *The Environmental Food Crisis* (Nairobi: 2009).

27. S. J. Scherr and S. Sthapit, *Mitigating Climate Change Through Food and Land Use*, Worldwatch Report 179 (Washington, DC: Worldwatch Institute, 2009).

28. S. J. Scherr and C. A.Wallace, *Dialogue Towards a Shared Action Framework for Agriculture, Food Security and Climate Change in Africa*, Workshop Report (Washington DC: EcoAgriculture Partners, New Partnership for Africa's Development, United Nations Foundation, and World Wide Fund for Nature, 2010).

Innovations in Rice Breeding in Madagascar

1. Ministère de l'Agriculture, de l'Elévage et de la Pêche, *Deuxième Rapport National sur l'Etat des Ressources Phytogénétiques pour l'Alimentation et l'Agriculture, Madagascar* (Antananarivo, Madagascar: 2009).

2. Unpublished data from collecting missions from 1986 to 1998 carried out with the support of the International Board for Plant Genetic Resources, the Japanese project, and the Swiss Development Corporation.

3. X. Rakotonjanahary, "New Rice Varieties for the Highlands of Madagascar: A Tool for Improving the Productivity and Income in Rice-based Farming Systems," in International Rice Research Institute, *Fragile Lives in Fragile Ecosystems: Proceedings of the International Rice Research Conference* (Manila: 1995); E. Ralambofetra, "Contribution à L'étude de la Valeur Nutritionnelle Comparée de Variétés de Riz de Madagascar," Thèse de 3ème cycle (Antananarivo, Madagascar: Université d'Antananarivo, 1983); Andrianilana Fidelis et al., "Grain Quality Characteristics of Rice in Madagascar Retail Markets," *Plant Foods for Human Nutrition*, 30 January 1990, pp. 21–30.

4. Rakotonjanahary, op. cit. note 3.

5. Sant S. Virmani, C. X. Mao, and B. Hardy, *Hybrid Rice for Food Security, Poverty Alleviation, and Environmental Protection* (Manila: International Rice Research Institute, 2003).

6. T. Defoer et al., "Rice-based Production Systems for Food Security and Poverty Alleviation in Sub-Saharan Africa," in N. Van Nguyen, ed., *Rice is Life, International Rice Commission Newsletter* 53 Proceedings of the FAO Conference Rice is Life (Rome: Food and Agriculture Organization, 2004), pp. 85–96.

7. Ibid.

8. Ibid.

Chapter 3. The Nutritional and Economic Potential of Vegetables

1. "Biotechnology and the Green Revolution: Norman Borlaug," ActionBioScience.org, updated 2002.

2. Beverly D. McIntyre et al., eds., *Synthesis Report: Agriculture at a Crossroads*, International Assessment of Agricultural Knowledge, Science and Technology for Development (Washington, DC: Island Press, 2009); Raj Patel, Eric Holt-Gimenez, and Annie Shattuck, "Ending Africa's Hunger," *The Nation*, 21 September 2009.

3. M. Ezzati et al., "Selected Major Risk Factors and Global and Regional Burden of Disease," *Lancet*, 2 November 2002, pp. 1347–60.

4. Ibid.

5. H. E. Bouis, "Breeding for Nutrition," *Public Interest Report*, July-August 1995, pp. 8–16; M. Lotfi et al., *Micronutrient Fortification of Foods: Current Practices, Research and Opportunities* (Wageningen, The Netherlands: The Micronutrient Initiative, International Agricultural Center, 1996); Federal Government of Nigeria and UNICEF, *The Nutritional Status of Women and Children in Nigeria* (Lagos, Nigeria: National Planning Commission and UNICEF Country Office, 1994).

6. Mark W. Rosegrant et al., *2020 Global Food Outlook: Trends, Alternates, and Choices* (Washington DC: International Food Policy Research Institute, 2001), p. 7; K. Weinberger and T. A. Lumpkin, *Horticulture for Poverty Alleviation—The Unfunded Revolution*, Working Paper No. 15 (Shanhua, Taiwan: AVRDC–The World Vegetable Center, 1995).

7.   Namanga Ngongi, "A New Green Revolution: Challenges and Opportunities in Linking
Smallholder Farmers," remarks at The Global Child
Nutrition Forum: Symposium on Global Agriculture and Food Security," Accra, Ghana, 1 June
2010.

8.   "Spotlight on AVRDC: Africa Indigenous
Vegetables," *Maendeleo Agricultural Technology
Fund Newsletter*, June 2006, pp. 12–13; "Healthy
Urban Fast Food—A New Maasai Enterprise,"
Point of Impact (AVRDC–The World Vegetable
Center), November 2008.

9.   Box 3–1 from the following: Population
growth from U.N. Population Division, *World Population Prospects: The 2002 Revision, Highlights*
(New York: 2002); crop productivity from D. Spielman and R. Pandya-Lorch, eds, *Millions Fed: Proven
Successes in Agricultural Development* (Washington, DC: International Food Policy Research Insti-
tute, 2009); modern varieties share from R. E.
Evenson and D. Gollin, "Assessing the Impact of
the Green Revolution, 1960 to 2000," *Science*, 2
May 2003, pp. 758–62; Corn Farmers' Coalition
from J. Eisenthal, "Corn Yield Trending
Higher," *Ethanol Today*, March/April 2010; R. S.
Zeigler and S. Mohantya, "Support for Interna-
tional Agricultural Research: Current Status and
Future Challenges," *New Biotechnology*, in press; W.
M. Fukuda and N. Saad, *Participatory Research in
Cassava Breeding with Farmers in Northeastern
Brazil*, Working Document No. 99 (Cruz das
Almas-Bahia, Brazil: National Centre for Research
in Cassava and Tropical Fruit Crops, 2001); N.
Saad et al., *Participatory Cassava Breeding in North-
east Brazil. Who Adopts and Why?* Working Docu-
ment no. 24 (Cali, Colombia: International Center
for Tropical Agriculture, 2006); L. Sperling, J. Lan-
con, and M. Loosvelt, eds., *Participatory Plant
Breeding and Participatory Plant Genetic Resource
Enhancement*, Proceedings of a Workshop in
Bouaké, Côte d'Ivoire, 7–10 May 2001 (Cali,
Colombia: CGIAR Systemwide Program on Participatory Research and Gender Analysis, 2004); P.
P. O. Ojwang et al., "Participatory Plant Breeding
Approach for Host Plant Resistance to Bean Fly in
Common Bean under Semi-arid Kenya Condi-
tions," *Euphytica*, vol. 170, no. 3 (2009), pp.
383–93; Pan-Africa Bean Research Alliance, "Bean
Seed Production in Rwanda: One Farmer's Story,"
at www.pabra.org/project07.html; Water Efficient
Maize for Africa Web site, at www.aatf-africa.org/
wema.

10.   Babel Isack, discussion with Danielle Nieren-
berg, 26 November 2009; Ronnie Vernooy and
Bob Stanley, "Breeding Better Barley—Together,"
in International Development Research Center,
Seeds That Give: Participatory Plant Breeding
(Ottawa: 2003).

11.   G. Keding et al., "Diversity, Traits and Use of
Traditional Vegetables in Tanzania," *Technical Bulletin No. 40* (Shanhua, Taiwan: AVRDC, 2007).

12.   Alpha Seeds is described in "Partnerships for
a Better African Tomato," *Point of Impact*
(AVRDC), November 2008.

13.   Andreas Ebert, Genebank Manager, AVRDC,
discussion with author, 2009.

14.   Marilyn L. Warburton et al., "Toward a Cost-
Effective Fingerprinting Methodology to Distin-
guish Maize Open-Pollinated Varieties," *Crop
Science*, March–April 2010, pp. 467–77.

15.   AVRDC, "Improvements That Pay Off: Tomatoes for Tanzania," AVRDC Factsheet, August
2006.

16.   Ibid.; "Improved Indigenous Vegetables Have
Market Potential," *Point of Impact* (AVRDC),
November 2008.

17.   Danielle Nierenberg and Bernard Pollock,
"Breeding Vegetables with Farmers in Mind," *Huff-
ington Post*, 8 December 2009.

18.   U.N. Food and Agriculture Organization
(FAO), International Fund for Agricultural Devel-
opment, and World Food Programme, "High Food
Prices: Impact and Recommendations," prepared for
meeting of Chief Executives Board for Coordina-
tion, Bern, Switzerland, 28–29 April 2008; J.
Aphane, M. L. Chadha, and M. O. Oluoch,
"Increasing the Consumption of Micronutrient-
rich Foods through Production and Promotion of
Indigenous Foods," *FAO-AVRDC International
Workshop Proceedings*, FAO and AVRDC-Regional
Center for Africa, Arusha, Tanzania, 5–8 March

2002. Box 3–2 from the following: Michael Burn-ham, "Kenya Provides Sharp Increase in Sustainable-Development Spending," *New York Times*, 1 July 2010; Mary O. Abukutsa-Onyango, discussion with Jeanne Roberts, 8 August 2010; Jeanne Roberts, "Solving Kenya's Food Crisis, One Indigenous Crop at a Time," *SolveClimate.com*, 2 September 2009; "Kenya: No Longer a Weed," *IRIN* (U.N. Office for the Coordination of Humanitarian Affairs), 7 August 2009.

19. "Healthy Urban Fast Food," op. cit. note 8.

20. "Improved Indigenous Vegetables," op. cit. note 16.

21. Ibid.

22. Ibid.

23. "A Surprising Nutritional Heritage," *Point of Impact* (AVRDC), November 2008; AVRDC, "How to Grow African Nightshade," flyer, Regional Center for Africa.

24. H. C. Bittenbender, R. P. Barrett, and B. M. Indire-Lavusa, "Beans and Cowpea as Leaf Vegetables and Grain Legumes," *Occasional Monograph Series No. 1* (East Lansing, MI: Michigan State University, 1984), pp. 1–21; Keding et al., op. cit. note 11; Danielle Nierenberg, "Vertical Farms: Finding Creative Ways to Grow Food in Kibera," *Nourishing the Planet Blog*, 11 November 2009.

25. Shayna Bailey and Danielle Nierenberg, "A Global Reason to Eat Locally," *Vancouver Sun*, 17 August 2010; Mel Oluoch, liason officer, Vegetable Breeding and Seed System Program, AVRDC–The World Vegetable Center, discussion with Danielle Nierenberg, 26 November 2009.

26. Oluoch quoted in Danielle Nierenberg and Abdou Tenkouano, "Cultivating Food Security in Africa," *Kansas City Star*, 18 February 2010.

Developing Innovations in School Cultivation

1. Slow Food International, *School Gardens in Uganda: Food Education Project* (Kampala, Uganda: 2009).

2. Ibid.

3. Ibid.

4. Ibid.

5. Ibid.

6. Ibid.

7. Ibid.

8. Ibid.

9. Ibid.

10. Danielle Nierenberg, "How to Keep Kids 'Down on the Farm'," *Nourishing the Planet Blog*, 9 December 2009; Slow Food International, op. cit. note 1.

11. Danielle Nierenberg, "Cultivating a Passion for Agriculture," *Nourishing the Planet Blog*, 15 December 2009.

12. Ibid.

13. Slow Food International, op. cit. note 1.

The One Acre Fund Puts Farmers First

1. Interviews with farmers in Chwele District, Kenya, and Nyamasheke District, Rwanda, December 2009.

2. One Acre Fund, *Fall 2009 Performance Report*, at www.oneacrefund.org/files/reports/OneAcreFund_SixMonthReport_Fall2009.pdf.

3. Ibid.

4. One Acre Fund, "Program Dashboard," at www.oneacrefund.org/our_results/program_dashboard.

5. Interviews with farmers in Chwele District, Kenya, January 2010.

6. One Acre Fund, "Leadership," at www.oneacrefund.org/about_us/leadership; One Acre Fund field staff in Rwanda and Kenya, discussions with

author, January 2010.

Chapter 4. Getting More Crop per Drop

1. Grain yields and irrigated area from U.N. Food and Agriculture Organization (FAO), *FAO-STAT Statistical Database*, at faostat.fao.org, viewed 13 August 2010.

2. Figure of 70 percent from FAO, *Aquastat Database*, at www.fao.org/NR/WATER/AQUA STAT/main/index.stm, viewed July 2010; review of global agricultural water use per country from www.fao.org/nr/water/aquastat/water_use/index 6.stm; Sandra Postel, *Pillar of Sand: Can the Irrigation Miracle Last?* (New York: W.W. Norton & Company, 1999).

3. FAO, *The State of Food Insecurity in the World* (Rome: 2010); 60 percent figure and majority on farms from David Molden, ed., *Water for Food, Water for Life: A Comprehensive Assessment of Water Management in Agriculture* (London and Colombo: Earthscan and International Water Management Institute (IWMI), 2007), pp. 7–8.

4. Postel, op. cit. note 2, pp. 209–10.

5. Figure 4–1 from FAO, op. cit. note 2.

6. Years of rain shortfalls and drought from Johan Rockström et al., "Managing Water in Rainfed Agriculture–The Need for a Paradigm Shift," *Agricultural Water Management*, April 2010, pp. 543–50; Paul Rogers, "Millions Facing Famine in Ethiopia as Rains Fail," *The Independent*, 30 August 2009.

7. Figure 4–2 from World Bank, *Climate Change Data Portal*, at beta.worldbank.org/climate change/data; World Bank, *Databank on World Development Indicators (WDIs) and Global Finance*, at databank.worldbank.org/ddp/home.do?Step= 12&id=4&CNO=2, viewed 9 July 2010; three quarters from "NIGER: Forced to Sell Cattle for a Handful of Dollars," *IRIN News*, 22 June 2010; livestock estimate from "NIGER: Chasing after Pastoralists with Truckloads of Aid," *IRIN News*, 4 August 2010; less rain with climate change from M. Boko et al., "Africa," in Intergovernmental Panel on Climate Change (IPCC), *Climate Change*

2007: Impacts, Adaptation and Vulnerability. Contribution of Working Group II to the Fourth Assessment Report (Cambridge, U.K.: Cambridge University Press, 2007).

8. Yield range from S.P Wani et al., "Rainfed Agriculture—Past Trends and Future Prospects," in Suhas P. Wani, Johan Rockström, and Theib Oweis, eds., *Rainfed Agriculture: Unlocking the Potential* (Wallingford, U.K.: CAB International, 2009); Molden, op. cit. note 3, p. 92.

9. Overview of methods from Molden, op. cit. note 3, p. 27. Table 4–1 from the following: International Development Enterprises (IDE), *2009 Annual Progress Report for the Bill and Melinda Gates Foundation*; "Super MoneyMaker," Kick-Start Web site, at www.kickstart.org; Ashley Dean, "Solar-powered Irrigation Systems Improve Diet and Income in Rural Sub-Saharan Africa, Stanford Study Finds," *Stanford University News*, 6 January 2010; "Projects," Solar Electric Light Fund (SELF) Web site, at www.self.org/benin.shtml; Netherlands Water Partnership et al., *Smart Water Harvesting Solution, Examples of Innovative Low-cost Technologies* (The Hague: 2007); Fidelis Zvomuya, "Harvesting Fog to Deal with Drought," *AlertNet*, 13 July 2010; SWITCH (Sustainable Water Management Improves Tomorrow's Cities' Health): Managing Water for the City of the Future, at www.switchurbanwater.eu; "Water for Urban Agriculture," *Urban Agriculture Magazine*, September 2008, pp. 7–8, 11–13; International Fund for Agricultural Development, "Niger: Managing Rainfall with Tassa," at www.ifad.org/english/water/ innowat/cases/niger.htm; Postel, op. cit. note 2, p. 204.

10. Total number of treadle pumps from Paul Polak, *Out of Poverty: What Works When Traditional Approaches Fail* (San Francisco: Berrett-Koehler Publishers, Inc., 2008), pp.104–07; background on treadle pump from ibid., and from Postel, op. cit. note 2, pp. 205–08.

11. Polak, op. cit. note 10, p. 105.

12. "Super MoneyMaker," op. cit. note 9; Michael Mills, KickStart, discussion with Alexandra Tung, Worldwatch Institute, 28 July 2010; shift to China from "Less Labour with Simple Irrigation System,"

Appropriate Technology, March 2010, pp. 20–22.

13. EnterpriseWorks/VITA (EWV), "$420 Million Water Pump: The Story Behind the Story," at www.enterpriseworks.org/pubs/ACF2FB9.pdf, viewed 11 July 2010; Jon Naugle, Technical Director of Relief International/EWV, discussion with Alexandra Tung, Worldwatch Institute, 9 August 2010; IDE, op. cit. note 9; Andy Vermouth, IDE, discussion with Alexandra Tung,Worldwatch Institute, 23 July 2010.

14. Sandra Postel et al., "Drip Irrigation for Small Farmers: A New Initiative to Alleviate Hunger and Poverty," *Water International*, March 2001, pp. 3–13; 600,000 sales from "Design for the Other 90%," at other90.cooperhewitt.org/Design/drip-irrigation-system, viewed 14 July 2010.

15. Bucket irrigation study is by H. R. Wallingford, United Kingdom, 2001, as cited in Polak, op. cit. note 10, p. 102; Ghana's irrigated area, according to FAO, op. cit. note 2, is 30,900 hectares; 8 million figure from Polak, op. cit. note 10, p. 102.

16. "Projects," op. cit. note 9.

17. Jennifer Burney et al., "Solar-powered Drip Irrigation Enhances Food Security in the Sudano-Sahel," *Proceedings of the National Academy of Sciences*, February 2010, pp. 1,848–53; Dean, op. cit. note 9; school attendance from "Projects," op. cit. note 9.

18. Rockström et al., op. cit. note 6.

19. See the knowledge base of World Overview of Conservation Approaches and Technologies, at www.wocat.net/en/knowledge-base/technologies approaches.html.

20. Johan Rockström et al., "Conservation Farming Strategies in East and Southern Africa: Yields and Rain Water Productivity from On-farm Action Research," *Soil & Tillage Research*, April 2009, pp. 23–32.

21. Postel, op. cit. note 2, p. 213.

22. William Critchley, Girish Negi, and Marit Brommer, "Local Innovation in 'Green Water'

Management," in Deborah Bossio and Kim Geheb, eds., *Conserving Land, Protecting Water* (Wallingford, U.K.: CAB International, 2008), pp. 107–18.

23. Question Box at questionbox.org; Ron Nixon, "Dialing for Answers Where Web Can't Reach," *New York Times*, 28 September 2009.

24. P. Drechsel et al., "Adoption Driver and Constraints of Resource Conservation Technologies in Sub-Saharan Africa," IWMI, FAO, and Humboldt University (Berlin), 2005, at westafrica2.iwmi.org/projects/Adoption%20Technology/Technology_Adoption-article.htm.

25. Ibid.

26. Will Critchley, *Looking After Our Land: Soil and Water Conservation in Dryland Africa* (Oxford: Oxfam, 1991); 50 percent figure from a 2000 report of the U.N. Environment Programme, cited in "Fanya Juu," in IWMI, FAO, and Humboldt University (Berlin), Technology Information Sheet, at westafrica2.iwmi.org/projects/Adoption%20Technology/RainWaterHarvesting/50-Fanya%20juu.htm.

27. Labor requirement and 70 percent figure from IWMI, FAO, and Humboldt University, op. cit. note 24; 1,000 kilometers from Critchley, op. cit. note 26; green beans from Fred Pearce, *Confessions of an Eco-Sinner: Tracking Down the Sources of My Stuff* (Boston: Beacon Press, 2008), pp. 72–73.

28. Figure of 1,500 tons is rounded average of virtual water content of paddy rice, wheat, and maize, from A. K. Chapagain and A. Y. Hoekstra, *Water Footprints of Nations, Vol. 1: Main Report* (Delft, Netherlands: UNESCO-IHE Delft, November 2004); food riots from Global Water Policy Project, based on Leonard Doyle, "Starving Haitians Riot as Food Prices Soar," (London) *The Independent*, 10 April 2008, on Rachelle Kliger, "Cairo Grapples with Bread Crisis," *Jerusalem Post*, 18 March 2008, on "Mauritania; High Food Prices Spark Protests," *Africa News*, 13 November 2007, on "Burkina Faso; Food Riots Shut Down Main Towns," *Africa News*, 22 February 2008, on "Senegal; Heavy Handed Response to Food Protesters," *Africa News*, 31 March 2008, and on other news sources.

29. IPCC, op. cit. note 7.

30. Molden, op. cit. note 3, p. 5.

Rainwater Harvesting

1. Comprehensive Assessment of Water Management in Agriculture, *Water for Food, Water for Life: A Comprehensive Assessment of Water Management in Agriculture* (London and Colombo, Sri Lanka: Earthscan and International Water Management Institute, 2007), p. 11.

2. The MDG Centre for East and Southern Africa, U.N. Development Programme Tanzania, and World Agroforestry Centre, *An Assessment of Rainwater Harvesting Potential in Zanzibar* (Nairobi: May 2007), p. 34.

3. SearNet Organization Profile, at worldagroforestry.org/projects/searnet/index.php?id=30.

4. Ministry of Agriculture and Animal Resources of Government of Rwanda and World Agroforestry Centre, *Action Plan for Implementation of Agricultural Rainwater Harvesting Interventions in Rwanda* (Nairobi: May 2007).

5. Rwanda Agricultural Development Authority, "Rainwater Harvesting for Agricultural Production–Rwanda," undated.

6. Joseph Sang and Caroline Wambui, *Rainwater Harvesting Project among the Maasai Community in Olepolos, Kajiado District in Kenya* (Nairobi: Regional Land Management Unit (RELMA) in ICRAF (World Agroforestry Centre), April 2006), p. 17.

7. Canadian Rotary Collaboration for International Development, "Rift Valley Water and Sanitation Program Update," London, ON, Canada, 8 February 2010.

8. Alex R. Oduor and Maimbo M. Malesu, eds., *Managing Water for Food Self Sufficiency*, Proceedings of Regional Rainwater Harvesting Seminar for Eastern and Southern Africa (Nairobi: RELMA in ICRAF, Netherlands Ministry of Foreign Affairs, and Swedish International Development Cooperation Agency (Sida), 2005), pp. 39–43.

9. Orodi J. Odhiambo, Alex R. Oduor, and Maimbo M. Malesu, *Impacts of Rainwater Harvesting* (Nairobi: RELMA in ICRAF, Netherlands Ministry of Foreign Affairs, and Sida, 2005).

10. Stephen N. Ngigi, *Climate Change Adaptation Strategies: Water Resources Management Options for Smallholder Farming Systems in Sub-Saharan Africa* (New York: The MDG Centre for East and Southern Africa and The Earth Institute at Columbia University, 2010), p. 136.

Chapter 5. Farmers Take the Lead in Research and Development

1. Eddy Ouko from Qureish Noordin and Subash Gumaste, "Training Report: Training on Farmer-Led Experimentation in FOCODEP (World Neighbors)," 2007.

2. Michael Malinga et al., "Farmer's Own and Joint Research on Alternative Ways to Grow Potatoes in South Africa," in Chesha Wettasinha and Ann Waters-Bayer, eds., *Farmer-led Joint Research* (Silang, Philippines, and Leusden, Netherlands: International Institute of Rural Reconstruction and Prolinnova International Secretariat, 2010); Ann Waters-Bayer, field notes, external evaluation of Adigrat Diocesan Development Action, Tigray, Ethiopia, 13 January–7 February 1996.

3. Eddy Ouko from Qureish Noordin, LISF follow-up visit with Local Steering Committee-FOCODEP, 2009.

4. World Neighbors, *East Africa Area Report 2008/2009* (Oklahoma City, OK: date unknown); Janet Wabwire from Daniel Omondi, meeting of change team leaders/farmer experimenters, 2009.

5. Saidou Magagi, Ekadé Roumanatou, and Saley Kanta, "Women's Innovation in Savings and Credit in Niger," in Chesha Wettasinha, Mariana Wongtschowski, and Ann Waters-Bayer, eds., *Recognising Local Innovation* (Silang, Philippines, and Leusden, Netherlands: International Institute of Rural Reconstruction and Prolinnova International Secretariat, 2008), pp. 17–18.

6. Ibid.

7.   Esther Omusi from Noordin, op. cit. note 3.

8.   Mariana Wongtschowski et al., "Towards a Farmer-Governed Approach to Agricultural Research for Development: Lessons from International Experiences with Local Innovation Support Funds," presented at International Symposium on Innovation for Sustainable Development in Agriculture and Food, 28 June–1 July 2010, Montpellier, France; Joe Ouko from Qureish Noordin, "Meeting Report: Awareness Creation Meeting on Asset Based Citizen-led Development," Onyuongo Village, 2009.

9.   Tesfahun Fenta et al., *The Ethiopian Experience in Piloting Local Innovation Support Funds, April 2006–March 2008* (Addis Ababa, Ethiopia: Prolinnova–Ethiopia, 2008).

10. Dorcas Wena from Noordin, op. cit. note 3; Vincent Dudi from Caroline Adera, "Field Day Report: Field Day on Method Establishment at FOCODEP," 2010.

11. Calistus Buluma from Qureish Noordin, visit to Muyafwa Village by participants during World Neighbors Annual Conference, 2007; Sivusimpilo Farmers Forum from Michael Malinga, Nicholas Madondo, and Maxwell Mudhara, "Farmer-Led Documentation: Report of a Pilot in Potshini in KwaZulu-Natal, South Africa" (Prolinnova, 2008); Takalafiya from discussion with Saidou Magagi, April 2010.

12. Phillip Kilaki from Ann Wanja, "Event Report: Farmer Innovators Forum in Eastern Kenya," Organized by PELUM Kenya, 2009.

13. Saidou Magagi et al., "Supporting Farmers in Documenting and Sharing Local Innovations in Niger" (Prolinnova, 2008); Joy Bruce, "Participatory Video to Document Farmer Innovation in North Ghana," in Wettasinha, Wongtschowski, and Waters-Bayer, op. cit. note 5, pp. 35–37; Anne Piepenstock et al., "Digital Technology Supports Farmer-led Documentation in Bolivia," in ibid., pp. 31–32.

14. Drip irrigation from PROFIEET (Promotion of Farmer Innovation and Experimentation in Ethiopia), *Catalogue of Farmer Innovations*, vol. 1 (Addis Ababa: AgriService Ethiopia, 2006); Hailu Araya et al., "Participatory Research That Builds on Local Innovation in Beekeeping to Escape Poverty," presented at Tropentag Conference on International Agricultural Research for Development, University of Bonn, 11–13 October 2006; Demekech Gera and Tesfahun Fenta, "Participatory Research Based on Farmer Innovation to Control *Enset* Bacterial Wilt," in Wettasinha and Waters-Bayer, op. cit. note 2. Box 5–1 from the following: Hailu Araya and Sue Edwards, *The Tigray Experience: A Success Story in Sustainable Agriculture*, Environment & Development Series 4 (Penang, Malaysia: Third World Network, 2006); Emiru Seyoum and Sue Edwards, "Re-Inventing Extension for Small Scale Farmers in Africa: Novelty or Necessity?" presented at International Workshops on Capacity Building for Global Competitiveness in Developing Economies: The Nexus of Technology Development and Transfer, Education and Culture, Ghana, 14–16 October 2009; Arefayne Asmelash, *Dekhu'i tefetro: intayn bkhemeyn* (Making Compost: What It Is, and How It Is Made), Tigray Bureau of Agriculture and Natural Resources and Institute for Sustainable Development; Sue Edwards et al., *The Impact of Compost Use on Crop Yields in Tigray, Ethiopia, 2000-2006*, Environment & Development Series 10 (Penang, Malaysia: Third World Network, 2007); Abreha from Hailu Araya et al., eds., *A Fund to Support Local Innovation: Experience of a Farmer in Tigray* (Addis Ababa, Ethiopia: Prolinnova–Ethiopia Secretariat, 2008).

15. World Neighbors, op. cit. note 4.

16. Hailu Araya, Sue Edwards, and Ann Waters-Bayer, "Agricultural Innovation: Do We Understand Who Wants What?" *Rural Development News*, vol. 2 (2006), pp. 39–43.

17. Mengistu Hailu, "My Name is Mawcha Gebremedhin: A Woman Innovator Speaks," *IK Notes* 70 (Washington, DC: World Bank Knowledge and Learning Center, 2004).

18. Niger institute from Saidou Magagi, April 2010; Kenyan fund from Agricultural Sector Coordination Unit Web site, at www.ascu.go.ke; Ethiopian fund from Ibrahim Mohammed, Ministry of Agriculture and Rural Development, Addis Ababa, Ethiopia, discussion with Ann Waters-Bayer, March 2010.

19. Ouko, op. cit. note 8.

Grain Trading in Zambia

1. Based on discussions with author, November 2009.

2. Common Market for Eastern and Southern Africa, at www.comesa.int; Alliance for Commodity Trade in Eastern and Southern Africa, at www.actesacomesa.org; "Food Security Group: Research, Policy Dialogue, and Training Projects," Michigan State University, at www.aec.msu.edu/fs2/index.htm.

Chapter 6. Africa's Soil Fertility Crisis and the Coming Famine

1. Discussions with author, Koboko Village, Mali, September 2009.

2. Ibid.

3. Craig Timberg, "Drought Magnifies Hunger, Suffering of Children in Malawi," *Washington Post*, 4 November 1995; discussions with author, op. cit., note 1.

4. Discussions with author, op. cit. note 1; T. Benson, J. Chamberlin, and I. Rhinehart, "An Investigation of the Spatial Determinants of the Local Prevalence of Poverty in Rural Malawi," *Food Policy*, vol. 30, no. 5–6 (2005), pp. 532–50.

5. Based on material from unpublished studies conducted by the author. These studies looked at the program impacts and needs of the villagers in programs supported by the Christian Reformed World Relief Committee and Oxfam America.

6. For information on amount of semihumid and arid areas, see Munyaradzi Chenje, "Chapter 3. Land," in U. N. Environment Programme, *Africa Environment Outlook 2* (Nairobi: 2006), pp. 78–118.

7. Cheryl A. Palm, Robert J. K. Myers, and Stephen M. Nandwa, "Combined Use of Organic and Inorganic Nutrient Sources for Soil Fertility Management and Replenishment," in Roland J. Buresh, Pedro A. Sanchez, and Frank Calhoun,

eds., *Replenishing Soil Fertility in Africa* (Indianapolis, IN: Soil Science Society of America, 1996), pp. 193–216.

8. Unpublished data drawn from author's work in 19 African nations over the last 30 years.

9. Eric M. A. Smailing, Stephen M. Nandwa, and Bert H. Jansen, "Soil Fertility in Africa Is at Stake," in Buresh, Sanchez, and Calhoun, op. cit. note 7, pp. 47–61.

10. R. Trostle, *Global Agricultural Supply and Demand: Factors Contributing to the Recent Increase in Food Commodity Prices* (Washington, DC: Economic Research Service, U.S. Department of Agriculture, July 2008).

11. The Fertilizer Institute, "The U.S. Fertilizer Industry and Climate Change Policy," at www.tfi.org/publications/climatechange.pdf.

12. Unpublished data, op. cit. note 8.

13. See endnote 5.

14. Population already short of food from "African Hunger," *AlertNet*, 11 November 2009; P. A. Sanchez, "Soil Fertility and Hunger in Africa," *Science*, 15 March 2002, pp. 2,019–20.

15. CARITAS Internationalis, "Food Crisis in Niger Worse than in 2005 as Millions Face Hunger," *Caritas.org*, 16 June 2010; see also Jon Gambrell, "10 Million Face Famine in West Africa," (London) *The Independent*, 30 May 2010; Eric deCarbonnel, "Catastrophic Fall in 2009 Global Food Production," Centre for Research on Globalization, 10 February 2009.

16. Famine Early Warning Systems Network, "The USAID FEWSNET Weather Hazards Impacts Assessment for Africa January 14, 2009 – January 20, 2010," at www.reliefweb.int/rw/fullmaps_af.nsf/luFullMap/0510EB48B8A8B51DC12576AB0027B643/$File/map.pdf?OpenElement.

17. See endnote 5.

18. Elizabeth Blunt, "Nigeria Shuts Benin Border," *BBC News*, 9 August 2003.

19. G. Baechler, "Environmental Degradation and Violent Conflict: Hypotheses, Research Agendas and Theory Building," in M. Suliman, ed., *Ecology, Politics and Violent Conflict* (London: Zed Books, 1999), pp. 76–112.

20. A. Dorward et al., "Towards 'Smart' Subsidies in Agriculture? Lessons from a Recent Experience in Malawi," *Natural Resource Perspectives No. 116* (London: Overseas Development Institute, October 2008).

21. See endnote 5.

22. Cheryl A. Palm, Robert J. K. Myers, and Stephen M. Nandwa, "Combined Use of Organic and Inorganic Nutrient Sources for Soil Fertility Management and Replenishment," in Buresh, Sanchez, and Calhoun, op. cit. note 7, pp. 193–216.

23. R. Bunch, "Adoption of Green Manure and Cover Crops," *LEISA Magazine*, vol. 19, no. 4 (2003), pp. 16–18.

24. Ibid.

25. Palm, Myers, and Nandwa, op. cit. note 22.

26. Peter J. A. Kleinman, Ray B. Bryant, and David Pimentel, "Assessing Ecological Sustainability of Slash-and-Burn Agriculture through Soil Fertility Indicators," *Agronomy Journal*, vol. 88, no. 2 (1996), pp. 122–27.

27. Unpublished data, op. cit. note 8.

28. Food and Agriculture Organization (FAO), "Honduras: People's Participation Brings Food Security," *FAO Focus*, at www. fao.org/FOCUS/ E/honduras/story-e.htm.

29. Unpublished data, op. cit. note 8.

30. FAO, "*Vigna unguiculata* (L.) Walp," and "*Lablab purpureus* (L.) Sweet," at www.fao .org/ag/AGP/agpc/doc/GBASE; Roland Bunch, "Tropical Green Manures/Cover Crops," *The Overstory, Agroforestry eJournal*, at www.agroforestry .net/overstory/overstory29.html.

31. Unpublished data, op. cit. note 8.

32. In an experiment carried out during a drought in Honduras, maize fertilized with chemical fertilizer died one month into the drought, maize fertilized with animal manure died about two weeks later, and maize fertilized with jackbean still managed to produce a rather small harvest.

33. Sharon Begley, "The Evolution of an Eco-Prophet: Al Gore's Views on Climate Change Are Advancing as Rapidly as the Phenomenon Itself," *Newsweek*, 9 November 2009.

34. Bunch, op. cit. note 23.

35. Ibid.

36. Ibid.

37. Discussions with author, Dogon villages.

38. Ibid.

39. Ibid.

New Cassava Varieties in Zanzibar

1. J. P. Legg et al., "Cassava Mosaic Virus Disease in East and Central Africa: Epidemiology and Management of a Regional Pandemic," *Advances in Virus Research*, vol. 67 (2006), pp. 355–418.

2. T. Alicai et al., "Re-emergence of Cassava Brown Streak Disease in Uganda," *Plant Disease*, January 2007, pp. 24–29.

3. Haji Saleh, discussion with author, 14 June 2010; "African Cassava Breeders Network Moves to Derail Spreading Epidemic of Devastating Crop Virus," press release (Nairobi: Alliance for a Green Revolution in Africa, 18 October 2007).

4. *Zanzibar Leo*, 18 March 2007; "Solution Found for Cassava Root-Rot Devastation in Africa," press release (Dar es Salaam: International Institute of Tropical Agriculture, 2 May 2007).

5. Saleh, op. cit. note 3.

6. Ibid.

7. Alicai et al., op. cit. note 2; Ramadhani Abdala

Ame, discussion with author, 14 June 2010.

8. Ame, op. cit. note 7.

9. Ibid.

10. Suleiman John Ndebe, discussion with author, 15 June 2010.

11. Ibid.

12. Salma Omar Mohamed, discussion with author, 16 June 2010; African Cassava Breeders Network," op. cit. note 3.

13. Edward Kanju, discussion with author, 10 June 2010; A. G. O. Dixon et al., "Cassava: From Poor Farmers' Crop to a Pacesetter of African Rural Development," *Chronica Horticulturae*, December 2003, pp. 8–15.

Chapter 7. Safeguarding Local Food Biodiversity

1. U.N. Food and Agriculture Organization (FAO), *FAO Rice Information, Volume 3* (Rome: December 2002).

2. Author's visit to Guinea-Bissau, 18–26 June 2010.

3. Tadesse Woldemariam Gole and Feyera Senbeta, *Sustainable Management and Promotion of Forest Coffee in Bale, Ethiopia* (Addis Ababa: SOS Sahel/FARM-Africa, August 2008); author's visit to Ethiopia, 1–10 November 2009.

4. Slow Food Foundation for Biodiversity, "Harenna Forest Wild Coffee, Ethiopia," at www.slowfoodfoundation.org.

5. Ibid.; Welsh from Danielle Nierenberg, "In Ethiopia, Learning from Past Mistakes," *Nourishing the Planet Blog*, 2 November 2009.

6. WorldFish Center, *Fish and Food Security in Africa*, Policy Brief (Penang, Malaysia: 2005).

7. Slow Food, "Meeting Convivia and Terra Madre Communities in Senegal," press release (Bra, Italy: 10 March 2008).

8. Ibid.

9. Seynabou Ndoye, president of Slow Food Sèelal Dundin, discussion with author, November 2009.

10. Box 7–1 from the following: R. L. Roothaert and R. Magado, "Revival of Cassava Production in Nakasongola District, Uganda," *International Journal of Agricultural Sustainability*, forthcoming; FAO, "What is Happening to Global Agrobiodiversity?" Economic and Social Development Department, at www.fao.org; World Hunger Education Service, "World Hunger and Poverty Facts and Statistics 2010," May 2010, at www.worldhunger.org; Roothaert and Magado, op. cit. this note; G. Muhanji et al., "African Indigenous Vegetable Enterprises and Market Development for Small Scale Farmers in East Africa," *International Journal of Agricultural Sustainability*, forthcoming; L. Smith and L. Haddad, "Explaining Child Malnutrition in Developing Countries: A Cross-Country Analysis," International Food Policy Research Institute, Washington, DC, 2000; A. Hassanali et al., "Integrated Pest Management: The Push–Pull Approach for Controlling Insect Pests and Weeds of Cereals, and Its Potential for Other Agricultural Systems Including Animal Husbandry," *Philosophical Transactions of the Royal Society B: Biological Sciences*, 12 February 2008, pp. 611–21; Jules Pretty, "Jules Pretty on Higher Food Production, Lower Impact on the Land," *Earth Sky*, April 2010; Jules Pretty, "Agroecological Approaches to Agricultural Development," in World Bank, *World Development Report 2008: Agriculture for Development* (Washington, DC: 2007), p. 23; Jules Pretty, *Regenerating Agriculture: Policies and Practices for Sustainability and Self-Reliance* (London: Earthscan, 1995); Jules Pretty, *Agri-Culture: Reconnecting People, Land and Nature* (London: Earthscan, 2002), pp. 84, 93; Jules Pretty, *The Earth Only Endures* (London: Earthscan, 2007).

11. Visit to Mali of Velia Lucidi, Slow Food Internatinal (Africa), 23 July–1 August 2010; Slow Food, "Dogon Somè Presdium," 24 June 2010 at multimedia.slowfood.com.

12. Visit to Mali, op. cit. note 11; Slow Food, op. cit. note 11.

13. Visit to Mali, op. cit. note 11; Slow Food, op. cit. note 11.

14. Visit to Mali, op. cit. note 11; Slow Food, op. cit. note 11.

15. Galdino Zara, Board of Trustees, Slow Food Italy, discussion with author, November 2009.

16. Table 7–1 from the following: Slow Food Foundation for Biodiversity, *Slow Food Presidium: Wenchi Volcano Honey* (Rome: 2008); Tim Truluck, "Presidium Project: Zulu Sheep/Izimvu," Slow Food Johannesburg Convivium: Presidium, 14 April 2009; Slow Food, *Imraguen Women's Mullet Bottarga*, Mauritania Slow Food Presidium (Rome: 2009); Mananara vanilla from Slow Food, "Traditional Vegetables and Solidarity with Small Slow Food Presidia Producers in Africa and South America," press release, 31 May 2007, and from Slow Food Foundation for Biodiversity, "Mananara Vanilla: Madagascar," at www.slowfoodfoundation.org; Slow Food Foundation for Biodiversity, op. cit. note 4; Slow Food Foundation for Biodiversity, "Andasibe Red Rice: Madagascar," at www.slowfoodfoundation.org; Slow Food Foundation for Biodiversity, "Dogon Somè: Mali," at www.slowfoodfoundation.org.

17. FAO, "FAO STAT: Natural Honey," at faostat.fao.org; Slow Food, "Wukro White Honey Presidium in Ethiopia," at www.slowfood.com.

18. Slow Food, op. cit. note 19.

19. Visit to Ethiopia of Slow Food International technical expert, September-October 2006.

20. Slow Food Foundation for Biodiversity, "Wenchi Volcano Honey in Ethiopia," at www.slowfoodfoundation.com.

21. Slow Food Foundation for Biodiversity, "Honey of Ethiopia," at www.slowfoodfoundation.com.

22. Slow Food, "School Gardens Food Education Project in Uganda," at www.slowfood.com; Slow Food Waitekere, "Seven Examples of Food Communities around the World," 17 September 2008, at slowfoodwaitakere.blogspot.com.

23. Slow Food Foundation for Biodiversity, "Slow Kenya," 19 January 2010, at www.slowfoodfoundation.org.

24. Terra Madre, "A Thousand Gardens in Africa," Slow Food International, Bra, Italy, October 2010; Lay Volunteers International Association, "LVIA Solidarity and International Cooperation," at www.lvia.it/en; Cooperazione Internazionale, at www.coopi.org/en; Network for Ecofarming in Africa, at www.necofa.org/6.0.html; "The eThekwini Municipality Green Roof Pilot Project," Greenroofs.com, at www.greenroofs.com/content/guest_features010.htm.

Threats to Animal Genetic Resources in Kenya

1. Jacob Wanyama, discussion with Danielle Nierenberg, 7 November 2009.

2. Walter Menya, "Drought Triggers Rise in Killings," (Nairobi) *Daily Nation*, 6 October 2009; Mwangi Ndirangu, "Herders Hard Hit as Skies Refuse to Open Up," (Nairobi) *Daily Nation*, 22 September 2009.

3. Pastoralist group, Samburu, Kenya, discussion with Danielle Nierenberg, 7 November 2010.

4. Pastoralist, Samburu, Kenya, discussion with Danielle Nierenberg, 7 November 2010.

The Benefits of Solar Cookers in Senegal

1. Eva Rehfuess, Sumi Mehta, and Annette Prüss-Üstün, "Assessing Household Solid Fuel Use: Multiple Implications for the Millennium Development Goals" *Environmental Health Perspectives*, March 2006, pp. 373–78; World Health Organization (WHO), *Global Health Atlas, 2007* (Geneva: 2007).

2. Rehfuess, Mehta, and Prüss-Üstün, op. cit. note 1; WHO, "Indoor Air Pollution and Health," Fact Sheet No. 292 (Geneva: June 2005).

3. World Bank, *The Welfare Impacts of Rural Electrification: A Reassessment of the Costs and Benefits* (Washington, DC: 2008), Appendix D.

4. Moussa Diop, *Energy Systems: Vulnerability–Adaptation–Resilience: Senegal* (Paris: Helio

International, 2009), p. 11; "Senegal," *Monga-bay.com*, at rainforests.mongabay.com/deforestation/2000/Senegal.htm.

5.   Abdoulaye Touré, "Proposal for Pilot Project Sites," SHE, Inc, Senegal, 2006; discussions with author, March 2007 and May 2008.

6.   Fatou Gueye, discussion with author, May 2008.

Chapter 8. Coping with Climate Change and Building Resilience

1.   D. B. Lobell et al., "Prioritizing Climate Change Adaptation Needs for Food Security in 2030," *Science*, 1 February 2008, pp. 607–10; W. Schlenker and D. B. Lobell, "Robust Negative Impacts of Climate Change on African Agriculture," *Environmental Research Letters*, January-March 2010.

2.   World Bank, *World Development Report 2010: Development and Climate Change* (Washington, DC: 2009).

3.   M. B. Burke, D. B. Lobell, and L. Guarino, "Shifts in African Crop Climates by 2050, and the Implications for Crop Improvement and Genetic Resources Conservation," *Global Environmental Change*, vol. 19, no. 3 (2009), pp. 317–25.

4.   E. Duflo, R. Glennerster, and M. Kremer, "Using Randomization in Development Economics: A Toolkit," in T. P. Schultz and J. Strauss, eds., *Handbook of Development Economics, Volume 4* (Amsterdam: North-Holland Press, 2008), Chapter 61.

5.   "Push for 'Great Green Wall of Africa' to Halt Sahara," *BBC News*, 17 June 2010; Billion Tree Campaign, at www.unep.org/billiontreecampaign.

6.   "Nigeria: Dead Baby Trees by the Millions as Reforestation Fails," *Reuters*, 8 April 2008.

7.   T. Adam et al., *Plus de Gens, Plus D'arbres: La Transformation des Systèmes de Production au Niger et Les Impacts des Investissements dans la Gestion des Ressources Naturelles* (Niamey, Niger: Comité Permanent Inter-Etats de Lutte contre la Sécheresse dans le Sahel (CILSS) and Université de Niamey, 2006).

8.   B. Yamba, *Ressources Ligneuses et Problèmes D'aménagement Forestier dans la Zone Agricole du Niger*, PhD dissertation (Bordeaux, France: Université de Bordeaux, 1995); M. Mortimore et al., *Synthesis of Long-term Change in Maradi Department 1960–2000*, Drylands Research Working Paper No. 39 (Crekerne, U.K.: Drylands Research, 2001); U.S. Agency for International Development, CILSS, and International Resources Group, *Investing in Tomorrow's Forests: Toward an Action Agenda for Revitalizing Forestry in West Africa* (Washington, DC, and Ouagadougou: 2002); World Resources Institute, *Roots of Resilience: Growing the Wealth of the Poor* (Washington, DC: 2008); C. Reij, G. Tappan, and M. Smale, *Agroenvironmental Transformation in the Sahel: Another Kind of "Green Revolution"* (Washington, DC: International Food Policy Research Institute, 2009).

9.   T. Abdoulaye and G. Ibro, *Analyse des Impacts Socio-économiques des Investissements dans la Gestion des Ressources Naturelles: Etude de Cas dans les Régions de Maradi, Tahoua et Tillabéry (Niger)* (Niamey, Niger: Centre Régional d'Enseignement Spécialisé en Agriculture, Université Abdou Moumouni, 2006).

10.   For basic information on the group, see www.cis.vu.nl/en/our-expertise/natural-resource-management/current-projects/africa-regreening-initiatives/index.asp. For updates, see africa-regreening.blogspot.com.

11.   P. Wright, "Water and Soil Conservation by Farmers," in H. W. Ohm and J. G. Nagy, eds., *Appropriate Technologies for Farmers in Semi-arid Africa* (West Lafayette, IN: Purdue University, Office of International Programs in Agriculture, 1985).

12.   Abdoulaye and Ibro, op. cit. note 9.

13.   H. Sawadogo et al., "Pits for Trees: How Farmers in Semi-arid Burkina Faso Increase and Diversify Plant Biomass," in C. Reij and A. Waters-Bayer, eds., *Farmer Innovation in Africa: A Source of Inspiration for Agricultural Development* (London: Earthscan, 2001). Ousséni Kindo is one of the

farmer innovators in agroforestry analyzed in this chapter.

14. SahelECO, *First Annual Report* (June 2009 –June 2010), about the initiative in Mali.

15. This is just an example of advocacy to increase awareness of high-level policymakers of farmer-managed re-greening and its multiple impacts. Its impact on decisionmaking is not yet clear. Achieving impact may require more regular and longer-term exposure of policymakers to achievements and impacts.

16. For the documentary "Trees Outside the Forest," see www.saheleco.net; Peter Weston, World Vision Australia, discussion with author, 2 August 2010.

17. M. Allen, "Regreening the Sahel: A Case Study of Farmer Managed Natural Regeneration in the Sahel," in preparation.

18. "Project de Promotion de l'Initiative Locale pour le Développement à Aguie," IFAD Africa, at www.fidafrique.net/rubrique121.html.

19. Tony Rinaudo, discussion with author, Addis Ababa, 22 July 2010.

20. Moctar Coulibaly, coordinator, Alliance des Radios Communautaires du Mali (Alliance of Community Radios in Mali), discussion with author.

21. SahelECO, op. cit. note 14.

22. Web Foundation, at www.webfoundation.org; 1.5 million subscribers from Carlos Sanogo, telecom firm ZAIN, at Web Alliance for Re-greening in Africa workshop, Ouagadougou, 3 February 2010.

23. For instance, the International Fund for Agricultural Development has funded a land rehabilitation project on the Central Plateau of Burkina Faso since 1989. It began as the Soil and Water Conservation: Agroforestry Project; the current phase is called Sustainable Rural Development Programme (2005–2013).

24. J.-M. Boffa, *Agroforestry Parkland in Sub-Saharan Africa*, FAO Conservation Guide 34

(Rome: 1999); R. R. B. Leakey et al. "Agroforestry Tree Products (AFTPs): Targeting Poverty Reduction and Enhanced Livelihoods," *International Journal of Agricultural Sustainability*, vol. 3, no. 1 (2005), pp. 1–23.

25. Shea butter cooperative, at www.iicd.org/projects/articles/KariICT; Leakey et al., op. cit. note 24.

26. Examples of coverage of re-greening include "Reboiser le Désert: et Si On Essayait?" (Reforesting the Desert: And If We Tried?), *Le Monde*, 21 August 2009; "Le Sahel Reverdit" (The Sahel Regreens), *Le Monde Diplomatique*, August 2010; "Regreening Africa," *The Nation*, 6 December 2009; and a BBC World 25-minute documentary about re-greening in Burkina Faso and Mali broadcast in August 2009.

27. "The Man Who Stopped the Desert," 1080 Films, at www.1080films.co.uk.

28. See endnote 23.

29. F. Hien and A. Ouedraogo, "Joint Analysis of the Sustainability of a Local SWC Technique in Burkina Faso," in Reij and Waters-Bayer, op. cit. note 13.

30. P. Uvin, "Fighting Hunger at the Grassroots: Paths to Scaling Up," *World Development*, vol. 23, no. 6 (1995), pp. 927–39.

31. See "Uncovering the Geographic Extent of Farmer-Managed Natural Regeneration," Annex in Reij, Tappan, and Smale, op. cit. note 8.

32. NOAA Satellite Information Service, National Oceanic and Atmospheric Administration, at www.ncdc.noaa.gov/oa/reports/billionz.html#chron; author's visit to New Forest Farm, July 2008.

33. U.N. Environment Programme (UNEP), *Assessing the Environmental Impacts of Consumption and Production: Priority Products and Materials* (Nairobi: 2010); Greenpeace International, *Slaughtering the Amazon* (Amsterdam: 2009).

34. Intergovernmental Panel on Climate Change, *Climate Change 2007: Fourth Assessment Report*

(Cambridge, U.K.: Cambridge University Press, 2007); Henning Steinfeld et al., *Livestock's Long Shadow: Environmental Issues and Options* (Rome: U.N. Food and Agriculture Organization, 2006).

35. Anna Lappé, *Diet for a Hot Planet: The Climate Crisis at the End of Your Fork and What You Can Do About It* (New York: Bloomsbury USA, 2010).

36. Tim J. LaSalle and Paul Hepperly, "Regenerative Organic Farming: A Solution to Global Warming," Rodale Institute, Kutztown, PA, 2008.

37. Ibid.

38. Catherine Badgley et al., "Organic Agriculture and the Global Food Supply," *Renewable Agriculture and Food Systems*, June 2007, pp. 86–108.

39. Jules Pretty, *Agroecological Approaches to Agricultural Development* (Santiago, Chile: Latin American Center for Rural Development, 2006); U.N. Conference on Trade and Development and UNEP, *Organic Agriculture and Food Security in Africa* (New York: 2008).

40. Discussion with author, 27 April 2010.

41. Environmental Working Group, *Farm Subsidy Database*, at farm.ewg.org/farm/regiondetail.php?fips=00000&summlevel=2.

42. Subsidies from Doug Gurian-Sherman, *CAFOs Uncovered: The Untold Costs of Confined Animal Feeding Operations* (Washington, DC: Union of Concerned Scientists, 2008); figure for percentage of corn supply used as domestic and foreign livestock feed from Office of Chief Economist, U.S. Department of Agriculture (USDA), "World Supply and Demand Estimates, 2008–2009," at www.usda.gov/oce/commodity/wasde/index.htm.

43. Timothy A. Wise, *Identifying the Real Winners from U.S. Agricultural Policies* (Medford, MA: Global Development and Environment Institute, Tufts University, 2005); Timothy A. Wise and Elanor Starmer, eds., *Feeding at the Trough: Industrial Livestock Firms Saved $35 Billion from Low Feed Prices* (Medford, MA: Global Development and Environment Institute, Tufts University, 2007); Gurian-Sherman, op. cit. note 42.

44. EQIP Organic Initiative from Catherine Green, Edward Slattery, and William D. McBride, "America's Organic Farmers Face Issues and Opportunities," *Amber Waves* (USDA), June 2010; research dollars from USDA Deputy Secretary Kathleen Merrigan, Testimony at the U.S. Senate Agriculture Committee Hearing on the 20th Anniversary of the Passage of the Organic Food Production Act, 15 September 2010.

45. USDA Farmers Market Nutrition Program Information Fact Sheet, at www.fns.usda.gov/wic/WIC-FMNP-Fact-Sheet.pdf.

An Evergreen Revolution for Africa

1. Stockholm Environment Institute, *Sustainable Pathways to Attain the Millennium Development Goals—Assessing the Role of Water, Energy and Sanitation*, prepared for the U.N. World Summit (Stockholm: 2005).

2. D. P. Garrity et al., "Evergreen Agriculture: A Robust Approach to Sustainable Food Security in Africa," *Food Security*, September 2010, pp. 197–214.

3. C. Pye-Smith, Farming Trees, *Banishing Hunger: How an Agroforestry Programme is Helping Smallholders in Malawi to Grow More Food and Improve Their Livelihoods* (Nairobi: World Agroforestry Centre, 2008), p. 10.

4. G. Sileshi et al., *Evidence for Impact of Green Fertilizers on Maize Production in Sub-Saharan Africa: A Meta-analysis*, ICRAF Occasional Paper No. 10 (Nairobi: World Agroforestry Centre, 2009).

5. Garrity, op. cit. note 2.

6. Pye-Smith, op. cit. note 3, pp. 2, 3.

7. Garrity, op. cit. note 2.

8. Ibid., p. 5; R. D. Barnes and C. W. Fagg, Faidherbia albida: *Monograph & Annotated Bibliography*, Tropical Forestry Papers No 41 (Oxford: Oxford Forestry Institute, 2003); F. K. Akinnifesi et al., "Synergistic Effect of Inorganic N & P Fertilizers & Organic Inputs from *Gliricidia Sepium* on Productivity of Intercropped Maize in Southern

Malawi," Plant and Soil, vol. 294, nos. 1–2 (2007), pp. 203–17; D. P. Garrity, "Agroforestry & the Achievement of the Millennium Development Goals," *Agroforestry Systems*, vol. 61–62 (2004), pp. 5–17; G. Sileshi and P. L. Mafongoya, "Long-term Effect of Legume-improved Fallows on Soil Invertebrates & Maize Yield in Eastern Zambia," *Agriculture, Ecosystems & Environment*, July 2006, pp. 69–78.

9. Garrity, op. cit. note 2, p. 5; J. M. Boffa, *Agroforestry Parklands in Sub-Saharan Africa*, FAO Conservation Guide 34 (Rome: U.N. Food and Agriculture Organization, 1999); P. W. Chirwa et al., "Soil Water Dynamics in Intercropping Systems Containing *Gliricidia Sepium*, Pigeonpea and Maize in Southern Malawi," *Agroforestry Systems*, vol. 69, no. 1 (2007) pp. 29–43; W. Makumba et al., "Long-term Impact of a *Gliricidia*-Maize Intercropping System on Carbon Sequestration in Southern Malawi," *Agriculture, Ecosystems & Environment*, vol. 118 (2007), pp. 237–43; S. Scherr and J. McNeely, eds., *Farming with Nature* (Washington, DC: Island Press, 2009), p. 473.

10. Garrity, op. cit. note 2.

11. Ibid.; P. Aagard, Conservation Farming Unit, Lusaka, Zambia, discussion with author, 2009.

12. A. R. Saka et al., "The Effects of *Acacia albida* on Soils and Maize Grain Yields under Smallholder Farm Conditions in Malawi," *Forest Ecology and Management*, vol. 64 (1994), pp. 217–30; Niger data from C. Reij, G. Tappan, and M. Smale, *Agroenvironmental Transformation in the Sahel: Another Kind of "Green Revolution"* (Washington, DC: International Food Policy Research Institute, 2009).

13. Pye-Smith, op. cit. note 3, p. 22.

14. D. P. Garrity, "Hope Is Evergreen," *Our Planet*, May 2010, pp. 28–30.

Chapter 9. Post-Harvest Losses: A Neglected Field

1. V. Smil, "Improving Efficiency and Reducing Waste in Our Food System," *Environmental Sciences*, vol. 1, no. 1 (2004), pp. 17–26.

2. "Post-Harvest Food Losses in Developing Countries: A New Study," *Food and Nutrition Bulletin*, vol. 1 (1979), p. 2; compare M. Grolleaud, *Overview of the Phenomenon of Losses during the Post-Harvest System* (Rome: U.N. Food and Agriculture Organization (FAO), 2001), chapter 1.

3. FAO, *Food Loss Prevention in Perishable Crops*, FAO Agricultural Services Bulletin No. 43, 1981; the resolution was passed in the 7th Special Session of the U.N. General Assembly in 1975.

4. Organisation for Economic Co-operation and Development, "Agriculture: Improving Policy Coherence for Development," *Policy Brief* (Paris: April 2008); U.K. Department for International Development, *Official Development Assistance to Agriculture* (London: 2004); C. Nellemann et al., eds., *The Environmental Food Crisis—The Environment's Role in Averting Future Food Crises. A UNEP Rapid Response Assessment* (Norway: GRID-Arendal and U.N. Environment Programme, 2009), p. 12; 5 percent from A. Kader and R. Rolle, *The Role of Post-Harvest Management in Assuring the Quality and Safety of Horticultural Produce* (Rome: FAO, 2004), p. 2; FAO, op. cit. note 3.

5. China from Smil, op. cit. note 1, and from L. Liang et al., "China's Post-Harvest Grain Losses and the Means of Their Reduction and Elimination," *Jingji Dili* (*Economic Geography*), vol. 1 (1993), pp. 92–96; Vietnam from World Resources Institute, *Disappearing Food: How Big Are Postharvest Losses?* (Washington, DC: 1998); losses across Asia from D. Calverley, *A Study of Loss Assessment in Eleven Projects in Asia Concerned with Rice* (Rome: FAO, 1996); losses in Brazil and Bangladesh from Grolleaud, op. cit. note 2, paragraph 3.2.1. Box 9–1 from the following: 11 tons a day and Institute estimate from Institute of Post Harvest Technology, *Annual Report* (Colombo, Sri Lanka: 2002), p. 5; for cooling systems in markets, see FAO, op. cit. note 3, Recommendation 5; underfunding from Institute of Post Harvest Technology, op. cit. this note, and from H. Senewiratne, "Rs. 9 Billion Worth Fruits, Vegetables Go to Waste," *Daily News* (Sri Lanka), 27 June 2006; India from Confederation of Indian Industry and McKinsey & Co., *Modernizing the Indian Food Chain: Food & Agriculture Integrated Development Action Plan* (New Delhi: 1997), and from World Bank, *World Development Report 2008:*

Agriculture for Development (Washington, DC: 2007); Mishra from "72% of India's Fruit, Vegetable Goes to Waste," *Economic Times*, 12 May 2008; mangoes in Pakistan from A. Khushk and A. Memon, "Making Harvesting of Mangoes Productive," *Dawn*, 8 May 2006.

6.   Smil, op. cit. note 1; Ricardo Sibrián, senior statistician, FAO, discussion with author, 2007; 4 percent from W. Bender, "An End Use Analysis of Global Food Requirements," *Food Policy*, vol. 19, no. 4 (1994), pp. 381–95.

7.   D. Proctor, ed., *Grain Storage Techniques: Evolution and Trends in Developing Countries*, FAO Agricultural Services Bulletin No. 109, 1994; V. Smil, *Feeding the World: A Challenge for the Twenty-First Century* (Cambridge, MA: The MIT Press, 2001), p. 187.

8.   M. W. Rosegrant and S. Meijer, "Appropriate Food Policies and Investments Could Reduce Child Malnutrition by 43% in 2020," *The Journal of Nutrition*, November 2002, pp. 3437S–40S; A. Muimba Kankolongo, Kerstin Hell, and Irene N. Nawa, "Assessment for Fungal, Mycotoxin and Insect Spoilage in Maize Stored for Human Consumption in Zambia," *Journal of the Science of Food and Agriculture*, vol. 89, no. 8 (2009), pp. 1366–75.

9.   Kankolongo, Hell, and Nawa, op. cit. note 8.

10.   Ibid.

11.   A. Muimba Kankolongo, discussion with author, 10 August 2010.

12.   Kankolongo, Hell, and Nawa, op. cit. note 8; compare K. Hell et al., "The Influence of Storage Practices on Aflatoxin Contamination in Maize in Four Agroecological Zones of Benin, W. Africa," *Journal of Stored Products Research*, vol. 36, no. 4 (2000), pp. 365–82.

13.   Ministry of Agriculture and Cooperatives, Government of the Republic of Zambia, *National Agricultural Policy 2004–2015* (November 2004), in FANR Directorate and SADC Secretariat, *Implementation and Coordination of Agricultural Research and Training (ICART) in the SADC Region: Situation Analysis of Agricultural Research and Training in the SADC Region* (Gaborone, Botswana: 2008), Annex II(a), pp. 55, 4, 25.

14.   Kankolongo, op. cit. note 11.

15.   U.S. Agency for International Development/Zambia, *Annual Report 2005* (Lusaka: 2004), p. 13.

16.   T. Armitage, "Post-Harvest Loss Costs East African Milk Market $90m," *Dairy Processing & Markets*, 27 October 2004.

17.   P. C. Turner et al., "Reduction in Exposure to Carcinogenic Aflatoxins by Postharvest Intervention Measures in West Africa: A Community-Based Intervention Study," *Lancet*, 4–10 June 2005, pp. 1950–56.

18.   Ibid.

19.   Naresh Magan et al., "Limiting Mycotoxins in Stored Wheat," *Food Additives and Contaminants*, May 2010, pp. 644–50; T. K. Jayasekara et al., "Effect of Volatile Constituents from *Securidaca longepedunculata* on Insect Pests of Stored Grain," *Journal of Chemical Ecology*, vol. 31, no. 2 (2005), pp. 303–13.

20.   M. Fehr et al., "A Practical Solution to the Problem of Household Waste Management in Brazil," *Resources, Conservation and Recycling*, September 2000, pp. 245–57.

21.   K. Tomlins et al., "On Farm Evaluation of Methods for Storing Fresh Sweet Potato Roots in East Africa," *Tropical Science*, vol. 47, no. 4 (2007), pp. 197–210; S. Mitra et al., "Impacts of Different Maturity Stages and Storage on Nutritional Changes in Raw and Cooked Tubers of Orange-Fleshed Sweet Potato (*Ipomoea batatas*) Cultivars," *ISHS Acta Horticulturae 858: III International Conference Postharvest Unlimited*, 2008.

22.   M. Katundu et al., "Can Sequential Harvesting Help Small Holder Organic Farmers Meet Consumer Expectations for Organic Potatoes?" *Food Quality and Preference*, vol. 21, no. 4 (2010), pp. 379–84.

23. KPMG-ASSOCHAM, *Food Processing and Agri Business* (New Delhi: 2009).

24. J. Rankins et al., "Solar Drying of Mangoes: Preservation of an Important Source of Vitamin A in French-Speaking West Africa," *Journal of the American Dietetic Association*, June 2008, p. 986–90.

25. A Taste of Freedom, at www.atasteoffreedom .org.uk.

26. R. C. Witthuhn, A. Cilliers, and T. J. Britz, "Evaluation of Different Preservation Techniques on the Storage Potential of Kefir Grains," *Journal of Dairy Research*, February 2005, pp. 125–28.

27. N. Terryn, G. Gheysen, and M. Van Montagu, "Increasing Food Security in Central Africa by Reducing Sweet Potato Losses due to Weevils and Viral Diseases Using Biotechnology," *Journal of Biotechnology*, vol. 131, no. 2 (2007).

28. J. Coulter, "Making the Transition to a Market-Based Grain Marketing System," undated, submitted for publication, at www.nri.org/docs/ grainmarket.pdf, pp.19–20; World Resources Institute, op. cit. note 5; Grolleaud, op. cit. note 2; compare Proctor, op. cit. note 7, Annex 1, on cost effectiveness.

29. Nigeria from M. Bokanga, "Cassava: Post-Harvest Operations," in FAO, *Compendium on Post-Harvest Operations* (Rome: 1996); World Resources Institute, op. cit. note 5; International Rice Research Institute, "Postproduction Management," Irrigated Rice Research Consortium, at www.irri.org/irrc/postharvest/index.asp; R. Bas, "Enthusiasms and Forebodings," *Manila Times*, 21 April 2008; United Nations Trust Fund for Human Security, "Timor-Leste: Reducing Post-Harvest Losses to Improve Food Security," 2007, ochaonline, at un.org/LinkClick.aspx?link=2125 &tabid=2110.

30. U. Baloch et al., "Loss Assessment and Loss Prevention in Wheat Storage—Technology Development and Transfer in Pakistan," in E. Highley, ed., *Stored Product Protection* (Wallingford, CT: CABI Publishing, 1994).

31. Figure 9–1 from Smil, op. cit. note 7.

Turning the Catch of the Day into Better Livelihoods

1. Danae Maniatis, "Retrospective Study of the Mangroves of the Tanbi Wetland Complex, The Gambia," Master's Thesis, Vrije University, Brussels, 19 August 2005.

2. Daniel Theisen, "Pilot Ba Nafaa Oyster Culture Project," 20 January 2010, at www.crc.uri .edu/download/Report_Oyster_Aquaculture_Train ing_2010.pdf.

3. U.S. Agency for International Development, Republic of The Gambia, Coastal Resources Center of the University of Rhode Island, and WWF West Africa Regional Office, *Gambia-Senegal Sustainable Fisheries Project, Year 1 Work Plan* (Narragansett, RI: Coastal Resources Center, undated), p. 21.

4. Oyster harvesters, Lamin, discussion with author, 2 July 2010.

5. Fatou Janha, TRY founder, discussion with author, 16 June 2010.

Chapter 10. Feeding the Cities

1. Alice Wairimu, discussion with authors, 13 July 2010.

2. UN-HABITAT, *State of the World Cities 2010/2011: Cities for All, Bridging the Urban Divide* (London: Earthscan, 2010).

3. René van Veenhuizen, ed., *Cities Farming for the Future: Urban Agriculture for Green and Productive Cities* (Manila: International Institute of Rural Reconstruction and ETC Urban Agriculture, 2006); Luc J. A. Mougeot, *Growing Better Cities: Urban Agriculture for Sustainable Development* (Ottawa: International Development Research Centre (IDRC), 2006).

4. Table 10–1 from the following: vertical farm from Urban Harvest, Nairobi, at uharvest.org, and from Danielle Nierenberg, "Vertical Farms: Finding Creative Ways to Grow Food in Kibera," *Nour-*

ishing the Planet Blog, 9 November 2009; tire garden from ECHO Farm, "Urban Garden," at www.echonet.org/content/globalFarm/864/Urban%20Garden, and from Danielle Nierenberg, "Growing Food in Urban 'Trash,'" *Nourishing the Planet Blog,* 1 September 2009; rooftop garden from Eagle Street Rooftop Farm, at rooftop farms.org; platform garden from ECHO Farm, op. cit. this note, and from Danielle Nierenberg, "Growing Food in Urban 'Trash,'" op. cit. this note; Community Supported Agriculture from Michael Levenston, "RUAF Update 15: Urban Agriculture News from Around the World," at www.city farmer.info/2010/07/15/ruaf-update-15-urban-agriculture-news-from-around-the-world, and from Abalimi Besekhaya, at www.abalimi.org.za.

5.   Daniel G. Maxwell, *The Political Economy of Urban Food Security in Sub-Saharan Africa,* FCND Discussion Paper No. 41 (Washington, DC: International Food Policy Research Institute, 1998).

6.   Paule Moustier and George Danso, "Local Economic Development and Marketing of Urban Produced Food," in van Veenhuizen, op. cit. note 3, pp. 174–91.

7.   G. W. Nasinyama, D. C. Cole, and D. Lee-Smith, "Health Impact Assessment of Urban Agriculture in Kampala," in Gordon Prain, Nancy Karanja, and Diana Lee-Smith, eds., *African Urban Harvest: Agriculture in and around African Cities, 2002–2006* (Ottawa and Nairobi: IDRC and CIP/Urban Harvest, 2010).

8.   Figure 10–1 from Alberto Zetta and Luca Tasciotti, "Urban Agriculture, Poverty, and Food Security: Empirical Evidence from a Sample of Developing Countries," *Food Policy,* August 2010, pp. 265–73; S. Haluna, "The Contribution of Urban Agriculture to Household Food Security in the Tamala Municipality," B.Sc. Project Report, 2002; Jac Smit and Martin Bailkey, "Urban Agriculture and the Building of Communities," in van Veenhuizen, op. cit. note 3; Luc J. A. Mougeot, "African City Farming from World Perspective," in Auxumite G. Egziabher et al., eds., *Cities Feeding People* (Ottawa: IDRC, 1994); M. Denninger, B. Egero, and D. Lee Smith, *Urban Food Production: A Survival Strategy of Urban Households,* Report of a Workshop on East and Southern Africa (Nairobi:

Mazingira Institute, 1998); O. Soemarwato, "Home Gardens in Indonesia," presented at the Fourth Pacific Science Inter-Congress, Singapore, September 1981.

9.   Mary Njenga, Nancy Karanja, and Janet Magoiya, "Urban Farmers Earn Income from Seed Production in Nairobi, Kenya," *Urban Grown* (newsletter of Kansas City Center for Urban Agriculture), August 2009.

10.   Winnie, Coordinator, Solidarites, discussion with authors, Nairobi, September 2010.

11.   C. Ssekyewa et al., "Vegetable Gardening in Primary Schools and Its Impact on Community Livelihoods in Uganda," *Journal of Sustainable Development in Africa,* vol. 9, no. 2 (2007), pp. 149–63.

12.   Alice Hovorka, Henk De Zeeuw, and Mary Njenga, eds., *Women Feeding Cities: Mainstreaming Gender in Urban Agriculture and Food Security* (Rugby, U.K.: Practical Action Publishing, 2009).

13.   Mary Mutola, "Urban Agriculture: A Sustainable Solution to Alleviating Urban Poverty, Addressing the Food Crisis, and Adapting to Climate Change," Case Study of Nairobi, Kenya, workshop, Nairobi, 21 July 2010.

14.   Eunice Ambani and Jane Okaka from N. Karanja et al., "Strengthening Capacity for Sustainable Livelihoods and Food Security through Urban Agriculture among HIV and AIDS Affected Households in Nakuru, Kenya," *International Journal of Agricultural Sustainability,* vol, 8. nos. 1 2 (2010), pp 40–53.

15.   Box 10–1 from the following: Mark Redwood, "Introduction: Greywater Use in the Middle East–The Story So Far," in Stephen McIlwaine and Mark Redwood, eds., *Greywater Use in the Middle East: Technical, Social, Economic and Policy Issues* (Rugby, U.K.; Ottawa; and Amman: Practical Action Publishing, IDRC, and Center for the Study of the Built Environment, 2010), p. 2; food production from Department of Statistics, *Jordan in Figures, Issue 4* (Amman: Hashemite Kingdom of Jordan, 2001); IDRC, *Dealing With the Water Deficit in Jordan,* Growing Better Cities Case Study

3 (Ottawa: 2006), pp. 1, 3, 4; Murad Bino, Shihab Al Beiruti, and Mohammad Ayesh, "Greywater Use in Rural Home Gardens in Karak, Jordan," in McIlwaine and Redwood, op. cit. this note, pp. 29, 31, 38; Kampala from IDRC, *From the Ground Up: Urban Agriculture Reforms Take Root*, Growing Better Cities Case Study 2 (Ottawa: 2006), p. 2.

16. Kenya study from D. Lee-Smith and D. Lamba, "The Potential of Urban Farming in Africa," *Ecodecision*, December 1991, pp. 37–40; Australian Academy of Technological Sciences and Engineering, *Water Recycling in Australia* (Victoria, Australia: 2004); B. Jimenez and T. Asano, "Acknowledge All Approaches: The Global Outlook on Reuse," *Water21*, December 2004, pp. 32–37; J. Smit, A. Ratta, and J. Nassr, *Urban Agriculture—Food, Jobs and Sustainable Cities*, Publication Series for Habitat II, Vol. I (New York: U.N. Development Programme, 1996).

17. S. Kiongo and J. Amend, "Linking (Peri) Urban Agriculture and Organic Waste Management in Dar es Salaam," presented at International IBSRAM-FAO Workshop on Urban and Peri-urban Agriculture, Accra, Ghana, 2–6 August 1999; O. Cofie, "Co-composting of Faecal Sludge and Solid Waste for Urban and Peri-urban Agriculture in Kumasi, Ghana," International Water Management Institute, Department of Water & Sanitation in Developing Countries of the Swiss Federal Institute for Environmental Science and Technology, Kwame Nkrumah University of Science and Technology, and Kumasi Metropolitan Assembly, Kumasi, 2003; Mary Njenga et al., "Nutrient Recovery from Solid Waste and Linkage to Urban and Peri Urban Agriculture in Nairobi, Kenya," in A. Bationo et al., eds., *Advances in Integrated Soil Fertility Management in Sub-Saharan Africa: Challenges and Opportunities* (Amsterdam: Springer, 2007), pp. 487–91.

18. Andra D. Johnson and Henry D. Gerhold, "Carbon Storage by Urban Tree Cultivars, in Roots and Above-ground," *Urban Forestry & Urban Greening*, vol. 2, no. 2 (2003), pp. 65–72; C. Liu, P. Zhou, and Y. Zhang, "Urban Forestry in China: Status and Prospects," in van Veenhuizen, op. cit. note 3.

19. American Planning Association, *Policy Guide on Community and Regional Food Planning* (Wash-

ington, DC: 2007).

20. IDRC, *Rosario, Argentina: A City Hooked on Urban Farming*, Growing Better Cities Case Study 6 (Ottawa: 2006); Minu Hemmati, *Multi-Stakeholder Processes for Governance and Sustainability: Beyond Deadlock and Conflict* (London: Earthscan, 2002).

21. Office of the Mayor, "Mayor Newsom Announces Regional Food Policy for San Francisco and Several New Food Initiatives," press release (San Francisco: City and County of San Francisco, 8 July 2009).

22. Municipal Development Partnership for East and Southern Africa, *The Harare Declaration on Urban and Peri-urban Agriculture*, Ministers' Conference on Urban and Peri-urban Agriculture, Harare, 2003.

23. Diana Lee-Smith, "The Contribution of Research-Development Partnerships to Building Urban Agriculture Policy," in Prain, Karanja, and Lee-Smith, op. cit. note 7; Republic of Kenya, Ministry of Lands Sessional Paper No. 3 of 2009 on National Land Policy.

24. Mougeot, op. cit. note 3; Daniel G. Maxwell, "Highest and Best Use? Access to Urban Land for Semi-subsistence Food Production," *Land Use Policy*, July 1996, pp. 181–95.

25. IDRC, Urban Management Program for Latin America and the Caribbean, and Promotion of Sustainable Development (Peru), "Urban Agriculture: Land Management and Physical Planning. Guidelines for Municipal Policymaking on Urban Agriculture," Ottawa, March 2003.

Promoting Safer Wastewater Irrigation in West Africa

1. International Water Management Institute (IWMI), *Recycling Realities: Managing Health Risks to Make Wastewater an Asset*, Water Policy Briefing 17 (Colombo, Sri Lanka: 2006); limited coverage in sub-Saharan Africa from World Health Organization (WHO), *Global Water Supply and Sanitation Assessment 2000 Report* (Geneva and New York: WHO and UNICEF, 2000).

2. Polluted stream water from B. Keraita et al., "Harnessing Farmers' Knowledge and Perceptions for Health Risk Reduction in Wastewater Irrigated Agriculture," in P. Drechsel et al., eds., *Wastewater Irrigation and Health: Assessing and Mitigating Risks in Low-income Countries* (London: Earthscan, International Development Research Centre (IDRC), and IWMI, 2010), pp. 337–54; H. Karg et al., "Facilitating the Adoption of Food Safety Interventions in the Street Food Sector and On Farm," in ibid., pp. 319–35.

3. P. Amoah et al., "From World Cafés to Road Shows: Using a Mix of Knowledge Sharing Approaches to Improve Wastewater Use in Urban Agriculture," *Knowledge Management for Development Journal*, December 2009, pp. 246–62; B. Keraita and P. Drechsel. "Agricultural Use of Untreated Urban Wastewater in Ghana," in C. Scott, N. I. Faruqui, and L. Raschid, eds., *Waste Water Use in Irrigated Agriculture: Confronting the Livelihood and Environmental Realities* (Wallingford, U.K.: CABI Publishing, IDRC, and IWMI, 2008).

4. Karg et al., op. cit. note 2.

5. Ibid.

6. Amoah et al., op. cit. note 3.

7. Ibid.

8. J. P. Ilboudo, "After 50 Years: The Role and Use of Rural Radio in Africa," in Bruce Girard, ed., *The One to Watch: Radio, New ICTs and Interactivity* (Rome: U.N. Food and Agriculture Organization, 2003); Amoah et al., op. cit. note 3.

9. Amoah et al., op. cit. note 3.

10. Ibid.

11. Ibid.; quote from discussion with Philip Amoah, IWMI Ghana.

An Agricultural Answer to Nature's Call

1. World Health Organization (WHO)/UNICEF Joint Monitoring Programme for Water Supply and Sanitation, *Water For Life: Making it Happen* (Geneva: 2005), p. 4; Emily White Johans-

son and Tessa Wardlaw, *Diarrhoea: Why Children Are Still Dying and What Can Be Done* (Geneva: WHO and UNICEF , 2009, p. v.

2. Sindya N. Bhanoo, "For Pennies, a Disposable Toilet That Could Help Grow Crops," *New York Times*, 1 March 2010; Peepoople, at www.peepoople.com/index.php.

3. Nicholas D. Kristof, "On the Ground with Nicholas Kristof: American Ingenuity in Haiti" (video), *New York Times*, 29 March 2009; Sustainable Organic Integrated Livelihoods (SOIL), at www.oursoil.org.

4. Danielle Nierenberg, "Improving Livelihoods and Nutrition with Permaculture," *Nourishing the Planet Blog*, 5 January 2010; Bhanoo, op. cit. note 2; Peepoople, op. cit. note 2; Rigel Technology Ltd., at www.rigel.com.sg/en/home, viewed 9 September 2010; Sulabh International Social Service Organisation, "Community Toilet Linked Biogas Plant," at www.sulabhinternational.org/st/community_toilet_linked_biogas_pant.php.

5. World Bank, *Changing the Face of the Waters: Meeting the Promise and Challenge of Sustainable Aquaculture* (Washington, DC: 2007), p. 26.

6. Nitin Jugran Bahuguna, "Walk of Shame Triggers Toilet Consciousness," UNICEF, at www.unicef.org/india/wes_2920.htm.

Chapter 11. Harnessing the Knowledge and Skills of Women Farmers

1. Imodale Caulker-Burnett, discussion with Dianne Forte, 7 June 2010.

2. World Bank, U.N. Food and Agriculture Organization (FAO), and International Fund for Agricultural Development (IFAD), *Agriculture and Rural Development: Gender in Agriculture Sourcebook* (Washington, DC: World Bank, 2009); Shaohua Chen and Martin Ravallion, *The Developing World Is Poorer Than We Thought, But No Less Successful in the Fight against Poverty*, Policy Research Working Paper 4703 (Washington, DC: World Bank Development Research Group, 2008); FAO, *The State of Food Insecurity in the World: Economic Crises—Impacts and Lessons Learned* (Rome:

2009); United Nations, Millennium Development Goals, at www.un.org/millenniumgoals.

3. AudienceScapes, "Are New Media in Africa Bridging the Gender Divide?" 2 July 2010, at www.audiencescapes.org/are-new-media-africa-bridging-gender-divide-gap-Kenya-Ghana-mobile-internet-radio-television; Marilyn Carr and Martha Chen, "Globalization, Social Exclusion and Gender," *International Labour Review*, vol. 143, no. 1–2 (2004), pp. 129–59; Pauline Tiffen et al., "From Tree-minders to Global Players: Cocoa Farmers in Ghana," in Marilyn Carr, ed., *Chains of Fortune: Linking Women Producers and Workers with Global Markets* (London: Commonwealth Secretariat, 2004), pp. 11–43; N. Kanji et al., "Cashing In on Cashew Nuts: Women Producers and Factory Workers in Mozambique," in ibid., pp. 75–102; Oxfam, "Make Trade Fair," at www.youtube.com/TTVCanada#p/a/f/0/9mgPEP8HAss, viewed by Dianne Forte, 26 June 2010.

4. Rose Hyde, co-founder, Agbanga Karite Women's Fair Trade Shea Butter Cooperative, discussion with Dianne Forte, 4 June 2010.

5. Marlene Elias and Judith Carney, "African Shea Butter: A Feminized Subsidy from Nature," *Africa: The Journal of the International African Institute*, vol. 77, no. 1 (2007), pp. 37–62.

6. Box 11–1 from Hyde, op. cit. note 4.

7. Delaney Greig, "Shea Butter: Connecting Rural Burkinabè Women to International Markets Through Fair Trade," *Development in Practice*, August 2006, pp. 465–75.

8. Lorenzo Cotula, *Gender and Law—Women's Rights in Agriculture*, FAO Legislative Study No. 76 (Rome: FAO, rev. 2007); "Burkina Faso," International Women's Rights Action Watch, University of Minnesota, at www1.umn.edu/humanrts/iwraw/burkina.htm; FAO, *Women, Agriculture and Rural Development: A Synthesis Report of the Africa Region* (Rome: 1995).

9. Elias and Carney, op. cit. note 5.

10. Carr and Chen, op. cit. note 3.

11. Jeffrey Sachs, "Internet and Mobile Phones Spur Development," *Real Clear Markets*, at www.realclearmarkets.com, 21 August 2008.

12. *Agricultural Education and Training in Africa* (AET) Web site, at www.aet-africa.org/?q=node/1.

13. Box 11–2 from the following: World Cocoa Foundation (WCF), "Sustainable Tree Crops Program," *The World Cocoa Foundation Annual Program Book* (Washington, DC: May 2010), pp. 12–13, 14–15; WCF, "Innovative Approaches," in *The ECHOES Alliance Quarter Five Report, October – December 2008* (Washington, DC: December 2008), pp. 11–12; WCF, "Success Stories," in *The ECHOES Alliance Quarter Two Report, January – March 2008* (Washington, DC: March 2008), pp. 27–28.

14. Royce Gloria Androa, *Assessment Report of Potential On-Farm, Off-Farm IGAs in Four Settlements in Karamoja*, for Gesellschaft für Technische Zusammenarbeit, Germany, unpublished, April 2010.

15. Ibid.

16. Susan Ocokoru, agricultural extension worker, Arua, Uganda, discussion with Royce Gloria Androa, 28 May 2010; Janet Asege, community development expert, Karamoja, Uganda, discussion with Royce Gloria Androa, 18 April 2010.

17. Sarah Parkinson, "Learning to Respond to Farmers," National Agricultural Advisory Services (NAADS) Secretariat, Kampala, Uganda, unpublished, May 2006.

18. NAADS Secretariat, *National Agricultural Advisory Services Annual Report 2006-2007* (Kampala, Uganda: August 2007).

19. D. Pearce et al., *Microfinance Institutions Moving into Rural Finance for Agriculture* (Washington, DC: World Bank Group, 2004).

20. Women and Population Division, "Women and Sustainable Food Security," FAO, at www.fao.org/sd/fsdirect/fbdirect/fsp001.htm, updated 2007; Fatma Denton et al., *Le Visage de la Pauvreté*

Energétique à Travers la Femme au Sénégal (Dakar, Senegal: Environment and Development Action in the Third World, 2005).

21. Dinnah Kapiza, discussion with Marie-Ange Binagwaho, 22 April 2010, with follow-up notes.

22. Ibid.

23. Ibid.

24. Ibid.

25. Dinnah Kapiza, dicsussion with Marie-Ange Binagwaho, 6 June 2010.

26. Ibid.

27. Global System of Mobile Communications Association (GSMA), *Universal Access: How Mobile Can Bring Communications to All* (London: 2008); AudienceScapes, op. cit. note 3.

28. Sokari Ekine, "SMS Uprising: Mobile Activism in Africa," *Pambazuka Press*, at www.pambazuka.org, 6 January 2010; International Telecommunications Union, *Telecommunication/ICT Markets and Trends in Africa* (Geneva: 2007).

29. GSMA, op. cit. note 27; Brandie Martin and Eric Abbott, "Development Calling: The Use of Mobile Phones in Agriculture Development in Uganda," conference paper, 2009; Helen Aitkin, *Rural Women and Telecommunication in Developing Countries*, 1998, at www.ardaf.org/NR/rdonlyres/049DC4A9-0D80-4A9A-9CB6-6B08A914A243/0/199813HelenAitkin.pdf.

30. Mark Williams, *Broadband for Africa: Developing Backbone Communications Networks* (Washington, DC: World Bank, 2010); Aitkin, op. cit. note 29; World Bank, FAO, and IFAD, op. cit. note 2; Janine Firpo, "Banking the Unbanked: Technology's Role in Delivering Accessible Financial Services to the Poor," SEMBA Consulting, undated; Gautam Bandyopadhyay, "Banking the Unbanked: Going Mobile in Africa," in Standard Chartered PLC, *Asia, Africa and the Middle East: The Guide to Working Capital Management 2009/2010* (2009), pp. 60–67.

31. Williams, op. cit. note 30.

32. IFAD, *Innovation Strategy: Enabling Poor Rural People to Overcome Poverty* (Rome: 2007).

Using Theater to Help Women Farmers

1. World Bank, *World Development Report 2008: Agriculture for Development* (Washington, DC: 2007).

2. FANRPAN Network, at www.fanrpan.org/about/network.

3. FANRPAN, "FANRPAN Launches Project to Strengthen the Capacity of Women Farmers' Influence in Agricultural Policy and Development Programmes in Southern Africa," press release (Pretoria, South Africa: 27 July 2009).

4. World Bank, Food and Agriculture Organization, and International Fund for Agricultural Development, *Agriculture and Rural Development: Gender in Agriculture Sourcebook* (Washington, DC: World Bank, 2009).

5. U.N. Development Programme/U.N. Economic Commission for Africa, *Local Governance for Poverty Reduction in Africa: Post-Maputo Follow-up Framework* (New York: October 2002).

6. "Women Accessing Realigned Markets (WARM) Project Launch," FANRPAN Web site, at www.fanrpan.org/documents/d00961.

7. Ibid.

8. Linda Nghatsane quoted in Vusumuzi Sifile, "Policy Makers Out of Touch with Farmers Reality," *Terraviva* (IPS Africa), 3 September 2009.

9. Chance Kabaghe and Cecilia Makota at WARM Project Launch, 3 September 2009.

10. Obed Dlamini at WARM Project Launch, 3 September 2009.

What Is an Appropriate Technology?

1. Gordon Conway and Jeff Waage, with Sara Delaney, *Science and Innovation for Development*

(London: U.K. Collaborative on Development Sciences, 2010); quote from London book launch, 19 January 2010.

2.   "Agriculture: Africa's 'Engine for Growth'—Plant Science and Biotechnology Hold the Key," Association of Applied Biologists Conference, Rothamsted International, Harpenden, U.K., 10–12 October 2009.

3.   Conway and Waage, op., cit. note 1, p. 358.

Chapter 12. Investing in Africa's Land: Crisis and Opportunity

1.   Robert Ziegler, discussion with author, 2009.

2.   Ibid.

3.   For the causes of the 2008 world food crisis, see U.N. Food and Agriculture Organization (FAO), *The State of Agricultural Commodity Markets: High Food Prices and the Food Crisis—Experiences and Lessons Learned* (Rome: 2009); 90 percent from Robert Thompson, University of Illinois, discussion with author, summer/fall 2009; Guinea savanna from World Bank and FAO, *Awakening Africa's Sleeping Giant: Prospects for Commercial Agriculture in the Guinea Savannah Zone and Beyond* (Washington, DC: 2009), pp. 152–53.

4.   FAO Subregional Office for Eastern Africa, *Soaring Food Prices in Ethiopia: Towards Balanced and Sustainable Solutions* (Addis Ababa: October 2008), p. 6; Nick Wadhams, "Kenyan Activists Fight Land Deal With Qatar," (Abu Dhabi) *The National*, 5 June 2009; "S. Korea in 'Tanzania Land Deal,'" *BBC*, 24 September 2009.

5.   Alexandra Spieldoch, Institute for Agriculture and Trade Policy, discussion with author, 2009.

6.   Sonja Vermeulen and Lorenzo Cotula, *Making the Most of Agricultural Investment: A Survey of Business Models That Provide Opportunities for Smallholders* (London, Rome, and Bern: International Institute for Environment and Development (IIED), FAO, International Fund for Agricultural Development (IFAD), and Swiss Agency for Development Cooperation, 2010).

7.   "About a million died" from Oxfam, "Oxfam Calls for Radical Shake-up of Aid System to Break Cycle of Hunger in Ethiopia," press release (Oxford, U.K.: 22 October 2009); for Ethiopia's agricultural potential, see World Bank, "Four Ethiopias: A Regional Characterization Assessing Ethiopia's Growth Potential and Development Obstacles," Washington, DC, 24 May 2004. News reports of the government's efforts to promote foreign investment in agriculture include K. S. Ramkumar, "Ethiopia Offers Huge Land for Saudis to Grow Cereals," *Arab News*, 7 August 2008; Tsegaye Tadesse, "Ethiopia Sets Aside Land for Foreign Investors," *Reuters*, 29 July 2009; Argaw Ashine, "Ethiopia: Hunger-Ridden Country Defends Land Grabs," *Business Daily*, 14 August 2009.

8.   Wudineh Zenebe, "Sheik's New Agro Firm Shells Out $80m," *Addis Fortune*, 12 October 2009.

9.   "Transcript: Barack Obama's Inaugural Address," *New York Times*, 20 January 2009.

10.   Susan Payne, CEO, Emergent Asset Management, discussion with author, 2009.

11.   Supervisor and workers at Mohammed Al Amoudi's farm in Ethiopia, discussion with author, June–July 2009.

12.   Ibid.; conversations with various Ethiopian journalists and civil society figures.

13.   Residents of Ethiopian village, discussion with author, 2009.

14.   For history of Ethiopian land tenure issues, see Dessalegn Rahmato, *The Peasant and the State: Studies in Agrarian Change in Ethiopia, 1950s–2000s* (Traverse City, MI: Custom Books Publishing, 2008).

15.   Michael Taylor, program manager, International Land Coalition, discussion with author, 2009.

16.   GRAIN, *Seized! The 2008 Land Grab for Financial and Food Security* (Barcelona: October 2008); Table 12–1 from Shepard Daniel with Anuradha Mittal, *(Mis)Investment in Agriculture: The Role of the International Finance Corporation in*

Global Land Grabs (Oakland, CA: Oakland Institute, 2010), and from GRAIN's cataloging Web site, at www.farmlandgrab.org; Javier Blas, "S. Koreans to Lease Farmland in Madagascar," *Financial Times*, 19 November 2008.

17. World Bank, "Data Catalog," at data.world bank.org/data-catalog.

18. World Bank and FAO, op. cit. note 3; World Bank, *World Development Report 2008: Agriculture for Development* (Washington, DC: 2007), p. 6.

19. World Bank and FAO, op. cit. note 3; Javier Blas, "UN Warns of Food 'Neo-colonialism,'" *Financial Times*, 18 August 2008.

20. Chido Makunike, presentation at Conference on Land Acquisition, Woodrow Wilson International Center for Scholars, Washington, DC, May 2009.

21. "G8 Backs Japan's Farmland Investment Principle Idea," *Reuters*, 8 July 2009.

22. World Bank and FAO, op. cit. note 3, pp. 152–53; Annual World Bank Conference on Land Policy and Administration, Washington, DC, 26–27 April 2010.

23. Lorenzo Cotula et al., *Land Grab or Development Opportunity? Agricultural Investment and International Land Deals in Africa* (London and Rome: IIED, FAO, and IFAD, 2009); "another Zimbabwe" comment from World Bank land tenure expert Klaus Deininger, Global Aginvesting Conference, New York, 23 June 2009.

24. World Bank and FAO, op. cit. note 3, p. 17; William Wallis, "Africa's Frontier Market Ready to Score," *Financial Times*, 1 June 2010.

25. David Hallam, "International Investments in Agricultural Production," presentation at the Expert Meeting on How to Feed the World in 2050, FAO, Rome, 24–26 June 2009; Davison Gumbo, "Do Outgrower Schemes Improve Rural Livelihoods? Evidence from Zambia," PowerPoint presentation at Annual World Bank Conference on Land Policy and Administration, Washington, DC, 26–27 April 2010.

26. Gemedo Tilago, discussion with author, 2009.

Better Food Storage

1. African Development Bank Group, "AfDB Delegation Makes Key Presentation at the High Level Conference in Abuja," press release (Tunis: 8 March 2010).

2. Ziyelesa Banda, discussion with Benedict Tembo, 1 March 2010; Sunduzwayo Banda, discussion with Benedict Tembo, 5 June 2010.

3. Sunduzwayo Banda, op. cit. note 2.

4. Ray Handema, acting executive director, National Institute for Scientific Research and Industrial Relations, discussion with Benedict Tembo, 25 February 2010.

5. Daniel Tesfaye Haileselassie, e-mail to Benedict Tembo, 18 March 2010.

6. AVRCDC–The World Vegetable Center, "How to Grow Cowpea," Regional Center for Africa, Tanzania, at www.avrdc.org/fileadmin/pdfs/Grow_Cowpea.pdf.

7. Danielle Nierenberg, "Innovation of the Week: Investing in Better Food Storage in Africa," *Nourishing the Planet Blog*, 21 January 2010.

8. Handema, op. cit. note 4.

9. Danielle Nierenberg, "Women Entrepreneurs: Adding Value," *Nourishing the Planet Blog*, 8 November 2009; Mazingira Institute, at www .mazinst.org.

10. East Africa Dairy Development, at eadairy .wordpress.com.

11. Jeffrey Gettleman, "With Flights to Europe Grounded, Kenya's Produce Wilts," *New York Times*, 19 April 2010.

Chapter 13. The Missing Links: Going Beyond Production

1. Rob Munro, U.S. Agency for International Development (AID) PROFIT (Production, Finance, and Technology), discussion with author, June 2010; "Zambia in Historic Bumper Maize Harvest," *Lusaka Times*, 24 May 2010.

2.   AID PROFIT, "2009–2010 Zambia Agricultural Statistics Data File," June 2010; "Zambia to Harvest 1.9 Million Metric Tones of Maize for 2008/2009 Season," *Lusaka Times*, 14 May 2009.

3.   Box 13–1 from the following: Eratus Kibugu, Uganda Country Director for Technoserve, discussion with author, May 2010; Ken Opala, "Kenyan Farmers Discover the Internet," *International Development Research Centre News*, 29 January 2004; Jenny C. Aker, "'Can You Hear Me Now?' How Cell Phones are Transforming Markets in Sub-Saharan Africa," *CGD Notes* (Washington, DC: Center for Global Development, October 2008); ESoko Web site, at www.esoko.com, viewed 7 May 2010; "Agricultural Applications Deployed," Grameen Foundation Technology Center, at www.grameenfoundation.applab.org/section/uganda-ag-apps; Zambia National Farmers Union Web site, at www.znfu.org.zm, viewed 7 May 2010; Katharina Felgenhauer, "Zambia—Leveraging Agricultural Potential," Organisation for Economic Co-operation and Development, at www.oecd.org/dataoecd/35/34/41302315.pdf.

4.   AID PROFIT, *Annual Report 2009* (Washington, DC: 2009), pp. 10–11.

5.   Thilo Thielke,"Zimbabwe's Displaced Farmers Find a New Home," *Spiegel Online International*, 27 December 2004; AID PROFIT, "Overview of Zambian Agricultural Sector," data from 2000 Zambia Census, p. 12.

6.   Number of farmers from AID PROFIT, op. cit. note 4; figure on net food purchases from Rob Munro, AID PROFIT, discussion with and e-mails to author, June 2010.

7.   Mabvuto Chisi, AID PROFIT, discussion with author, June 2010; AID PROFIT, op. cit. note 5, p. 13.

8.   Chisi, op. cit. note 7; AID PROFIT, op. cit. note 2.

9.   Wilson Mwape, discussion with author, June 2010; Zambia Food Security Research Project, Michigan State University, "What's Behind Zambia's Record Maize Crop," PowerPoint presentation, slide 9; Figures 13–1 and 13–2 from U.N. Food and Agriculture Organization (FAO), FAO Statistical Database, at faostat.fao.org, updated 2 September 2010, from Zambia Ministry of Agriculture and Cooperatives (MACO) and Central Statistical Office (CSO), *Patterns of Maize Farming Behavior and Performance Among Small- and Medium-Scale Smallholders in Zambia: A Review of Statistical Data from the CSO/MACO Crop Forecast Survey 2000/2001 to 2007/2008 Production Seasons*, Working Draft for Comments, 20 June 2008, and from MACO and CSO, *2009/2010 Agricultural Statistics* (Lusaka, Zambia: 2010).

10.   Justine Chiyesu, discussion with author, June 2010.

11.   Ibid., with yield calculations by author.

12.   Ibid.

13.   Ibid.

14.   Ibid.

15.   Ibid.

16.   FAO, "Change in Extent of Forest and Other Wooded Land 1990–2005" (Table), *Forestry Resources Assessment 2005*, at www.fao.org/forestry/32033/en.

17.   Lytton Zulu, managing director, CropServe, discussion with author, June 2010; AID PROFIT, op. cit. note 4, pp. 12–13.

18.   AID PROFIT, *Conservation Agriculture in Zambia* (Washington, DC: undated), p. 2.

19.   According to interviews with CropServe, one of the herbicides commonly used in Zambian maize fields is atrazine; while used around the world, it is banned in the European Union and under review by the U.S. Environmental Protection Agency; www.epa.gov/pesticides/reregistration/atrazine/atrazine_update.htm.

20. Author observation; James Luhana, AID PROFIT, discussion with author, June 2010; Box 13–2 from Graham Lettner, Mobile Transactions, Lusaka, Zambia.

21. For the damage done by humanitarian food imports, see Roger Thurow and Scott Kilman, *Enough: Why the World's Poorest Starve in an Age of Plenty* (New York: Public Affairs, 2009); Felix Edwards, World Food Programme, Lusaka, Zambia, discussion with author, June 2010; additional details from Munro, op. cit. note 1, and from AID PROFIT, op. cit. note 4, p. 33.

22. AID PROFIT, op. cit. note 4, p. 37; details on exchange from Edwards, op. cit. note 21, and from Brian Tembo, managing director, Zamace, June 2010.

23. Munro, op. cit. note 1; Tembo, op. cit. note 22; Jan Joost Nijhoff, Michigan State University Regional Program Coordinator at the Common Market for Southern and Eastern Africa on government agricultural policies, discussion with author, June 2010.

24. For a discussion of Zambian spending in agriculture, see J. Govereh et al., *Raising the Productivity of Public Investments in Zambia's Agricultural Sector*, Working Paper No. 20 (Lusaka, Zambia: Food Security Research Project, December 2006).

Churches Moving Beyond Hunger Relief

1. Peter Cunningham, e-mails to author, July 2010; Serving in Mission Web site, at www.sim .org/index.php/project/97355.

2. Cunningham, op. cit. note 1; Serving in Mission, op. cit. note 1.

3. Peter Cunningham, "Farmer Managed Agroforestry Farming Systems," *ECHO Technical Note*, August 2010.

4. Educational Concerns for Hunger Organization (ECHO), author's visit, 39 March–1 April 2009; ECHO Web site, at www.echonet.org.

5. ECHO, author's visit, op. cit. note 4; ECHO Web site, op. cit. note 4.

6. ECHO, author's visit, op. cit. note 4; ECHO Web site, op. cit. note 4.

7. ECHO, author's visit, op. cit. note 4; ECHO Web site, op. cit. note 4.

8. Stan Doerr, ECHO, discussion with author, 30 March 2009.

9. Ibid.

10. "A Discussion with Robin Denney, Agriculture Consultant, Episcopal Church of Sudan," Berkley Center for Religion, Peace, & World Affairs, Georgetown University, 16 April 2010, at berkleycenter.georgetown.edu.

11. Ellen Davis, discussion with author, 14 July 2010.

12. Ibid.

13. Ibid.

14. Martin Price, discussion with author, 1 April 2009.

Chapter 14. Improving Food Production from Livestock

1. Christopher Delgado et al., *Livestock to 2020: The Next Food Revolution*, Food, Agriculture, and the Environment Discussion Paper 28 (Washington, DC: International Food Policy Research Institute, 1999).

2. Table 14–1 is based on Mario Herrero et al., "Livestock, Livelihoods and the Environment: Understanding the Trade-offs," *Current Opinion in Environmental Sustainability*, vol. 1 (2009), pp. 111–20.

3. K. Homewood et al., eds., *Staying Maasai: Livelihoods Transitions Livelihoods, Conservation and Development in East African Rangelands* (Germany: Springer, 2009).

4. S. Gizah et al., *Sheep and Goat Production and Marketing Strategies in Ethiopia: Characteristics and Strategies for Improvement*, IPMS Working Paper 53 (Nairobi: International Livestock Research Institute, 2010).

5. M. Blummel and P. Pathasarathy Rao, "Economic Value of Sorghum Stover Traded as Fodder for Urban and Peri-urban Dairy Production in Hyderabad, India," *International Sorghum and Millet Newsletter*, vol. 47 (2006), pp. 97–99.

6. G. R. Thomson et al., "International Trade in Livestock and Livestock Products: The Need for a Commodity-Based Approach," *Veterinary Record*, 2 October 2004, pp. 429–33.

7. L. H. Taylor et al., "Risk Factors for Human Disease Emergence," *Philosophical Transactions of the Royal Society of London B: Biological Sciences*, 29 July 2001, pp. 983–89.

8. D. Grace et al., "Characterisation and Validation of Farmers' Knowledge and Practice of Cattle Trypanosomosis Management in the Cotton Zone of West Africa," *Acta Tropica*, August 2009, pp. 137–43.

9. Ana Riviere-Cinnamond, "Animal Health Policy and Practice: Scaling-up Community-based Animal Health Systems, Lessons from Human Health," Pro-Poor Livestock Policy Initiative Working Paper 23775 (Rome: U.N. Food and Agriculture Organization, 2005).

10. I. Capua et al., "Development of a DIVA (Differentiating Infected from Vaccinated Animals) Strategy Using a Vaccine Containing a Heterologous Neuraminidase for the Control of Avian Influenza," *Avian Pathology*, February 2003, pp. 47–55; Box 14–1 is based Danielle Nierenberg's visit to Kyeema Foundation in Maputo, Mozambique, February 2010; see also "Improving Access to Livestock Disease Prevention," *Nourishing the Planet Blog*, 2 February 2010, and R. G. Alders, B. Bagnol, and M. P. Young, "Technically Sound and Sustainable Newcastle Disease Control in Village Chickens: Lessons Learnt over Fifteen Years," *World's Poultry Science Journal*, vol. 66, no. 3 (2010), pp. 433–40.

11. Christine C. Jost et al., "Epidemiological Assessment of the Rift Valley Fever Outbreak in Kenya and Tanzania in 2006 and 2007," *American Journal of Tropical Medicine and Hygiene*, vol. 83, 2 supplement (2010), pp. 65–72.

12. Homewood et al., op. cit. note 3.

13. Herrero et al., op. cit. note 2.

14. M. E. Hellmuth et al., eds., *Index Insurance and Climate Risk: Prospects for Development and Disaster Management*, Climate and Society No. 2 (New York: International Research Institute for Climate and Society, Columbia University, 2009).

15. Andrew Mude et al., *Insuring against Drought-Related Livestock Mortality: Piloting Index Based Livestock Insurance in Northern Kenya and Southern Ethiopia* (Nairobi: International Livestock Research Institute, 2009).

Small-Scale Livestock Production in Rwanda

1. Danielle Nierenberg, visit to Rwanda, 7 December 2009; Kigali Memorial Centre, at www.kigalimemorialcentre.org/old/genocide/index.html.

2. Dr. Dennis Karamuzi, programs manager, Heifer International Rwanda, discussion with Danielle Nierenberg, 7 December 2009.

3. Holindintwali Cyprien, Heifer International beneficiary and farmer, discussion with Danielle Nierenberg, 8 December 2009.

4. Karamuzi, op. cit. note 2.

5. Rwanda Ministry of Infrastructure, at mininfra.gov.rw/index.php?option=com_content&task=view&id=115&Itemid=143.

6. Helen Bahikwe, Heifer International beneficiary and farmer, discussion with Danielle Nierenberg, 8 December 2009.

7. Cyprien, op. cit. note 3.

8. Ibid.

9. Rwanda Animal Resources Development Authority, at www.rarda.gov.rw/spip.php?rubrique12; Karamuzi, op. cit. note 2.

Chapter 15. A Road Map for Nourishing the Planet

1. Gross world product growth from World Bank, *World Development Indicators Database*; fish resources from B. Worm et al., "Impacts of Biodiversity Loss on Ocean Ecosystem Services," *Science*, 3 November 2006, pp. 787–90; oil production from U.S. Department of Energy, Energy Information Agency, *International Energy Statistics* (Washington, DC), and from International Energy Agency (IEA), *World Energy Outlook 2009* (Paris: 2009); water withdrawals from McKinsey & Company, *Charting Our Water Future: Economic Frameworks to Inform Decision Making* (Washington, DC: 2009).

2. Water withdrawals from McKinsey & Company, op. cit. note 1; greenhouse gases from World Bank, *World Development Report 2008: Agriculture for Development* (Washington, DC: 2007), and from U.N. Framework Convention on Climate Change, at www.unfccc.int; 13 million hectares of forest loss from U.N. Food and Agriculture Organization (FAO), *State of the World's Forests* (Rome: 2009); agricultural encroachment from U.N. Environment Programme (UNEP), *Green Jobs: Towards Decent Work in a Sustainable, Low-Carbon World* (Geneva: 2008); population and growth projections from UNEP/GRID-Arendal, *The Environmental Food Crisis: The Environment's Role in Averting Future Food Crises* (Norway: 2009).

3. K. Saeed, *Towards Sustainable Development: Essays on System Analysis of National Policy* (Aldershot, U.K.: Ashgate Publishing Company, 1998); International Assessment of Agricultural Knowledge, Science and Technology for Development (IAASTD), *Agriculture at a Crossroads, Synthesis Report* (Washington, DC: Island Press, 2009).

4. Increased productivity from J. N. Pretty et al., "Resource-Conserving Agriculture Increases Yields in Developing Countries," *Environmental Science & Technology*, vol. 40, no. 4 (2006), pp. 1114–19, and from C. Badgley and I. Perfecto, "Can Organic Agriculture Feed the World?" *Renewable Agriculture and Food Systems*, June 2007, pp.

80–86; employment creation from UNEP, op. cit. note 2, and from GHK Consulting, in association with Cambridge Econometrics and Institute of European Environmental Policy, *Links between the Environment, Economy and Jobs* (London: 2007); lower emissions from Pretty et al., op. cit. this note.

5. A. Markandya et al., *The Costs of Achieving the Millennium Development Goals through Adopting Organic Agriculture*, ADBI Working Paper No. 193 (Tokyo: Asian Development Bank Institute, January 2010).

6. A. M. Bassi et al., *Assessing Future Prospects of the Agriculture Sector Using an Integrated Approach* (Arlington, VA: Millennium Institute, 2010).

7. Residues readily available from IEA, *Sustainable Production of Second-Generation Biofuels* (Paris: 2010).

8. United Nations, Millennium Development Goals, at www.un.org/millenniumgoals.

9. Box 15–1 from the following: data on research expenditures from Board on Agriculture, *Investing in Research: A Proposal to Strengthen the Agricultural, Food, and Environmental System* (Washington, DC: National Research Council, 1989), "Appendix B: Private Sector Research Activities and Prospects." Totals exclude Forest Service and Economic Research Service R&D and do not count research by the food processing industry. Company expenditures from Monsanto, "Corporate Profile," at www.monsanto.com/investors/corporate_profile.asp and from Syngenta Global, "Research & Development," at www2.syngenta.com/en/investor_relations/thisissyngenta_randd.html. Part of the growth in private sector R&D reflects the increasing globalization of the agricultural inputs industry. Thus it would be more appropriate to compare total global private-sector R&D to total worldwide public-sector R&D, including expenditures at the country level and by multilateral institutions. While the private-sector share of the total might be somewhat lower, the overall trend toward a much larger role for the private sector would still be unmistakable.

10. C. Benbrook, "Principles Governing the Long-Run Risks, Benefits, and Costs of Agricultural

Biotechnology," in Charles McManis, ed., *Biodiversity and the Law: Intellectual Property, Biotechnology, and Traditional Knowledge* (London: Earthscan, 2007).

11. J. K. Bourne, "The Global Food Crisis: The End of Plenty," *National Geographic*, June 2009.

12. R. L. Mulvaney, S. A. Khan, and T. R. Ellsworth, "The Browning of the Green Revolution," *State of Science: Commentaries* (Boulder, CO: The Organic Center, March 2010).

13. M. Stevenson, "Malawi Reaps the Reward of Returning to Age-Old, Chemical-Free Farming," *Theecologist.org*, 22 June 2010.

14. P. C. Ronald and R. W. Adamchak, *Tomorrow's Table: Organic Farming, Genetics, and the Future of Food* (Oxford: Oxford University Press, 2008).

15. R. Lal, "Enhancing Crop Yields in the Developing Countries Through Restoration of the Soil Organic Carbon Pool in Agricultural Lands," *Land Degradation & Development*, March/April 2006, pp. 197–209; R. E. Evans and D. Gollin, "Assessing the Impact of the Green Revolution, 1960–2000," *Science*, 2 May 2003, pp. 758–62.

16. FAO, "925 Million in Chronic Hunger Worldwide," press release (Rome: 14 September 2010); Daniel Shepard with A. Mittal, *The Great Land Grab: Rush for World's Farmland Threatens Food Security for the Poor* (Oakland, CA: Oakland Institute, 2009).

17. IAASTD, op. cit. note 3.

18. Ibid.; M. Ishii-Eiteman, "Food Sovereignty and the International Assessment of Agricultural Knowledge, Science and Technology for Development," *Journal of Peasant Studies*, July 2009, pp. 689–700.

19. Anne-Marie Izac et al., "Options for Enabling Policies and Regulatory Environments," in IAASTD, *Agriculture at a Crossroads: The Global Report* (Washington, DC: Island Press, 2009); U.N. Conference on Trade and Development (UNCTAD) Secretariat, *Tracking the Trend towards Market Concentration: The Case of the Agricultural Input Industry* (Geneva: 2006); F. Dreyfus et al., "Historical Analysis of the Effectiveness of AKST Systems in Promoting Innovation," in IAASTD, op. cit. this note.

20. C. Badgley et al., "Organic Agriculture and the Global Food Supply," *Renewable Agriculture and Food Systems*, June 2007, pp. 86–108; IAASTD, *Agriculture at a Crossroads: Global Summary for Decision Makers* (Washington, DC: Island Press, 2009).

21. Jules Pretty, "Agroecological Approaches to Agricultural Development," Background Paper for *World Development Report 2008* (Santiago, Chile: Latin American Center for Rural Development, 2006); UNCTAD/UNEP, *Organic Agriculture and Food Security in Africa* (New York and Geneva: 2008).

22. IAASTD, op. cit. note 20; J. Berdegue, "'Learning to Beat Cochrane's Treadmill: Public Policy, Markets and Social Learning in Chile's Small Scale Agriculture," in C. Leeuwis and R. Pyburn, eds., *Wheelbarrows Full of Frogs: Social Learning and Rural Resource Management* (Wageningen, Netherlands: Agricultural University of Wageningen, 2002).

23. Cathy Rozel Farnworth, Emyr Vaughn Thomas, and Janice Jiggins, "Towards a New Agenda," in Cathy Rozel Farnworth, Janice Jiggins, and Emyr Vaughn Thomas, eds., *Creating Food Futures: Trade, Ethics and the Environment* (Aldershot, U.K.: Gower Publishing, 2008), pp. 229–36.

24. Aletheia Harper et al., *Food Policy Councils: Lessons Learned* (Oakland, CA: Food First/Institute for Food and Development Policy, 2009); Mark Redwood, "Urban Agriculture and Changing Food Markets," in Jennifer Clapp and Marc Cohen, eds., *The Global Food Crisis: Governance Challenges and Opportunities* (Waterloo, Canada: Centre for International Governance Innovation and Wilfrid Laurier University Press, 2008), pp. 205–16; Syed Miftahul Hasnat, "Arvari Sansad: The Farmers' Parliament," *LEISA Magazine*, December 2005.

25. Jérôme Ballet, Jean-Luc Dubois, and François-Régis Mahieu, "Responsibility in Value Chains and Capability Structures," in Farnworth, Jiggins, and

Thomas, op. cit. note 23, pp. 189–202; Fabrice Dreyfus et al., "Historical Analysis of the Effectiveness of AKST Systems in Promoting Innovation," in IAASTD, op. cit. note 19; M. Hendrickson et al., "Changes in Agriculture and Food Production in NAE since 1945," in IAASTD, op. cit. note 19; Izac et al., op. cit. note 19.

26. Olivier De Schutter, "Countries Tackling Hunger with a Right to Food Approach: Significant Progress in Implementing the Right to Food at National Scale in Africa, Latin America and South Asia," Briefing Note 01 (New York: United Nations, May 2010); IAASTD, op. cit. note 19.

27. Industry size and employment from World Wildlife Fund, "Agriculture," at www.worldwildlife.org/what/globalmarkets/agriculture; FAO, op. cit. note 16.

28. "Bill Gates—2009 World Food Symposium," 15 October 2009, Bill & Melinda Gates Foundation, at www.gatesfoundation.org.

29. Grants from Bill & Melinda Gates Foundation, at www.gatesfoundation.org.

30. Agricultural Biotechnology Support Program, at www.absp2.cornell.edu/consortiumpartners; Southern Africa Regional Biosafety Programme, at www.usaid.gov/press/factsheets/2003/fs030623_7.html; U.S. Agency for International Development, "Pest Resistant Eggplant: India, Bangladesh, Philippines," Fact Sheet, Washington, DC, undated.

31. World Future Council, "Belo Horizonte: A City Abolishes Hunger," at www.worldfuturecouncil.org/future_policy_award_shortlist.html.

32. Frances Moore Lappé, "The City that Ended Hunger," *YES! Magazine*, spring 2009.

33. Ibid.

34. Anuradha Mittal, "The 2008 Food Price Crisis: Rethinking Food Security Policies," G24 Discussion Paper (Geneva: UNCTAD, 2009).

35. Frederic Mousseau, *The High Food Price Challenge: A Review of Responses to Combat Hunger* (Oakland, CA: Oakland Institute, 2010).

36. Z. R. Khan and J. A. Pickett, "The 'Push-Pull' Strategy for Stemborer Management: A Case Study in Exploiting Biodiversity and Chemical Ecology," in Geoff M. Gurr, Steve D. Wratten, and Miquel A. Altieri, eds., *Ecological Engineering for Pest Management: Advances in Habitat Manipulation for Arthropods* (Ithaca, NY: Cornell University Press, 2004), pp. 155–64.

37. Z. R. Khan et al., "Economic Performance of the 'Push-Pull' Technology for Stemborer and *Striga* Control in Smallholder Farming Systems in Western Kenya," *Crop Protection*, vol. 27 (2008), pp. 1084–97.

38. Office of the Compliance Advisor/Ombudsman, at www.cao-ombudsman.org.

39. "Indonesia/Wilmar Group–01/West Kalimantan," Office of the Compliance Advisor/Ombudsman, at www.cao-ombudsman.org/cases/case_detail.aspx?id=76.

40. *Ben & Jerry's Social and Environmental Assessment Report*, at www.benjerry.com/company/sear.

41. High Level Task Force on the Global Food Security Crisis, *Comprehensive Framework for Action* (New York: July 2008); FAO, "Declaration of the World Summit on Food Security," Rome, November 2009; World Bank, "Five Countries Receive Food Security Support Through Multi-Donor Fund," press release (Washington, DC: 23 June 2010); Feed the Future, at www.feedthefuture.gov.

42. Committee on Economic, Social and Cultural Rights, "General Comment 12: The Right to Food (Article 11)," United Nations, 12 May 1999; Daryll E. Ray, "Battling Global Hunger by Increasing Global Production?" *Policy Pennings*, Agricultural Policy Analysis Center, University of Tennessee, 2 April 2010.

43. Action Aid International, *Impact of Agro-Import Surges on Developing Countries* (Johannesburg: July 2008).

44. Ibid.

45. Organisation for Economic Co-operation and Development (OECD) and FAO, *OECD-FAO Agricultural Outlook 2010–2019* (Paris: OECD, 2010); H.R. 4173 Dodd-Frank Wall Street Reform and Consumer Protection Act, at www.open congress.org/bill/111-h4173/show; Institute for Agriculture and Trade Policy, "Wall Street Reform Bill Signed Today Will Limit Excessive Speculation in Agriculture: New Rules to Curb Wall Street's Influence over Food and Farming,"press release (Minneapolis, MN: 21 July 2010).

46. East Africa Grain Council, "Approved Warehouses," at www.eagc.org/warehouses.asp; The Sahel and West Africa Club (SWAC/OECD), "2010 SWAC Forum: Call for Contributions," at www.oecd.org/document/8/0,3343,en_3823374 1_38242551_45431968_1_1_1_1,00.html; Riza Bernabe, "The Need for a Rice Reserve Mechanism in Southeast Asia," for the Asian Farmers' Association, PowerPoint prepared for Food Reserves: Sta-

bilizing Markets, Investing in Farmers and Achieving Food Security Conference, Brussels, 1–2 June 2010; Joachim von Braun, "Time to Regulate Food Markets," *Financial Times*, 9 August 2010.

47. World Bank, *Rising Global Interest in Farmland: Can it Yield Sustainable and Equitable Benefits?* (Washington, DC: September 2010); Alexandra Spieldoch, *Global Land Grab* (Washington, DC: Foreign Policy in Focus, 18 June 2009); FAO et al., "Principles for Responsible Agricultural Investment that Respects Rights, Livelihoods and Resources," Discussion Note, Rome, 25 January 2010.

48. FAO, *Guide to Conducting a Right to Food Assessment* (Rome: 2009).

49. De Schutter, op. cit. note 26.

50. Ibid.

Index

A

A Taste of Freedom, 106
Abebe, Tsegaye, 140
Abreha, Malede, 56
Abukutsa-Onyango, Mary O., 34
ACDI/VOCA, 72–73
adaché savings program, 53
African Agricultural Carbon Facility, 11
African Agricultural Land Fund, 135
African Agricultural Technology Foundation, 31
African eggplant, 33, 35
African nightshade, 35
African Re-greening Initiatives, 87–88, 90–92
African Union, 86
African Wildlife Foundation, 22
Agbanga Association, 123
agribusiness. *See* food production
Agricultural Biotechnology Support Program, USAID, 176
agricultural development
  churches and Christian development organizations, new approaches of, 153–54
  collective action in, 13–14
  decreasing levels of funding for, 5, 101
  evaluating projects, 169–72
  farmers and farmer groups, lessons for development practitioners from, 57
  foreign investment in agricultural land and, 138–40
  green versus business-as-usual investments, 167–68
  input-intensive farming systems, economic unsustainability of, 171–72
  measuring success in, 13–14
Agricultural Farm Labor Federation, Bangladesh, 173

agricultural investment
  foreign arable land. *See* international agricultural land acquisition
  policy issues, 181–82
Agricultural Policy Analysis Center, University of Tennessee, 180
agricultural research
  evaluating projects, 169–72
  farmer participation in. *See* farmers and farmer groups
  modern varieties, use of, 30
  seed varieties, focus on, 7–8
Agricultural Sector Coordination Unit, Kenya, 57
agricultural trade barriers, 58
AgriService Ethiopia, 54
agroecology, 15–24
  biodiversity and, 15, 17, 20
  chemical fertilizer use discouraging, 169–70
  churches and Christian development organizations, new approaches of, 153–54
  climate change and, 15–16, 23–24, 93–96
  current programs and organizations, 21–22
  defined, 16–17
  energy use and generation, 94
  evaluating agricultural R&D projects in light of, 169–72
  greenhouse gas emissions, counterbalancing, 11, 22, 83, 93–96
  holistic approach to landscape ecology, 17–20
  hunger and malnutrition, combating, 6–7
  landscape measurement issues, 21
  local food biodiversity, importance of preserving, 72
  mainstreaming agroecological practices, 23–24
  potential benefits of, 20–21

reasons for pursuing, 15–16
rice, 20, 25
small-scale farmers, 149–50
soil fertility and, 15, 24
types of, 17
water supply management and conservation in,
    15, 18
agroforestry
    climate change, effects on, 11, 83, 86–93
    defined, 17
    farmer-managed natural regeneration of tree
        cover, 86–93
    fertilizer trees, 97–98, 149–50, 153
    Great Green Wall, 86, 92–93
    greenhouse gas emissions, counterbalancing,
        11, 22, 83, 93–96
    holistic approach to landscape ecology, 18–19,
        20
    potential benefits of, 21
    training in, 88–89, 153–54
    urban agriculture and, 114
AID. See U.S. Agency for International Develop-
    ment
Akissi, Sopi, 125
Alaffia, 123
Alliance for a Green Revolution in Africa, 28, 70,
    130, 175
Alliance for Commodity Trade in Eastern and
    Southern Africa, 58
Alpha Seed, 176
amaranth, 33
Ambani, Eunice, 113
Ame, Ramadhani Abdala, 69–70
American Planning Association, 115
Al Amoudi, Mohammed, 135–36
animals, domestic. See livestock
appropriate technology, 132
aquifers. See water supply management and con-
    servation
Argentina, 115
Asege, Janet, 126
Asia. See also specific countries
    agricultural development in, 13, 14
    emergency rice reserve in, 181
    green manure/cover crops, 65
    Green Revolution in, 13, 27, 29
    hunger levels in, 4
    iron deficiency in, 75
    post-harvest food loss in, 101, 102
    rinderpest control in, 14
    urban agriculture in, 10, 110

Asociación Nacional de Mujeres Rurales e
    Indígenas, Chile, 174
Associated Chamber of Commerce and Industry,
    105
Association Songtaab-Yalgre, Burkina Faso, 123
Australia, 21, 153, 161
AVRDC–The World Vegetable Center, 29, 32,
    33, 35

B
Ba Nafaa, 108
Bahikwe, Helen, 164
bananas, 106, 145, 176
Banda, Enos, 151
Banda, Sunduzwayo, 141
Banda, Ziyelesa, 141
Bangladesh, 42–43, 47, 101, 173, 176
banking services, access to, 129, 151. See also
    loan mechanisms for farmers
Barasa, Martha, 38
Barnes, Gunnar, 42, 43
Bayer Crop Science, 106, 176
Belo Horizonte, Brazil, 176
Ben & Jerry's, 178–79
Benin, 44, 45, 83, 106
Bill & Melinda Gates Foundation, 141, 146,
    175, 176
Billion Tree Campaign, 86
biodiversity
    agroecology and, 15, 17, 20
    global benefits of, 7
    livestock, 17, 81
    local foods. See local food biodiversity
    seed varieties, focus on, 7
biofuel development, 168
biogas source, manure as, 164
biomass fuel use in sub-Saharan Africa, 82
biotechnology and food preservation, 106
Borlaug, Norman, 27
Brazil
    agroecological rice husbandry in, 25
    agroforestry in, 18–19, 93
    cassava yields in, 30–31
    Fome Zero (Zero Hunger Strategy), 182
    governance innovation in, 177
    green manure/cover crops, 64
    post-harvest food loss in, 101
Brazilian Agricultural Association, 30–31
brown streak (cassava disease), 69, 75
bucket irrigation, 43–44
Buluma, Calistus, 54

bumper crops, dealing with, 143–44, 148–49,
    152
Burkina Faso, 13, 43, 87–91, 123

C

Cameroon, 67, 181
carbon content of soil, increasing, 6, 24, 94
carbon dioxide. *See* greenhouse gas emissions
Care International, 103
CARITAS International, 62
Carr, Marilyn, 124
cashews, 72
cassava
    disease-resistant new varieties of, 69–70
    genetically engineered, 176
    millet glumes as fertilizer for, 54
    mosaic disease in, 69
    post-harvest food loss prevention, 106
    yields in Brazil, 30–31
cattle. *See* livestock
Caulker-Burnett, Imodale, 121, 122
cell phones, 128, 146, 147, 151
Center for International Cooperation,
    Amsterdam, 91
Central Africa, 28, 69
Centre National de la Recherche Appliquée au
    Développement Rural, Madagascar, 25
Centro Internacional de Agricultura Tropical.
    See International Institute of Tropical
    Agriculture
Chanyenga, Tembo, 98
chemical fertilizers
    agricultural research and development
        investment in, 7–8
    agroecological approaches, discouraging,
        169–70
    energy prices affecting costs of, 61
    green manure/cover crops comparison, 67
    overuse of, 170
    reducing reliance on, 56
    small-scale farmers' use of, 149
    subsidization, problems associated with, 63–64
    system dynamics model comparing organic and
        chemical products, 167
Chen, Martha, 124
children. *See also* education and schools
    fuel gathering by, 82
    hunger levels for, 4, 177
    links between farmers and markets, 145–46
Chilean Asociación Nacional de Mujeres Rurales
    e Indígenas, 174

China
    agroecology in, 21
    household farming, return to, 13
    international agricultural land acquired by, 12
    Moneymaker water pumps, manufacture of, 43
    post-harvest food loss in, 101
    rice aquaculture in, 75
    urban agroforestry in, 114
    water demand in, 39
Chisi, Mabvuto, 146
Chiyembekezo (Hope), 127
Chiyesu, Justine, 9, 147–50, 152
chocolate manufacturing, use of shea butter in,
    124
churches and Christian development
    organizations, 153–54
climate change, 83–96
    agnostic approach to project design, 11, 83,
        84–85
    agroecology and, 15–16, 23–24, 93–96
    agroforestry and, 11, 83, 86–93
    carbon content of soils, improving, 6
    global impact of agriculture on, 11
    indigenous vegetables and, 33, 34
    industrial food production system and, 83,
        93–96
    livestock affected by, 155–56
    livestock and, 155–56, 161–63
    soil fertility affected by, 61
    water supply and management issues, 47–48
CNFA, 127
cocoa-growing communities, fostering women's
    involvement in, 125
coffee, wild, harvesting, 72–73
collaborative/collective action. *See also* farmers
    and farmer groups
    agricultural development, 13–14
    agroecology, 18–19
    banana farmers, 145
    milk processing centers, cooperative, 103–04,
        142
    village-level dealer networks, 147–50
Committee on World Food Security, FAO, 179
Common Africa Agriculture Development
    Programme, 130
common agricultural policy, Economic Commu-
    nity of West African States, 177–78
Common Market for Eastern and Southern
    Africa, 58
community building, urban agriculture as means
    of, 112–13

community food gardens, 80
Community Knowledge Service, 21–22
Community Markets for Conservation, 141
complex systems, innovations in understanding, 166–68
compost. *See* fertilizer
Comprehensive Framework for Action, 179
Congo, Democratic Republic of, 58, 146
conservation agriculture, 17, 25, 97, 149. *See also* agroecology
Conservation Farming Unit, Zambia, 98
Consultative Group on International Agricultural Research
    seed varieties, focus on, 7
    soil fertility crisis and, 61–62, 63
    vegetable research, 28
    wastewater farming, 115, 118
Conway, Gordon, 132
coolbot technology, 126
cooperative action. *See* collaborative/collective action
copper wire, water dowsing by, 50
Corn Farmers' Coalition, 30
Cornell University, 94, 176
Côte d'Ivoire, 79–80, 125
cover crops/green manure, 64–68
cowpeas, 6, 35, 65, 68, 141
crop diversity. *See* biodiversity
cross-breeding livestock, 81
cultural issues. *See* food and farming culture
Cunningham, Peter, 153
Cyprien, Holimdintwoli and Donatilla, 164

D
Daewoo Logistics, 136
dairy produce
    cooperative milk processing centers, 103–04, 142
    imported products, reducing need for, 104
    kefir, 106
pasteurization of, 142
Dakar, Senegal, rooftop gardening cooperative, 6
Davis, Ellen, 154
de Schutter, Olivier, 8, 176
Democratic Republic of Congo, 58, 146
Denney, Robin, 154
Dialogue Towards a Shared Action Framework for Agriculture, Food Security and Climate Change in Africa, 24
diseases and pests. *See also* specific diseases and pests

appropriate technology for, 132
cassava, mosaic and brown streak diseases in, 69, 75
enset, bacterial wilt in, 55
grassy-stunt virus in rice, 75
livestock, 159–61
local food biodiversity as means of combating, 74, 75–76
monoculture encouraging, 75
post-harvest food loss from. *See* food storage; post-harvest food loss
push-pull systems to control, 75, 178
rinderpest control, 14
dispersed shade/trees systems, 66, 67
DIVA vaccines for livestock, 160
diversity. See biodiversity
Dlamini, Obed, 131
Doerr, Stan, 154
Dogon people, 68, 74–77
dried fruits, 106, 142
drip irrigation, 43–44, 55, 132
DrumNet, 146
Dudi, Vincent, 54
Duke Divinity School, 154
Dunavant, 150, 151
Dwivedi, Gaurav, 120

E
East Africa
    agroecology in, 21, 22
    indigenous vegetables, commercial farming of, 35
    indigenous water conservation techniques in, 46
    livestock in, 81, 160, 163
    pest control in, 178
    post-harvest food loss in, 104
East Africa Grain Council, 181
East African Dairy Development project, 142
ECHO Technical Notes, 154
ecoagriculture. *See* agroecology
EcoAgriculture Partners, 21
ecological conservation. *See* agroecology; agroforestry; environmental conservation
Economic Community of West African States, 177–78
economic unsustainability of input-intensive farming systems, 171–72
Ecuador, 182
Edith (Rwandan farmer), 38
education and schools. *See also* training

agricultural R&D, university involvement in, 170
bicycles for girls attending school, 123
feeding programs in schools, 10, 182
growing, cooking, and eating of indigenous
    vegetables, 10, 35, 36–37, 80
theological education, including sustainable
    agricultural development as part of, 154
urban agriculture, community building
    through, 112–13
women farmers, extension services for, 124–26,
    127
Educational Concerns for Hunger Organization,
    153–54
eggplant, African, 33, 35
Egypt, 160
Emergent Asset Management, 135
Empowering Cocoa Households, 125
endangered food species in Africa, 77–78
energy. See also solar energy
    agroecological practices and, 94
    biofuel development, 168
    biomass fuel use in sub-Saharan Africa, 82
    chemical fertilizers, energy prices affecting
        costs of, 61
    manure as biogas source, 164
enset, 55
environmental conservation. See also agroecology;
    agroforestry
    commercial agriculture, as ecological culprit,
        166
    urban agriculture contributing to, 113–14
Environmental Quality Incentives Program, U.S.,
    96
Episcopal Church of Sudan, 154
Ethiopia
    agricultural development potential in, 138
    agroforestry in, 87, 91
    farmers and farmer groups in, 52, 54, 55, 56
    international acquisition of agricultural land in,
        135–36, 139, 140
    livestock in, 158–59
    local food biodiversity in, 73, 78–79
    water and soil conserving tillage methods,
        45–46
    water-driven famines in, 40
Ethiopian Coffee Exchange, 72
Europe/European Union, 10, 86, 101
evergreen agriculture, 17, 97–98. See also agro-
    forestry
extension services for women farmers, 124–26,
    127

F
Faidherbia (fertilizer tree), 97, 98, 149–50
fair trade market in shea butter, 122–24
fallowing practices, 60–61, 63, 67
Family Support Scholarship Program, ECHOES,
    125
Famine Early Warning Systems Network, 62
Farm Bill (U.S.), 95–96
FarmAfrica, 76
Farmer Innovation Fund, 57
farmer-managed natural regeneration of tree
    cover, 86–93
farmers and farmer groups, 51–57. See also links
    between farmers and markets; loan
    mechanisms for farmers; women/women
    farmers
    banana farmers, 145
    development practitioners, lessons for, 57
    disseminating agricultural innovations via,
        54–55, 56
    hunger and malnutrition, combating, 11
    institutional support for, 173
    middle-aged professionals as, 31
    One Acre Fund providing loans to, 38
    reasons for supporting, 55–56
    supporting and encouraging innovation by,
        52–54
    vegetables, involvement in participatory
        research on, 28–29, 30–31
    wastewater farming, improving safety of,
        118–19
    water supply and management practices, adopt-
        ing, 44–47
farming. See agriculture
Feed Foundation, 12
Feed the Future, 5, 179
fertilizer. See also chemical fertilizers; manure
    solid waste used for composting, 113–14, 120
    system dynamics model comparing organic and
        chemical products, 167
    trees, nitrogen-fixing, 97–98, 149–50, 153
financial incentives encouraging sustainable
    practices, 173
fisheries and seafood
    Gulf of Mexico dead zone, 12
    local food biodiversity, encouraging, 73–74
    overfishing, 73
    oyster beds, preservation of, 3–4, 108
    percentage of dietary protein provided by, 4
    rice paddies, 75
    yeet, 73–74

Fome Zero (Zero Hunger Strategy), Brazil, 182
fonio, 68, 74, 79
Food, Agriculture and Natural Resources Policy
  Analysis Network, 130–31
food aid
  high food prices affecting, 4
  moving beyond, 153
  sources of food provided by, 10–11
Food Aid Convention, 181
Food and Agriculture Organization, U.N.
  Committee on World Food Security, 179
  hunger report (2010), 3, 4–5
  international acquisitions of agricultural land,
    134, 138, 139, 140
  post-harvest food loss, 100, 101, 104
  Principles on Responsible Agricultural Invest-
    ment, 181
  right to food assessment guide, 182
  unused arable land in Africa, 134, 137
  women farmers, 130
  women's access to microcredit, 127
food and farming culture
  earlier hunger programs ignoring, 7
  human waste composting, 120
  indigenous vegetables, 35
  overabundance and waste, 99–100, 107
  participatory agricultural research and, 28–29
  water supply management and conservation,
    46–47
food insecurity. *See* hunger and malnutrition,
  combating
food policies, setting, 173
food preservation techniques, 104–06. *See also*
  post-harvest food loss
food prices
  aid programs affected by, 4
  bumper crops, dealing with, 143–44, 148–49,
    152
  crisis of 2008, 101, 180
  foreign land acquisition as means of
    controlling, 133
  indigenous vegetables, 33
  overall increases in, 4
  small-scale farmers and, 146
  upward pressures on, 5
food production
  climate change and industrial food system, 83,
    93–96
  conservation efforts, reinforcing. *See*
    agroecology
  Green Revolution. *See* Green Revolution

hunger and malnutrition, combating, 8–10
indigenous vegetables, 33
links between farmers and markets. *See* links
  between farmers and markets
post-harvest losses, as means of preventing,
  106, 142
soil fertility crisis and drop in, 61
value-added to agricultural products in Africa,
  9
food reserves, 151, 181
food security
  Green Revolution, resulting from, 13, 27, 30,
    39
  urban agriculture as means of ensuring,
    111–12
food sovereignty, 177
food storage
  agribusiness technologies for, 99
  cowpeas, 6, 141
  metal grain storage containers, 107
  mold and fungus problems, 103
  poor storage in developing countries, 100,
    101, 141
  sweet potatoes, 105
  technologies for developing nations, 141
food waste. *See* post-harvest food loss
foreign acquisition of agricultural land. *See*
  international agricultural land acquisition
forestry. *See* agroforestry
Forestry Research Institute of Malawi, 98
Forum on Agricultural Research in Africa, 55
Friends of Katuk Odeyo, Kenya, 54
Fulani people, 63, 68, 155

G
The Gambia, 3–4, 108
Gates, Bill, 175
Gates Foundation, 141, 146, 175, 176
Gebremedhin, Mawcha, 55
genetic engineering, 106, 132, 171, 176
Germany, 103, 129
Ghana
  micro-irrigation in, 44
  Millennium Development Goals for hunger in,
    4
  urban areas and urban poor in, 9, 110
  urban wastewater farming in, 118–19
  women farmers in, 123, 125, 128
Gilbert (Rwandan farmer), 38
Global Agriculture and Food Security Program,
  World Bank, 179

Global Crop Diversity Trust, 10
global financial crisis of 2008–09, 140
global warming. *See* climate change
globalized food market
    climate change, responsibility for, 47–48
    corporate and foreign ownership of agricultural
        land. *See* international agricultural land
        acquisition
    hunger and malnutrition, combating, 10–12,
        180
    Icelandic volcanic eruptions, food and flower
        transport disrupted by, 142
    local/indigenous/traditional foods in, 76–79
    locavore/local food movements, 7, 22
    percentage of agricultural lands and food pro-
        duction entering, 23
    water imports, grain imports as, 47
    women farmers in, 122–24, 131
Google Trader, 146
governance issues, 175–79
GRAIN, 11, 136
grain trading, 58
GrainPro, Inc., 141
Grameen Bank, 106
Grameen Foundation, 146
grassland restoration, 19
gray water (wastewater) farming, 109, 113,
    114–15, 118–19
Great Green Wall, 86, 92–93
green manure/cover crops, 64–68
Green Revolution
    increased crop yields and food security result-
        ing from, 13, 27, 30, 39
    "miracle rice" developed by, 133–34
    persistence of hunger despite, 4–5
    semidwarf wheat and rice varieties developed
        in, 26, 30
    single-avenue approach of, 40, 47
    vegetables' role in African version of, 27–28
    water requirements, 39–40
greenhouse gas emissions, 173, 178
    agroecology and agroforestry
        counterbalancing, 11, 22, 83, 93–96, 114
    carbon content of soil, increasing, 6, 24, 94,
        167
    commercial agriculture's contribution to, 166
    livestock-produced, 94, 157–59, 161–63
    urban agriculture reducing, 114
groundnuts, 104, 142
GTZ, 129
Gueye, Fatou, 82

Guindo, Mamadou, 76
Guinea, 104
Guinea-Bissau, 71–72
Guinea savannah zone, 134
Gulf of Mexico dead zone, 12
Gustafson, Ellen, 12

H
Haileselassie, Daniel Tesfaye, 141
Haiti, 120
Hallam, David, 140
Handema, Ray, 141, 142
Harare Declaration, 116
Heartlands Program, African Wildlife
    Foundation, 22
Heifer International Rwanda, 164
herding peoples (pastoralists), 81, 156, 158,
    160–61
herding societies. *See* pastoralists
HIV/AIDS, 14, 113, 159
Honduras, 64
honey production in Ethiopia, 78–79
human-powered water pumps, 8, 41–43, 47, 49,
    145
human waste, composting, 120
hunger and malnutrition, 3–12
    agroecology, 6–7
    children, levels of, 4, 177
    churches and Christian development organiza-
        tions, new approaches of, 153–54
    FAO hunger report (2010), 3, 4–5
    farmers and farmer groups, role of, 11
    food production, 8–10
    global nature of food market and, 10–12, 180
    local food biodiversity and, 10, 75
    Millennium Development Goals for, 4, 168
    political economy of, 172–75
    post-harvest food loss and, 8–9, 101, 107
    problematic aspects of earlier programs, 7
    seed varieties, focus on, 7–8
    urban agriculture as means of, 9–10, 110
    vegetables, nutritional value of, 28
    water and soil issues, 6, 7–8
    women, levels of, 4, 121–22
Hyde, Rose, 123

I
Ibero-American Model Forest Network, 22
Ideal Woman Shea Butter Producers and Pickers
    Association, Ghana, 123
Imperata grass, 64

India
   agroecology in, 20, 22
   genetically engineered agricultural products in,
      176
   Green Revolution in, 30
   human waste processing in, 120
   livestock in, 159
   micro-irrigation in, 44
   post-harvest food loss in, 102, 105
   water demand in, 39
indigenous peoples. *See also* specific groups, e.g.
      Maasai people
   Asociación Nacional de Mujeres Rurales e
      Indígenas, Chile, 174
   pastoralists, 81, 156, 158, 160–61
   territorial development strategies, 22
indigenous plants and foods. *See* local food
   biodiversity
indigenous water conservation techniques, 46
Indonesia, 177
industrial-scale agribusiness. *See* food
   production
information technology
   agroforestry and re-greening initiatives, 90
   ECHO Technical Notes, 154
   links between farmers and markets, providing,
      146
   mobile phones, 128, 146, 147, 151
   women farmers' access to, 128–29
innovations, 165–82
   in evaluating agricultural research and develop-
      ment projects, 169–72
   by farmers and farmer groups, 52–54
   farmers and farmer groups disseminating,
      54–55, 56
   in governance, 175–79
   in institutional support, 172–75
   in political economy of hunger and food
      systems, 172–75
   in rice breeding, 25–26, 132, 133–34
   in understanding complex systems, 166–68
   in urban agriculture, 110, 111
   of women/women farmers, 52, 53, 55
input-intensive farming systems, economic unsustainability of, 171–72
Insect Resistant Maize for Africa Project, Kenya
   Agricultural Research Institute, 176
Institute for Agriculture and Trade Policy, 134,
   181
Institute for Sustainable Development, Ethiopia,
   56

Institute of Post-Harvest Technology, Sri Lanka,
   102
institutional support, innovations in, 172–75
insurance for livestock, 162
integrated landscape initiatives, 22
intellectual property rights, 174, 176
Inter-Islamic Network on Water Resources
   Development, 114
Intergovernmental Panel on Climate Change, 48
Intermedia, 128
international agricultural land acquisition,
   133–40
   development advantages and drawbacks,
      138–40
   food prices, as effort to control, 133
   hunger and malnutrition, combating, 11–12
   land rights issues, 136, 139
   land rush in Ethiopia, 135–36
   local labor, use of, 135–36
   outgrower model, 140
   policy controls for, 181–82
   proposed and completed investments, 137–38
International Assessment of Agricultural Knowledge, Science and Technology for Development, 12, 16, 95, 173, 175
International Center of Insect Physiology and
   Ecology, 178
International Crops Research Institute for the
   Semi-Arid Tropics, 45
International Development Enterprises, 43–44
International Development Research Centre, 29,
   114, 115
International Finance Corporation, 150, 178
International Food Policy Research Institute, 28
International Fund for Agricultural Development
   climate change, 89, 90, 91
   farmers and farmer groups, 55
   links between farmers and markets, 146
   Principles on Responsible Agricultural Invest-
      ment, 181
   women farmers, 129
International Institute of Tropical Agriculture,
   69, 106, 125, 176
International Land Coalition, 136
International Landcare, 21
International Maize and Wheat Center, 31
International Monetary Fund, 140
International Potato Center, 106, 176
International Red Cross, 112
International Rice Research Institute, 30, 132,
   133–34

International Rural Poultry Center, Kyeema
    Foundation, Mozambique, 161
International Water Management Institute, 41,
    118
Internet. *See* information technology
investment, agricultural
    in foreign arable land. *See* international
        agricultural land acquisition
    policy issues, 181–82
irrigation. *See* water supply management and con-
    servation
Isack, Babel, 29
Ishii-Eiteman, Marcia, 95

J

Jane, Nassaazi, 37
Japan, 73, 103
Jischke, Martin C., 141
Jomo Kenyatta University of Agriculture and
    Technology, Nairobi, 34
Jordan, 114–15

K

Kabaghe, Chance, 131
Kampala Urban Food Security, Agriculture, and
    Livestock Coordinating Committee,
    Uganda, 115
Kanananji, 127–28
Kanju, Edward, 70
Kankolongo, Ambayeba Muimba, 103
Kapiza, Dinnah, 127–28
Karamuzi, Dennis, 164
Karanja, Nancy, 10
Kenya
    agroecology in, 15, 16, 17, 19–20
    agroforestry in, 91
    cassava agriculture in, 70
    climate change in, 83
    farmers and farmer groups in, 51–55, 57
    food production in, 142
    indigenous vegetables and climate change in,
        34
    information technology, women farmers' access
        to, 128, 129
    international acquisition of agricultural land in,
        134, 136
    links between farmers and markets in, 145–46
    livestock in, 81, 161, 163
    local food biodiversity in, 75–76, 80
    One Acre Fund, 38
    pest control in, 178

    Rift Valley fever in, 160
    soil fertility in, 60
    urban agriculture in, 9–10, 109, 111–13, 116
    urban areas and urban poor, 4, 110
    water supply and management in, 40, 47, 49,
        50
Kenya Agricultural Research Institute, 176
Kibugu, Eratus, 145
KickStart, 43
Kijabe Environmental Volunteers, Kenya, 15
Kilaki, Phillip, 54
Kindo, Ousséni, 88
Kizimbani Research Station, Zanzibar, 70
Kuria, David, 15, 16
Kyeema Foundation, Mozambique, 161

L

land acquisition, international. *See* international
    agricultural land acquisition
The Land Coalition, 11
Landcare, 21
landscape ecology, ecoagriculture as part of,
    17–20
landscape measurement, 21
LaSalle, Timothy, 94
Latin America. *See also* specific countries
    economic unsustainability of input-intensive
        farming systems in, 172
    green manure/cover crops, 64, 65
    Green Revolution in, 13, 27, 29
    territorial development strategies, 22
links between farmers and markets, 143–52
    agroecological issues, 149–50
    bumper crops, dealing with, 143–44, 148–49,
        152
    commercial farm practices, 144
    grain exchanges, 150–52
    grain trading, 58
    hunger and malnutrition, combating, 9
    loan mechanisms for improving, 150
    post-harvest food loss prevention, 142
    small-scale farmers, 144–47
    value chains, 144, 145
    village-level dealer networks, 147–50
livestock, 155–63. *See also* manure
    agroforestry benefits for, 87
    as assets, 156, 158
    biodiversity in, 17, 81
    climate change and, 155–56, 161–63
    communal grassland restoration and, 19
    cross-breeding and mixed breeds, 81

developing world, changing role in, 156–58
diseases and pests, controlling, 159–61
feeding strategies, 158–59
greenhouse gas emissions, 94, 157–59, 161–63
insurance for, 162
integrated landscape initiatives, 22
methane emissions, 94
overnighting in agricultural fields, 68
recovery program in Rwanda, 164
solid waste used as feed for, 113
urban agriculture involving, 109, 113, 115,
    157
U.S. subsidies for industrial production of,
    95–96
women farmers and, 158–59, 161
loan mechanisms for farmers
    financial incentives encouraging sustainable
        practices, 173
    food preservation and loss prevention, 106
    innovation, supporting and encouraging,
        53–54
    links between farmers and markets, improving,
        150
    microcredit, 106, 126–28, 145
    One Acre Fund, 38
    social credit programs, 53
    women farmers, 53, 126–28, 129–30
local food biodiversity, 71–80
    climate change and indigenous vegetables, 33,
        34
    combating hunger and malnutrition, 10, 75
    community access to, 79–80
    decline in, 71–72
    diseases and pests, combating, 74, 75–76
    Dogon condiments (somè), 74–77
    endangered food species in Africa, 77–78
    globalized food market and, 76–79
    importance of preserving, 72–74
    schools, growing, cooking, and eating of
        indigenous vegetables in, 10, 35, 36–37, 80
    vegetables and vegetable research, 32–35, 76
locavore/local food movements, 7, 22
L'Occitane, 122, 123
Loess Plateau Watershed Rehabilitation Project,
    China, 21
Luhana, James, 150

M
Maasai people, 81, 155, 158, 160–61
Macharia, Michael, 109
Madagascar, 25–26, 40, 106, 136, 138–39

Maifa, Esther Mjoki, 142
Mailaka (rice variety), 26
maize
    bumper crops, dealing with, 143–44, 148–49,
        152
    conservation agriculture and, 25
    conservation farming of, 149
    evergreen agriculture and, 17, 97–98
    fodder and soil conservation grasses planted
        with, 75–76
    genetic modification of, 132
    high-yield varieties, 84
    hybrid corn industry, U.S., 30
    indigenous grains as replacements for, 34
    international trade in, 58
    One Acre Fund, yield gains following assistance
        from, 38
    post-harvest losses, 102–3
    push-pull pest control intercropping technolo-
        gies, use of, 178
    soil and water conservation practices leading to
        yield gains in, 8, 45–46, 47
Majoni, Mariko, 97
Makerere University, Uganda, 115
Makota, Cecilia, 131
Makumbi, Winnie, 115
Makunike, Chido, 138
Malawi
    agroecology in, 17
    chemical fertilizer subsidies, 63
    climate change in, 83
    composting human waste in, 120
    fertilizer trees in, 97–98
    mobile phone banking in, 151
    Moneymaker water pumps in, 43
    small-scale irrigation techniques in, 46
    soil fertility in, 59–60
    women farmers in, 127–28, 130–31
    yield-boosting techniques in, 6
Mali
    agroforestry in, 87–90
    local food biodiversity in, 74–77
    small-scale irrigation techniques in, 46
    soil fertility issues in, 8, 60, 62, 68
    treadle pumps in, 43
malnutrition. See hunger and malnutrition,
    combating
Malthus, Thomas Robert, 137
Mamati, Francis, 38
mangoes, 102, 106
manure

as biogas source, 164
scarcity due to low livestock numbers, 60
soil fertility and use of, 60, 63, 68
markets and farmers, links between. *See* links
    between farmers and markets
Mars Corporation, 22
Mawoubé (woman farmer), 122, 123
Mazingira Institute, Kenya, 142
methane. *See* greenhouse gas emissions
Mexico, 30
Michigan State University, 58, 176
microcredit, 106, 126–28, 145
Microloan Foundation, 127, 128
Mid-American Consortium, 176
Mike (grain trader), 58
milk and milk products. *See* dairy produce
Millennium Development Goals, 4, 122, 168
Ministers' Conference on Urban and Periurban
    Agriculture in East and Southern Africa,
    116
Mishra, P. K., 102
mixed-breed livestock, 81
mobile phones, 128, 146, 147, 151
Mobile Transactions, 151
Mohamed, Salma Omar, 70
Molden, David, 41
Moneymaker water pumps, 8, 43
monoculture food production, 23, 75, 178
Monsanto, 31, 170, 176
"More People, More Trees" (documentary), 91
mosaic disease in cassava, 69, 75
Mosi-O-Tunya water pump, 8, 43
Mozambique, 17, 130–31, 139–40, 161
msangu trees, 149–50
Multilateral Investment Guarantee Agency, 178
Munai, Simon, 38
Munro, Rob, 143, 152
Musila, Lydia, 38
Mutola, Mary, 112, 113
Muyafwa Development Program, Kenya, 52, 55
Mwape, Wilson, 147

N

National Agricultural Advisory Services, Uganda,
    37, 126
National Agricultural Research Centers, Africa,
    31
National Agricultural Research Institute, Niger,
    56–57
National Agricultural Research Organization,
    Uganda, 115

National Federation of Fishworkers, Sri Lanka,
    173
National Institute for Scientific Research and
    Industrial Relations, 141–42
Natural Biogas Program, Rwanda, 164
Ndebe, John, 70
Ndiaye, Cisse, 82
Ndoye, Seynabou, 73–74
Nelspruit Agricultural Development Association,
    South Africa, 131
Nepal, 44
Nestle, 22
NetHope, 129
Network of Eco-Farming in Africa, 80
Network of Farmers' and Agricultural Producers'
    Organisations of West Africa, 174
New Forest Farm, Wisconsin, 93
New Zealand, 21, 94
Newcastle disease in poultry, 160, 161
Newsom, Gavin, 116
Nghatsane, Linda, 131
Ngongi, Namanga, 28
Nicaragua, 21
Niger
    agroforestry in, 86–90, 92
    churches and Christian development organiza-
        tions, new approaches of, 153
    collective action in agricultural development in,
        13
    farmers and farmer groups in, 53–57
    fertilizer trees in, 98
    links between farmers and markets in, 146
    soil fertility in, 60, 64
    treadle pumps in, 43
    water vulnerabilities in, 40
Nigeria, 28, 40, 86, 106
Njenga, Mary, 10
Nyando Dairy Goats Farmers Group, Kenya, 54,
    57

O

Obama, Barack, 10, 135, 179, 181
Ocokoru, Susan, 126
Office of the Compliance Advisor/Ombudsman,
    IFC, 178
Okaka, Jane, 113
Oluoch, Mel, 35
ombudsmen, 178
Omusi, Esther, 53
One Acre Fund, 38
One Cow Per Poor Household Program,

Rwanda, 164
Open Mind, 46
open-pollinated seed varieties, 32
organic agriculture, 17, 20, 96, 171. *See also*
    agroecology
organic beauty products market, 122–23
Ouedraogo, Fatou, 123
Ouko, Eddy, 51, 52
Ouko, Joe, 54, 57
overabundance, culture of, 99–100, 107
Oxfam, 87, 120
oyster beds, preservation of, 3–4, 108

P
Pakistan, 30, 39, 102, 107
Pan-Africa Bean Research Alliance, 31
participatory research, involving farmers in,
    28–29, 30–31
Pasternak, Dov, 45
pasteurization, 142
pastoralists, 81, 156, 158, 160–61
Payne, Susan, 135
Peepoo, 120
PELUM-Kenya, 11, 53, 54
pesticides. *See* diseases and pests
Philippines, 21, 22, 106, 175
Pimentel, David, 94
planting pits (*zaï*), 91, 132
Polak, Paul, 43
policies
    establishing for food, 173
    for agricultural R&D, 169–72
    governance issues, 175–79
    institutional support for development of,
        172–75
    urban agriculture, 115–16
post-harvest food loss, 99–107
    dairy produce, 103–04, 106, 142
    food production as means of preventing, 106,
        142
    hunger and malnutrition, combating, 8–9,
        101, 107
    investments and assistance to prevent, 106–7
    local markets, developing, 142
    low-cost alternatives to synthetic preservatives,
        104–06
    overabundance, culture of, 99–100, 107
    as problem in developing world, 100–04
    storage techniques. *See* food storage
    women farmers' concern with, 124–26
poultry. *See* livestock

preservation of food, 104–06. *See also* post-
    harvest food loss
Pretty, Jules, 20
Price, Martin, 154
prices. *See* food prices
Principles on Responsible Agricultural
    Investment, 181
private agricultural R&D, 170
private investment in foreign arable land. *See*
    international agricultural land acquisition
processing food. *See* food production
Production, Finance, and Technology program,
    AID, 9, 144, 145, 148–50, 152
Project DISC, Uganda, 10, 36–37
Project for the Promotion of Local Initiative for
    Development in Aguié, IFAD, 89
Prolinnova, 11, 53, 54
Promoting Farmer Innovation, 46
protective tariffs, 177, 180–81
pumps, human powered, 8, 41–43, 47, 49, 145
Purchase for Progress initiative, 150
Purdue Improved Cowpea Storage, 141
push-pull systems, 75, 178

Q
Qatar, 134

R
radio broadcasting, 89, 119, 128
Rainforest Alliance, 20
rainwater. *See* water supply management and con-
    servation
Rangpur Dinajpur Rural Service, Bangladesh, 43
Ray, Daryll, 180
re-greening initiatives. *See* agroforestry
Red Cross, 112
Relief International, 43
religion-based development organizations,
    153–54
Renk Theological College, Sudan, 154
research. *See* agricultural research
Reseau MARP, 87–88, 91
reserves of food, 151, 181
rice
    Asian emergency rice reserve, 181
    biodiversity of traditional varieties, 71, 75
    breeding innovations, 25–26, 132, 133–34
    genetically engineered, 176
    imported, 71, 79
    International Rice Research Institute, 30, 132,
        133–34

post-harvest loss and loss prevention, 101, 106
sustainable rice intensification, 20, 25
trade liberalization and self-sufficiency in, 177
Rift Valley, 50, 140
Rift Valley fever, 160–61
Rigel Technology, 120
rights-based approach to food, 175, 177, 180, 182
Rinaudo, Tony, 89
rinderpest control, 14
Rockefeller Foundation, 176
Rockström, Johan, 44
Rodale Institute, 94–95
roof water catchment tanks, 49–50
Rotary International of Canada, 49
Rothamsted Research Station, U.K., 178
Rural Agricultural Input Supply Expansion Program, CNFA, 127
rural areas
    agroecology and rural livelihoods, 15
    hunger levels in, 4
    soil fertility crisis and abandonment of, 62–63
Rural Capacity Building Project, World Bank, 57
rural mobile money networks, 151
Rwanda, 38, 49, 164

S

Sabuloni, Mary, 97
Sachs, Jeffrey, 124
Sahara, southward movement of, 86
Sahel region
    agroecology in, 153
    climate change, planting trees to combat, 83, 86–93
    green manure/cover crops in, 67
    shea butter and, 122
    soil fertility crisis, emerging signs of, 8, 63
    water vulnerabilities of, 40, 48
Sahel Regreening Initiative, 87
SahelECO, 88–90
Saleh, Haji, 69
San Francisco Urban-Rural Roundtable, 116
sanitation services and composting, 120
Saudi Arabia, 12, 133–34, 135, 139
Saudi Star Agricultural Development, 135
Sawadogo, Yacouba, 91
schools. See education and schools
Schutter, Olivier de, 8, 176
seafood. See fisheries and seafood
SearNet, 49

Securidaca longepedunculata (natural pest deterrent), 104
seed availability, 29–32
seed varieties, focus on, 7–8
Senegal
    agroforestry in, 89
    local food biodiversity in, 73–74, 79
    rooftop gardening cooperative, Dakar, 6
    solar cookers in, 82
    treadle pumps in, 43
    women farmers in, 127
Serving in Mission, 153
shallots, 74
shea nuts and shea butter, 90, 122–24
Shepard, Mark, 93, 94, 95
Siddimallaiah (Indian farmer), 20
Sierra Leone, 121
Singh, A. K., 159
Sivusimpilo Farmers Forum, 54
slash-and-burn systems of agriculture, 61, 65
Slow Food International, and local chapters, 10, 35, 36, 72–73, 78, 79, 80
slums, urban. See urban areas
small-scale irrigation, 46
Smil, Vaclav, 101
social audits, 178–79
social credit programs, 53
Soil Association, 8
soil fertility, 59–68. See also fertilizer
    agroecology and, 15, 24
    agroforestry benefits for, 87
    animal manure, use of, 60, 63, 68
    carbon content of soil, increasing, 6, 24, 94, 167
    climate change affecting, 61
    emerging signs of crisis in, 61–63
    fallowing practices, 60–61, 63, 67
    green manure/cover crops, 64–68
    home-grown versus technology-driven approaches to improving, 169–70
    hunger and malnutrition, combating, 6, 7–8
    new land, efforts to find and use, 60, 62, 63
    rural areas, abandonment of, 62–63
    solid waste used for composting, 113–14, 120
    threats to, 60–61
SOIL/SOL, 120
Solar Electric Light Fund, 44, 45
solar energy
    cookers, solar-powered, 82
    coolbot technology, 126

food preservation through solar heat drying,
    104, 106
micro-irrigation systems, solar-powered, 44, 45
Solar Household Energy Inc., 82
solid waste used for composting, 113–14, 120
Solidarites, 112
Somali pastoralists, 160–61
somè (Dogon condiments), 74–77
South Africa
    agroecology in, 21, 22
    farmers and farmer groups in, 51, 54, 55
    grain trade, 58
    irrigated land in, 40
    post-harvest food loss prevention, 105, 106
South Korea, 134, 136, 138–39
Southern Africa Regional Biosafety Programme,
    176
Southern and Eastern Africa Rainwater Network,
    49
Sowing Seeds of Change in the Sahel, 153–54
Spieldoch, Alexandra, 134
Sri Lanka, 102, 173
Stanford University, 44, 45
stem borers, 75, 76, 178
Stockholm Environment Institute, 44
Striga (parasitic weed), 64, 76, 132, 178
sub-Saharan Africa. *See also* specific countries and
        regions
    agriculture in. *See* agriculture
    biomass fuel use in, 82
    endangered food species in, 77–78
    food price crisis of 2008 in, 101, 180
    modern varieties of plants, low levels of use of,
        30
    value-added to agricultural products in, 9
Sudan, 40, 154
Super Moneymaker water pump, 43
Sustainable Agriculture Initiative Platform, 20
sustainable farming. *See* agroecology
sustainable rice intensification, 20, 25
Sustainable Tree Crops Programme,
        International Institute of Tropical
        Agriculture, 125
Swedish International Development Agency, 47,
    49
sweet potatoes, 105, 106, 142, 176
Syngenta, 170, 176

T
talc powder, as pesticide, 141
Tanbi National Park, The Gambia, 108

Tanzania
    agroecology in, 17
    cassava agriculture in, 70
    indigenous vegetables in, 33
    international acquisition of agricultural land in,
        134
    livestock in, 161
    local food biodiversity in, 76
    urban agriculture in, 110
    vegetable seeds and varieties in, 32
tariffs, protective, 177, 180–81
Taylor, Michael, 136
Tchala, Olowo–n'djo, 122, 123
tea plantations, agroecology in, 20
technology, appropriate, 132
TechnoServe, 145
tef, 8, 45–46
TerrAfrica, 22
territorial development strategies, 22
Thailand, 71, 79
theater, women farmers project using, 130–31
theological education, including sustainable agri-
        cultural development as part of, 154
30 Project, Feed Foundation, 12
Tilago, Gemedo, 140
tillage
    minimization of, 149
    tractors, 150
    water and soil conserving methods, 45–46
    zero-tillage cultivation, 13, 67
Timor, 107
Tisaiwale Trading, 127
Tithonia diversifolia, 52
Togo, 110, 122, 123
toilets, composting, 120
Toucas, Matthieu, 76
trade liberalization, 58, 101, 124, 177, 180–81
traditional foods, preserving. *See* local food
        biodiversity
training. *See also* education and schools
    agroforestry, 88–89, 153–54
    churches and Christian development organiza-
        tions, new approaches of, 153–54
    food loss prevention, 104
    women farmers, extension services for, 124–26,
        127
treadle pumps, 8, 42–43, 47, 49, 145
trees. *See* agroforestry
TRY Women's Oyster Harvesting Association,
        The Gambia, 3–4, 108

U

Uganda
  cassava agriculture in, 69, 70
  indigenous vegetables in, 33
  links between farmers and markets in, 145, 146
  local food biodiversity in, 79
  post-harvest food loss in, 104
  Project DISC, 10, 36–37
  soil fertility in, 60, 64
  urban agriculture in, 110, 115, 116
  women farmers in, 124–26, 128
UNICEF, 120
UNIFEM, 123
Unilever Tea Company, 20
United Kingdom, 94, 178
United Nations
  FAO. *See* Food and Agriculture Organization, U.N.
  food storage projects, 107
  greenhouse gas emissions from livestock, 95
  International Assessment of Agricultural Knowledge, Science and Technology for Development, 12, 16, 95, 173, 175
  irrigation statistics, 44
  Millennium Development Goals, 4, 122, 168
  right to food, 176, 180, 182
  World Food Summit (2009), 179
United Nations Conference on Trade and Development, 95, 181
United Nations Environment Programme, 49, 86, 95
United States. *See also* U.S. Agency for International Development
  agricultural R&D spending in, 170
  agroecology versus industrialized food production in, 93, 95–96
  Feed the Future initiative, 5, 179
  food aid from, 10
  global implications of American diet, 12
  hybrid corn industry in, 30
  school-provided meals in, 10
  urban agriculture in, 116
  Wall Street Reform and Consumer Protection Act, 181
University of Essex, U.K., 94
University of Michigan, 94
University of Tennessee, 180
urban agriculture, 109–17
  community building, as means of, 112–13
  environmental benefits from, 113–14
  food security, as means of ensuring, 111–12
  future developments in, 116–17
  Harare Declaration on, 116
  hunger and malnutrition, combating, 9–10, 110
  indigenous vegetables, 35
  innovations in, 110, 111
  livestock, 109, 113, 115, 157
  policies for, 115–16
  solid waste used for composting, 113–14, 120
  vertical basket gardens, 112
  wastewater farming, 109, 113, 114–15, 118–19
  women's involvement in, 109, 112, 113, 117
urban areas
  contrast between rich and poor in, 110
  food supply for, 101, 105
  hunger levels for poor in, 4, 9
  soil fertility and abandonment of rural areas for, 62–63
Urban Harvest, 113
U.S. Agency for International Development
  food prices affecting programs of, 4
  genetic engineering programs supported by, 176
  links between farmers and markets, 143–48, 150, 152
  oyster beds, preservation of, 108
  post-harvest food loss prevention aid, 103
  PROFIT program, 9, 144, 145, 148–50, 152
  warehouse and warehouse receipting programs, 181
Uvin, Peter, 92

V

vaccines for livestock, 160, 161
value-added to agricultural products in Africa, 9
value chains, 144, 145
vegetables, 27–35
  Green Revolution in Africa, necessary role in, 27–28
  indigenous, 32–35, 76
  nutritional value of, 28
  participatory research, involving farmers in, 28–29, 30–31
  post-harvest losses, preventing, 104–06
  seed availability, 29–32
  water supply and management, 49
vertical integration, 148
Via Campesina, 10
Video Viewing Clubs, 125
Vietnam, 101

Village Community Granaries Scheme,
  Madagascar, 106
Vitamin A deficiency, 28
VU University, Amsterdam, 91

W
Waage, Jeff, 132
Wabwire, Janet, 52
Wairimu, Alice, 109
Wall Street Reform and Consumer Protection Act
  (U.S.), 181
warehouse and warehouse receipting programs,
  181
waste products, composting, 113–14, 120
wasted food. *See* post-harvest food loss
wastewater farming, 109, 113, 114–15,
  118–19
Water Efficient Maize for Africa, 31
water supply management and conservation,
  39–48
  agroecology and, 15, 18
  catchment tanks and ponds, 49–50
  climate change and, 47–48
  effective rainfall management and harvesting,
    44–47, 49–50
  farming culture affecting, 46–47
  grain imports, as water imports, 47
  green manure/cover crops, 66–67
  Green Revolution, irrigation requirements of,
    39–40
  groundwater location devices, 50
  human-powered water pumps, 8, 41–43, 47,
    49, 145
  hunger and malnutrition, combating, 7–8
  livestock, 81
  low-cost, simple technology methods, 41, 42
  micro-irrigation technologies, 43–44, 55,
    132
  vulnerabilities and advantages in Africa,
    40–41
  wastewater farming, 109, 113, 114–15,
    118–19
Watson, Robert, 16
weeding, green manure/cover crops reducing,
  66
weevils, 101, 106, 141
Welsh, Joe, 73
Wena, Dorcas, 54
Wenchi honey, Ethiopia, 78–79
West Africa
  cocoa production in, 125

Economic Community of West African States,
  common agricultural policy of, 177–78
  fisheries and seafood in, 73
  Network of Farmers' and Agricultural
    Producers' Organisations of, 174
  post-harvest losses, preventing, 6, 106
  shea nut gathering in, 90
  Vitamin A deficiency in, 28
wetlands, as waste treatment centers, 120
wheat, zero-tillage cultivation of, 13
WIC Farmers Market Nutrition Program, 96
Wilmar Group, 178
Winrock International, 125
Women Accessing Realigned Markets project,
  130–31
women/women farmers, 121–29
  Chilean Asociación Nacional de Mujeres
    Rurales e Indígenas, 174
  in cocoa-growing communities, 125
  earlier hunger programs ignoring contributions
    of, 7
  extension services for, 124–26, 127
  fuel gathering by, 82
  globalized food market and, 122–24, 131
  hunger levels, 4, 121–22
  indigenous vegetables, 33, 35
  information technology, access to, 128–29
  livestock and, 158–59, 161
  loan mechanisms for, 53, 126–28, 129–30
  local food biodiversity and, 73–74, 80
  post-harvest food loss, concern with, 124–26
  shea nut gathering, 90
  shea nuts and shea butter, 90, 122–24
  single-parent households, 145
  solar cookers, use of, 82
  somè (Dogon condiments), knowledge about,
    74, 77
  supporting and encouraging innovation by, 52,
    53, 55
  urban agriculture, involvement in, 109, 112,
    113, 117
  WARM project, 130–31
  water supply and management, 45, 47,
    49–50
  weeding as women's work, 66
Women's Oyster Harvesting Association, The
  Gambia, 3–4, 108
World Agroforestry Centre, 49, 52, 87
World Bank
  agricultural development funding, importance
    of, 5, 130, 137

arable land in Guinea savannah zone, 134
Global Agriculture and Food Security
  Program, 179
land rights, 139
Multilateral Investment Guarantee Agency,
  178
Principles on Responsible Agricultural
  Investment, 181
Rural Capacity Building Project, 57
trade liberalization encouraged by, 101
World Cocoa Foundation, 125
World Food Conference, 100
World Food Prize Symposium (2009), 174
World Food Programme, 10, 11, 150–52,
  181
World Neighbors, 52, 54
World Vision Australia, 89
World Vision Senegal, 89
World Wide Web Foundation, 90
Wukro honey, Ethiopia, 78–79

Y

yeet, 73–74
yield increases
  agroecology producing, 6, 20–21
  cassava yields in Brazil, 30–31
  fertilizer trees and, 97
  Green Revolution, 13, 27, 30, 39
  maize, soil and water conservation practices
    affecting, 8, 45–46, 47
  Malawi, yield-boosting techniques in, 6
  rice, 26

Z

Zamace grain exchange, 150–52
Zambia
  agroecology in, 17
  fertilizer trees in, 98
  food storage in, 141
  grain trade, 58, 131
  international acquisition of agricultural land in,
    140
  links between farmers and markets in, 9,
    143–52. *See also* links between farmers and
    markets
  micro-irrigation in, 44
  mobile phone banking in, 151
  post-harvest food loss in, 102–4
  soil fertility in, 60
  treadle pumps in, 43, 145
Zambia National Farmers Union, 146
Zantiébougou Women Shea Butter Producers
    Cooperative, Mali, 90
Zanzibar, 69–70
Zara, Galdino, 76–77
Zeigler, Robert, 133–34
Zenawi, Meles, 135
Zero Hunger Strategy (Fome Zero), Brazil, 182
zero-tillage cultivation, 13, 67
Zimbabwe
  agroecology in, 17, 19
  grain trade, 131
  Internet access services in, 129
  micro-irrigation in, 44
  small-scale irrigation techniques in, 46
  urban agriculture in, 110
Zulu, Lytton, 149